4th New Frontiers in Summarization Workshop (NewSumm 2023)

Singapore
6 December 2023

ISBN: 978-1-7138-8603-7

Printed from e-media with permission by:

Curran Associates, Inc.
57 Morehouse Lane
Red Hook, NY 12571

Some format issues inherent in the e-media version may also appear in this print version.

Printed with permission by Curran Associates, Inc. (2024)

For permission requests, please contact the Association for Computational Linguistics at the address below.

Association for Computational Linguistics
209 N. Eighth Street
Stroudsburg, Pennsylvania 18360

Phone: 1-570-476-8006
Fax: 1-570-476-0860

acl@aclweb.org

Additional copies of this publication are available from:

Curran Associates, Inc.
57 Morehouse Lane
Red Hook, NY 12571 USA
Phone: 845-758-0400
Fax: 845-758-2633
Email: curran@proceedings.com
Web: www.proceedings.com

NewSumm 2023

Proceedings of The 4th New Frontiers in Summarization Workshop

Proceedings of EMNLP Workshop

December 6, 2023

Order copies of this and other ACL proceedings from:

Association for Computational Linguistics (ACL)
209 N. Eighth Street
Stroudsburg, PA 18360
USA
Tel: +1-570-476-8006
Fax: +1-570-476-0860
acl@aclweb.org

Message from the Workshop Chairs

The development of intelligent systems capable of producing concise, fluent, and accurate summaries is a longstanding objective in natural language processing. This workshop serves as a forum for the exchange of ideas towards achieving this aim. It brings together experts from various disciplines, including summarization, language generation, and cognitive and psycholinguistics, to discuss key issues in automatic summarization. The agenda covers a wide array of topics, such as innovative paradigms and frameworks, multilingual and cross-lingual setups, shared tasks, information integration, novel evaluation methods, applied research, and future research directions. The workshop is aimed at fostering a cohesive research community, expediting the transfer of knowledge, and developing new tools, datasets, and resources to meet the needs of academia, industry, and government.

This fourth edition of the workshop, following our previous workshops at EMNLP 2017, EMNLP 2019, and EMNLP 2021, received 31 paper submissions, with acceptance rates of 42%. We are honored to host five distinguished speakers: Kathleen McKeown (Columbia University), Jackie Cheung (McGill University), Rui Zhang (Penn State University), Iz Beltagy (AI2), Chenguang Zhu (Zoom), who collectively represent a wide spectrum of expertise in summarization and text generation fields. We extend our gratitude to these speakers, as well as to our program committee members and workshop attendees.

NewSumm Organizing Committee
Yue Dong,
Wen Xiao,
Lu Wang,
Fei Liu,
Giuseppe Carenini

Organizing Committee

General Chair, Publication Chair

Yue Dong, University of California, Riverside, USA

Vice General Chair, Presentation Chair

Wen Xiao, Microsoft Azure AI, Canada

Advisory Chair

Wang Lu, University of Michigan, USA
Fei Liu, Emory University, USA
Giuseppe Carenini, University of British Columbia, Canada

Program Committee

Program Committee

Niyathi Allu, University of California, Riverside
Kristjan Arumae, University of Central Florida
Susana Bautista, Universidad Francisco de Vitoria
Florian Boudin, Nantes University
Hou Pong Chan, University of Macau
Ido Dagan, Bar-Ilan University
Felice Dell'orletta, ItaliaNLP Lab @ Institute for Computational Linguistics Antonio Zampolli", ILC - CNR
Yuntian Deng, Allen Institute for AI
Richard Evans, University of Wolverhampton
Alex Fabbri, Salesforce AI Research
Tobias Falke, Amazon Alexa AI
Pengcheng He, Microsoft
Zhe Hu, Baidu
Xinyu Hua, Bloomberg
Patrick Huber, University of British Columbia
Masoud Jalili Sabet, Center for Information and Speech Processing, Ludwig Maximilian University of Munich
Jing Jiang, Singapore Management University
Wojciech Kryscinski, Salesforce Research
Yang Liu, Microsoft
Elena Lloret, University of Alicante
Wencan Luo, Google
Margot Mieskes, University of Applied Sciences, Darmstadt
Tadashi Nomoto, National Institute of Japanese Literature
Naoaki Okazaki, Tokyo Institute of Technology
Manabu Okumura, Tokyo Institute of Technology
Jessica Ouyang, University of Texas at Dallas
Maxime Peyrard, EPFL
Simone Paolo Ponzetto, University of Mannheim
Ori Shapira, Amazon
Priyanshu Sharma, University of California, Riverside
Kaiqiang Song, Tencent AI Lab
Arpit Sood, Meta Inc.
Juan-Manuel Torres-Moreno, LIA Avignon
Giulia Venturi, Institute of Computational Linguistics Antonio Zampolli"(ILC-CNR)
Esau Villatoro-Tello, Idiap Research Institute
Linzi Xing, University of British Columbia
Xinnuo Xu, University of Edinburgh
Jiacheng Xu, Salesforce AI Research
Haopeng Zhang, University of California, Davis
Rui Zhang, Penn State University
Ming Zhong, University of Illinois Urbana-Champaign

Keynote Talk: Invited Speaker 1

Kathleen McKeown
Columbia University

Keynote Talk: Invited Speaker 2

Jackie Cheung
McGill University

Keynote Talk: Invited Speaker 3

Rui Zhang
Penn State University

Keynote Talk: Invited Speaker 4

Iz Beltagy
AI2

Keynote Talk: Invited Speaker 5

Chenguang Zhu
Zoom

Table of Contents

Program

Wednesday, December 6, 2023

08:50 - 09:00	*Opening Remarks*
09:00 - 09:45	*Keynote I - Kathleen McKeown (Columbia University)*
09:45 - 10:30	*Keynote II - Jackie Cheung (McGill University)*
10:30 - 11:00	*Coffee Break*
11:00 - 11:45	*Keynote III - Rui Zhang (Penn State University)*
11:45 - 12:30	*Keynote IV - Iz Beltagy (Allen Institute for AI)*
12:30 - 14:00	*Lunch Break*
14:00 - 14:45	*Keynote V - Chenguang Zhu (Zoom)*
14:45 - 15:30	*Ligntning Talk (Workshop papers and Findings papers)*
15:30 - 16:00	*Coffee Break*
16:00 - 17:30	*Afternoon Session II - Poster Session (Workshop papers and Findings papers)*

Is ChatGPT a Good NLG Evaluator? A Preliminary Study

Jiaan Wang[1*†] Yunlong Liang[2*] Fandong Meng[3]
Zengkui Sun[2], Haoxiang Shi[4], Zhixu Li[5], Jinan Xu[2], Jianfeng Qu[1] and Jie Zhou[3]
[1]Soochow University, Suzhou, China [2]Beijing Jiaotong University, Beijing, China
[3]Pattern Recognition Center, WeChat AI, Tencent Inc, China
[4]Waseda University, Tokyo, Japan [5]Fudan Unversity, Shanghai, China

jawang.nlp@gmail.com {yunlongliang, zengksun}@bjtu.edu.cn
fandongmeng@tencent.com hollis.shi@toki.waseda.jp

Abstract

Recently, the emergence of ChatGPT has attracted wide attention from the computational linguistics community. Many prior studies have shown that ChatGPT achieves remarkable performance on various NLP tasks in terms of automatic evaluation metrics. However, the ability of ChatGPT to serve as an evaluation metric is still underexplored. Considering assessing the quality of natural language generation (NLG) models is an arduous task and NLG metrics notoriously show their poor correlation with human judgments, we wonder *whether ChatGPT is a good NLG evaluation metric.*

In this report, we provide a preliminary meta-evaluation on ChatGPT to show its reliability as an NLG metric. In detail, we regard ChatGPT as a human evaluator and give task-specific (*e.g.*, summarization) and aspect-specific (*e.g.*, relevance) instruction to prompt ChatGPT to evaluate the generated results of NLG models. We conduct experiments on five NLG meta-evaluation datasets (including summarization, story generation and data-to-text tasks). Experimental results show that compared with previous automatic metrics, ChatGPT achieves state-of-the-art or competitive correlation with human judgments in most cases. In addition, we find that the effectiveness of the ChatGPT evaluator might be influenced by the creation method of the meta-evaluation datasets. For the meta-evaluation datasets which are created greatly depending on the reference and thus are biased, the ChatGPT evaluator might lose its effectiveness. We hope our preliminary study could prompt the emergence of a general-purposed reliable NLG metric.[1]

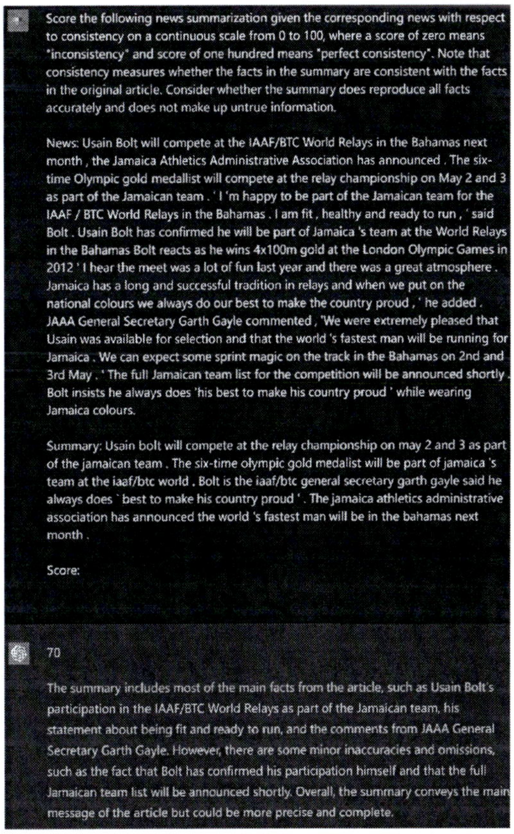

Figure 1: Prompting ChatGPT as an evaluator to score the generated results of NLG models (taking news summarization as an example).

1 Introduction

Pre-trained large language models (LLMs; *e.g.*, GPT-3.5, ChatGPT and GPT-4), which are performed through chatting (or asking) with it, have obtained promising results on various natural language understanding (NLU) and natural language generation (NLG) downstream tasks (Ouyang et al., 2022; Kocoń et al., 2023; Qin et al., 2023; Huang et al., 2023; Yang et al., 2023; Rao et al., 2023; Bang et al., 2023; Zuccon and Koopman, 2023). For example, Zhong et al. (2023) show that ChatGPT can attain the comparable understanding abil-

*Equal Contribution. Work was done when Wang and Liang was interning at Pattern Recognition Center, WeChat AI, Tencent Inc, China.

†Corresponding author.

[1]We have released the used data at https://github.com/krystalan/chatgpt_as_nlg_evaluator.

Proceedings of The 4th New Frontiers in Summarization Workshop, pages 1–11
December 6, 2023 ©2023 Association for Computational Linguistics

ity to some fine-tuned BERT-style models on NLU tasks while failing to surpass current task-specific NLU models. Wei et al. (2023) prove that ChatGPT can achieve good performance and even surpasses some full-shot models on several datasets through a multi-turn question-answering manner. For NLG tasks, Jiao et al. (2023) claim that ChatGPT performs competitively with commercial translation products (*e.g.*, Google Translator) on high-resource European languages. Wang et al. (2023a) demonstrate that ChatGPT can balance well between informativeness and conciseness, and generate great cross-lingual summaries. Although impressive performance on these tasks in terms of automatic evaluation metrics has been shown, it is still not clear *whether ChatGPT can evaluate the quality of textual generations as a human does.*

Recently, using pre-trained language models as NLG evaluation metric, *e.g.*, MoverScore (Zhao et al., 2019), BERTScore (Zhang et al., 2020), COMET (Rei et al., 2020), BLEURT (Sellam et al., 2020), BARTScore (Yuan et al., 2021) and MAUVE (Pillutla et al., 2022), receives increasing attention since it offers a decent human-related judgment from a deep semantic perspective. Given the powerful ability of ChatGPT as an intelligent conversational LLM, researchers also attempt to investigate whether it can evaluate the translation quality as a human evaluator (Kocmi and Federmann, 2023). However, the automated assessment of the general generation quality of NLG models still remains underexplored.

In this report, we aim to answer the following research question: *Is ChatGPT a good NLG evaluator?* To this end, we regard ChatGPT as a human evaluator and give task-specific (*e.g.*, summarization) and aspect-specific (*e.g.*, relevance) instruction to prompt ChatGPT to evaluate the generation of NLG models. As the example shows in Figure 1, we also attempt different scoring criteria and whether to provide golden references in the prompts to systematically test the reliability of the ChatGPT evaluator. We conduct experiments on five widely-used NLG meta-evaluation datasets (including summarization, story generation and data-to-text tasks). Experimental results show that ChatGPT exhibits a high correlation with human judgment in most cases especially for the story generation task, indicating its potential as an NLG metric. In addition, we find that the ChatGPT evaluator is sensitive to the prompts, and for different tasks or aspects, the prompts should be carefully designed. Moreover, the creation method of the meta-evaluation datasets has a significant influence on the effectiveness of different evaluation metrics. If a meta-evaluation dataset is created greatly depending on the reference, the similarity between model generation and references serves as a strong signal to reflect human judgments, where simple similarity-based metrics (*e.g.*, ROUGE) can achieve very strong performance. Therefore, the ChatGPT evaluator might lose its effectiveness in such situations.

Our main contributions are concluded as follows:

- To our knowledge, we are the first to utilize ChatGPT as a general NLG evaluation metric to study its correlations with human judgments.
- We use task-specific and aspect-specific prompts to guide ChatGPT to perform as a reference-free or reference-based NLG metric, and evaluate its effectiveness on five widely-used meta-evaluation datasets covering three NLG tasks.
- We find that the ChatGPT evaluator has a high correlation with humans in most cases, especially for creative NLG tasks (*e.g.*, story generation) where multiple generations can satisfy humans.
- We find that the ChatGPT evaluator is sensitive to the prompts. For different tasks and aspects, the prompt should be carefully designed.
- We find that the involved biases of the NLG meta-evaluation datasets also influence the effectiveness of NLG metrics, and might lead to the limited effectiveness of the ChatGPT evaluator.

2 Related Work

2.1 NLG Metrics

A good automatic NLG metric can effectively indicate the quality of the textual generations and thus can save lots of human labor from conducting human evaluation. Therefore, it is vital to design automatic evaluation metrics for NLG tasks, *e.g.*, text summarization, story generation, data-to-text generation, machine translation, and many others. Generally, the score that points out how well the systems perform on each task is computed by comparing the system texts with one or more reference texts for semantic matching. In the literature, the metrics can be roughly categorized into four types:

n-gram-based Metrics. Essentially, the n-gram-based metrics aim to measure the lexical overlap between a generated text and a reference text.

The standard n-gram overlap-based metrics generally include ROUGE (Lin, 2004), BLEU (Papineni et al., 2002), Distinct-n (Li et al., 2016), and METEOR (Denkowski and Lavie, 2011). For example, ROUGE is the dominant metric in the summarization evaluation area. Its variants consider the overlap of unigrams (ROUGE-1) and bigrams (ROUGE-2), among others. BLEU metric is the common practice for the machine translation evaluation area. Although these metrics achieve good correlations (typically large overlaps) with golden references, they are not general enough because a system summary might convey the same meaning while using different surface forms.

Embedding-based Metrics. To further improve semantic similarity between a generated text and a reference text, embedding-based metrics are proposed based on the word embeddings (*e.g.*, WMD (Kusner et al., 2015)) or sentence embeddings (*e.g.*, BERTScore (Zhang et al., 2020) and MoverScore (Zhao et al., 2019)). These metrics further bridge the gap with human-related judgment while they largely depend on the quality of embeddings, which may limit their potential.

LLM-based Metrics. With the development of LLMs, some researchers show that LLMs could achieve great correlation with human judgment, *i.e.*, BARTScore (Yuan et al., 2021), and GPTScore (Fu et al., 2023). However, ChatGPT, as a more powerful conversational LLM, has not been investigated to evaluate the quality of the NLG model outputs.

Other Metrics. In different research fields, there are some paraphraser-based or task-specific metrics. For example, PRISM (Thompson and Post, 2020) is proposed to evaluate translation outputs based on the pre-trained paraphrase models. StoryER (Chen et al., 2022), a learning metric, mimics human preference when judging a story by three steps: Ranking, Rating, and Reasoning based on a specific story-generation dataset. Besides, a specifically developed metric named PARENT (Dhingra et al., 2019) is designed for the table2text generation. Other statistical indicators, such as omission errors, hallucination errors, addition errors, duplication errors, and extrinsic errors, are also applied in the table2text task. Although these metrics have obtained impressive results, human evaluation is still inevitable in table2text.

2.2 Research on ChatGPT

In recent years, from BERT (Devlin et al., 2019) to ChatGPT (OpenAI, 2022), a large number of pretrained language models have been proposed one after another. Both their parameters and ability are gradually increased, facilitating much-advanced techniques. In particular, ChatGPT, which shows us a revolutionary change as an intelligent conversational large language model, sends shock waves through the research community and industries that have continued to reverberate to this day. With the emergence of ChatGPT, there are two growing research interests related to it: (1) leveraging ChatGPT to deal with various NLP tasks and evaluating its performance using traditional task-specific metrics (*i.e.*, evaluation), and (2) using as a metric to evaluate the outputs of other task-specific models (*i.e.*, evaluator) (Kocmi and Federmann, 2023).

Evaluation. Generally, the evaluation tasks on ChatGPT can be divided into two categories, *i.e.*, natural language understanding (NLU) and natural language generation (NLG). For NLU tasks, some researchers find that ChatGPT covers almost all NLU tasks (*e.g.*, sentiment analysis, textual similarity and textual entailment) and achieves competitive or even better performance (Qin et al., 2023; Bang et al., 2023; Zhong et al., 2023). For NLG tasks, machine translation (Jiao et al., 2023), summarization (Yang et al., 2023), query generation (Wang et al., 2023b), and radiology report simplification (Jeblick et al., 2022) are involved. Different from them, we regard ChatGPT as a human evaluator to automatically assess the quality of general textual generations rather than using it for solving tasks.

Evaluator. As an evaluator, there are two studies that evaluate the quality of translation (Kocmi and Federmann, 2023) and human personalities (Rao et al., 2023) by prompting ChatGPT. However, in this work, we aim to evaluate the more general textual outputs to further show the ability of ChatGPT as a general NLG metric.

3 ChatGPT for NLG Evaluation

In this section, we discuss how to prompt ChatGPT to serve as a reference-free NLG metric (§ 3.1) or a reference-based NLG metric (§ 3.2) to evaluate the generation quality of NLG models. We take the news summarization task as an example, and give the details of the prompt templates.

3.1 Reference-free Metric

To evaluate the generation quality of NLG models, we regard ChatGPT as a human evaluator and give it evaluation instruction via different prompts. Each prompt should specify (1) which NLG task (*e.g.*, summarization) needs to be evaluated and (2) which aspect (*e.g.*, fluency) of the generation result should be assessed currently.

Inspired by Kocmi and Federmann (2023), we utilize the following two prompts: direct assessment (**DA**) and one-to-five stars ranking (**star**).

> (DA Prompt)
> Score the following `[task-ins]` with respect to `[aspect]` on a continuous scale from 0 to 100, where a score of zero means "`[ant-aspect]`" and score of one hundred means "perfect `[aspect]`". Note that `[aspect]` measures `[aspect-ins]`.
>
> `[Conditioned Text]`
> `[Generated Text]`
> Scores:

> (Star Prompt)
> Score the following `[task-ins]` with respect to `[aspect]` with one to five stars, where one star means "`[ant-aspect]`" and five stars means "perfect `[aspect]`". Note that `[aspect]` measures `[aspect-ins]`.
>
> `[Conditioned Text]`
> `[Generated Text]`
> Stars:

where `[task-ins]` and `[aspect-ins]` are the instructions of the current task and aspect, respectively. `[aspect]` and `[ant-aspect]` denote the evaluated aspect and its antonym, respectively. `[Conditioned Text]` is the input of NLG models while `[Generated Text]` is the output. For example, when evaluating news summarization models in terms of fluency, the DA prompt may be like this:

> Score the following news summarization given the corresponding news with respect to fluency on a continuous scale from 0 to 100, where a score of zero means "disfluency" and score of one hundred means "perfect fluency". Note that fluency measures the quality of individual sentences, are they well-written and grammatically correct. Consider the quality of individual sentences.
>
> News: [a news article]
> Summary: [one generated summary]
> Scores:

In this manner, both the details of the task and the evaluation aspect are given to ChatGPT. Next, ChatGPT will give its judgment (*e.g.*, "score: 70") and the corresponding illustrative description (*e.g.*, "the summary covers the main points of the news, but ..."). A specific example is shown in Figure 1. Finally, the numerical scores could be extracted via several simple heuristic rules.

3.2 Reference-based Metric

In addition to reference-free metrics, we explicitly mention the golden references in the prompts to make ChatGPT a reference-based NLG metric:

> (DA Prompt w/ Reference)
> Score the following `[task-ins]` with respect to `[aspect]` on a continuous scale from 0 to 100, where a score of zero means "`[ant-aspect]`" and score of one hundred means "perfect `[aspect]`". Note that `[aspect]` measures `[aspect-ins]`.
>
> `[Conditioned Text]`
> Human reference: `[A Reference]`
> `[Generated Text]`
> Scores:

The star prompt with reference is also formed in a similar way:

> (Star Prompt w/ Reference))
> Score the following `[task-ins]` with respect to `[aspect]` with one to five stars, where one star means "`[ant-aspect]`" and five stars means "perfect `[aspect]`". Note that `[aspect]` measures `[aspect-ins]`.
>
> `[Conditioned Text]`
> Human reference: `[A Reference]`
> `[Generated Text]`
> Stars:

In this way, the ChatGPT evaluator will make its judgment and give the evaluation results under the consideration of the golden references.

Metrics	Coherence			Relevance			Consistency			Fluency			Avg.		
	Spear.	Pear.	Kend.	Spear.	Pear.	Kend.	Spear.	Pear.	Kend.	Spear.	Pear.	Kend.	Spear.	Pear.	Kend.
ROUGE-1	0.167	0.160	0.126	0.326	0.359	0.252	0.160	0.224	0.130	0.115	0.158	0.094	0.192	0.225	0.150
ROUGE-2	0.184	0.174	0.139	0.290	0.327	0.219	0.187	0.246	0.155	0.159	0.185	0.128	0.205	0.233	0.160
ROUGE-L	0.128	0.102	0.099	0.311	0.342	0.237	0.115	0.189	0.092	0.105	0.141	0.084	0.165	0.194	0.128
BERTScore	0.283	0.310	0.211	0.311	0.346	0.243	0.110	0.152	0.090	0.192	0.209	0.158	0.224	0.254	0.175
MoverScore	0.159	0.167	0.118	0.318	0.371	0.244	0.157	0.224	0.127	0.129	0.176	0.105	0.191	0.234	0.148
PRISM	0.249	0.258	0.196	0.212	0.232	0.163	0.345	0.352	0.285	0.254	0.264	0.205	0.265	0.276	0.212
BARTScore	0.322	0.345	0.250	0.264	0.290	0.197	0.311	0.321	0.256	0.248	0.260	0.203	0.286	0.304	0.227
BARTScore+CNN	0.448	0.458	0.342	0.356	0.369	0.273	0.382	0.422	0.315	0.356	0.407	0.292	0.385	0.414	0.305
BARTScore+CNN+Para	0.424	0.442	0.325	0.313	0.364	0.241	0.401	0.487	0.332	0.378	**0.448**	0.311	0.379	0.435	0.302
ChatGPT (DA w/o ref)	0.451	0.456	0.383	0.439	0.473	**0.379**	**0.432**	0.512	**0.399**	**0.380**	0.443	**0.351**	**0.425**	**0.471**	**0.378**
ChatGPT (Stars w/o ref)	0.470	0.484	0.403	0.428	0.454	0.374	0.419	0.517	0.389	0.353	0.415	0.329	0.417	0.468	0.374
ChatGPT (DA w/ ref)	0.420	0.435	0.346	**0.448**	**0.474**	0.378	0.424	**0.534**	0.384	0.316	0.381	0.285	0.402	0.456	0.348
ChatGPT (Stars w/ ref)	**0.474**	**0.491**	**0.407**	0.430	0.457	0.378	0.403	0.489	0.375	0.339	0.409	0.319	0.411	0.461	0.370

Table 1: Sample-level Spearman correlation (Spear.) correlation, Pearson (Pear.) correlation and Kendall's Tau (Kend.) of different aspects on SummEval (a text summarization meta-evaluation dataset). " Avg. " indicates the average performance. The **bold** indicates the best correlation.

4 Experiments

4.1 Experimental Setup

Metrics. To evaluate how well automatic metrics correlate with human judgment. Two widely-used correlation measures are adopted: (1) *Spearman correlation* (Zar, 2005) assesses the monotonic relationships between two variables; (2) *Pearson correlation* (Mukaka, 2012) measures the linear relationships between two sets of data; (3) *Kendall's Tau* (Kendall, 1938) evaluates the ordinal association between two measured quantities.

Evaluation Strategy. When calculating the correlation scores, there are different aggregation methods. Given a set of conditioned text $\{c_1, c_2, ..., c_n\}$ (*e.g.*, source documents in text summarization task) and M NLG models. The generated text of m-th model for the i-th condition text is denoted as $g_{i,m}$. (1) *Sample-level* evaluation strategy calculates the correlation scores as follows:

$$\text{Corr}_{\text{sample}} = \frac{1}{n}\sum_{1}^{n}(\rho([f_{\text{auto}}(g_{i,1}), ..., f_{\text{auto}}(g_{i,M})], [f_{\text{human}}(g_{i,1}), ..., f_{\text{human}}(g_{i,M})])) \quad (1)$$

where ρ denotes the correlation metrics like Spearman correlation. f_{auto} and f_{human} indicate the automatic evaluation and human judgment functions, respectively.

(2) *Dataset-level* evaluation strategy calculates the correlation as follows:

$$\text{Corr}_{\text{dataset}} = \rho([f_{\text{auto}}(g_{1,1}), ..., f_{\text{auto}}(g_{n,M})], [f_{\text{human}}(g_{1,1}), ..., f_{\text{human}}(g_{n,M})]) \quad (2)$$

4.2 Baselines

We compare the ChatGPT evaluator with the following widely-used automatic NLG metrics to provide deeper analyses:

- ROUGE-1, ROUGE-2 and ROUGE-L (Lin, 2004) measure the lexical overlap between the generated text and corresponding references based on unigram, bigram and longest common subsequence, respectively.
- BERTScore (Zhang et al., 2020) and MoverScore (Zhao et al., 2019) evaluate the semantic similarity via pre-trained BERT model (Devlin et al., 2019).
- PRISM (Thompson and Post, 2020) is used to evaluate NLG models via pre-trained paraphrase models.
- BARTScore (Yuan et al., 2021) is a state-of-the-art NLG metrics based on vanilla pre-trained BART model (Lewis et al., 2020).
- BARTScore+CNN (Yuan et al., 2021) could be regarded as an enhanced version of BARTScore. This metric is based on the BART fine-tuned on the CNN/DM dataset (Hermann et al., 2015).
- BARTScore+CNN+Para (Yuan et al., 2021) is another enhanced version of BARTScore. The metric is based on the BART fine-tuned on both CNN/DM and Paraphrase2.0 (Hu et al., 2019).
- Perplexity (PPL) is a commonly-used NLG metric to evaluate whether the generation result is grammatical and fluent.

4.3 Text Summarization

We conduct meta-evaluation on SummEval (Fabbri et al., 2021), NewsRoom (Grusky et al., 2018) and

Metrics	Coherence			Relevance			Informativeness			Fluency			Avg.		
	Spear.	Pear.	Kend.	Spear.	Pear.	Kend.	Spear.	Pear.	Kend.	Spear.	Pear.	Kend.	Spear.	Pear.	Kend.
ROUGE-1	0.095	-0.071	0.076	0.147	-0.001	0.112	0.130	-0.039	0.099	0.104	-0.074	0.082	0.119	-0.046	0.092
ROUGE-2	0.026	-0.108	0.009	0.091	-0.056	0.065	0.079	-0.087	0.052	0.048	-0.101	0.032	0.061	-0.088	0.092
ROUGE-L	0.064	-0.091	0.051	0.106	-0.034	0.083	0.089	-0.068	0.064	0.072	-0.090	0.061	0.083	-0.071	0.065
BERTScore	0.147	0.043	0.116	0.162	0.080	0.126	0.130	0.044	0.105	0.171	0.046	0.128	0.152	0.053	0.119
MoverScore	0.161	0.008	0.127	0.195	0.077	0.157	0.188	0.045	0.151	0.120	-0.008	0.086	0.166	0.030	0.130
PRISM	0.573	0.605	0.478	0.553	0.636	0.460	0.561	0.629	0.472	0.532	0.547	0.443	0.555	0.604	0.463
BARTScore	**0.679**	**0.709**	**0.568**	**0.604**	**0.744**	**0.507**	**0.646**	**0.749**	**0.543**	**0.670**	**0.662**	**0.564**	**0.650**	**0.716**	**0.545**
BARTScore+CNN	0.653	0.690	0.547	0.567	0.718	0.478	0.616	0.712	0.510	0.640	0.653	0.540	0.619	0.693	0.519
BARTScore+CNN+Para	0.657	0.675	0.544	0.562	0.739	0.465	0.614	0.727	0.507	0.652	0.630	0.545	0.621	0.693	0.515
ChatGPT (DA w/o ref)	0.469	0.487	0.405	0.461	0.587	0.392	0.578	0.645	0.498	0.507	0.524	0.427	0.504	0.561	0.430
ChatGPT (Stars w/o ref)	0.428	0.424	0.375	0.402	0.488	0.348	0.557	0.602	0.487	0.451	0.448	0.385	0.460	0.490	0.399
ChatGPT (DA w/ ref)	0.431	0.494	0.369	0.436	0.535	0.372	0.429	0.484	0.368	0.459	0.490	0.387	0.439	0.501	0.374
ChatGPT (Stars w/ ref)	0.423	0.424	0.369	0.443	0.506	0.395	0.404	0.463	0.352	0.503	0.504	0.430	0.443	0.474	0.387

Table 2: Sample-level Spearman correlation (Spear.) correlation, Pearson (Pear.) correlation and Kendall's Tau (Kend.) of different aspects on NewsRoom (a text summarization meta-evaluation dataset). " Avg. " indicates the average performance. The **bold** indicates the best correlation.

Metrics	Sample-level			Dataset-level		
	Spear.	Pear.	Kend.	Spear.	Pear.	Kend.
ROUGE-1	**0.498**	**0.526**	**0.408**	**0.533**	**0.555**	**0.383**
ROUGE-2	0.423	0.449	0.353	0.514	0.513	0.369
ROUGE-L	0.488	0.515	0.403	**0.533**	0.549	**0.383**
BERTScore	0.441	0.477	0.347	0.503	0.517	0.358
MoverScore	0.372	0.400	0.290	0.427	0.451	0.303
PRISM	0.411	0.458	0.324	0.478	0.494	0.339
BARTScore	0.441	0.467	0.342	0.467	0.458	0.327
BARTScore+CNN	0.475	0.500	0.374	0.436	0.455	0.306
BARTScore+CNN+Para	0.471	0.512	0.374	0.499	0.515	0.357
ChatGPT (DA w/o ref)	0.173	0.179	0.152	0.185	0.193	0.145
ChatGPT (Stars w/o ref)	0.145	0.162	0.129	0.170	0.179	0.136
ChatGPT (DA w/ ref)	0.184	0.208	0.154	0.276	0.288	0.206
ChatGPT (Stars w/ ref)	0.195	0.207	0.174	0.224	0.261	0.181

Table 3: Sample-level and Dataset-level correlation on RealSumm (a text summarization meta-evaluation dataset) (Spear.: Spearman correlation; Pear.: Pearson correlation; Kend.: Kendall's Tau). The **bold** indicates the best correlation.

RealSumm (Bhandari et al., 2020) to evaluate the performance of ChatGPT as an NLG metric for text summarization. SummEval collects 16 model-generated summaries on the CNN/DM dataset and annotates human judgments upon these summaries covering aspects of coherence, relevance, consistency and fluency. Newsroom, as a text summarization dataset, also provides human judgments on 7 model-generated summaries, including coherence, relevance, informativeness and fluency. RealSumm evaluates the pyramid (Nenkova and Passonneau, 2004) recall of 25 model-generated summaries.

The Potentiality of ChatGPT. Table 1 and Table 2 show the sample-level evaluation results on SummEval and NewsRoom, respectively (dataset-level evaluation results on SummEval and NewsRoom also shown in Table 4 and Table 5 with the similar trends). Experimental results show that ChatGPT achieves a new state-of-the-art correlation in most aspects of SummEval, demonstrating its potential of serving as an NLG metric. For results on Newsroom, ChatGPT also outperforms dominant summarization metrics (*i.e.*, ROUGE and BERTScore) by a large margin. Note that our experiments only estimate the lower bound of ChatGPT's performance, and better performances would like to be achieved once using better prompts or updated versions of ChatGPT.

The Impact of Dataset Biases. As shown in Table 3, we find that the experimental results on RealSumm show different trends from those on SummEval, *i.e.*, ChatGPT significantly underperforms other baseline metrics. For example, ChatGPT (Stars w/ ref) achieves 0.195 sample-level Spearman correlation, which is far behind the counterpart of ROUGE-1 (*i.e.*, 0.498). We conjecture this is because the human judgments in RealSumm are collected via pyramid method (Nenkova and Passonneau, 2004). In detail, this method first requires human evaluators to extract semantic content units from golden references, and then score each system summary based on how many extracted semantic content units are mentioned in the system summary.

In this manner, the more similarity between one generated summary and the corresponding golden reference, the more human evaluation scores will be achieved. Therefore, this reference-oriented annotation method makes the traditional n-gram-based metric (such as ROUGE) already achieve well correlations with human judgments, which we named as *lexical biases*. As for SummEval and NewsRoom, human evaluators are required to directly score different summaries without comparing them with the golden references, and thus do

Metrics	Coherence			Relevance			Consistency			Fluency			Avg.		
	Spear.	Pear.	Kend.	Spear.	Pear.	Kend.	Spear.	Pear.	Kend.	Spear.	Pear.	Kend.	Spear.	Pear.	Kend.
ROUGE-1	0.184	0.193	0.129	0.302	0.341	0.217	0.137	0.175	0.108	0.080	0.143	0.062	0.176	0.213	0.129
ROUGE-2	0.145	0.140	0.102	0.245	0.254	0.175	0.129	0.152	0.102	0.062	0.092	0.048	0.145	0.160	0.107
ROUGE-L	0.141	0.148	0.100	0.284	0.318	0.204	0.109	0.152	0.086	0.079	0.132	0.061	0.153	0.188	0.113
BERTScore	0.317	0.326	0.224	0.362	0.381	0.262	0.117	0.146	0.092	0.150	0.196	0.117	0.237	0.262	0.174
MoverScore	0.178	0.177	0.125	0.294	0.328	0.211	0.150	0.171	0.118	0.119	0.160	0.092	0.185	0.209	0.136
PRISM	0.286	0.281	0.204	0.280	0.297	0.202	0.323	0.297	0.256	0.236	0.248	0.184	0.281	0.281	0.212
BARTScore	0.335	0.357	0.241	0.363	0.386	0.263	0.269	0.276	0.212	0.187	0.206	0.146	0.288	0.306	0.215
BARTScore+CNN	0.408	0.434	0.292	0.394	0.423	0.286	0.334	0.377	0.264	0.285	0.354	0.223	0.355	0.397	0.266
BARTScore+CNN+Para	0.424	0.430	0.304	0.398	0.431	0.289	**0.379**	0.452	0.301	**0.346**	**0.410**	**0.271**	**0.387**	0.431	0.291
ChatGPT (DA w/o ref)	0.394	0.399	0.310	0.455	0.435	0.365	0.339	0.500	0.300	0.286	0.380	0.250	0.368	0.428	0.306
ChatGPT (Stars w/o ref)	0.435	0.438	0.353	0.448	0.459	0.366	0.356	**0.515**	**0.320**	0.300	0.385	0.268	0.385	**0.449**	0.327
ChatGPT (DA w/ ref)	0.418	0.426	0.327	**0.494**	**0.506**	**0.389**	0.363	0.507	0.315	0.237	0.329	0.203	0.378	0.442	0.308
ChatGPT (Stars w/ ref)	**0.465**	**0.472**	**0.385**	0.458	0.476	0.381	0.333	0.475	0.299	0.285	0.385	0.258	0.385	0.452	**0.331**

Table 4: Dataset-level Spearman correlation (Spear.) correlation, Pearson (Pear.) correlation and Kendall's Tau (Kend.) of different aspects on SummEval (a text summarization meta-evaluation dataset). " Avg. " indicates the average performance. The **bold** indicates the best correlation.

Metrics	Coherence			Relevance			Informativeness			Fluency			Avg.		
	Spear.	Pear.	Kend.	Spear.	Pear.	Kend.	Spear.	Pear.	Kend.	Spear.	Pear.	Kend.	Spear.	Pear.	Kend.
ROUGE-1	0.100	0.015	0.070	0.122	0.061	0.084	0.149	0.043	0.106	0.064	-0.009	0.043	0.109	0.028	0.076
ROUGE-2	0.080	0.033	0.060	0.124	0.071	0.092	0.158	0.060	0.119	0.045	0.018	0.032	0.102	0.045	0.076
ROUGE-L	0.079	-0.010	0.055	0.101	0.031	0.069	0.136	0.018	0.098	0.045	-0.030	0.029	0.090	0.002	0.063
BERTScore	0.169	0.138	0.122	0.176	0.158	0.127	0.196	0.153	0.141	0.154	0.129	0.109	0.174	0.145	0.125
MoverScore	0.173	0.119	0.122	0.192	0.156	0.132	0.232	0.148	0.166	0.112	0.091	0.076	0.177	0.129	0.124
PRISM	0.483	0.485	0.350	0.540	0.550	0.398	0.567	0.569	0.414	0.420	0.421	0.303	0.503	0.506	0.366
BARTScore	**0.656**	**0.666**	**0.495**	**0.588**	**0.700**	**0.439**	**0.645**	**0.710**	**0.485**	**0.615**	**0.610**	**0.464**	**0.626**	**0.671**	**0.471**
BARTScore+CNN	0.623	0.640	0.466	0.557	0.665	0.411	0.592	0.665	0.440	0.596	0.592	0.448	0.592	0.641	0.441
BARTScore+CNN+Para	0.621	0.639	0.465	0.575	0.692	0.427	0.615	0.694	0.459	0.593	0.577	0.444	0.601	0.650	0.449
ChatGPT (DA w/o ref)	0.383	0.418	0.297	0.491	0.541	0.392	0.527	0.576	0.413	0.401	0.398	0.309	0.451	0.483	0.353
ChatGPT (Stars w/o ref)	0.370	0.374	0.294	0.422	0.444	0.343	0.518	0.527	0.423	0.381	0.362	0.302	0.423	0.427	0.341
ChatGPT (DA w/ ref)	0.381	0.407	0.292	0.434	0.458	0.339	0.377	0.412	0.291	0.386	0.403	0.298	0.394	0.420	0.305
ChatGPT (Stars w/ ref)	0.370	0.355	0.295	0.425	0.426	0.342	0.373	0.400	0.301	0.439	0.425	0.353	0.402	0.402	0.323

Table 5: Dataset-level Spearman correlation (Spear.) correlation, Pearson (Pear.) correlation and Kendall's Tau (Kend.) of different aspects on NewsRoom (a text summarization meta-evaluation dataset). " Avg. " indicates the average performance. The **bold** indicates the best correlation.

Metrics	Sample-level			Dataset-level		
	Spear.	Pear.	Kend.	Spear.	Pear.	Kend.
ROUGE-1	0.014	0.020	0.013	-0.023	-0.010	-0.016
ROUGE-2	0.035	0.041	0.035	0.009	0.012	0.007
ROUGE-L	0.013	0.021	0.014	-0.016	-0.004	-0.011
BERTScore	0.140	0.120	0.105	0.081	0.084	0.056
BARTScore	-0.065	-0.082	-0.061	-0.065	-0.092	-0.045
BARTScore+CNN	0.049	0.026	0.041	0.047	0.053	0.033
BARTScore+CNN+Para	0.064	0.050	0.062	0.062	0.074	0.043
PPL	0.324	0.330	0.265	0.306	0.255	0.213
ChatGPT (DA w/o ref)	**0.507**	**0.533**	**0.439**	**0.471**	**0.494**	**0.366**
ChatGPT (Stars w/o ref)	0.472	0.490	0.427	0.415	0.439	0.342
ChatGPT (DA w/ ref)	0.411	0.434	0.357	0.363	0.375	0.281
ChatGPT (Stars w/ ref)	0.478	0.493	0.435	0.346	0.372	0.291

Table 6: Sample-level and Dataset-level correlation on OpenMEVA (a story generation meta-evaluation dataset) (Spear.: Spearman correlation; Pear.: Pearson correlation; Kend.: Kendall's Tau).

not involve such lexical biases.

The Impact of Different Prompt. In this work, we attempt four prompts to guide ChatGPT to evaluate the generation of NLG models. As we can see, the performances of ChatGPT are sensitive to the prompt design. For different aspects, the prompt should be carefully designed, just like formulating instructions for human evaluators.

4.4 Story Generation

Story generation is another NLG task with more emphasis on open-ended generation compared with text summarization, which also means for a given beginning of a story, various generated storylines and different plots could satisfy people. Therefore, story generation models are extremely challenging to evaluate. The automatic similarity-based metrics between the generated storylines and so-called references cannot fully evaluate the quality of the storylines since they do not consider creativity.

To show the effectiveness of ChatGPT as an NLG metric for the story generation task, we conduct experiments on OpenMEVA-ROC (Guan et al., 2021). The OpenMEVA-ROC dataset manually annotates five model-generated storylines under the consideration of their overall quality.

Metrics	Informativeness			Naturalness			Quality			Avg.		
	Spear.	Pear.	Kend.	Spear.	Pear.	Kend.	Spear.	Pear.	Kend.	Spear.	Pear.	Kend.
ROUGE-1	0.092	0.093	0.073	0.265	0.274	0.206	0.235	0.234	0.184	0.197	0.200	0.154
ROUGE-2	0.133	0.137	0.103	0.233	0.241	0.177	0.192	0.192	0.145	0.186	0.190	0.142
ROUGE-L	0.079	0.084	0.063	0.237	0.255	0.183	0.210	0.216	0.163	0.175	0.185	0.136
BERTScore	0.231	0.261	0.174	0.288	0.327	0.216	0.264	0.304	0.197	0.261	0.297	0.196
MoverScore	**0.284**	**0.276**	0.209	0.189	0.189	0.140	0.152	0.161	0.114	0.208	0.209	0.154
PRISM	0.255	0.268	0.189	0.301	0.350	0.223	0.308	0.337	0.226	0.288	0.318	0.213
BARTScore	0.234	0.270	0.174	0.221	0.280	0.164	0.186	0.245	0.139	0.214	0.265	0.159
BARTScore+CNN	0.237	0.253	0.177	0.312	0.382	0.233	0.294	0.357	0.219	0.281	0.331	0.210
BARTScore+CNN+Para	0.240	0.266	0.177	**0.335**	**0.416**	0.248	**0.343**	**0.383**	0.255	**0.306**	**0.355**	0.227
ChatGPT (DA w/o ref)	-	-	-	0.243	0.293	0.202	0.310	0.319	0.260	-	-	-
ChatGPT (Stars w/o ref)	-	-	-	0.316	0.389	**0.269**	0.307	0.367	**0.266**	-	-	-
ChatGPT (DA w/ ref)	0.247	0.255	0.198	0.305	0.344	0.248	0.269	0.343	0.215	0.274	0.314	0.220
ChatGPT (Stars w/ ref)	0.266	0.262	**0.224**	0.293	0.374	0.235	0.276	0.328	0.239	0.278	0.321	**0.233**

Table 7: Dataset-level Spearman correlation (Spear.) correlation, Pearson (Pear.) correlation and Kendall's Tau (Kend.) of different aspects on BAGEL (a data-to-text generation meta-evaluation dataset). " Avg. " indicates the average performance. The **bold** indicates the best correlation.

The Potentiality of ChatGPT. As shown in Table 6, ChatGPT achieves the best performance in terms of all correlations, and significantly outperforms the second-best metric (*i.e.*, PPL). For example, ChatGPT (DA w/o ref) achieves 0.507 sample-level Spearman correlation, while PPL only achieves 0.324 sample-level Spearman correlation. In addition, we also find that all similarity-based metrics (*i.e.*, ROUGE-1, ROUGE-2, ROUGE-L, BERTScore and BARTScore) show their weak correlations with the human judgments. This finding indicates that the ChatGPT evaluator has more powerful and reliable judgments on the open-ended and creative text generation tasks, where many diversified generated results could also be regarded as high-quality.

The Impact of Different Prompt. The results in Table 6 also show the sensitivity of the correlation results led by the different prompts. For example, there are large performance gaps between ChatGPT (DA w/o ref) and ChatGPT (DA w/ ref). This finding is also consistent with that in text summarization (Section 4.3). More recently, some researchers also discuss the robustness of LLMs on different (adversarial) prompts (Zhu et al., 2023), and we think this under-explored LLM research direction deserves more research attention.

4.5 Data-to-Text Generation

Data-to-text generation aims at generating a fluent free-text description for a given structured table. We conduct experiments on BAGEL (Mairesse et al., 2010) to show the effectiveness of the ChatGPT evaluator on data-to-text generation.

Table 7 shows the experimental results, where ChatGPT achieves competitive correlations compared with the previous state-of-the-art baselines, indicating its strong potentiality serving as a metric for data-to-text generation. It is worth noting that we do not provide reference-free ChatGPT performance in terms of informativeness because informativeness in BAGEL is defined as "whether the system generation contains all the information in the gold reference", which also means that when evaluating informativeness the golden references must be given.

5 Conclusion

In this technical report, we explore a research question: *"Is ChatGPT a good NLG evaluator?"*. To this end, we design task-specific as well as aspect-specific prompts to guide ChatGPT to perform as an NLG metric. Experimental results on five widely-used meta-evaluation datasets, covering text summarization, story generation and data-to-text tasks, show the potentiality of ChatGPT as an NLG metric. ChatGPT achieves the new state-of-the-art correlations (with human judgments) on SummEval and OpenMEVA meta-evaluation datasets, and obtains competitive results on NewsRoom and BAGEL datasets.

In addition, we also find that the lexical biases involved in the meta-evaluation datasets would influence the effectiveness of NLG metrics, and might lead to the limited performance of the ChatGPT evaluator. Besides, the performances of ChatGPT as an NLG evaluator are sensitive to the format of the prompt, for different tasks and aspects, the prompt should be carefully designed.

We believe that ChatGPT will exceed its current performance and provide a reliable NLG metric for the research community in the near future.

Limitations

While we show that ChatGPT achieves state-of-the-art or competitive correlation with human judgments on various NLG tasks, there are limitations that provide avenues for future work: (1) ChatGPT's performance as an NLG metric is related to prompts, and future work could explore more powerful prompts to achieve better performance; (2) This preliminary report misses experiments on some mainstream NLG tasks, *e.g.*, dialogue generation and report generation; (3) When we did the experiments, the OpenAI ChatGPT did not release the official API. Thus, we conducted the experiments on the ChatGPT website with default temperature, making the results difficult to reproduce. All experiments related to ChatGPT are conducted between February 24 to February 27, 2023; and March 17 to March 22. (4) The experiments are only conducted on the English NLG meta-evaluation datasets, and future work could extend this method into other languages or cross-lingual scenes. (5) The correlation between the ChatGPT evaluator and humans is also related to the quality and challenge of the corresponding meta-evaluation datasets. Our experiments are conducted on the traditional NLG meta-evaluation datasets (that appear before the LLM era). Recently, Zeng et al. (2023) propose LLM-BAR, a challenging meta-evaluation benchmark to test the ability of an LLM evaluator. Future work could adapt our method to other challenging datasets and study the performance of the ChatGPT evaluator.

Acknowledgement

We thank anonymous reviewers for their constructive suggestions and comments.

References

Yejin Bang, Samuel Cahyawijaya, Nayeon Lee, Wenliang Dai, Dan Su, Bryan Wilie, Holy Lovenia, Ziwei Ji, Tiezheng Yu, Willy Chung, et al. 2023. A multitask, multilingual, multimodal evaluation of chatgpt on reasoning, hallucination, and interactivity. *arXiv preprint arXiv:2302.04023*.

Manik Bhandari, Pranav Narayan Gour, Atabak Ashfaq, Pengfei Liu, and Graham Neubig. 2020. Re-evaluating evaluation in text summarization. In *Proceedings of the 2020 Conference on Empirical Methods in Natural Language Processing (EMNLP)*, pages 9347–9359, Online. Association for Computational Linguistics.

Hong Chen, Duc Vo, Hiroya Takamura, Yusuke Miyao, and Hideki Nakayama. 2022. StoryER: Automatic story evaluation via ranking, rating and reasoning. In *Proceedings of the 2022 Conference on Empirical Methods in Natural Language Processing*, pages 1739–1753, Abu Dhabi, United Arab Emirates. Association for Computational Linguistics.

Michael Denkowski and Alon Lavie. 2011. Meteor 1.3: Automatic metric for reliable optimization and evaluation of machine translation systems. In *Proceedings of the Sixth Workshop on Statistical Machine Translation*, pages 85–91, Edinburgh, Scotland. Association for Computational Linguistics.

Jacob Devlin, Ming-Wei Chang, Kenton Lee, and Kristina Toutanova. 2019. BERT: Pre-training of deep bidirectional transformers for language understanding. In *Proceedings of the 2019 Conference of the North American Chapter of the Association for Computational Linguistics: Human Language Technologies, Volume 1 (Long and Short Papers)*, pages 4171–4186, Minneapolis, Minnesota. Association for Computational Linguistics.

Bhuwan Dhingra, Manaal Faruqui, Ankur Parikh, Ming-Wei Chang, Dipanjan Das, and William Cohen. 2019. Handling divergent reference texts when evaluating table-to-text generation. In *Proceedings of the 57th Annual Meeting of the Association for Computational Linguistics*, pages 4884–4895, Florence, Italy. Association for Computational Linguistics.

Alexander R. Fabbri, Wojciech Kryściński, Bryan McCann, Caiming Xiong, Richard Socher, and Dragomir Radev. 2021. SummEval: Re-evaluating summarization evaluation. *Transactions of the Association for Computational Linguistics*, 9:391–409.

Jinlan Fu, See-Kiong Ng, Zhengbao Jiang, and Pengfei Liu. 2023. Gptscore: Evaluate as you desire.

Max Grusky, Mor Naaman, and Yoav Artzi. 2018. Newsroom: A dataset of 1.3 million summaries with diverse extractive strategies. In *Proceedings of the 2018 Conference of the North American Chapter of the Association for Computational Linguistics: Human Language Technologies, Volume 1 (Long Papers)*, pages 708–719, New Orleans, Louisiana. Association for Computational Linguistics.

Jian Guan, Zhexin Zhang, Zhuoer Feng, Zitao Liu, Wenbiao Ding, Xiaoxi Mao, Changjie Fan, and Minlie Huang. 2021. OpenMEVA: A benchmark for evaluating open-ended story generation metrics. In *Proceedings of the 59th Annual Meeting of the Association for Computational Linguistics and the 11th International*

Joint Conference on Natural Language Processing (Volume 1: Long Papers), pages 6394–6407, Online. Association for Computational Linguistics.

Karl Moritz Hermann, Tomás Kociský, Edward Grefenstette, Lasse Espeholt, Will Kay, Mustafa Suleyman, and Phil Blunsom. 2015. Teaching machines to read and comprehend. In *Advances in Neural Information Processing Systems 28: Annual Conference on Neural Information Processing Systems 2015, December 7-12, 2015, Montreal, Quebec, Canada*, pages 1693–1701.

J. Edward Hu, Abhinav Singh, Nils Holzenberger, Matt Post, and Benjamin Van Durme. 2019. Large-scale, diverse, paraphrastic bitexts via sampling and clustering. In *Proceedings of the 23rd Conference on Computational Natural Language Learning (CoNLL)*, pages 44–54, Hong Kong, China. Association for Computational Linguistics.

Fan Huang, Haewoon Kwak, and Jisun An. 2023. Is chatgpt better than human annotators? potential and limitations of chatgpt in explaining implicit hate speech.

Katharina Jeblick, Balthasar Schachtner, Jakob Dexl, Andreas Mittermeier, Anna Theresa Stüber, Johanna Topalis, Tobias Weber, Philipp Wesp, Bastian Sabel, Jens Ricke, and Michael Ingrisch. 2022. Chatgpt makes medicine easy to swallow: An exploratory case study on simplified radiology reports.

Wenxiang Jiao, Wenxuan Wang, Jen-tse Huang, Xing Wang, and Zhaopeng Tu. 2023. Is chatgpt a good translator? a preliminary study. *arXiv preprint arXiv:2301.08745*.

Maurice G Kendall. 1938. A new measure of rank correlation. *Biometrika*, 30(1/2):81–93.

Tom Kocmi and Christian Federmann. 2023. Large language models are state-of-the-art evaluators of translation quality. *arXiv preprint arXiv:2302.14520*.

Jan Kocoń, Igor Cichecki, Oliwier Kaszyca, Mateusz Kochanek, Dominika Szydło, Joanna Baran, Julita Bielaniewicz, Marcin Gruza, Arkadiusz Janz, Kamil Kanclerz, Anna Kocoń, Bartłomiej Koptyra, Wiktoria Mieleszczenko-Kowszewicz, Piotr Miłkowski, Marcin Oleksy, Maciej Piasecki, Łukasz Radliński, Konrad Wojtasik, Stanisław Woźniak, and Przemysław Kazienko. 2023. Chatgpt: Jack of all trades, master of none.

Matt Kusner, Yu Sun, Nicholas Kolkin, and Kilian Weinberger. 2015. From word embeddings to document distances. In *Proceedings of the 32nd International Conference on Machine Learning*, volume 37 of *Proceedings of Machine Learning Research*, pages 957–966, Lille, France. PMLR.

Mike Lewis, Yinhan Liu, Naman Goyal, Marjan Ghazvininejad, Abdelrahman Mohamed, Omer Levy, Veselin Stoyanov, and Luke Zettlemoyer. 2020. BART: Denoising sequence-to-sequence pre-training for natural language generation, translation, and comprehension. In *Proceedings of the 58th Annual Meeting of the Association for Computational Linguistics*, pages 7871–7880, Online. Association for Computational Linguistics.

Jiwei Li, Michel Galley, Chris Brockett, Jianfeng Gao, and Bill Dolan. 2016. A diversity-promoting objective function for neural conversation models. In *Proceedings of the 2016 Conference of the North American Chapter of the Association for Computational Linguistics: Human Language Technologies*, pages 110–119, San Diego, California. Association for Computational Linguistics.

Chin-Yew Lin. 2004. ROUGE: A package for automatic evaluation of summaries. In *Text Summarization Branches Out*, pages 74–81, Barcelona, Spain. Association for Computational Linguistics.

François Mairesse, Milica Gašić, Filip Jurčíček, Simon Keizer, Blaise Thomson, Kai Yu, and Steve Young. 2010. Phrase-based statistical language generation using graphical models and active learning. In *Proceedings of the 48th Annual Meeting of the Association for Computational Linguistics*, pages 1552–1561, Uppsala, Sweden. Association for Computational Linguistics.

Mavuto M Mukaka. 2012. A guide to appropriate use of correlation coefficient in medical research. *Malawi medical journal*, 24(3):69–71.

Ani Nenkova and Rebecca Passonneau. 2004. Evaluating content selection in summarization: The pyramid method. In *Proceedings of the Human Language Technology Conference of the North American Chapter of the Association for Computational Linguistics: HLT-NAACL 2004*, pages 145–152, Boston, Massachusetts, USA. Association for Computational Linguistics.

OpenAI. 2022. Introducing chatgpt. `https://openai.com/blog/chatgpt`.

Long Ouyang, Jeff Wu, Xu Jiang, Diogo Almeida, Carroll L Wainwright, Pamela Mishkin, Chong Zhang, Sandhini Agarwal, Katarina Slama, Alex Ray, et al. 2022. Training language models to follow instructions with human feedback. *arXiv preprint arXiv:2203.02155*.

Kishore Papineni, Salim Roukos, Todd Ward, and Wei-Jing Zhu. 2002. Bleu: A method for automatic evaluation of machine translation. In *Proceedings of the 40th Annual Meeting on Association for Computational Linguistics*, ACL '02, page 311–318, USA. Association for Computational Linguistics.

Krishna Pillutla, Lang Liu, John Thickstun, Sean Welleck, Swabha Swayamdipta, Rowan Zellers, Sewoong Oh, Yejin Choi, and Zaid Harchaoui. 2022. Mauve scores for generative models: Theory and practice.

Chengwei Qin, Aston Zhang, Zhuosheng Zhang, Jiaao Chen, Michihiro Yasunaga, and Diyi Yang. 2023. Is chatgpt a general-purpose natural language processing task solver? *arXiv preprint arXiv:2302.06476*.

Haocong Rao, Cyril Leung, and Chunyan Miao. 2023. Can chatgpt assess human personalities? a general evaluation framework.

Ricardo Rei, Craig Stewart, Ana C Farinha, and Alon Lavie. 2020. COMET: A neural framework for MT evaluation. In *Proceedings of the 2020 Conference on Empirical Methods in Natural Language Processing (EMNLP)*, pages 2685–2702, Online. Association for Computational Linguistics.

Thibault Sellam, Dipanjan Das, and Ankur Parikh. 2020. BLEURT: Learning robust metrics for text generation. In *Proceedings of the 58th Annual Meeting of the Association for Computational Linguistics*, pages 7881–7892, Online. Association for Computational Linguistics.

Brian Thompson and Matt Post. 2020. Automatic machine translation evaluation in many languages via zero-shot paraphrasing. In *Proceedings of the 2020 Conference on Empirical Methods in Natural Language Processing (EMNLP)*, pages 90–121, Online. Association for Computational Linguistics.

Jiaan Wang, Yunlong Liang, Fandong Meng, Zhixu Li, Jianfeng Qu, and Jie Zhou. 2023a. Cross-lingual summarization via chatgpt. *arXiv preprint*.

Shuai Wang, Harrisen Scells, Bevan Koopman, and Guido Zuccon. 2023b. Can chatgpt write a good boolean query for systematic review literature search?

Xiang Wei, Xingyu Cui, Ning Cheng, Xiaobin Wang, Xin Zhang, Shen Huang, Pengjun Xie, Jinan Xu, Yufeng Chen, Meishan Zhang, Yong Jiang, and Wenjuan Han. 2023. Zero-shot information extraction via chatting with chatgpt.

Xianjun Yang, Yan Li, Xinlu Zhang, Haifeng Chen, and Wei Cheng. 2023. Exploring the limits of chatgpt for query or aspect-based text summarization. *arXiv preprint arXiv:2302.08081*.

Weizhe Yuan, Graham Neubig, and Pengfei Liu. 2021. Bartscore: Evaluating generated text as text generation.

Jerrold H Zar. 2005. Spearman rank correlation. *Encyclopedia of biostatistics*, 7.

Zhiyuan Zeng, Jiatong Yu, Tianyu Gao, Yu Meng, Tanya Goyal, and Danqi Chen. 2023. Evaluating large language models at evaluating instruction following. *arXiv preprint arXiv:2310.07641*.

Tianyi Zhang, Varsha Kishore, Felix Wu, Kilian Q. Weinberger, and Yoav Artzi. 2020. Bertscore: Evaluating text generation with BERT. In *8th International Conference on Learning Representations, ICLR 2020, Addis Ababa, Ethiopia, April 26-30, 2020*. OpenReview.net.

Wei Zhao, Maxime Peyrard, Fei Liu, Yang Gao, Christian M. Meyer, and Steffen Eger. 2019. MoverScore: Text generation evaluating with contextualized embeddings and earth mover distance. In *Proceedings of the 2019 Conference on Empirical Methods in Natural Language Processing and the 9th International Joint Conference on Natural Language Processing (EMNLP-IJCNLP)*, pages 563–578, Hong Kong, China. Association for Computational Linguistics.

Qihuang Zhong, Liang Ding, Juhua Liu, Bo Du, and Dacheng Tao. 2023. Can chatgpt understand too? a comparative study on chatgpt and fine-tuned bert.

Kaijie Zhu, Jindong Wang, Jiaheng Zhou, Zichen Wang, Hao Chen, Yidong Wang, Linyi Yang, Wei Ye, Neil Zhenqiang Gong, Yue Zhang, et al. 2023. Promptbench: Towards evaluating the robustness of large language models on adversarial prompts. *arXiv preprint arXiv:2306.04528*.

Guido Zuccon and Bevan Koopman. 2023. Dr chatgpt, tell me what i want to hear: How prompt knowledge impacts health answer correctness.

Zero-Shot Cross-Lingual Summarization via Large Language Models

Jiaan Wang[1]*†, Yunlong Liang[2]*, Fandong Meng[3], Beiqi Zou[4]
Zhixu Li[5], Jianfeng Qu[1] and Jie Zhou[3]

[1]Soochow University, Suzhou, China [2]Beijing Jiaotong University, Beijing, China
[3]Pattern Recognition Center, WeChat AI, Tencent Inc, China [4]Princeton University, NJ, USA
[5]Fudan Unversity, Shanghai, China

jawang.nlp@gmail.com yunlongliang@bjtu.edu.cn
fandongmeng@tencent.com bzou@cs.princeton.edu

Abstract

Given a document in a source language, cross-lingual summarization (CLS) aims to generate a summary in a different target language. Recently, the emergence of Large Language Models (LLMs), such as GPT-3.5, ChatGPT and GPT-4, has attracted wide attention from the computational linguistics community. However, it is not yet known the performance of LLMs on CLS. In this report, we empirically use various prompts to guide LLMs to perform zero-shot CLS from different paradigms (*i.e.*, end-to-end and pipeline), and provide a preliminary evaluation on the generated summaries. We find that ChatGPT and GPT-4 originally prefer to produce lengthy summaries with detailed information. These two LLMs can further balance informativeness and conciseness with the help of an interactive prompt, significantly improving their CLS performance. Experimental results on three widely-used CLS datasets show that GPT-4 achieves state-of-the-art zero-shot CLS performance, and performs competitively compared with the fine-tuned mBART-50.

Moreover, we also find some multi-lingual and bilingual LLMs (*i.e.*, BLOOMZ, ChatGLM-6B, Vicuna-13B and ChatYuan) have limited zero-shot CLS ability. Due to the composite nature of CLS, which requires models to perform summarization and translation simultaneously, accomplishing this task in a zero-shot manner is even a challenge for LLMs. *Therefore, we sincerely hope and recommend future LLM research could use CLS as a testbed.*

1 Introduction

Cross-Lingual Summarization (CLS) aims to provide a target-language (*e.g.*, Chinese) summary for a lengthy document in a different source language (*e.g.*, English) (Leuski et al., 2003; Wan et al., 2010; Yao et al., 2015; Zhu et al., 2019, 2020; Ladhak et al., 2020; Perez-Beltrachini and Lapata, 2021; Bai et al., 2021a; Liang et al., 2022b; Feng et al., 2022; Hasan et al., 2021; Wang et al., 2022a,b; Liang et al., 2022a; Liu et al., 2022; Zheng et al., 2022; Aumiller et al., 2022). This task could help people quickly capture their interests from foreign documents.

Figure 1: An example of zero-shot CLS via ChatGPT.

In recent years, a number of powerful multi-lingual pre-trained generative models have been proposed one after another, such as mBART (Liu et al., 2020), mBART-50 (Tang et al., 2021), mT5 (Xue et al., 2021) and BLOOM (Scao et al., 2022). The parameters in these models have gradually increased from million levels (*e.g.*, 580M in mT5-base and 610M in mBART-Large) to billion levels (*e.g.*, 3.7B in mT5-XL, 13B in mT5-XXL and 176B in BLOOM), facilitating various research topics (*e.g.*, machine translation and CLS) in the multi-lingual world. Besides, large language mod-

* Equal Contribution. Work was done when Wang and Liang was interning at Pattern Recognition Center, WeChat AI, Tencent Inc, China.

† Corresponding author.

Proceedings of The 4th New Frontiers in Summarization Workshop, pages 12–23
December 6, 2023

els (LLMs) have been key to strong performance when transferring to new tasks by simply conditioning on a few input-label pairs (*in-context learning*) (Dong et al., 2022; Min et al., 2022) or short sentences describing crucial reasoning steps (*chain-of-thoughts*) (Fu et al., 2022; Zhang et al., 2022).

More recently, ChatGPT and GPT-4 (OpenAI, 2023) have attracted great attention from both the research communities and industries. Similar to InstructGPT (Ouyang et al., 2022), ChatGPT is created by fine-tuning a GPT-3.5 series model via reinforcement learning from human feedback (RLHF) (Christiano et al., 2017). GPT-4, as a multi-modal LLM that can accept image and text inputs and produce text outputs, exhibits human-level performance on various benchmark datasets (OpenAI, 2023). With the emergence of ChatGPT and GPT-4, there is growing interest in leveraging LLMs for various NLP tasks (Qin et al., 2023; Jiao et al., 2023; Bang et al., 2023; Yang et al., 2023; Zhong et al., 2023; Wang et al., 2023; Bubeck et al., 2023; Tan et al., 2023; Peng et al., 2023; Liu et al., 2023; Yong et al., 2023). Nevertheless, the exploration of LLMs on CLS is still lacking.

In this report, we present a preliminary evaluation of LLMs' zero-shot CLS performance, including GPT-3.5, ChatGPT, GPT-4, BLOOMZ, ChatGLM-6B, Vicuna-13B and ChatYuan. In detail, we design various prompts to guide LLMs to perform CLS in an end-to-end manner with or without chain-of-thoughts (CoT). Figure 1 gives an example of prompting ChatGPT to perform zero-shot CLS. To further exploit the interaction capability of conversational LLMs (*e.g.*, ChatGPT and GPT-4), we leverage an interactive prompt to let them produce more concise summaries. Moreover, to provide a deeper analysis of LLMs' zero-shot CLS performance, we compare them with fine-tuned mBART-50 (Tang et al., 2021) which has shown its superiority in many previous CLS works (Wang et al., 2022a; Feng et al., 2022; Perez-Beltrachini and Lapata, 2021). Experimental results on three CLS datasets, covering three domains (news, how-to guide and dialogue) and two cross-lingual directions (En⇒Zh and En⇒De)[1], show that GPT-4 achieves the best zero-shot performance but is still worse than the fine-tuned mBART-50 model in terms of ROUGE scores and BERTScore. We also conduct case studies to show that ChatGPT and GPT-4 could absorb the core idea of the given source-language documents and generate fluent and concise target-language summaries.

In addition, we find that the current open-source LLMs (*i.e.*, BLOOMZ, ChatGLM-6B, Vicuna-13B and ChatYuan) achieve limited zero-shot CLS performance, which is significantly worse than that of GPT-4. This leads us to conclude that the composite end-to-end CLS prompts are difficult for them to follow, and there is still a challenge for LLMs to perform zero-shot CLS in an end-to-end manner which requires simultaneously carrying out translation and summarization. Based on the finding, we suggest that future multi-lingual or bilingual LLM research uses CLS as a testbed to evaluate LLMs' capabilities to follow composite instructions as well as combine their different abilities.

Our main contributions are concluded as follows:

- To the best of our knowledge, we are the first to explore the zero-shot CLS performance of LLMs. To achieve that, we design various prompts to guide LLMs to perform CLS in an end-to-end manner with or without chain-of-thoughts.
- Experimental results on three widely-used CLS benchmark datasets, covering various domains and languages, show several LLMs (especially ChatGPT and GPT-4) achieve competitive results compared with the strong fine-tuned baseline.
- We also find the current open-source LLMs generally achieve limited zero-shot CLS performance, making us think CLS could be used as a testbed for future LLM research due to its challenges.

2 Methodology

2.1 Cross-Lingual Summarization Prompts

We heuristically design 3 prompts to guide LLMs to perform zero-shot CLS in an end-to-end manner, which is shown as follows with an example from an English document to a Chinese summary:

- The direct (**Dir**) prompt guides LLMs straightforwardly output the corresponding target-language summary without chain-of-thoughts (CoT):

```
Please summarize the
following text in
Chinese:  [English Doc]
```

  where `[English Doc]` indicates a given English document.

- The translate-then-summarize (**TS**) CoT prompt

[1] Since a CLS dataset might contain multiple source and target languages, we use "X⇒Y" to indicate the source language and target language are X and Y, respectively. En: English; Zh: Chinese; De: German.

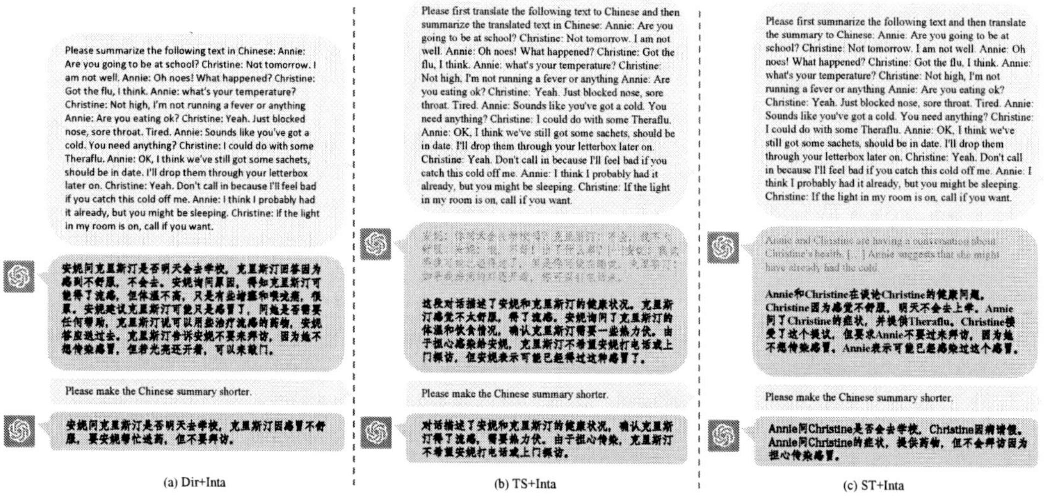

Figure 2: An illustration of all prompts used to guide LLMs to perform zero CLS (take ChatGPT as an example).

makes LLMs first translate the given document from the source language to the target language, and then summarize the translated document to perform CLS:

```
Please first translate
the following text
to Chinese and then
summarize the translated
text in Chinese:
[English Doc]
```

- The summarize-then-translate (**ST**) CoT prompt lets LLMs first summarize the given document and then translate the output summary to the target language:

```
Please first summarize
the following text
and then translate the
summary to Chinese:
[English Doc]
```

Note that though the TS and ST CoT prompts guide LLMs to perform CLS step by step, the behaviors are end-to-end since the target-language summaries are generated within a single turn.

To further exploit the potentiality of conversational LLMs, inspired by Bang et al. (2023), after prompting with Dir, TS or ST prompt, we adopt an interactive (**Inta**) prompt to make the preliminarily generated summary more concise:

```
Please make the Chinese
summary shorter.
```

and the whole process is denoted as "**Dir+Inta**", "**TS+Inta**" or "**ST+Inta**".

2.2 Large Language Models

We explore the CLS ability of the following LLMs:

- **Davinci-003** is the most advanced GPT-3.5 model with 175B parameters. We evaluate its performance by requesting the official API provided by OpenAI with default settings.[2]
- **ChatGPT** is created by fine-tuning a GPT-3.5 series model via reinforcement learning from human feedback (RLHF) (Christiano et al., 2017). We conduct experiments on the ChatGPT platform[3] between February 17 to February 19, 2023.
- **GPT-4**, as a multi-modal LLM that can accept image and text inputs and produce text outputs, exhibits human-level performance on various benchmark datasets (OpenAI, 2023). We assess GPT-4 on the ChatGPT platform between March 15 to March 19, 2023.
- **BLOOMZ** (Muennighoff et al., 2022) is an open-source multi-lingual LLM with 176B parameters. The model supports 59 languages, and is created by fine-tuning BLOOM (Scao et al., 2022) on an instruction corpus (*i.e.*, XP3).
- **ChatGLM-6B**[4] is an open-source bilingual (*i.e.*, Chinese and English) language model based on General Language Model (GLM) framework (Du

[2]https://platform.openai.com/docs/models/gpt-3-5

[3]https://chat.openai.com/

[4]https://github.com/THUDM/ChatGLM-6B

Dataset	Src Lang.	Trg Lang.	Domain	Example	Doc. Length	Sum. Length
CrossSum	English	Chinese	News	3981 / 497 / 50 out of 497	814.2	35.6
WikiLingua	English	Chinese	How-to guide	13211 / 1886 / 50 out of 3775	538.6	53.2
		German		40839 / 5833 / 50 out of 11669	526.1	63.4
XSAMSum	English	Chinese	Dialogue	14732 / 818 / 50 out of 819	140.1	27.6
		German		14732 / 818 / 50 out of 819	140.1	31.7

Table 1: Statistics of CLS datasets used in experiments. "*Src Lang.*" and "*Trg Lang*" denote the source and the target languages. "*Doc. Length*" and "*Sum. Length*" show the average length of source documents and target summaries (token level). "*Example*" lists the number of samples in each dataset w.r.t training, validation and test sets.

et al., 2022). The model suffers from both instruction tuning and RLHF.

- **Vicuna-13B**[5] is an open-source LLM created by fine-tuning LLaMA (Touvron et al., 2023) on user-shared conversations collected from ChatGPT. We evaluate the model via its demo platform[6] between March 31 to April 2, 2023.
- **ChatYuan**[7] is an open-source bilingual (*i.e.*, Chinese and English) LLM with 7.7B parameters. The training process of this model includes instruction tuning and RLHF.

Among the above LLMs, ChatGPT, GPT-4, ChatGLM-6B, Vicuna-13B and ChatYuan are conversational LLMs while Davinci-003 and BLOOMZ are not. When evaluating their zero-shot CLS performance, we only equip conversational LLMs with the interactive prompt.

3 Experiments

3.1 Experimental Setup

Datasets. We evaluate LLMs on the following three CLS datasets: CrossSum (En⇒Zh) (Hasan et al., 2021), WikiLingua (En⇒Zh/De) (Ladhak et al., 2020) and XSAMSum (En⇒Zh/De) (Wang et al., 2022a). CrossSum is collected from BBC news website, it contains 3,981 English news reports paired with Chinese summaries. WikiLingua involves 18,887 English how-to guides paired with Chinese summaries, and 58,375 English how-to guides paired with German summaries. Note that both CrossSum and WikiLingua also provide CLS samples in other cross-lingual directions, and we only utilize En⇒Zh or (and) En⇒De samples in this work. XSAMSum contains 16,369 English dialogues paired with both Chinese and German summaries. The detailed statistics of these datasets are listed in Table 1. Since ChatGPT, GPT-4 and Vicuna-13B can only be interacted with manually when we conduct experiments, evaluating their performance is time-consuming. Thus, we randomly sample 50 documents from the test set of each CLS dataset for evaluation.

Metrics. We adopt ROUGE-1/2/L (R-1/2/L) (Lin, 2004) and BERTScore (B-S) (Zhang et al., 2020) in our experiments. The ROUGE scores measure the lexical overlap between the generated summaries and corresponding references based on the unigram, bigram and longest common subsequence, while the BERTScore measures the semantic similarity. For ROUGE scores, we use *multi-lingual rouge*[8] toolkit. For BERTScore, we use *bert-score*[9] toolkit, and the score is calculated based on *bert-base-multilingual-cased*[10] model.

Baselines. We also compare zero-shot LLMs with fine-tuned mBART-50 (Tang et al., 2021) to provide a deeper analysis. mBART-50 is a multi-lingual version of BART (Lewis et al., 2020) with the vanilla transformer encoder-decoder architecture (Vaswani et al., 2017). This model has been pre-trained on large-scale multi-lingual unlabeled corpora with BART-like denoising objectives.

3.2 Implementation Details

For ChatGPT, GPT-4 and Vicuna-13B, we manually evaluate their results via the corresponding platform and demo websites. Among them, the demo website of Vicuna-13B cannot support the long input sequences, and it will automatically truncate the long sequences, thus we only evaluate Vicuna-13B on XSAMSum (En⇒Zh/De). For Davinci-003, we use the official API with default settings.

[5]https://vicuna.lmsys.org/

[6]https://chat.lmsys.org/

[7]https://github.com/clue-ai/ChatYuan

[8]https://github.com/csebuetnlp/xl-sum/tree/master/multilingual_rouge_scoring

[9]https://github.com/Tiiiger/bert_score

[10]https://huggingface.co/bert-base-multilingual-cased

Model	CrossSum (En⇒Zh)				WikiLingua (En⇒Zh)				WikiLingua (En⇒De)				XSAMSum (En⇒Zh)				XSAMSum (En⇒De)			
	R-1	R-2	R-L	B-S	R-1	R-2	R-L	B-S	R-1	R-2	R-L	B-S	R-1	R-2	R-L	B-S	R-1	R-2	R-L	B-S
mBART-50	26.1	7.4	22.1	65.4	32.1	10.4	26.8	68.5	26.8	7.7	20.5	62.5	40.6	14.4	33.9	74.5	42.4	18.9	35.4	73.7
ChatYuan-7.7B (Dir)	0.3	0.0	0.3	51.7	4.1	1.2	2.6	54.4	-	-	-	-	0.8	0.3	0.7	48.5	-	-	-	-
ChatYuan-7.7B (Dir+Inta)	0.2	0.0	0.2	52.0	4.7	1.6	3.4	51.6	-	-	-	-	0.3	0.1	0.3	47.0	-	-	-	-
ChatYuan-7.7B (TS)	0.4	0.0	0.4	46.6	8.2	2.7	5.4	56.0	-	-	-	-	11.3	4.2	8.7	49.5	-	-	-	-
ChatYuan-7.7B (TS+Inta)	2.0	0.5	1.4	46.9	6.9	2.1	4.3	53.4	-	-	-	-	9.5	3.2	6.9	52.3	-	-	-	-
ChatYuan-7.7B (ST)	0.5	0.0	0.4	49.6	6.9	2.1	4.2	56.1	-	-	-	-	7.5	2.5	5.5	49.6	-	-	-	-
ChatYuan-7.7B (ST+Inta)	1.2	0.4	0.9	49.7	7.3	2.3	4.6	55.5	-	-	-	-	6.0	2.0	3.9	48.5	-	-	-	-
ChatGLM-6B (Dir)	5.7	2.3	2.4	53.9	14.5	5.3	9.9	59.5	-	-	-	-	20.4	9.1	15.3	58.8	-	-	-	-
ChatGLM-6B (Dir+Inta)	7.9	2.4	5.3	55.6	14.6	5.1	9.5	59.1	-	-	-	-	18.0	8.0	14.0	59.5	-	-	-	-
ChatGLM-6B (TS)	8.4	2.9	4.8	54.1	14.6	5.3	9.8	59.7	-	-	-	-	21.5	9.6	16.6	57.9	-	-	-	-
ChatGLM-6B (TS+Inta)	9.6	3.0	6.1	55.2	14.9	5.1	9.4	59.1	-	-	-	-	18.7	8.1	15.0	58.6	-	-	-	-
ChatGLM-6B (ST)	5.8	1.8	3.6	53.2	15.6	5.5	10.2	59.9	-	-	-	-	19.8	8.3	14.7	58.1	-	-	-	-
ChatGLM-6B (ST+Inta)	2.2	0.6	1.7	53.8	9.8	3.3	6.1	57.0	-	-	-	-	12.7	5.1	9.9	56.8	-	-	-	-
Vicuna-13B (Dir)	-	-	-	-	-	-	-	-	-	-	-	-	19.5	7.2	14.5	60.1	22.5	4.9	17.6	58.5
Vicuna-13B (Dir+Inta)	-	-	-	-	-	-	-	-	-	-	-	-	24.1	9.7	18.9	63.0	28.7	7.8	22.0	60.5
Vicuna-13B (TS)	-	-	-	-	-	-	-	-	-	-	-	-	18.3	7.1	14.6	61.6	25.0	5.9	18.2	59.4
Vicuna-13B (TS+Inta)	-	-	-	-	-	-	-	-	-	-	-	-	22.0	7.9	17.4	64.3	31.7	8.9	24.2	61.2
Vicuna-13B (ST)	-	-	-	-	-	-	-	-	-	-	-	-	17.5	6.1	13.6	59.6	27.3	6.8	20.4	59.3
Vicuna-13B (ST+Inta)	-	-	-	-	-	-	-	-	-	-	-	-	19.8	7.4	15.4	62.2	31.6	9.4	24.1	61.9
BLOOMZ-176B (Dir)	0.7	0.1	0.7	29.2	0.3	0.0	0.2	8.9	0.0	0.0	0.0	3.3	21.4	11.2	17.8	65.3	13.0	1.2	11.9	56.2
BLOOMZ-176B (TS)	2.1	1.3	1.6	21.5	0.4	0.0	0.3	5.6	0.0	0.0	0.0	5.0	30.4	15.0	25.2	64.8	12.5	0.7	11.4	54.4
BLOOMZ-176B (ST)	3.0	1.2	2.4	33.8	0.3	0.0	0.2	9.0	0.0	0.0	0.0	3.3	28.1	13.4	23.4	66.3	13.8	1.3	12.8	54.8
Davinci-003 (Dir)	18.7	3.6	14.7	60.2	23.6	3.8	17.8	60.9	18.8	2.6	12.2	60.7	24.4	8.0	20.7	63.4	35.5	12.4	27.3	62.4
Davinci-003 (TS)	22.9	8.9	13.5	59.6	23.7	8.2	15.1	61.0	16.9	2.0	10.9	59.2	33.3	**17.1**	26.6	64.7	34.7	11.5	26.1	62.0
Davinci-003 (ST)	**26.2**	**9.3**	**16.9**	61.3	24.2	8.4	15.9	61.2	19.8	2.8	13.1	60.4	34.1	**18.2**	26.4	68.1	35.7	11.7	26.9	63.0
ChatGPT (Dir)	14.2	3.3	10.3	60.3	20.9	5.6	15.5	62.7	16.9	2.1	10.7	60.1	21.3	5.5	17.1	63.5	32.0	10.3	24.5	61.4
ChatGPT (Dir+Inta)	22.1	3.8	15.6	61.8	28.4	6.5	22.1	64.5	22.4	2.8	14.7	61.3	27.2	6.9	22.9	67.5	39.6	**16.0**	31.4	**64.3**
ChatGPT (TS)	15.8	3.3	11.9	60.9	24.8	5.4	19.1	62.9	19.4	2.4	12.6	60.0	26.0	7.3	21.2	66.4	33.2	9.6	25.3	61.1
ChatGPT (TS+Inta)	22.6	4.1	**16.9**	62.7	26.1	5.3	19.7	63.7	21.6	2.4	15.1	60.8	27.4	6.7	22.4	67.1	39.4	13.5	29.4	63.3
ChatGPT (ST)	16.5	3.8	12.0	60.8	27.2	7.3	20.3	64.3	21.3	3.5	14.4	60.9	26.8	7.7	21.3	66.7	31.7	8.8	23.5	60.8
ChatGPT (ST+Inta)	21.6	3.5	15.5	61.7	30.1	8.1	**22.4**	64.9	21.4	3.1	15.4	60.6	31.4	11.5	28.1	70.1	35.9	13.2	29.0	62.8
GPT-4 (Dir)	13.7	3.7	10.1	59.7	23.1	9.1	15.5	63.5	20.4	3.3	13.8	62.2	24.5	7.1	19.5	66.1	34.7	13.4	25.3	61.7
GPT-4 (Dir+Inta)	20.3	4.4	14.1	61.9	30.4	11.7	20.9	**65.7**	**24.8**	3.9	17.0	**63.5**	31.3	7.3	26.5	70.7	**40.5**	13.4	30.8	64.2
GPT-4 (TS)	19.4	3.6	14.3	60.9	28.5	11.4	18.2	64.2	23.1	3.8	16.3	62.7	**34.7**	12.5	**28.5**	71.0	38.9	11.9	29.0	63.3
GPT-4 (TS+Inta)	22.7	4.3	16.1	62.2	29.2	**12.6**	20.3	64.9	23.6	3.9	17.3	62.9	30.8	6.5	25.6	70.9	39.1	13.5	**32.6**	64.1
GPT-4 (ST)	19.0	4.3	14.1	61.7	30.2	12.2	19.5	64.2	23.4	3.8	16.4	63.0	32.1	10.7	26.4	70.7	38.6	12.3	29.5	63.2
GPT-4 (ST+Inta)	22.6	4.9	16.8	**63.1**	**30.5**	11.9	21.3	65.2	23.1	**4.2**	**17.4**	62.7	29.2	8.2	25.4	**71.4**	39.0	11.5	31.2	63.7

Table 2: Experimental results on CrossSum, WikiLingua and XSAMSum. Pink denotes the fine-tuned baseline. Light blue and blue denote the zero-shot performance of open-source and non-open-source LLMs, respectively. Green indicates the zero-shot result is better than that of the fine-tuned baseline. "-" denotes the model cannot be evaluated in the corresponding dataset.

For BLOOMZ, ChatGLM-6B and ChatYuan, we download the corresponding checkpoints and evaluate their performances following the officially released codes. The 176B BLOOMZ makes use of 5*80G GPUs to load with FP16 precision. We use a sampling decoding strategy and set the temperature to 0.7. We only evaluate ChatGLM-6B and ChatYuan on En⇒Zh cross-lingual direction due to their bilingualism (*i.e.*, Chinese and English).

For mBART-50 baseline, inspired by Feng et al. (2022) and Wang et al. (2022a), we employ `mBART-large-50-many-to-many-mmt` model[11] via the implementation of Huggingface Transformers (Wolf et al., 2020). This model is fine-tuned with 4 batch size, 5e-6 learning rate and 10 epochs on each CLS dataset.

[11]`https://huggingface.co/facebook/mbart-large-50-many-to-many-mmt`

3.3 Main Results

Table 2 lists the experimental results. As we can see, Davinci-003, ChatGPT and GPT-4 achieve competitive results with the fine-tuned mBART-50.

The Effect of Each CLS Prompt. Among three end-to-end prompts (*i.e.*, Dir, ST and TS), the CoT prompts lead to better performance than the direct prompt, indicating the effectiveness of CoT. It also indicates that it is still challenging for a single model to directly perform CLS without giving any crucial or helpful instructions.

The Effect of Interactive Prompt. Further, with the help of the interactive prompt, the performance of ChatGPT and GPT-4 significantly improve and even outperform mBART-50 in several automatic metrics. As shown in Table 3, more concise summaries can be generated after inputting the interactive prompt, *e.g.*, 183.7 tokens generated by ChatGPT (Dir) on CrossSum, while the counterpart of ChatGPT (Dir+Inta) is 66.4 tokens. Figure 3

English Dialogue	Generated Summaries
Boris: Due to the number of PTO requests this week, we had to decide who will be allowed to take off based on seniority. Sarah: I understand. Boris: Unfortunately, you are too low on the totem pole and we will have to deny your request. Sarah: Oh, that's too bad! Is there any compromise? I really wanted to have some time with my family. Boris: I can give you first choice of dates the week after, but that's the best I can do. Sarah: What if someone cancels? Boris: That is a rare, but yes, I will come to you first. Sarah: Thank you. Boris: Again, I'm very sorry. Sarah: Could you amend my request for the following week, Monday through Wednesday? Boris: Certainly. That should be no problem. Sarah: That's great, at least I'll have a long weekend! Boris: Very true. No problems from my side. Sarah: Do I need to initial the change? Boris: Yes, please come see my assistant at your earliest convenience. Sarah: Certainly, no problem. Boris: Thank you for being so flexible. Sarah: Sure, I understand we can't all be off. You are just trying to be fair. Boris: That's it exactly. Sarah: Thank you again for explaining it so well. Boris: My pleasure. Have a nice holiday and enjoy your time off. Sarah: Thank you!	**ChatGPT (Dir):** Boris通知Sarah由于请假请求众多，公司不得不按资历高低来决定谁可以休假。由于Sarah资历不够高，公司不得不拒绝她的请求。Sarah想知道是否有妥协的余地，Boris答应给她下周第一批可以选择的日期，但这是他所能做的最好安排。Sarah问如果有人取消假期怎么办，Boris说这是很少见的，但如果确实发生，他会优先通知Sarah。最后，Sarah改变了请假日期，Boris同意了，并建议她尽快与他的助手联系确认。他们互相道别，Sarah感谢Boris的解释，Boris祝她假期愉快。 **ChatGPT (Dir+Inta):** Sarah想请假，但因资历不够高被拒绝。Boris答应给她下周第一批可以选择的日期，如果有人取消假期，会优先通知她。最后，Sarah改变了请假日期，Boris同意了。 **ChatGPT (TS):** 对于申请休假的员工，由于请假申请数量较多，公司根据资历来决定谁可以休假，导致低资历的员工被拒绝休假请求。员工虽然表示遗憾，但同意公司的决定并愿意接受推迟的休假时间，直到后来有机会更改休假时间并获得了首选日期。公司对员工的灵活性表示感谢，并向员工祝福愉快的假期。 **ChatGPT (TS+Inta):** 公司根据资历决定员工休假，低资历员工被拒绝休假请求。员工同意公司决定并愿意推迟休假时间，后来获得了首选日期。公司感谢员工的灵活性，祝愿员工假期愉快。 **ChatGPT (ST):** 鲍里斯告诉萨拉，由于请假申请太多，他必须根据资历批准休假，但很遗憾，萨拉的请求不能被批准。然而，鲍里斯提供萨拉选择下周的日期，如果有人取消。萨拉问能否修改为下周的请求，鲍里斯同意了。他们以积极的态度结束了谈话，鲍里斯祝萨拉度过愉快的假期，萨拉感谢他的理解。 **ChatGPT (ST+Inta):** 因请假申请太多，鲍里斯按资历批准休假，未能批准萨拉的请求。但鲍里斯提供了选择下周日期的机会。萨拉同意改为下周休假，他们友好结束谈话。 **GPT-4 (Dir):** Boris通知Sarah由于请假请求众多，公司不得不按资历高低来决定谁可以休假。由于Sarah资历不够高，公司不得不拒绝她的请求。Sarah想知道是否有妥协的余地，Boris答应给她下周第一批可以选择的日期，但这是他所能做的最好安排。Sarah问如果有人取消假期怎么办，Boris说这是很少见的，但如果确实发生，他会优先通知Sarah。最后，Sarah改变了请假日期，Boris同意了，并建议她尽快与他的助手联系确认。他们互相道别，Sarah感谢Boris的解释，Boris祝她假期愉快 **GPT-4 (Dir+Inta):** Sarah想请假，但因资历不够高被拒绝。Boris答应给她下周第一批可以选择的日期，如果有人取消假期，会优先通知她。最后，Sarah改变了请假日期，Boris同意了。 **GPT-4 (TS):** 由于本周请假申请众多，鲍里斯根据员工资历决定谁能休假，萨拉的申请被拒。经过沟通，鲍里斯同意在下周给萨拉优先选择日期，若有人取消，也会优先考虑萨拉。最后，鲍里斯帮助萨拉将申请更改为下周一至周三。萨拉表示理解公平性并感谢鲍里斯的帮助。 **GPT-4 (TS+Inta):** 鲍里斯因员工请假申请多而根据资历拒绝了萨拉的请求。经沟通，鲍里斯同意下周给萨拉优先选择日期，若有人取消，也会优先考虑。萨拉表示理解公平性并感谢鲍里斯。 **GPT-4 (ST):** 由于本周休假申请数量众多，鲍里斯不得不根据资历来决定谁可以休假，因此拒绝了萨拉的申请。他们讨论了潜在的妥协方案，最终同意萨拉在下周一至周三休假。如果有人取消休假，鲍里斯将首先向萨拉提供名额。萨拉需要在鲍里斯的助手那里签署更改。 **GPT-4 (ST+Inta):** 鲍里斯因资历问题拒绝了萨拉的休假申请。他们商量后同意萨拉下周一至三休假。若有人取消，鲍里斯会优先通知萨拉。萨拉需在助手处确认更改。

Figure 3: Example dialogue document in XSAMSum and summaries generated by ChatGPT and GPT-4.

also shows an example English document with the corresponding summaries generated by ChatGPT and GPT-4 via different prompts. Therefore, the conversational LLMs prefer to generate lengthy summaries probably due to the RLHF training process, and the interactive prompt further helps them balance informativeness and conciseness, and significantly improves their zero-shot CLS ability.

Best Zero-Shot LLM vs. Fine-Tuned mBART. GPT-4 achieves state-of-the-art zero-shot CLS performance among all LLMs, justifying its superiority. But the model is still slightly worse than the fine-tuned mBART-50 in terms of automatic evaluation metrics. One possible reason is that zero-shot LLMs are not aware of the text style of the golden summaries when performing zero-shot CLS on each dataset. However, lower automatic scores do not indicate worse performance. For example, as discussed by Goyal et al. (2022), the news summaries generated by GPT-3 achieve lower ROUGE scores than fine-tuned models but higher in human evaluation. Thus, the comparison between LLMs and fine-tuned mBART-50 in CLS needs human evaluation, which we reserve for the future.

Limited Performance of Open-Source LLMs. For open-source LLMs, *i.e.*, BLOOMZ, ChatGLM-6B, Vicuna-13B and ChatYuan-7.7B, they perform poorly on CrossSum and WikiLingua datasets whose documents typically contain more lengthy content than those of XSAMSum. Although they perform decently on XSAMSum, there is still a

Method	CrossSum	WikiLingua		XSAMSum	
	En⇒Zh	En⇒Zh	En⇒De	En⇒Zh	En⇒De
mBART-50	32.7	46.6	75.4	22.3	27.9
Davinci-003 (Dir)	83.3	78.5	149.1	61.8	62.5
Davinci-003 (TS)	82.1	76.2	148.6	53.4	65.8
Davinci-003 (ST)	44.7	49.1	91.7	43.4	52.1
ChatGPT (Dir)	183.7	176.6	273.5	68.6	75.3
ChatGPT (Dir+Inta)	66.4	50.0	80.7	28.7	42.5
ChatGPT (TS)	155.1	82.1	149.3	48.2	60.9
ChatGPT (TS+Inta)	63.4	46.2	70.0	30.3	41.1
ChatGPT (ST)	132.7	94.3	124.2	54.9	68.1
ChatGPT (ST+Inta)	57.8	50.1	71.6	29.3	37.5
GPT-4 (Dir)	227.1	170.5	193.1	70.4	74.4
GPT-4 (Dir+Inta)	102.2	58.7	75.1	30.1	38.3
GPT-4 (TS)	93.9	85.6	114.7	44.1	53.8
GPT-4 (TS+Inta)	56.5	45.4	66.5	26.3	33.8
GPT-4 (ST)	106.6	87.8	109.5	43.6	53.7
GPT-4 (ST+Inta)	62.7	48.0	65.1	26.7	33.3
Golden	36.1	50.0	66.8	23.9	29.6

Table 3: The average length (token level) of the generated summaries on the test set of each CLS dataset. Light green indicates the length of golden summaries.

large gap compared to GPT-4. Thus, we conclude that zero-shot CLS is challenging for LLMs to perform due to its composite nature that requires models to perform summarization and translation simultaneously. In this situation, we suggest future bilingual or multi-lingual LLM research adopt CLS as a testbed to evaluate the LLMs' capabilities to follow composite instructions as well as combine their different ability.

3.4 LLM-based Evaluation

It is worth noting that conducting human evaluation on the generated summaries of both LLMs and fine-tuned models is not trivial since human evaluators

	XSAMSum (En⇒Zh)				XSAMSum (En⇒De)			
	Coherence	Relevance	Consistency	Fluency	Coherence	Relevance	Consistency	Fluency
mBART-50	54.0	32.3	36.6	55.8	54.6	36.0	45.3	52.1
ChatYuan-7.7B (Dir)	44.6	17.3	40.3	53.6	-	-	-	-
ChatYuan-7.7B (Dir+Inta)	43.6	21.0	37.3	52.0	-	-	-	-
ChatYuan-7.7B (TS)	41.0	17.0	24.8	48.8	-	-	-	-
ChatYuan-7.7B (TS+Inta)	39.0	15.3	17.3	41.5	-	-	-	-
ChatYuan-7.7B (ST)	47.3	19.6	36.3	54.6	-	-	-	-
ChatYuan-7.7B (ST+Inta)	48.6	15.3	33.0	52.0	-	-	-	-
ChatGLM-6B (Dir)	58.8	31.0	49.0	61.0	-	-	-	-
ChatGLM-6B (Dir+Inta)	60.6	35.3	55.1	60.8	-	-	-	-
ChatGLM-6B (TS)	52.0	22.0	25.3	54.0	-	-	-	-
ChatGLM-6B (TS+Inta)	55.0	31.6	46.5	58.5	-	-	-	-
ChatGLM-6B (ST)	58.6	27.0	37.3	56.5	-	-	-	-
ChatGLM-6B (ST+Inta)	59.3	34.0	53.1	63.8	-	-	-	-
Vicuna-13B (Dir)	50.3	28.0	39.6	52.8	64.3	53.6	67.1	63.8
Vicuna-13B (Dir+Inta)	55.5	36.0	43.0	56.8	63.8	49.0	62.0	63.6
Vicuna-13B (TS)	57.1	44.6	57.3	56.5	68.3	55.6	69.3	66.5
Vicuna-13B (TS+Inta)	55.1	35.6	49.3	52.1	66.6	56.3	66.3	64.0
Vicuna-13B (ST)	54.6	33.6	46.3	56.6	65.0	54.0	62.8	62.1
Vicuna-13B (ST+Inta)	53.6	37.0	44.3	55.1	69.5	57.3	67.6	66.3
BLOOMZ-176B (Dir)	53.5	38.3	44.3	54.3	63.1	51.0	61.0	63.8
BLOOMZ-176B (TS)	52.3	37.0	37.6	53.6	59.3	48.3	61.3	58.8
BLOOMZ-176B (ST)	54.3	37.3	44.3	55.5	59.5	48.0	60.3	60.3
Davinci-003 (Dir)	60.0	33.0	55.0	59.3	71.3	60.6	76.6	69.5
Davinci-003 (TS)	56.3	26.6	38.6	54.3	68.5	54.3	68.6	68.3
Davinci-003 (ST)	62.8	46.6	54.0	61.5	68.6	61.6	77.0	70.1
ChatGPT (Dir)	63.1	45.3	**70.0**	65.3	74.0	64.0	82.0	71.6
ChatGPT (Dir+Inta)	58.0	45.0	58.0	60.6	68.3	65.3	76.0	69.1
ChatGPT (TS)	63.0	49.6	59.0	62.8	71.5	62.0	77.6	71.8
ChatGPT (TS+Inta)	64.5	49.3	61.3	60.5	70.0	59.0	77.0	69.8
ChatGPT (ST)	64.3	51.6	64.0	62.3	72.3	63.6	77.0	74.0
ChatGPT (ST+Inta)	64.1	51.0	60.6	65.3	69.1	60.3	73.6	67.0
GPT4 (Dir)	64.0	48.6	67.6	**67.0**	**75.3**	68.0	**83.6**	**74.5**
GPT4 (Dir+Inta)	62.0	50.6	57.3	63.1	70.0	**68.6**	77.6	70.3
GPT4 (TS)	**66.0**	**55.3**	63.3	65.6	73.6	**68.6**	79.0	72.0
GPT4 (TS+Inta)	62.3	48.6	59.0	63.8	65.1	60.3	69.3	68.3
GPT4 (ST)	63.0	52.6	64.0	62.3	72.8	67.3	80.3	72.3
GPT4 (ST+Inta)	60.6	46.3	56.3	63.5	70.8	62.6	79.0	70.1

Table 4: Evaluation results (judged by ChatGPT) on XSAMSum. Pink denotes the fine-tuned baseline. Light blue and blue denote the zero-shot performance of open-source and non-open-source LLMs, respectively. "-" denotes the model cannot be evaluated in the corresponding dataset.

can easily realize which summaries are generated by LLMs or fine-tuned models. In this manner, the evaluators may have biases during scoring each summary. To ensure the fairness of human judgment, Stiennon et al. (2020) only retain the generated summaries whose length belongs to a certain range, and then collect human judgment on these summaries to minimize the potential evaluation bias caused by summary length. In our scene, the text styles of LLMs and fine-tuned models are quite different, which might also lead to bias. Thus, the human evaluation of comparing zero-shot LLMs and fine-tuned models on CLS needs more carefully designed.

As an alternative to human evaluation, recent studies (Liu et al., 2023; Kocmi and Federmann, 2023; Wang et al., 2023) show that the natural language generation (NLG) results evaluated by LLMs could achieve better correlations with humans. Following Wang et al. (2023), we utilize ChatGPT to score the generated summaries in a reference-free manner on four aspects, *i.e.*, coherence, relevance, consistency and fluency. An example prompt is shown in Figure 4, and please refer to Wang et al. (2023) for prompts of all aspects. The instruction of each aspect (marked in purple in Figure 4) is inspired by SummEval (a widely-used summarization meta-evaluation benchmark dataset) (Fabbri et al., 2021). We utilize the official

Score the following dialogue summarization given the corresponding dialogue with respect to fluency on a continuous scale from 0 to 100, where a score of zero means "disfluency" and score of one hundred means "perfect fluency". Note that fluency measures the quality of individual sentences, are they well-written and grammatically correct. Consider the quality of individual sentences.

Dialogue: [a given dialogue]
Summary: [one generated summary]
Scores:

Figure 4: An example prompt used to guide ChatGPT to score the summarization results in the aspect of fluency. Purple indicates the detailed instruction of the corresponding aspect.

APIs provided by OpenAI[12] to conduct the experiments with `gpt-3.5-turbo` model, and set the temperature to 0 to eliminate the randomness of evaluation results.

Table 4 shows the evaluation results on XSAMSum (En⇒Zh/De). As we can see, GPT-4 achieves the best performance in most aspects, showing its superiority. Besides, compared with the fine-tuned mBART-50 baseline, several zero-shot LLMs, including ChatGLM-6B, Vicuna-13B, Davinci-003, ChatGPT and GPT-4, achieve better results in all aspects, demonstrating the potentiality of performing zero-shot CLS via LLMs. For example, ChatGLM-6B (Dir+Inta) achieves 60.6, 35.3, 55.1 and 60.8 scores in aspects of coherence, relevance, consistency and fluency respectively on XSAMSum (En⇒Zh), while the counterparts of mBART-50 are 54.0, 32.3, 36.6 and 55.8, respectively. For GPT-4 (Dir), the corresponding scores even reach 64.0, 48.6, 67.6 and 67.0, significantly better than the fine tuned mBART-50.

Moreover, while we show the interactive prompt can improve the performance of zero-shot LLM in terms of ROUGE scores and BERTScore, we do not find the same trend in the LLM-based evaluation results. In some cases, the interactive prompt even leads to worse LLM-based scores. We conjecture that the interactive prompt would force zero-shot LLMs to reduce the length of the generated summaries, and the models cannot make a good trade-off between conciseness and other aspects, which is also hard for humans.

[12]`https://platform.openai.com/docs/guides/gpt/chat-completions-api`

4 Related Work

4.1 Cross-Lingual Summarization

Given documents in one language, cross-lingual summarization (CLS) generates summaries in another language. Early work typically focuses on pipeline methods (Leuski et al., 2003; Orăsan and Chiorean, 2008; Wan et al., 2010; Wan, 2011; Yao et al., 2015), *i.e.*, translation and then summarization or summarization and then translation. Recently, with the availability of large-scale CLS datasets (Zhu et al., 2019; Ladhak et al., 2020; Perez-Beltrachini and Lapata, 2021; Wang et al., 2022a; Zheng et al., 2022), many researchers shift the research attention to end-to-end CLS models. According to a comprehensive CLS review (Wang et al., 2022b), the end-to-end models involve multi-task learning (Cao et al., 2020; Bai et al., 2021b; Liang et al., 2022b), knowledge distillation (Nguyen and Luu, 2022), resource-enhanced (Zhu et al., 2020; Jiang et al., 2022) and pre-training (Xu et al., 2020; Chi et al., 2021) frameworks. However, none of them explore LLMs performance on CLS. To our knowledge, we are the first to explore *can LLMs perform zero-shot CLS* and *how their results are*.

4.2 Large Language Models

Recently, there are growing interest in leveraging LLMs for various NLP tasks. Bang et al. (2023), Qin et al. (2023) and Zhong et al. (2023) conduct systematic investigations of ChatGPT's performance on various downstream tasks. Jiao et al. (2023) and Peng et al. (2023) evaluate ChatGPT on machine translation. Yong et al. (2023) show that ChatGPT could generate high-quality code-mixed text. Tan et al. (2023) explore the performance of ChatGPT on knowledge-based question answering (KBQA). Some works (Kocmi and Federmann, 2023; Wang et al., 2023; Liu et al., 2023; Ji et al., 2023) utilize ChatGPT or GPT-4 as an evaluation metric to assess task-specific model performance.

5 Conclusion and Future Work

In this technical report, we evaluate the zero-shot performance of mainstream bilingual and multilingual LLMs on cross-lingual summarization. We find that Davinci-003, ChatGPT and GPT-4 can combine the ability to summarize and translate to perform zero-shot CLS, and achieve competitive results with the fine-tuned baseline (*i.e.*, mBART-50). In addition, the current open-source LLMs (*i.e.*, BLOOMZ, ChatGLM-6B, Vicuna-13B and ChatYuan) generally show their limited ability to perform CLS in an end-to-end manner, showing the challenge of performing zero-shot CLS still exists.

In the future, we would like to unleash the potentiality of LLMs and leverage LLMs to perform CLS in few-shot learning manners.

Limitations

While we evaluate the performance of LLMs on the cross-lingual summarization task, there are some limitations worth noting: (1) We only evaluate the lower threshold of these models' CLS performance. Prompts are important to guide LLMs to perform specific tasks, and future work could explore better prompts to obtain better results. (2) This report only uses two cross-lingual directions (En⇒Zh and En⇒De) in experiments, and all the languages are considered high-resource languages in the world. The performance of LLMs on low-resource languages still needs to be explored. According to Jiao et al. (2023), the machine translation ability of ChatGPT is limited on low-resource languages. We conjecture that the same situation might exist in CLS. (3) Though the general trend of the evaluation results should be correct, the comparisons between LLMs are not rigorous due to the decoding strategies of these models are not the same.[13] This is one of the major reasons leading to the limited soundness of this work. (4) In the future, we would like to conduct human evaluation to give more analyses.

Acknowledgement

We thank anonymous reviewers for their constructive suggestions and comments.

References

Dennis Aumiller, Ashish Chouhan, and Michael Gertz. 2022. EUR-lex-sum: A multi- and cross-lingual dataset for long-form summarization in the legal domain. In *Proceedings of the 2022 Conference on Empirical Methods in Natural Language Processing*, pages 7626–7639, Abu Dhabi, United Arab Emirates. Association for Computational Linguistics.

Yu Bai, Yang Gao, and Heyan Huang. 2021a. Cross-lingual abstractive summarization with limited parallel resources. In *Proceedings of the 59th Annual Meeting of the Association for Computational Linguistics and the 11th International Joint Conference on Natural Language Processing (Volume 1: Long Papers)*, pages 6910–6924, Online. Association for Computational Linguistics.

Yu Bai, Heyan Huang, Kai Fan, Yang Gao, Zewen Chi, and Boxing Chen. 2021b. Bridging the gap: Cross-lingual summarization with compression rate. *ArXiv preprint*, abs/2110.07936v1.

Yejin Bang, Samuel Cahyawijaya, Nayeon Lee, Wenliang Dai, Dan Su, Bryan Wilie, Holy Lovenia, Ziwei Ji, Tiezheng Yu, Willy Chung, et al. 2023. A multitask, multilingual, multimodal evaluation of chatgpt on reasoning, hallucination, and interactivity. *arXiv preprint arXiv:2302.04023*.

Sébastien Bubeck, Varun Chandrasekaran, Ronen Eldan, Johannes Gehrke, Eric Horvitz, Ece Kamar, Peter Lee, Yin Tat Lee, Yuanzhi Li, Scott Lundberg, et al. 2023. Sparks of artificial general intelligence: Early experiments with gpt-4. *arXiv preprint arXiv:2303.12712*.

Yue Cao, Hui Liu, and Xiaojun Wan. 2020. Jointly learning to align and summarize for neural cross-lingual summarization. In *Proceedings of the 58th Annual Meeting of the Association for Computational Linguistics*, pages 6220–6231, Online. Association for Computational Linguistics.

Zewen Chi, Li Dong, Shuming Ma, Shaohan Huang, Saksham Singhal, Xian-Ling Mao, Heyan Huang, Xia Song, and Furu Wei. 2021. mT6: Multilingual pretrained text-to-text transformer with translation pairs. In *Proceedings of the 2021 Conference on Empirical Methods in Natural Language Processing*, pages 1671–1683, Online and Punta Cana, Dominican Republic. Association for Computational Linguistics.

Paul F Christiano, Jan Leike, Tom Brown, Miljan Martic, Shane Legg, and Dario Amodei. 2017. Deep reinforcement learning from human preferences. *Advances in neural information processing systems*, 30.

Qingxiu Dong, Lei Li, Damai Dai, Ce Zheng, Zhiyong Wu, Baobao Chang, Xu Sun, Jingjing Xu, and Zhifang Sui. 2022. A survey for in-context learning. *arXiv preprint arXiv:2301.00234*.

Zhengxiao Du, Yujie Qian, Xiao Liu, Ming Ding, Jiezhong Qiu, Zhilin Yang, and Jie Tang. 2022. Glm: General language model pretraining with autoregressive blank infilling. In *Proceedings of the 60th Annual Meeting of the Association for Computational Linguistics (Volume 1: Long Papers)*, pages 320–335.

Alexander R. Fabbri, Wojciech Kryściński, Bryan McCann, Caiming Xiong, Richard Socher, and Dragomir Radev. 2021. SummEval: Re-evaluating Summarization Evaluation. *Transactions of the Association for Computational Linguistics*, 9:391–409.

[13]Currently, we cannot set the decoding strategy of GPT-4 when manually evaluating it on the ChatGPT platform. Besides, it is difficult to ensure the decoding strategies of LLMs are totally the same when using online platforms or demos.

Xiachong Feng, Xiaocheng Feng, and Bing Qin. 2022. MSAMSum: Towards benchmarking multi-lingual dialogue summarization. In *Proceedings of the Second DialDoc Workshop on Document-grounded Dialogue and Conversational Question Answering*, pages 1–12, Dublin, Ireland. Association for Computational Linguistics.

Yao Fu, Hao Peng, Ashish Sabharwal, Peter Clark, and Tushar Khot. 2022. Complexity-based prompting for multi-step reasoning. *arXiv preprint arXiv:2210.00720*.

Tanya Goyal, Junyi Jessy Li, and Greg Durrett. 2022. News summarization and evaluation in the era of gpt-3. *arXiv preprint arXiv:2209.12356*.

Tahmid Hasan, Abhik Bhattacharjee, Wasi Uddin Ahmad, Yuan-Fang Li, Yong-Bin Kang, and Rifat Shahriyar. 2021. Crosssum: Beyond english-centric cross-lingual abstractive text summarization for 1500+ language pairs. *ArXiv preprint*, abs/2112.08804v1.

Yunjie Ji, Yan Gong, Yiping Peng, Chao Ni, Peiyan Sun, Dongyu Pan, Baochang Ma, and Xiangang Li. 2023. Exploring chatgpt's ability to rank content: A preliminary study on consistency with human preferences. *arXiv preprint arXiv:2303.07610*.

Shuyu Jiang, Dengbiao Tu, Xingshu Chen, R. Tang, Wenxian Wang, and Haizhou Wang. 2022. Clue-GraphSum: Let key clues guide the cross-lingual abstractive summarization. *ArXiv preprint*, abs/2203.02797v2.

Wenxiang Jiao, Wenxuan Wang, Jen-tse Huang, Xing Wang, and Zhaopeng Tu. 2023. Is chatgpt a good translator? a preliminary study. *arXiv preprint arXiv:2301.08745*.

Tom Kocmi and Christian Federmann. 2023. Large language models are state-of-the-art evaluators of translation quality. *arXiv preprint arXiv:2302.14520*.

Faisal Ladhak, Esin Durmus, Claire Cardie, and Kathleen McKeown. 2020. WikiLingua: A new benchmark dataset for cross-lingual abstractive summarization. In *Findings of the Association for Computational Linguistics: EMNLP 2020*, pages 4034–4048, Online. Association for Computational Linguistics.

Anton Leuski, Chin-Yew Lin, Liang Zhou, Ulrich Germann, Franz Josef Och, and Eduard H. Hovy. 2003. Cross-lingual c*st*rd: English access to hindi information. *ACM Trans. Asian Lang. Inf. Process.*, 2:245–269.

Mike Lewis, Yinhan Liu, Naman Goyal, Marjan Ghazvininejad, Abdelrahman Mohamed, Omer Levy, Veselin Stoyanov, and Luke Zettlemoyer. 2020. BART: Denoising sequence-to-sequence pre-training for natural language generation, translation, and comprehension. In *Proceedings of the 58th Annual Meeting of the Association for Computational Linguistics*, pages 7871–7880, Online. Association for Computational Linguistics.

Yunlong Liang, Fandong Meng, Jinan Xu, Jiaan Wang, Yufeng Chen, and Jie Zhou. 2022a. Summary-oriented vision modeling for multimodal abstractive summarization. *arXiv preprint arXiv:2212.07672*.

Yunlong Liang, Fandong Meng, Chulun Zhou, Jinan Xu, Yufeng Chen, Jinsong Su, and Jie Zhou. 2022b. A variational hierarchical model for neural cross-lingual summarization. In *Proceedings of the 60th Annual Meeting of the Association for Computational Linguistics (Volume 1: Long Papers)*, pages 2088–2099, Dublin, Ireland. Association for Computational Linguistics.

Chin-Yew Lin. 2004. ROUGE: A package for automatic evaluation of summaries. In *Text Summarization Branches Out*, pages 74–81, Barcelona, Spain. Association for Computational Linguistics.

Nayu Liu, Kaiwen Wei, Xian Sun, Hongfeng Yu, Fanglong Yao, Li Jin, Guo Zhi, and Guangluan Xu. 2022. Assist non-native viewers: Multimodal cross-lingual summarization for how2 videos. In *Proceedings of the 2022 Conference on Empirical Methods in Natural Language Processing*, pages 6959–6969, Abu Dhabi, United Arab Emirates. Association for Computational Linguistics.

Yang Liu, Dan Iter, Yichong Xu, Shuohang Wang, Ruochen Xu, and Chenguang Zhu. 2023. Gpteval: Nlg evaluation using gpt-4 with better human alignment. *arXiv preprint arXiv:2303.16634*.

Yinhan Liu, Jiatao Gu, Naman Goyal, Xian Li, Sergey Edunov, Marjan Ghazvininejad, Mike Lewis, and Luke Zettlemoyer. 2020. Multilingual denoising pre-training for neural machine translation. *Transactions of the Association for Computational Linguistics*, 8:726–742.

Sewon Min, Xinxi Lyu, Ari Holtzman, Mikel Artetxe, Mike Lewis, Hannaneh Hajishirzi, and Luke Zettlemoyer. 2022. Rethinking the role of demonstrations: What makes in-context learning work? In *Proceedings of the 2022 Conference on Empirical Methods in Natural Language Processing*, pages 11048–11064, Abu Dhabi, United Arab Emirates. Association for Computational Linguistics.

Niklas Muennighoff, Thomas Wang, Lintang Sutawika, Adam Roberts, Stella Biderman, Teven Le Scao, M Saiful Bari, Sheng Shen, Zheng-Xin Yong, Hailey Schoelkopf, et al. 2022. Crosslingual generalization through multitask finetuning. *arXiv preprint arXiv:2211.01786*.

Thong Thanh Nguyen and Anh Tuan Luu. 2022. Improving neural cross-lingual abstractive summarization via employing optimal transport distance for knowledge distillation. *Proceedings of the AAAI Conference on Artificial Intelligence*, 36(10):11103–11111.

OpenAI. 2023. Gpt-4 technical report. *ArXiv*, abs/2303.08774.

Constantin Orăsan and Oana Andreea Chiorean. 2008. Evaluation of a cross-lingual Romanian-English multi-document summariser. In *Proceedings of the Sixth International Conference on Language Resources and Evaluation (LREC'08)*, Marrakech, Morocco. European Language Resources Association (ELRA).

Long Ouyang, Jeff Wu, Xu Jiang, Diogo Almeida, Carroll L Wainwright, Pamela Mishkin, Chong Zhang, Sandhini Agarwal, Katarina Slama, Alex Ray, et al. 2022. Training language models to follow instructions with human feedback. *arXiv preprint arXiv:2203.02155*.

Keqin Peng, Liang Ding, Qihuang Zhong, Li Shen, Xuebo Liu, Min Zhang, Yuanxin Ouyang, and Dacheng Tao. 2023. Towards making the most of chatgpt for machine translation. *Available at SSRN 4390455*.

Laura Perez-Beltrachini and Mirella Lapata. 2021. Models and datasets for cross-lingual summarisation. In *Proceedings of the 2021 Conference on Empirical Methods in Natural Language Processing*, pages 9408–9423, Online and Punta Cana, Dominican Republic. Association for Computational Linguistics.

Chengwei Qin, Aston Zhang, Zhuosheng Zhang, Jiaao Chen, Michihiro Yasunaga, and Diyi Yang. 2023. Is chatgpt a general-purpose natural language processing task solver? *arXiv preprint arXiv:2302.06476*.

Teven Le Scao, Angela Fan, Christopher Akiki, Ellie Pavlick, Suzana Ilić, Daniel Hesslow, Roman Castagné, Alexandra Sasha Luccioni, François Yvon, Matthias Gallé, et al. 2022. Bloom: A 176b-parameter open-access multilingual language model. *arXiv preprint arXiv:2211.05100*.

Nisan Stiennon, Long Ouyang, Jeffrey Wu, Daniel Ziegler, Ryan Lowe, Chelsea Voss, Alec Radford, Dario Amodei, and Paul F Christiano. 2020. Learning to summarize with human feedback. *Advances in Neural Information Processing Systems*, 33:3008–3021.

Yiming Tan, Dehai Min, Yu Li, Wenbo Li, Nan Hu, Yongrui Chen, and Guilin Qi. 2023. Evaluation of chatgpt as a question answering system for answering complex questions. *arXiv preprint arXiv:2303.07992*.

Yuqing Tang, Chau Tran, Xian Li, Peng-Jen Chen, Naman Goyal, Vishrav Chaudhary, Jiatao Gu, and Angela Fan. 2021. Multilingual translation from denoising pre-training. In *Findings of the Association for Computational Linguistics: ACL-IJCNLP 2021*, pages 3450–3466, Online. Association for Computational Linguistics.

Hugo Touvron, Thibaut Lavril, Gautier Izacard, Xavier Martinet, Marie-Anne Lachaux, Timothée Lacroix, Baptiste Rozière, Naman Goyal, Eric Hambro, Faisal Azhar, Aurelien Rodriguez, Armand Joulin, Edouard Grave, and Guillaume Lample. 2023. Llama: Open and efficient foundation language models. *arXiv preprint arXiv:2302.13971*.

Ashish Vaswani, Noam Shazeer, Niki Parmar, Jakob Uszkoreit, Llion Jones, Aidan N. Gomez, Lukasz Kaiser, and Illia Polosukhin. 2017. Attention is all you need. In *Advances in Neural Information Processing Systems 30: Annual Conference on Neural Information Processing Systems 2017, December 4-9, 2017, Long Beach, CA, USA*, pages 5998–6008.

Xiaojun Wan. 2011. Using bilingual information for cross-language document summarization. In *Proceedings of the 49th Annual Meeting of the Association for Computational Linguistics: Human Language Technologies*, pages 1546–1555, Portland, Oregon, USA. Association for Computational Linguistics.

Xiaojun Wan, Huiying Li, and Jianguo Xiao. 2010. Cross-language document summarization based on machine translation quality prediction. In *Proceedings of the 48th Annual Meeting of the Association for Computational Linguistics*, pages 917–926, Uppsala, Sweden. Association for Computational Linguistics.

Jiaan Wang, Yunlong Liang, Fandong Meng, Haoxiang Shi, Zhixu Li, Jinan Xu, Jianfeng Qu, and Jie Zhou. 2023. Is chatgpt a good nlg evaluator? a preliminary study. *arXiv preprint arXiv:2303.04048*.

Jiaan Wang, Fandong Meng, Ziyao Lu, Duo Zheng, Zhixu Li, Jianfeng Qu, and Jie Zhou. 2022a. ClidSum: A benchmark dataset for cross-lingual dialogue summarization. In *Proceedings of the 2022 Conference on Empirical Methods in Natural Language Processing*, pages 7716–7729, Abu Dhabi, United Arab Emirates. Association for Computational Linguistics.

Jiaan Wang, Fandong Meng, Duo Zheng, Yunlong Liang, Zhixu Li, Jianfeng Qu, and Jie Zhou. 2022b. A Survey on Cross-Lingual Summarization. *Transactions of the Association for Computational Linguistics*, 10:1304–1323.

Thomas Wolf, Lysandre Debut, Victor Sanh, Julien Chaumond, Clement Delangue, Anthony Moi, Pierric Cistac, Tim Rault, Remi Louf, Morgan Funtowicz, Joe Davison, Sam Shleifer, Patrick von Platen, Clara Ma, Yacine Jernite, Julien Plu, Canwen Xu, Teven Le Scao, Sylvain Gugger, Mariama Drame, Quentin Lhoest, and Alexander Rush. 2020. Transformers: State-of-the-art natural language processing. In *Proceedings of the 2020 Conference on Empirical Methods in Natural Language Processing: System Demonstrations*, pages 38–45, Online. Association for Computational Linguistics.

Ruochen Xu, Chenguang Zhu, Yu Shi, Michael Zeng, and Xuedong Huang. 2020. Mixed-lingual pre-training for cross-lingual summarization. In *Proceedings of the 1st Conference of the Asia-Pacific Chapter of the Association for Computational Linguistics and the 10th International Joint Conference on Natural Language Processing*, pages 536–541, Suzhou, China. Association for Computational Linguistics.

Linting Xue, Noah Constant, Adam Roberts, Mihir Kale, Rami Al-Rfou, Aditya Siddhant, Aditya Barua, and Colin Raffel. 2021. mT5: A massively multilingual pre-trained text-to-text transformer. In *Proceedings of the 2021 Conference of the North American Chapter of the Association for Computational Linguistics: Human Language Technologies*, pages 483–498, Online. Association for Computational Linguistics.

Xianjun Yang, Yan Li, Xinlu Zhang, Haifeng Chen, and Wei Cheng. 2023. Exploring the limits of chatgpt for query or aspect-based text summarization. *arXiv preprint arXiv:2302.08081*.

Jin-ge Yao, Xiaojun Wan, and Jianguo Xiao. 2015. Phrase-based compressive cross-language summarization. In *Proceedings of the 2015 Conference on Empirical Methods in Natural Language Processing*, pages 118–127, Lisbon, Portugal. Association for Computational Linguistics.

Zheng-Xin Yong, Ruochen Zhang, Jessica Zosa Forde, Skyler Wang, Samuel Cahyawijaya, Holy Lovenia, Lintang Sutawika, Jan Christian Blaise Cruz, Long Phan, Yin Lin Tan, et al. 2023. Prompting large language models to generate code-mixed texts: The case of south east asian languages. *arXiv preprint arXiv:2303.13592*.

Tianyi Zhang, Varsha Kishore, Felix Wu, Kilian Q. Weinberger, and Yoav Artzi. 2020. Bertscore: Evaluating text generation with BERT. In *8th International Conference on Learning Representations, ICLR 2020, Addis Ababa, Ethiopia, April 26-30, 2020*. OpenReview.net.

Zhuosheng Zhang, Aston Zhang, Mu Li, and Alex Smola. 2022. Automatic chain of thought prompting in large language models. *arXiv preprint arXiv:2210.03493*.

Shaohui Zheng, Zhixu Li, Jiaan Wang, Jianfeng Qu, An Liu, Lei Zhao, and Zhigang Chen. 2022. Long-document cross-lingual summarization. *arXiv preprint arXiv:2212.00586*.

Qihuang Zhong, Liang Ding, Juhua Liu, Bo Du, and Dacheng Tao. 2023. Can chatgpt understand too? a comparative study on chatgpt and fine-tuned bert. *arXiv preprint arXiv:2302.10198*.

Junnan Zhu, Qian Wang, Yining Wang, Yu Zhou, Jiajun Zhang, Shaonan Wang, and Chengqing Zong. 2019. NCLS: Neural cross-lingual summarization. In *Proceedings of the 2019 Conference on Empirical Methods in Natural Language Processing and the 9th International Joint Conference on Natural Language Processing (EMNLP-IJCNLP)*, pages 3054–3064, Hong Kong, China. Association for Computational Linguistics.

Junnan Zhu, Yu Zhou, Jiajun Zhang, and Chengqing Zong. 2020. Attend, translate and summarize: An efficient method for neural cross-lingual summarization. In *Proceedings of the 58th Annual Meeting of the Association for Computational Linguistics*, pages 1309–1321, Online. Association for Computational Linguistics.

SimCSum: Joint Learning of Simplification and Cross-lingual Summarization for Cross-lingual Science Journalism

Mehwish Fatima[†], **Tim Kolber**[†], **Katja Markert**[‡] and **Michael Strube**[†]
[†]Heidelberg Institute for Theoretical Studies, Heidelberg, Germany
[‡]Department of Computational Linguistics, Heidelberg University
Heidelberg, Germany
(mehwish.fatima|tim.kolber|michael.strube)@h-its.org
markert@cl.uni-heidelberg.de

Abstract

Cross-lingual science journalism is a recently introduced task that generates popular science summaries of scientific articles different from the source language for non-expert readers. A popular science summary must contain salient content of the input document while focusing on coherence and comprehensibility. Meanwhile, generating a cross-lingual summary from the scientific texts in a local language for the targeted audience is challenging. Existing research on cross-lingual science journalism investigates the task with a pipeline model to combine text simplification and cross-lingual summarization. We extend the research in cross-lingual science journalism by introducing a novel, multi-task learning architecture that combines the aforementioned NLP tasks. Our approach is to jointly train the two high-level NLP tasks in SIMCSUM for generating cross-lingual popular science summaries. We investigate the performance of SIMCSUM against the pipeline model and several other strong baselines with several evaluation metrics and human evaluation. Overall, SIMCSUM demonstrates statistically significant improvements over the state-of-the-art on two non-synthetic cross-lingual scientific datasets. Furthermore, we conduct an in-depth investigation into the linguistic properties of generated summaries and an error analysis.

1 Introduction

Cross-lingual science journalism is a recently introduced task that produces science summaries in a target language from scientific documents in a source language while emphasizing simplification (Fatima and Strube, 2023). A real-world example of cross-lingual science journalism is Spektrum der Wissenschaft[1]. It is the German version of Scientific American and an acclaimed bridge between local readers and the latest scientific research in Germany. Spektrum's target audience are non-expert adults, so their journalists summarize complex scientific concepts in easy-to-understand terms in their local language. These scientific summaries are distinctive from other scientific texts/abstracts due to their length, which is more concise than regular scientific articles, containing non-complex and simplified terms, and are generated in a different language from their source.

Previous work on science journalism, including monolingual and cross-lingual, is quite limited. Monolingual science journalism has been investigated as a downstream task of abstractive summarization (Dangovski et al., 2021; Zaman et al., 2020) with customized monolingual datasets (Zaman et al., 2020; Goldsack et al., 2022). These datasets are, unfortunately, not suitable for cross-lingual science journalism. Moreover, cross-lingual science journalism has been investigated as a fusion of cross-lingual summarization and text simplification with a pipeline model (Fatima and Strube, 2023) with cross-lingual scientific datasets (Fatima and Strube, 2021). In the dawn of cross-lingual summarization, various pipeline models (Ouyang et al., 2019; Zhu et al., 2019, 2020) with synthetic cross-lingual datasets have been introduced to explore the task. Later, cross-lingual summarization models have been focused towards Multi-Task Learning (MTL) (Cao et al., 2020; Bai et al., 2021, 2022) and direct cross-lingual summarization with non-synthetic datasets (Ladhak et al., 2020; Fatima and Strube, 2021).

Due to the limited prior work in cross-lingual science journalism, this task needs further investigation. Fatima and Strube (2023) introduce the cross-lingual science journalism task with a pipeline-based model - SELECT, SIMPLIFY and REWRITE (SSR). SSR consists of three components - an extractive summarizer as SELECT, a reinforcement simplification model as SIMPLIFY, and a cross-lingual abstractive summarizer as REWRITE. SSR is a plug-and-play model which shows promising

[1]https://www.spektrum.de/magazin

Proceedings of The 4th New Frontiers in Summarization Workshop, pages 24–40
December 6, 2023 ©2023 Association for Computational Linguistics

results for cross-lingual science journalism. However, this model has a few limitations. The SELECT component is not a trainable model and cannot be fine-tuned for the training data. The SIMPLIFY and REWRITE components require independent training and hyper-parameter settings. Therefore, these models cannot learn the mutual representations for simplification and cross-lingual summarization. We find this as a research gap. To the best of our knowledge, there are no available models for cross-lingual science journalism that can be trained at once on training data for simplification and cross-lingual summarization.

To fill this gap, we propose an MTL-based model - SIMCSUM that jointly trains for simplification and cross-lingual summarization to generate cross-lingual popular science summaries. SIMCSUM consists of one shared encoder and two independent decoders for each task based on a transformer architecture, where we consider cross-lingual summarization as our main task and simplification as our auxiliary task. The proposed model also leads us to two important research questions. **(RQ1)** Can jointly trained models learn and perform better than pipeline models for cross-lingual science journalism? **(RQ2)** Which linguistic features can effectively measure conciseness and readability to compare cross-lingual science journalism models? To investigate these research questions, we empirically evaluate the performance of SIMCSUM against SSR and several existing cross-lingual summarization models on two cross-lingual scientific datasets. We conduct a human evaluation to find the linguistic qualities of generated summaries. We further analyze the outputs for various lexical, readability and syntactic-based linguistic features. We also perform an error analysis to assess the quality of outputs.

2 Related Work

2.1 Scientific Summarization

This section focuses on the datasets for scientific summarization. Most science summarization datasets are collected from English scientific papers paired with abstracts: ARXIV (Kim et al., 2016; Cohan et al., 2018), PUBMED (Cohan et al., 2018; Nikolov et al., 2018), MEDLINE (Nikolov et al., 2018) and science blogs (Vadapalli et al., 2018b,a). Some work has been conducted for extreme summarization with monolingual dataset (Cachola et al., 2020), extended for cross-lingual extreme summarization (Takeshita et al., 2022). The extreme summarization task generates a one/two-line summary from a scientific abstract/paper, which makes it different from science journalism.

Cross-lingual scientific summarization is an understudied area due to its challenging nature. We find two studies: a synthetic dataset from English to Somali, Swahili, and Tagalog with round trip translation (Ouyang et al., 2019), two real cross-lingual datasets from Wikipedia Science Portal and Spektrum der Wissenschaft for English-German (Fatima and Strube, 2021).

2.2 Cross-lingual Summarization

This section focuses on MTL-based cross-lingual summarization. Zhu et al. (2019) develop an MTL model for English-Chinese cross-lingual summarization. They develop two variations of the transformer model (Vaswani et al., 2017), where the encoder is shared, and two decoders are independent. Cao et al. (2020) present a MTL model for cross-lingual summarization by joint learning of alignment and summarization. Their model consists of two encoders and two decoders, each dedicated to one task while sharing contextual representations. The authors evaluate their model on synthetic cross-lingual datasets for the English-Chinese language pairs. Takase and Okazaki (2022) introduce an MTL framework for cross-lingual abstractive summarization by augmenting (monolingual) training data with translations for three pairs: Chinese-English, Arabic-English, and English-Japanese. The model consists of a transformer encoder-decoder model with prompt-based learning in which each training instance is affixed with a special prompt to signal example type. Bai et al. (2021) develop a variation of multi-lingual BERT for English-Chinese cross-lingual abstractive summarization. The model is trained with a few shots of monolingual and cross-lingual examples. Bai et al. (2022) extend their work by introducing a MTL model to improve cross-lingual summaries by combining cross-lingual summarization and translation rates. They add a compression scoring method at the encoder and decoder of their model. They augment their datasets for different compression levels of summaries. One variation consists of cross-lingual and monolingual summarization decoders, while the other consists of cross-lingual and translation decoders.

Most of these studies focus on English-Chinese synthetic datasets emphasizing summarization and translation (Zhu et al., 2019; Xu et al., 2020; Chen et al., 2023; Bai et al., 2021, 2022). By architecture, SIMCSUM is similar to Zhu et al. (2019) model as it also consists of one shared encoder and two task-specific decoders.

2.3 Science Journalism

This section focuses on science journalism models. Zaman et al. (2020) develop an extension of PGN (See et al., 2017) by modifying the loss function, so the model is trained for joint simplification and summarization. It is not a MTL model but a summarization model with an added loss for simplification. Moreover, the model is trained for monolingual science journalism on a customized dataset that contains simplified summaries from the Eureka Alert science news website. Dangovski et al. (2021) introduce monolingual science journalism as a downstream task of abstractive summarization and story generation. They apply BERT-based models with a prompting method for data augmentation on a monolingual dataset collected from Science daily press releases and scientific papers. They use three existing models for their work: SCI-BERT, a CNN-based sequence-to-sequence model and a story generation model.

Fatima and Strube (2023) propose cross-lingual science journalism as a downstream task of text simplification and cross-lingual summarization. They investigate the task on two non-synthetic cross-lingual scientific datasets with a pipeline-based model - SELECT, SIMPLIFY and REWRITE (SSR). To the best of author's knowledge, there is no other cross-lingual science journalism model to-date.

3 Proposed Model

Our model jointly trains for **Sim**plification and Cross-lingual **Sum**marization (SIMCSUM). We first define MTL and our tasks, and then discuss the architecture of our proposed model.

3.1 Multi-Task Learning

MTL is an approach in deep learning which improves generalization by learning different noise patterns from data related to different tasks. We define our MTL-based model trained on two tasks: simplification and cross-lingual summarization. We adopt hard parameter sharing as it improves the positive transfer and reduces the risk of overfitting (Ruder, 2017).

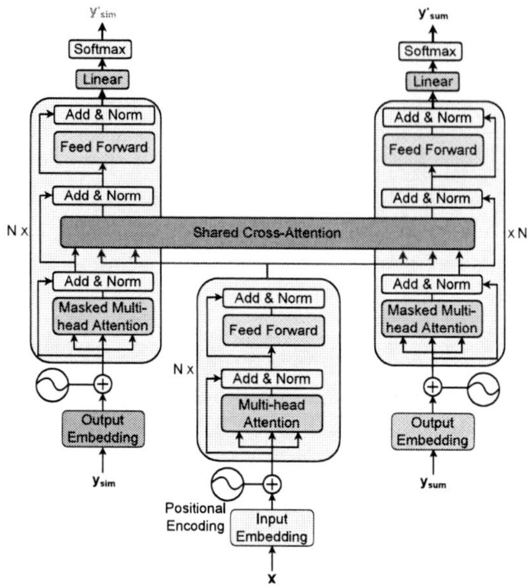

Figure 1: Architecture of SIMCSUM.

3.2 Summarization

We define single-document abstractive summarization as follows. Given a text $X = \{x_1, \cdots, x_m\}$ with m number of sentences comprising of a set of words (vocabulary) $W_X = \{w_1, \cdots, w_X\}$, an (encoder-decoder-based) abstractive summarizer generates a summary $Y = \{y_1, \cdots, y_n\}$ with n sentences that contain salient information of X, where $m \gg n$ and Yconsisting of a set of words $W_Y = \{w_1, \cdots, w_Y | \exists w_i \notin W_X\}$. The decoder learns the conditional probability distribution over the given input and all previously generated words, where t denotes the time step.

$$P_\theta(Y|X) = \log P(y_t|\, y_{<t}, X) \tag{1}$$

Cross-lingual summarization adds another dimension of language for simultaneous translation and summarization. Given a text $X^l = \{x_1^l, \cdots, x_m^l\}$ in a language l with m sentences comprising of a vocabulary $W_X^l = \{w_1^l, \cdots, w_X^l\}$, a cross-lingual summarizer generates a summary $Y^k = \{y_1^k, \cdots, y_n^k\}$ in a language k that contains salient information in X, where $m \gg n$ and Y consisting of a vocabulary $W_Y^k = \{w_1^k, \cdots, w_Y^k | \exists w_i \notin W_X^l\}$. The conditional probability is the same as in Eq.1, the only difference being that the language on the decoder side is different from the encoder side.

3.3 Simplification

We define the document-level (lexical and syntactic) simplification task as follows. Given a

Algorithm 1 Training of SIMCSUM for Simplification and Cross-lingual Summarization

```
Input:
  for each d ∈ trainset do
  ▷ Process each instance d of dataset D for tuples I of input
  x and targets for each task T
     Create I⟨x, y_T⟩
  end for

  Initialize model parameters θ
  Set maximum Epoch Ep
  for epoch 1 to Ep do
     for b ∈ trainset do
     ▷ b is a mini-batch containing I from trainset
     ▷ SIMCSUM consists of Encoder E, two Decoders D_T
        Feed x to E and get the cross-attention
        Feed y_T to D_T
        Feed the cross-attention to D_T [eq. (2)]
        t ← 0
        while θ_t is not converged do
           t ← t + 1
           Compute L(θ) [eq. (3)]
           Compute gradient ∇(θ_t)
           Update θ_t ← θ_{t−1} − η∇(θ)
        end while
     end for
  end for
```

text $X = \{x_1, \cdots, x_m\}$ with m sentences comprising of a vocabulary $W_X = \{w_1, \cdots, w_X\}$, a simplification model generates the output text $Y = \{y_1, \cdots, y_n\}$ that retains the primary meaning of X, yet more comprehensible as compared to X, where $m \approx n$ and Y consisting of a vocabulary $W_Y = \{w_1, \cdots, w_Y | \exists w_i \notin W_X\}$. The conditional probability is also the same as in Eq.1.

3.4 SimCSum

We illustrate the framework of SIMCSUM[2] in Figure 1. SIMCSUM jointly trains on simplification and cross-lingual summarization. SIMCSUM adopts hard parameter sharing where the encoder is shared between the tasks while having two task-specific decoders. The decoders only share the cross-attention layer, and the loss is combined to update the parameters (θ). We opt for two decoders because each task's output language and length differ. The training method is described in Algorithm 1. Here we discuss the further details of SIMCSUM. For all mathematical definitions, $\mathcal{T} \in \{sim, sum\}$ denotes a task.

3.4.1 Architecture

Considering the excellent text generation performance of multi-lingual Bart (mBART) (Liu et al., 2020), we implement the SIMCSUM model based on it and modify it for two decoding sides for each task. Each encoder and decoder stack consists of 12 layers.

Self-Attention. Each layer of encoder/decoder has its self-attention, consisting of keys, values, and queries generated from the same sequence.

$$A(Q, K, V) = Softmax(\frac{Q \cdot K^T}{\sqrt{d_k}}) \cdot V$$

where Q is a query, K^T is transposed K (key) and V is the value. All parallel attentions are concatenated to generate multi-head attention scaled with a weight matrix W.

$$MH(Q, K, V) = Concat(A_1, \cdots, A_h) \cdot W^O$$

Cross-attention. The cross-attention connects the encoder and decoder and provides the decoder with a weight distribution at each step, indicating the importance of each input token in the current context. We concatenate the cross-attention of both decoders.

$$A(E, D_{\mathcal{T}}) = Concat(Softmax(\frac{D_{\mathcal{T}} \cdot E^T}{\sqrt{d_k}}) \cdot E) \quad (2)$$

where E is the encoder representation, $D_{\mathcal{T}}$ is the task-specific decoder contextual representation, and d_k is the model size.

3.4.2 Training Objective

We train our model end-to-end to maximize the conditional probability of the target sequence given a source sequence. We define the task-specific loss as follows.

$$\mathcal{L}_{\mathcal{T}}(\theta) = \sum_{n=1}^{N} \log P(y_{\mathcal{T}_t} | y_{\mathcal{T}_{<t}}, x; \theta)$$

where x represents the input, y is the target, N is the mini-batch size, t is the time step and θ denotes learnable parameters. We define the total loss of our model by task-specific losses where $\lambda_{\mathcal{T}}$ is an assigned weight to each task.

$$\mathcal{L}(\theta) = \sum \lambda_{\mathcal{T}} \cdot \mathcal{L}_{\mathcal{T}}(\theta) \quad (3)$$

3.5 Comparison with SSR

Here, we discuss the key differences between SSR (Fatima and Strube, 2023) and SIMCSUM. SSR is a component-based approach that combines three distinct modules: SELECT, SIMPLIFY and REWRITE. Each of these components addresses

[2]https://github.com/MehwishFatimah/SimCSum

a specific aspect of cross-lingual science journalism. It allows for fine-grained control over each step of the process, making it easier to analyze the individual contributions of these components. However, SIMCSUM is a unified model, where a single model is trained to handle both simplification and summarization. It needs to learn to balance and optimize these tasks simultaneously. It leverages synergies between the two tasks, potentially improving performance by learning shared representations between simplification and summarization. Furthermore, SSR introduces a degree of complexity due to its multi-component nature but allows for more control and transparency in the overall process. While SIMCSUMcan simplify the pipeline as it employs a single jointly trained model, potentially reducing complexity and taking benefits of shared representations.

4 Experiments

4.1 Datasets

4.1.1 Summarization

WIKIPEDIA. It is harvested from Wikipedia Science Portal for English and German (Fatima and Strube, 2021). Wikipedia Science Portal contains articles in various science fields. The WIKIPEDIA dataset consists of 50,132 English articles (avg. 1572 words) and German summaries (avg. 100 words).

SPEKTRUM. It is collected from Spektrum der Wissenschaft (Fatima and Strube, 2021). Spektrum is a famous science magazine (Scientific American) in Germany. It covers various topics in diverse science fields: astronomy, biology, chemistry, archaeology, mathematics, physics, *etc*. The SPEKTRUM dataset contains 1510 English articles (avg. 2337 words) and German summaries (avg. 361 words).

4.1.2 Simplification

We construct a synthetic WIKIPEDIA dataset for the simplification task by applying Keep-It-Simple (KIS) (Laban et al., 2021). To create the simplified WIKIPEDIA, we fine-tune KIS on WIKIPEDIA English articles as KIS is an unsupervised model and does not require parallel data. The simplified WIKIPEDIA consists of the original English articles paired with simplified English articles.

4.2 Split and Usage

We use WIKIPEDIA for training, validation and testing (80/10/10), while we use SPEKTRUM for zero-shot adaptability as a case study. All PLM baselines are trained on WIKIPEDIA where each instance I in the training set consists of $< x, y >$ where x is the input English text and y is the target German summary. SIMCSUM is trained on WIKIPEDIA where each instance I in the training set contains $< x, y_{sim}, y_{sum} >$ where x denotes the input English article and y_{sim} refers to the simplified English article and y_{sum} is the target German summary.

4.3 Models

Baselines. Almost all cross-lingual MTL models in §2 are based on translation and summarization, and none of them applies simplification. So we select several PLMs that accept long input texts as baselines. We fine-tune the following baselines: (1) mT5 (Xue et al., 2021), (2) mBART (Liu et al., 2020), (3) PEGASUS (Zhang et al., 2020a), (4) LongFormer-Encoder-Decorder (LONG-ED) (Beltagy et al., 2020), and (5) XLSUM (Hasan et al., 2021) and (6) BIGBIRD (Zaheer et al., 2020). We also consider SSR as a strong baseline for cross-lingual science journalism.

SimCSum. We set $\lambda_{Sum} = 0.75$ for SIMCSUM based on the best results on the WIKIPEDIA validation set.

4.4 Training and Inference

The libraries, hardware and training time details are presented in Appendix A. Here, we discuss hyper-parameters.

Baselines. We fine-tune all models for a maximum of 25 epochs and average the results of 5 runs for each model. We use a batch size of 4-16, depending on the model size. We use a learning rate (LR) of $5e^{-5}$ and 100 warm-up steps to avoid over-fitting of the fine-tuned models. We use the Adam optimizer with a LR linearly decayed LR scheduler. The encoder language is set to English, and the decoder language is German.

SimCSum. We adopt similar settings as used for baselines, except for the batch size fixed to 4. We only generate tokens from the Summarization decoder side in the inference period. We use beam search of size 5 and a tri-gram block during the decoding stage to avoid repetition.

4.5 Evaluation

Automatic. We evaluate all models with three metrics. ROUGE (Lin, 2004) is a standard metric for summarization. BERT-score (Zhang et al., 2020b)

MODELS	R1	R2	RL	BS	FRE
GOLD	-	-	-	-	36.93
mT5	26.79	12.65	23.40	69.12	45.42
mBART	31.43	13.20	25.12	70.52	44.67
PEGASUS	29.30	13.93	24.62	69.83	43.39
XLSUM	31.91	13.30	24.14	70.04	37.83
BIGBIRD	29.23	13.72	24.60	69.19	41.42
LONG-ED	15.11	06.82	13.67	63.94	24.48
SSR	32.17	13.56	25.01	70.60	**48.34**†
SIMCSUM	**34.50**†	**14.36**†	**25.85**†	**71.60**†	46.86

Table 1: The WIKIPEDIA results for all baselines and SIMCSUM. GOLD denotes the reference summaries. **Bold**† denotes the best overall results with significant improvements ($p < .001$).

MODELS	R1	R2	RL	BS	FRE
GOLD	-	-	-	-	40.76
mT5	09.21	00.75	06.50	58.52	38.18
mBART	16.16	01.47	13.89	62.11	39.17
PEGASUS	11.49	00.95	08.01	60.56	37.93
XLSUM	17.10	01.63	09.79	62.25	33.83
BIGBIRD	12.28	01.04	08.65	59.97	36.24
LONG-ED	01.32	00.11	01.18	51.85	30.16
SSR	**21.14**†	**04.34**†	**15.15**†	63.09	41.01
SIMCSUM	20.98	03.82	14.16	**63.47**†	**41.03**†

Table 2: The SPEKTRUM results for all baselines and SIMCSUM. GOLD denotes the reference summaries. **Bold**† denotes the best overall results with significant improvements ($p < .001$).

(BS) is a recent metric for summarization and simplification as an alternative metric to n-gram-based metrics and applies contextual embeddings. For readability, we use Flesch Kincaid Reading Ease (FRE) (Kincaid et al., 1975) (Appendix B §B.2).

Human. We conduct a human evaluation to compare the outputs of SIMCSUM with mBART (baseline) for the same linguistic properties. Our annotators are two university students from the Computational Linguistics department with fluent German and English skills. It is worth mentioning that human evaluation of long cross-lingual scientific text is challenging and costly because it requires bi-lingual annotators with a scientific background.

5 Results

5.1 WIKIPEDIA

We report F-score of ROUGE and BERT-score and FRE of all models in Table 1. The first block includes the fine-tuned PLM models, the second block presents the pipeline baseline, and the last block includes SIMCSUM. From Table 1, we note that SIMCSUM outperforms all baselines for every metric except FRE. We compute the statistical significance of the results with the Mann-Whitney two-tailed test for a p-value $p < .001$. Interestingly, WIKIPEDIA summaries are not simplified compared to SPEKTRUM summaries; still, SIMCSUM performs better on WIKIPEDIA than the baselines. We interpret that the simplification auxiliary task helps SIMCSUM to learn a better contextual representation and produce more relevant German words. We deduce from the results that joint learning of simplification and cross-lingual summarization improves the quality of summaries.

Among the baselines, almost all models demonstrate comparable performance except LONG-ED. For R1, SSR perform better than other models, however, mBART and XLSUM perform also similar. PEGASUS takes the lead for R2, and mBART shows higher performance for RL. SSR and mBART take the lead for BS among the baselines. For FRE, a score between $30 - 50$ is the readability level best understood by college graduates. The WIKIPEDIA summaries fall in this range. For FRE, SSR performs the best among all models. Interestingly, almost all baselines except BIGBIRD and XLSUM demonstrate good performance.

5.2 Case Study: SPEKTRUM

Table 2 presents the results of all models on SPEKTRUM. We find a similar pattern that SIMCSUM outperforms all baselines except SSR for ROUGE-scores. We also compute the statistical significance of these results with the same procedure. The SPEKTRUM results are on the lower side compared to the WIKIPEDIA results due to zero-shot adaptability, especially for R2. This is because the ROUGE score computes n-gram overlap (Ng and Abrecht, 2015). The SPEKTRUM summaries have higher FRE scores compared to WIKIPEDIA. Interestingly, we note that all baselines perform lower than the GOLD summaries. However, the SIMCSUM score is similar to the GOLD summaries.

Human Evaluation. We compare the SIMCSUM and mBART outputs for analyzing linguistic qualities because SIMCSUM's architecture is based on mBART. We provide 30×2 (for each model) random summaries with their original texts. We ask two annotators to evaluate each document for three linguistic properties on a Likert scale from $1 - 5$. The first five samples are used to calibrate the an-

MODELS	FLUENCY	RELEVANCE	SIMPLICITY
mBART	2.28 (0.64)	1.64 (0.70)	1.86 (0.56)
SIMCSUM	2.62 (0.87)	2.76 (0.78)	2.88 (0.81)

Table 3: The SPEKTRUM human evaluation for mBART and SIMCSUM. The average scores (Krippendorff's α) for each linguistic feature are presented here.

notations of annotators, and then each annotator provides independent judgments on the rest of the samples.

Table 3 shows the human evaluation results. The samples used for calibration are not used for computing the scores (guidelines in Appendix C). We compute the inter-rater reliability by using Krippendorff's α[3]. We find that SIMCSUM improves the fluency, relevance and readability of outputs. We present a few comparative examples of SIMCSUM and mBART in Appendix E.

6 Readability Analysis: SPEKTRUM

The automatic evaluation of models show higher performance of SIMCSUM for ROUGE and BERT-score for WIKIPEDIA. However, it is not the case for FRE. Interestingly, for SPEKTRUM, SIMCSUM shows better performance for FRE. So we decide to further investigate readability with lexical diversity, readability scores and syntactic analysis to determine the quality of generated summaries. These types of analyses are well-known in NLP for textual analysis (Aluisio et al., 2010; Hancke et al., 2012; Vajjala and Lučić, 2018; Mosquera, 2022; Weiss and Meurers, 2022). The lexical diversity and readability scores are computed over all SPEKTRUM's reference summaries (Gold) and outputs of mBART, SSR and SIMCSUM. The gold summaries' score is a guideline for how similar the models' outputs are to gold summaries.

6.1 Lexical Diversity

Lexical diversity estimates the overall language distribution and computes cohesion through synonyms in the text. It is a good indicator of the readability of a text. We calculate Shannon Entropy Estimation (SEE) (Shannon, 1948) and Measure of Textual Lexical Diversity (MTLD) (McCarthy, 2005) to find lexical diversity (see Appendix B.1 for the formula).

SEE presents a text's "informational value" and language diversity. It is a language-dependent feature, and its value varies for different languages.

[3]https://github.com/LightTag/simpledorff

FEATURES	GOLD	mBART	SSR	SIMCSUM
Lexical Diversity				
SEE ↓	4.25	4.26	4.25	4.25
MTLD ↑	201	65.13	90.32	91.75
Readability scores				
CLI ↓	18.45	21.64	19.98	20.96
ARI ↓	18.99	21.07	21.16	20.26

Table 4: Lexical diversity and readability features' average scores.

Higher SEE scores suggest higher lexical diversity. We aim to get similar SEE as Gold summaries. Table 4 shows SEE scores of all three models which are similar to Gold summaries suggesting the similar informational value of all summaries.

MTLD is considered a robust version of the type-token ratio (TTR) and calculates lexical diversity without considering text length. Higher MTLD represents the greater vocabulary richness. Table 4 presents MTLD scores of all three models. The gold summaries have the highest scores, while SIMCSUM is the second highest, SSR has a slightly lower score than SIMCSUM, and mBART has the lowest score. These scores suggest that the lexical richness of all groups is not similar, in contrast to SEE results. The SIMCSUM outputs are more lexically diverse than the SSR and mBART outputs. We deduce from the improved SIMCSUM scores that joint learning of simplification and cross-lingual summarization impacts word generation. These results also suggest that MTLD provides a better estimation of lexical diversity for our summaries.

6.2 Readability Scores

Readability scores measure comprehension levels of the text. One of the syllables-based readability scores is already presented in §5. Coleman and Liau (1975) suggests that word length in letters is a better predictor of readability than syllables. We calculate Coleman Liau Index (CLI) (Coleman and Liau, 1975) and Automated Readability Index (ARI) (Senter and Smith, 1967) as these do not rely on syllables (see Appendix B.1 for the formula).

CLI computes scores on word lengths. ARI computes scores on characters, words and sentences. For both CLI and ARI, the lower score is better as it shows the ease of reading and understanding. From Table 4, we note that Gold summaries have the lowest score, SIMCSUM and SSR have similar scores, while mBART has the highest score. We deduce from these scores that joint learning of simplifica-

FEATURES↓	GOLD	mBART	SSR	SIMCSUM
ASL	24.09	24.15	22.65	20.97
ADD	3.60	4.16	3.95	3.91
ADW	0.93	0.95	0.94	0.94
ATH	8.32	8.72	8.60	8.57

Table 5: Syntactic features' average scores.

ERROR TYPES	mBART	SIMCSUM
Non-German words	83	35
Wrong name entities	1	2
Unfaithful information	3	3

Table 6: Error occurrences for mBART and SIMCSUM summaries which may contain multiple errors.

tion and cross-lingual summarization has an impact on both word and sentence level because CLI only focuses on words, while ARI includes sentences also.

6.3 Syntactic Analysis

Syntactic analysis elaborates on how words and phrases are related in a sentence structure. We perform it with constituency trees on 25×3 (for each model) random summaries from mBART, SIMCSUM and the gold summaries. The total number of sentences for mBART is 70, for SSR is 120, for SIMCSUM is 80 and for gold is 131. Table 5 presents four syntactic features (see Appendix B.2 for definitions).

We note from the average sentence length (ASL) that SIMCSUM produces shorter sentences among all models, which exhibits syntactic simplicity. A small average dependency distance (ADD) shows that words with a dependency relation are close together, making the text easier to understand. Table 5 shows that SIMCSUM summaries have a smaller average dependency than SSR and mBART, much closer to gold summaries. Fewer dependents per word (ADW) make a text less ambiguous and thus easier to follow. Table 5 shows both SSR and SIMCSUM outputs have fewer dependents than the mBART outputs and are similar to gold summaries. The average tree height (ATH) explains the syntactic structural complexity of a sentence. Table 5 shows that SIMCSUM outputs are less structurally complex than SSR and mBART outputs, however, gold summaries have the least average tree height. We deduce from the syntactic analysis that joint learning of simplification and cross-lingual summarization positively impacts the syntactic properties of summaries.

7 Error Analysis

To further explore the challenges of generating cross-lingual science summaries, we consider the base model - mBART and SIMCSUM for analyzing the produced errors. We randomly select 25×2 (for each model) summaries from the SIMCSUM and mBART outputs. We note three main categories of errors in the manual inspection. Table 6 presents the occurrences of these errors in each model. Appendix D presents some examples from the error analysis and its guidelines.

Non-German Words. This is the error type where the models either produce non-existent German words or partially English-German or words in another language. We find that mBART is more prone to produce such errors. We note that it is due to the imbalance between the pre-trained and fine-tuned dataset sizes. These models are pre-trained on many languages and usually fine-tuned on comparatively smaller data. SIMCSUM tends to produce fewer errors due to data augmentation (simplification data) during the training.

Wrong Named Entities. This is the error type where the models produce wrong named entities, such as cities or country names and persons' first and last names. We find that both models tend to produce such errors, however, the percentage of such errors is quite low. We note that the models overestimate or underestimate the probability of word sequences present in data.

Unfaithful Information. This is the error type where we find some (new) information in generated summaries that is not faithful to the source documents. We note that this error is caused by long inputs where the model tends to hallucinate and generates some content that cannot be verified from the source. We find that SIMCSUM makes similar errors as mBART for this error type.

8 Conclusions

In this paper, we investigate a recently introduced task - cross-lingual science journalism. We propose a novel multi-task model - SIMCSUM- that combines two high-level NLP tasks, simplification and cross-lingual summarization. SIMCSUM jointly trains for reducing linguistic complexity and cross-lingual abstractive summarization. Our empirical investigation shows the significantly superior performance of SIMCSUM over the pipeline-based SSR model and other baselines on two non-synthetic cross-lingual scientific datasets. This is confirmed by human evaluation. Furthermore, our in-depth linguistics analysis shows how multi-task learning in SIMCSUM has lexical and syntactic impacts on the generated summaries. We perform error analysis to find what kind of errors has been produced by the model. In the future, we plan to add modules for linguistically informed simplification.

9 Limitations

We proposed SIMCSUM for the cross-lingual science journalism task and verified its performance for WIKIPEDIA and SPEKTRUM datasets for the English-German language pair. We believe that SIMCSUM is adaptable for other domains and languages. However, we have not verified it experimentally and limited our experiments to English-German scientific texts.

Our model jointly trains on two high-level NLP tasks, which takes slightly more time than its base model - mBART, as it has more parameters to learn during the training. However, it takes much less time in training than SSR. Furthermore, our model is trained on synthetic simplification data, which may create a dependency on the simplification model - Keep-it-Simple (Laban et al., 2021). Therefore, we plan to add linguistically informed simplification modules in our model as our future work. We also find during error analysis that both mBART and SIMCSUM have problems (repetition or unfaithful information) with long inputs, which need further investigation that how we can mitigate such errors.

10 Ethical Consideration

Reproducibility. We discussed all relevant parameters, training details, and hardware information in §4.4 and Appendix A.

Legal Consent. We obtained legal consent from Spektrum der Wissenschaft to use their dataset. We adopted the public implementations with mostly recommended settings, wherever applicable.

Acknowledgements

The work was carried out at Heidelberg Institute for Theoretical Studies (supported by the Klaus Tschira Foundation), Heidelberg, Germany, under the collaborative Ph.D. scholarship scheme between the Higher Education Commission of Pakistan (HEC) and Deutscher Akademischer Austausch Dienst (DAAD). We would like to express our sincere gratitude to the reviewers whose feedback and insights greatly contributed to the quality of this work. We also extend our appreciation to the human annotators whose valuable contributions were essential for the success of this project.

References

Sandra Aluisio, Lucia Specia, Caroline Gasperin, and Carolina Scarton. 2010. Readability assessment for text simplification. In *Proceedings of the NAACL HLT 2010 fifth workshop on innovative use of NLP for building educational applications*, pages 1–9.

Yu Bai, Yang Gao, and He-Yan Huang. 2021. Cross-lingual abstractive summarization with limited parallel resources. In *Proceedings of the 59th Annual Meeting of the Association for Computational Linguistics and the 11th International Joint Conference on Natural Language Processing (Volume 1: Long Papers)*, pages 6910–6924.

Yu Bai, Heyan Huang, Kai Fan, Yang Gao, Yiming Zhu, Jiaao Zhan, Zewen Chi, and Boxing Chen. 2022. Unifying cross-lingual summarization and machine translation with compression rate. In *Proceedings of the 45th International ACM SIGIR Conference on Research and Development in Information Retrieval*, pages 1087–1097.

Iz Beltagy, Matthew E Peters, and Arman Cohan. 2020. Longformer: The long-document transformer. *arXiv preprint arXiv:2004.05150*.

Isabel Cachola, Kyle Lo, Arman Cohan, and Daniel Weld. 2020. TLDR: Extreme summarization of scientific documents. In *Findings of the Association for Computational Linguistics: EMNLP 2020*, pages 4766–4777, Online. Association for Computational Linguistics.

Yue Cao, Hui Liu, and Xiaojun Wan. 2020. Jointly learning to align and summarize for neural cross-lingual summarization. In *Proceedings of the 58th annual meeting of the association for computational linguistics*, pages 6220–6231.

Yulong Chen, Huajian Zhang, Yijie Zhou, Xuefeng Bai, Yueguan Wang, Ming Zhong, Jianhao Yan, Yafu Li, Judy Li, Xianchao Zhu, et al. 2023. Revisiting cross-lingual summarization: A corpus-based study and a new benchmark with improved annotation. In *Proceedings of the 61st Annual Meeting of the Association for Computational Linguistics (Volume 1: Long Papers)*, pages 9332–9351.

Arman Cohan, Franck Dernoncourt, Doo Soon Kim, Trung Bui, Seokhwan Kim, Walter Chang, and Nazli Goharian. 2018. A discourse-aware attention model for abstractive summarization of long documents. In *Proceedings of the 2018 Conference of the North*

American Chapter of the Association for Computational Linguistics: Human Language Technologies, Volume 2 (Short Papers), pages 615–621, New Orleans, Louisiana. Association for Computational Linguistics.

Meri Coleman and Ta Lin Liau. 1975. A computer readability formula designed for machine Scoring. *Journal of Applied Psychology*, 60(2):283.

Rumen Dangovski, Michelle Shen, Dawson Byrd, Li Jing, Desislava Tsvetkova, Preslav Nakova, and Marin Soljacic. 2021. We Can Explain Your Research in Layman's Terms: Towards Automating Science Journalism at Scale. In *Proceedings of the AAAI Conference on Artificial Intelligence*, volume 35, pages 12728–12737, Online.

Mehwish Fatima and Michael Strube. 2021. A novel Wikipedia based dataset for monolingual and cross-lingual summarization. In *Proceedings of the Third Workshop on New Frontiers in Summarization*, pages 39–50, Online and in Dominican Republic. Association for Computational Linguistics.

Mehwish Fatima and Michael Strube. 2023. Cross-lingual science journalism: Select, simplify and rewrite summaries for non-expert readers. In *Proceedings of the 61st Annual Meeting of the Association for Computational Linguistics (Volume 1: Long Papers)*, pages 1843–1861.

Tomas Goldsack, Zhihao Zhang, Chenghua Lin, and Carolina Scarton. 2022. Making science simple: Corpora for the lay summarisation of scientific literature. In *Proceedings of the 2022 Conference on Empirical Methods in Natural Language Processing*, pages 10589–10604.

Julia Hancke, Sowmya Vajjala, and Detmar Meurers. 2012. Readability classification for german using lexical, syntactic, and morphological features. In *Proceedings of COLING 2012*, pages 1063–1080.

Tahmid Hasan, Abhik Bhattacharjee, Md Saiful Islam, Kazi Mubasshir, Yuan-Fang Li, Yong-Bin Kang, M Sohel Rahman, and Rifat Shahriyar. 2021. Xl-sum: Large-scale multilingual abstractive summarization for 44 languages. In *Findings of the Association for Computational Linguistics: ACL-IJCNLP 2021*, pages 4693–4703.

Minsoo Kim, Dennis Singh Moirangthem, and Minho Lee. 2016. Towards abstraction from extraction: Multiple timescale gated recurrent unit for summarization. In *Proceedings of the 1st Workshop on Representation Learning for NLP*, pages 70–77, Berlin, Germany. Association for Computational Linguistics.

J Peter Kincaid, Robert P Fishburne Jr, Richard L Rogers, and Brad S Chissom. 1975. Derivation of new readability formulas (automated readability index, fog count and flesch reading ease formula) for navy enlisted personnel. Technical report, Naval Technical Training Command Millington TN Research Branch.

Philippe Laban, Tobias Schnabel, Paul Bennett, and Marti A. Hearst. 2021. Keep it simple: Unsupervised simplification of multi-paragraph text. In *Proceedings of the 59th Annual Meeting of the Association for Computational Linguistics and the 11th International Joint Conference on Natural Language Processing (Volume 1: Long Papers)*, pages 6365–6378, Online. Association for Computational Linguistics.

Faisal Ladhak, Esin Durmus, Claire Cardie, and Kathleen McKeown. 2020. WikiLingua: A new benchmark dataset for cross-lingual abstractive summarization. In *Findings of the Association for Computational Linguistics: EMNLP 2020*, pages 4034–4048, Online. Association for Computational Linguistics.

Chin-Yew Lin. 2004. ROUGE: A package for automatic evaluation of summaries. In *Text Summarization Branches Out*, pages 74–81, Barcelona, Spain. Association for Computational Linguistics.

Yinhan Liu, Jiatao Gu, Naman Goyal, Xian Li, Sergey Edunov, Marjan Ghazvininejad, Mike Lewis, and Luke Zettlemoyer. 2020. Multilingual denoising pre-training for neural machine translation. *Transactions of the Association for Computational Linguistics*, 8:726–742.

Philip M McCarthy. 2005. *An assessment of the range and usefulness of lexical diversity measures and the potential of the measure of textual, lexical diversity (MTLD)*. Ph.D. thesis, The University of Memphis.

Alejandro Mosquera. 2022. Tackling data drift with adversarial validation: An application for german text complexity estimation. In *Proceedings of the GermEval 2022 Workshop on Text Complexity Assessment of German Text*, pages 39–44.

Jun-Ping Ng and Viktoria Abrecht. 2015. Better summarization evaluation with word embeddings for rouge. In *Proceedings of the 2015 Conference on Empirical Methods in Natural Language Processing*, pages 1925–1930.

Nikola I Nikolov, Michael Pfeiffer, and Richard HR Hahnloser. 2018. Data-driven Summarization of Scientific Articles. In *Proceedings of the Eleventh International Conference on Language Resources and Evaluation (LREC 2018)*, Miyazaki, Japan. European Language Resources Association (ELRA).

Jessica Ouyang, Boya Song, and Kathy McKeown. 2019. A robust abstractive system for cross-lingual summarization. In *Proceedings of the 2019 Conference of the North American Chapter of the Association for Computational Linguistics: Human Language Technologies, Volume 1 (Long and Short Papers)*, pages 2025–2031, Minneapolis, Minnesota. Association for Computational Linguistics.

Sebastian Ruder. 2017. An overview of multi-task learning in deep neural networks. *arXiv preprint arXiv:1706.05098*.

Abigail See, Peter J. Liu, and Christopher D. Manning. 2017. Get To The Point: Summarization with Pointer-Generator Networks. In *Proceedings of the 55th Annual Meeting of the Association for Computational Linguistics (Volume 1: Long Papers)*, pages 1073–1083, Vancouver, Canada. Association for Computational Linguistics.

RJ Senter and Edgar A Smith. 1967. Automated readability index. Technical report, Cincinnati Univ OH.

Claude Elwood Shannon. 1948. A mathematical theory of communication. *The Bell system technical journal*, 27(3):379–423.

Sho Takase and Naoaki Okazaki. 2022. Multi-task learning for cross-lingual abstractive summarization. In *Proceedings of the Thirteenth Language Resources and Evaluation Conference*, pages 3008–3016.

Sotaro Takeshita, Tommaso Green, Niklas Friedrich, Kai Eckert, and Simone Paolo Ponzetto. 2022. X-scitldr: cross-lingual extreme summarization of scholarly documents. In *Proceedings of the 22nd ACM/IEEE Joint Conference on Digital Libraries*, pages 1–12.

Raghuram Vadapalli, Bakhtiyar Syed, Nishant Prabhu, Balaji Vasan Srinivasan, and Vasudeva Varma. 2018a. Sci-blogger: A step towards automated science journalism. In *Proceedings of the 27th ACM International Conference on Information and Knowledge Management, CIKM 2018, Torino, Italy, October 22-26, 2018*, pages 1787–1790. ACM.

Raghuram Vadapalli, Bakhtiyar Syed, Nishant Prabhu, Balaji Vasan Srinivasan, and Vasudeva Varma. 2018b. When science journalism meets artificial intelligence : An interactive demonstration. In *Proceedings of the 2018 Conference on Empirical Methods in Natural Language Processing: System Demonstrations*, pages 163–168, Brussels, Belgium. Association for Computational Linguistics.

Sowmya Vajjala and Ivana Lučić. 2018. Onestopenglish corpus: A new corpus for automatic readability assessment and text simplification. In *Proceedings of the thirteenth workshop on innovative use of NLP for building educational applications*, pages 297–304.

Ashish Vaswani, Noam Shazeer, Niki Parmar, Jakob Uszkoreit, Llion Jones, Aidan N Gomez, Łukasz Kaiser, and Illia Polosukhin. 2017. Attention is all you need. In *Advances in Neural Information Processing Systems 30: Annual Conference on Neural Information Processing Systems 2017, December 4-9, 2017, Long Beach, CA, USA*, pages 5998–6008.

Zarah Weiss and Detmar Meurers. 2022. Assessing sentence readability for german language learners with broad linguistic modeling or readability formulas: When do linguistic insights make a difference? In *Proceedings of the 17th Workshop on Innovative Use of NLP for Building Educational Applications (BEA 2022)*, pages 141–153.

Ruochen Xu, Chenguang Zhu, Yu Shi, Michael Zeng, and Xuedong Huang. 2020. Mixed-lingual pre-training for cross-lingual summarization. In *Proceedings of the 1st Conference of the Asia-Pacific Chapter of the Association for Computational Linguistics and the 10th International Joint Conference on Natural Language Processing*, pages 536–541.

Linting Xue, Noah Constant, Adam Roberts, Mihir Kale, Rami Al-Rfou, Aditya Siddhant, Aditya Barua, and Colin Raffel. 2021. mT5: A massively multilingual pre-trained text-to-text transformer. In *Proceedings of the 2021 Conference of the North American Chapter of the Association for Computational Linguistics: Human Language Technologies*, pages 483–498, Online. Association for Computational Linguistics.

Manzil Zaheer, Guru Guruganesh, Kumar Avinava Dubey, Joshua Ainslie, Chris Alberti, Santiago Ontanon, Philip Pham, Anirudh Ravula, Qifan Wang, Li Yang, et al. 2020. Big bird: Transformers for longer sequences. *Advances in Neural Information Processing Systems*, 33:17283–17297.

Farooq Zaman, Matthew Shardlow, Saeed-Ul Hassan, Naif Radi Aljohani, and Raheel Nawaz. 2020. Htss: A novel hybrid text summarisation and simplification architecture. *Information Processing & Management*, 57(6):102351.

Jingqing Zhang, Yao Zhao, Mohammad Saleh, and Peter Liu. 2020a. PEGASUS: pre-training with extracted gap-sentences for abstractive summarization. In *Proceedings of the 37th International Conference on Machine Learning, ICML 2020, 13-18 July 2020, Virtual Event*, volume 119 of *Proceedings of Machine Learning Research*, pages 11328–11339. PMLR.

Tianyi Zhang, Varsha Kishore, Felix Wu, Kilian Q Weinberger, and Yoav Artzi. 2020b. Bertscore: Evaluating text generation with BERT. In *8th International Conference on Learning Representations, ICLR 2020, Addis Ababa, Ethiopia, April 26-30, 2020*. OpenReview.net.

Junnan Zhu, Qian Wang, Yining Wang, Yu Zhou, Jiajun Zhang, Shaonan Wang, and Chengqing Zong. 2019. NCLS: Neural cross-lingual summarization. In *Proceedings of the 2019 Conference on Empirical Methods in Natural Language Processing and the 9th International Joint Conference on Natural Language Processing (EMNLP-IJCNLP)*, pages 3054–3064, Hong Kong, China. Association for Computational Linguistics.

Junnan Zhu, Yu Zhou, Jiajun Zhang, and Chengqing Zong. 2020. Attend, translate and summarize: An efficient method for neural cross-lingual summarization. In *Proceedings of the 58th Annual Meeting of the Association for Computational Linguistics*, pages 1309–1321, Online. Association for Computational Linguistics.

A Training and Inference

Libraries. We train all models with Pytorch[4], Hugging Face[5] integrated with DeepSpeed[6] for parallel model training with ZeRO-2. We apply ZeRO-2[7] to enable model parallelism. ZeRO-2 reduces the memory footprints for gradients and optimizer because it shards the optimizer states and gradients across GPUs.

Hardware. For all models, we complete training and inference on 4 Tesla P40 GPUs each with 24GB memory.

Training Time. We use the maximum length capacity at the encoder side and set length of 200 tokens at the decoder side. mBART takes 1 day and 17 hours, mT5 takes 10 hours, PEGASUS takes 1 day and 8 hours, XLSUM takes 1 day and 3 hours, LONG-ED takes almost 4 days, and BIGBIRD takes 2 days to complete 25 epochs. SIMCSUM takes 2 days to complete 25 epochs.

B Analysis: SPEKTRUM

B.1 Lexical Diversity

SEE is calculated with a frequency table as follows.

$$H(x) = \sum_{i=1}^{n} p(x_i) log_2 \frac{1}{p(x_i)}$$

where $H(x)$ is the total amount of information in an entire probability distribution. $P(x_i)$ refers to the frequency of a token appearing in the text, and $1/p(x)$ denotes the information of each case.

MTLD divides the texts into sequences having the same TTR and then calculates the mean length of the sequences.

B.2 Readability

FRE is calculated as follows:

$$FRE = 180 - ASL - (58.5 \times ASW)$$

where average sentence length (ASL) is the number of words divided by the number of sentences in the text. The average number of syllables per word (ASW) is the number of syllables divided by the number of words in the text. The numeric values are language-dependent constants.

CLI is calculated as follows:

$$CLI = 5.88 \times \frac{L}{W} - 29.6 \times \frac{S}{W} - 15.8$$

where L is the total number of characters (including numbers and punctuation), W is the total number of words, and S is the total number of sentences in a given text.

ARI is computed as follows:

$$ARI = 4.71 \times \frac{L}{W} + 0.5 \times \frac{W}{S} - 21.43$$

where L is the total number of characters (including numbers and punctuation), W is the total number of words, and S is the total number of sentences in a given text.

B.3 Syntactic Analysis

We use Stanza[8] to extract dependency relations and Stanford Parser [9] to extract constituency trees for each summary. Before tree generation, we replace all German umlauts (ä, ö, ü and ß) in the summaries with their replacements (ae, oe, ue and ss) due to encoding issues of the Stanford Parser.

Average Sentence Length. It is the number of tokens in the sentences averaged over the number of sentences in a summary.

Average Dependency Distance. It is the averaged dependency distance over the sentences, which means the distance between the dependency heads and their dependents.

Average Dependents per Word. It computes the average number of dependents for each word.

Average Tree Height. For computing the average tree height of a summary, we calculate the height of every tree and average it over the sentences.

C Human Evaluation

C.1 Task

We provided annotators with 30 examples of documents paired with a reference summary and two system-generated summaries. The models' identities had not been revealed. The annotators had to rate each model summary for the following linguistic properties after reading the English document and the German summaries. We asked annotators to use the first 5 examples to resolve the annotator's conflict and to find a common consensus for rating the linguistic aspects. However, the rest of the examples were annotated independently.

[4] https://pytorch.org/

[5] https://huggingface.co/

[6] https://www.microsoft.com/en-us/research/project/deepspeed/

[7] Initially, we used ZeRO-3 offload with FP16 evaluation, and the training became quite slow as it consumes a lot of time for offloading during evaluation.

[8] https://stanfordnlp.github.io/stanza/constituency.html

[9] https://nlp.stanford.edu/software/lex-parser.shtml

C.2 Linguistic Properties

We asked annotators to annotate each summary for the following linguistic properties.

Relevance. A summary delivers adequate information about the original text. Relevance determines the content relevancy of the summary.

Fluency. The words and phrases fit together within a sentence, and so do the sentences. Fluency determines the structural and grammatical properties of a summary.

Simplicity. Lexical (word) and syntactic (syntax) simplicity of sentences. A simple summary should have minimal use of complex words/phrases and sentence structure.

C.3 Scale

We use a Likert scale from 1 to 5 to score each property (1:worst | 2:bad | 3:ok | 4:good | 5:best). These scores should be assigned by comparing the outputs of both models.

D Error Analysis

D.1 Guidelines

We define our informal guidelines for the error analysis as follows. To find the errors in the mBART and SIMCSUM outputs, we compare them to each other, to the SPEKTRUM German gold summary and the original English text.

Non-German Words. To find them, it is sufficient to read through our model outputs and look up any unknown words. If one of the unknown words turns out to be a non-German word, we mark them in red.

Wrong named entities. We find wrong named entities by comparing the names in both system outputs to the reference summary. If the names differ, we verify with the original text that they refer to the same person and thus represent a mistake by the model, and we mark them in blue.

Unfaithful information. We note new/unfaithful information by looking up every piece of information in the model outputs in the reference summary. We search for this information in the original text, and if it is not present there, it is clear that the model produced new information that is not faithful to the source text. We mark this information in orange.

D.2 Examples

Target: im freigehege aufzuwachsen und sich dort im schlamm zu suhlen, stärkt offenbar das immunsystem von schweinen : verglichen mit artgenossen, die in einem stall gehalten wurden, hatten freilandschweine eine höhere anzahl von gesundheitsfördernden darmbakterien. zu diesem ergebnis kommen jetzt wissenschaftler um denise kelly von der university of aberdeen. auch gene, die auf entzündungsreaktionen hindeuten, waren bei tieren, die im außenbereich lebten, wesentlich weniger aktiv. [...]   **Translation:** Growing up in an outdoor enclosure and wallowing in the mud there apparently strengthens the immune system of pigs : compared to conspecifics that were kept in a pen, free-range pigs had a higher number of health-promoting intestinal bacteria. scientists led by denise kelly from the university of aberdeen are now coming to this conclusion. genes that indicate inflammatory responses were also significantly less active in animals that lived outdoors. [...]
mBART: als fruehmikrobielle kolonisation wird dieabdeckung der brustdruese von schweinen bei der fruehen entwicklung des erwachsenen menschen bezeichnet. sie wird in der medizin, der mikrobiologie und der pathologie erforscht. early microbial colonization of the gut reduced the incidence of infectious, entzuendlichen und autoimmunischen diseasen reduced the incidence of infectious, inflammatory and autoimmune diseases.   **Translation:** the covering of the mammary gland of pigs during the early development of the adult human is referred to as early microbial colonization. it is researched in medicine, microbiology and pathology. early microbial colonization of the gut reduced the incidence of infectious, inflammatory and autoimmune diseases reduced the incidence of infectious, inflammatory and autoimmune diseases.
SIMCSUM : die fruehzeitshygiene ist ein begriff aus der entwicklungsbiologie und bezeichnet das phaenomen, dass die fruehzeitliche besiedlung des darmes durch krankheitserreger verhindert wird. die fruehzeitshygiene unterscheidet sich von anderen entwicklungsbiologischen forschungsgebieten wie der entwicklungsphysiologie, der haematologie und der palaeontologie dadurch, dass in ihrer gesamtheit zur fruehen entwicklungsphase die mikrobielle vielfalt des darmes zaehlt.   **Translation:** early hygiene is a term from developmental biology and describes the phenomenon that prevents early colonization of the intestines by pathogens. early hygiene differs from other developmental biological research areas such as developmental physiology, haematology and palaeontology in that the microbial diversity of the intestine counts in its entirety for the early development phase.

Table D.1: An example of SPEKTRUM output, where mBART produces non-German words (marked as red) and SIMCSUM generates the summary with wrong attention on hygiene. The summaries are translated via Google translate.

Target: nicht nur stress und genetische faktoren tragen zu essstörungen bei, sondern auch vorübergehende hungerphasen. nun stießen forscher vom europäischen zentrum für hirnforschung in rom auf einen möglichen grund dafür - und zwar in den gehirnen von labormäuse, die sich auch durch schmerzen nicht vom naschen abbringen ließen. die psychologin rossella ventura und ihre kollegen trainierten mäuse darauf, in einer von zwei kammern nach einer belohnung in form von schokolade zu suchen. dann versetzten sie den tieren ausgerechnet in dem raum, wo die leckerei lockte, schmerzhafte elektroschocks. die mäuse mieden fortan die schokolade und hielten sich vorwiegend in der anderen kammer auf - außer jene, die zuvor einige zeit lang kaum futter bekommen hatten. [...]   **Translation:** Not only stress and genetic factors contribute to eating disorders, but also periods of starvation. now researchers from the european center for brain research in rome have discovered a possible reason for this - namely in the brains of laboratory mice, which were not deterred from snacking even by pain. psychologist rossella ventura and her colleagues trained mice to look for a chocolate reward in one of two chambers. then they gave the animals painful electric shocks in the room where the treat lured them. From then on, the mice avoided the chocolate and mainly stayed in the other chamber - except for those that had hardly received any food for a while. [...]
mBART: eating disorders (engl. "ess-stoerungen") nennt man eine vielzahl von ursachen und mechanismen, die zur auspraegung von essstoerungen fuehren koennen.   **Translation:** eating disorders are a number of causes and mechanisms that can lead to the development of eating disorders.
SIMCSUM : als essverhalten oder magersucht werden die verhaltensweisen von menschen und tieren bezeichnet, die excessive (vergoren) oder chronisch (z.b. nach unfaellen oder erkrankungen) zu es verlangen oder dieses verhalten unterdruecken. essverhalten kann zu verhaltensstoerungen fuehren, die ursache fuer die entstehung von essstoerungen sind innere oder aeussere ursachen des essverhaltens.   **Translation:** eating habits or anorexia are the behaviors of people and animals that demand excessive (fermented) or chronic (e.g. after accidents or illnesses) or suppress this behavior. eating behavior can lead to behavioral disorders, the cause of eating disorders are internal or external causes of eating behavior.

Table D.2: An example of SPEKTRUM output, where mBART produces non-German words (marked as red) and quite short summary. While SIMCSUM generates also generates a non-German word. The summaries are translated via Google translate.

Target: der tod kam auf dem höhepunkt der macht : cangrandei. della scala, der berühmteste spross der scaliger aus verona, hatte in zahlreichen kriegerischen auseinandersetzungen die herrschaft über ganz venetien an sich gerissen. doch kurz nach seinem triumphalen einzug in die norditalienische stadt treviso am 18. juli 1329 begannen mit durchfall und erbrechen die ersten symptome einer tödlichen erkrankung. [...]
Translation: death came at the height of power : cangrandei. della scala, the most famous offspring of the scaliger family from verona, seized control of all of veneto in numerous military conflicts. but shortly after his triumphant entry into the northern italian city of treviso on july 18, 1329, the first symptoms of a fatal illness began with diarrhea and vomiting. [...]

mBART: **alberto** cangrande (* 1291 oder 1329 in verona ; † 29. oktober 1329 ebenda) war ein italienischer dichter, schriftsteller und politiker der flämischen republik. in der zeit der italienischen republik bestieg er von seinen brudern die dynastie der scaliger i. bei der eroberung der elfenbeinküste 1311 wurde er zum maßgebenden gründer der faction in rom. ab 1314 war er herrscher im königreich venedig. cangrande gilt als vater der italienischen
Translation: **alberto** cangrande (b. 1291 or 1329 in verona ; † october 29, 1329 ibid) was an italian poet, writer and politician of the flemish republic. in the time of the italian republic he ascended from his brothers the dynasty of the scaligeri. when he conquered the ivory coast in 1311, he became the main founder of the faction in rome. from 1314 he was ruler of the kingdom of venice. cangrande is considered the father of the italian

SIMCSUM : cangrande della scala oder cangrande **cangrande** (* 9. märz 1291 in verona ; † 22. juli 1329 ebenda) war ein begründer der von den scaligeri beeinflussten dynastie, der unter den herrschern von verona von 1308 bis 1387 regierte. der sohn des veronaer stadtbegründers und stadtmeisters alberto della scala (genannt „ albert “ oder „ adelsmann “), der nur als unterstellt war, wurde nach seinem tod 1301 zum bruder von alberto verbannte.
Translation: cangrande della scala or cangrande **cangrande** (born march 9, 1291 in verona ; † july 22, 1329 ibid) was a founder of the dynasty influenced by the scaligeri, who reigned under the rulers of verona from 1308 to 1387. the son of verona's founder and mayor alberto della scala (called " albert " or " nobleman "), who was only subordinate, was banished to alberto's brother after his death in 1301.

Table D.3: An example of SPEKTRUM output, where mBART generates a wrong named entity. SPEKTRUM, on the other hand, gets it right but generates a wrong alias for this person. The summaries are translated via Google translate.

Target: inoffizieller weltrekordhalter im nicht - frieren trotz eisiger kälte ist der niederländer wimhof : er lief bereits ziemlich nackt halbmarathons nördlich des polarkreises und nahm das längste eisbad seit beginn der aufzeichnungen - ohne sich ernsthaft zu beklagen. wissenschaftliche untersuchungen des eismannes hatten bisher keine körperlichen auffälligkeiten gefunden, die erklären könnten, warum hof mit kälte offensichtlich besser umgeht als der durchschnittsmensch. [...]
Translation: the unofficial world record holder for not freezing despite the icy cold is the dutchman wimhof : he ran half marathons north of the arctic circle quite naked and took the longest ice bath since records began - without seriously complaining. scientific examinations of the ice cream man had not found any physical abnormalities that could explain why hof obviously deals with the cold better than the average person. [...]

mBART: wim hof (* 20. april 1959) ist ein niederländischer sportler, der sich unter anderem mit eisschwimmern beschäftigt.
Translation: wim hof (born april 20, 1959) is a dutch athlete who is involved with ice swimmers, among other things.

SIMCSUM : wim hof (* 20. april 1959), auch als eismann bekannt, ist ein niederländischer swimmer und ein ehemaliger olympiateilnehmer. er hält seit dem 28. februar 2015 den bislang längsten direkten kontakt menschlichen körpers mit eis.
Translation: Wim Hof (born April 20, 1959), also known as Eismann, is a Dutch swimmer and a former Olympic competitor. since february 28, 2015, he has been in the longest direct contact between the human body and ice.

Table D.4: An example of SPEKTRUM output, where both mBART and SIMCSUM produce unfaithful information. Marked in orange is unfaithful information to the original text. The summaries are translated via Google translate.

E SIMCSUM Examples and Results

Here we present some examples showing the difference between SIMCSUM and mBART.

Target: für menschen ist der einbeinige stand immer eine wackelpartie , vor allem bei geschlossenen augen . um nicht umzukippen , müssen die muskeln permanent die leichten schwankungen ausgleichen . nicht so bei flamingos : sie kostet es weniger kraft , auf einem bein zu stehen als auf zweien . deswegen können sie auch beruhigt auf einem bein ein schläfchen machen , ohne dabei umzukippen . [...]
Translation: standing on one leg is always a shaky game for humans, especially with closed eyes. in order not to tip over , the muscles have to constantly compensate for the slight fluctuations . Not so with flamingos: it takes less strength for them to stand on one leg than on two. that's why you can take a nap on one leg without tipping over. [...]

---

mBART: die biogerontologie (von griech. bíos ,, leben " und lat. protes ,, befestigt ") beschäftigt sich mit dem verhältnis von körpergewicht und körperhaltung. so untersucht die biogerontologie das verhältnis von körpergewicht und körperhaltung : welche gewichtszustände und welche muskeln notwendig sind, um einen pilz, der einer krankheit ausgesetzt ist, zu tragen? wie sehr wichtig es ist, den jeweiligen körpergewichtszustand zu messen. dies wird in der
Translation: biogerontology (from greek bíos "life" and lat. protes "fixed") deals with the relationship between body weight and posture. this is how biogerontology examines the relationship between body weight and posture: which weight conditions and which muscles are necessary to carry a fungus that is exposed to a disease? how very important it is to measure the respective body weight condition. this will be in the

---

SIMCSUM : flamingos (phoenicopteridae) oft sitzen auf einem bein, um eine muskelkontraktion zu erzeugen. sie haben die fähigkeit, das körpergewicht aufzunehmen und zu tragen, ohne dabei eine muskelaktive wirkung auszuüben.
Translation: Flamingos (phoenicopteridae) often perch on one leg to produce muscle contraction. they have the ability to absorb and carry body weight without exerting a muscle-active effect.

Table E.1: An example of SPEKTRUM output, where SIMCSUM generates a better summary than mBART . In this case, the mBART summary misses the article's point by focusing on biogerontology which has no relevancy in this case, and SIMCSUM generates a summary that better captures the idea and main focus of the original text. Marked in orange is unfaithful information to the original text. The summaries are translated via Google translate.

Target: eine besondere strategie, seinen fressfeinden zu entkommen, hat der bombardierkäfer pheropsophus jessoensis entwickelt. er wehrt sich sogar noch, nachdem er eigentlich schon verloren hat, und das sogar recht erfolgreich, wie jetzt shinji sugiura und takuya sato von der universität kobe in den biology letters berichten. gerade verschluckt, schießt der käfer im magen der kröte einen strahl heißes, ätzendes sekret aus der afterdrüse - eine strategie, die den bombardierkäfern ihren namen eingebracht hat. normalerweise allerdings dient die waffe zur abschreckung. in diesem fall jedoch ätzen sich die käfer mit ihrer hilfe quasi zurück in die freiheit : das sekret lässt die kröten erbrechen ; und der eigentlich schon verspeiste käfer entkommt. [...]
Translation: the bombardier beetle pheropsophus jessoensis has developed a special strategy for escaping its predators. he even defends himself after he has actually already lost, and even quite successfully, as shinji sugiura and takuya sato from the university of kobe now report in the biology letters. just swallowed, the beetle in the toad's stomach shoots a jet of hot, caustic secretion out of the anal gland - a strategy that has given the bombardier beetle its name. normally, however, the weapon serves as a deterrent. in this case, however, the beetles etch their way back to freedom with your help: the toads vomit the secretion; and the actually already eaten beetle escapes. [...]

---

mBART: unter zoologischer kompatibilitaet versteht man in der biologie die faehigkeit von beutetieremischlingen, nach einem laubabschweif von artgenossen in den verdauungstrakt von artgenossen zu entweichen. die oekologische kompatibilitaet ist ein wesentlicher bestandteil der erfolgreichen entstehung von beutegreifern.beim laubabschweifexperiment mit hilfe des insektenpheropsophus jessoensis aus zwei kaeferarten, dem bufo japonicus und dem b. torrenticola, konnte nachgewiesen werden, dass der kaefer pheropsophus jessoensis unter laboratorischen bedingungen eine in den magensaftgastropfen der jagdsekten einschleudern kann.
Translation: in biology, zoological compatibility means the ability of hybrid prey animals to escape into the digestive tract of conspecifics after the leaves have drifted away from conspecifics. ecological compatibility is an essential part of the successful emergence of predators.in the leaf-dropping experiment with the help of the insect pheropsophus jessoensis from two beetle species, the bufo japonicus and the b. torrenticola, it could be proven that the beetle pheropsophus jessoensis can inject one into the gastric juice droplets of the hunting sects under laboratory conditions.

SIMCSUM : als wehrverhalten oderverteidigungsverhalten bezeichnet man in der verhaltensbiologie verschiedene verhaltensweisen von tieren, die wehren gegen die fressfeinde oder andere fresstiere bilden. nicht zu verwechseln ist das wehrverhalten mit der phylogenetik, die sich aus der evolutionsgeschichte entwickelt hat.
Translation: in behavioral biology, defensive behavior is the term used to describe various behaviors of animals that defend themselves against predators or other predators. the defensive behavior should not be confused with the phylogenetics that have developed from the history of evolution.

Table E.2: An example of SPEKTRUM output, both SIMCSUM and mBART produce reasonable summaries. The SIMCSUM summary is preferred because it explains the basic idea of the beetle defending itself against predators. The mBART summary is filled with complex words that do not make sense or are unnecessary for this context. These words are marked in orange. The summaries are translated via Google translate.

Target: manche farben bleiben besser im gedächtnis haften als andere, doch auf die erinnerung an den entsprechend gefärbten gegenstand hat das keinen einfluss. das zeigt nun eine studie von psychologen um christof kuhbandner von der universität regensburg. die ergebnisse machen deutlich, dass der gegenstand selbst und dessen eigenschaften vom gehirn nicht immer als einheit betrachtet werden. die wissenschaftler testeten für ihre studie das gedächtnis ihrer versuchspersonen. dabei variierten sie sowohl, was zu merken war, als auch, wie es dargeboten wurde. insbesondere präsentierten sie wörter und gegenstände in unterschiedlichen farben. [...] **Translation:** some colors stick in the memory better than others, but this has no influence on the memory of the correspondingly colored object. this is now shown by a study by psychologists led by christof kuhbandner from the university of regensburg. the results make it clear that the object itself and its properties are not always viewed as a unit by the brain. for their study, the scientists tested the memory of their subjects. they varied both what was to be remembered and how it was presented. in particular, they presented words and objects in different colors. [...]
mBART: die farbpsychologie ist ein teilgebiet der psychologie und beschäftigt sich mit der wirkung von farben auf die wahrnehmung und das gedächtnis. **Translation:** color psychology is a branch of psychology and deals with the effect of colors on perception and memory.
SIMCSUM : die farbe ist ein farbmuster, das uns wahrnehmungen und die sinneswahrnehmung durch das sehen vermittelt. die farbwahrnehmung gehört zu den kognitionswissenschaften. wir sehen sie nicht nur als eindimensionales spektrum möglicher farben, sondern auch als eindimensionales, oftmals auch als „ visuelles system “, das die sinneswahrnehmung mitanpasst. [...] **Translation:** color is a color pattern that conveys perceptions and sensory perception to us through seeing. Color perception is one of the cognitive sciences. we see them not only as a one-dimensional spectrum of possible colors, but also as a one-dimensional, often also as a " visual system " that also adapts the sensory perception. [...]

Table E.3: An example of SPEKTRUM output, where mBART performs better than SIMCSUM . mBART generates a summary that is too short but which better recapitulates the main idea. The orange marked words in the SIMCSUM summary are incoherent and are not faithful to the original text. The summaries are translated via Google translate.

Extract, Select and Rewrite: A Modular Sentence Summarization Method

Shuo Guan
UBS AG
New York, NY 10010
shuo.guan@ubs.com

Vishakh Padmakumar
New York University
New York, NY 10012
vishakh@nyu.edu

Abstract

A modular approach has the advantage of being compositional and controllable, comparing to most end-to-end models. In this paper we propose Extract-Select-Rewrite (*ESR*), a three-phase abstractive sentence summarization method. We decompose summarization into three stages: (i) knowledge extraction, where we extract relation triples from the text using off-the-shelf tools; (ii) content selection, where a subset of triples are selected; and (iii) rewriting, where the selected triple are realized into natural language. Our results demonstrates that ESR is competitive with the best end-to-end models while being more faithful. Being modular, ESR's modules can be trained on separate data which is beneficial in low-resource settings and enhancing the style controllability on text generation.[1]

1 Introduction

While end-to-end models are dominating text generation tasks today, modular or pipelined approaches have the advantage of greater controllability and interpretability (Kedzie and McKeown, 2020). Prior work on abstractive summarization adopts a two-step process of first generating a plan (e.g., a semantic representation) of the target summary and then generating the summary conditioned on both the plan and the input document (Narayan et al., 2021, 2022). In this paper, we present a three-phase extract-select-rewrite pipeline, or ESR, for abstractive sentence summarization, where the plan is restricted to be a subset of knowledge triples extracted from the document. Specifically, we decompose the task into three subtasks: knowledge extraction, content selection and rewriting. To implement the three modules, we extract knowledge triples from the source document using off-the-shelf tools. Then, we train a classifier to select important triples representing content of the summary. Finally, we train a rewriter to convert the selected triples into natural language text (Figure 1).

There is extensive prior work that uses structured content extracted from the document to help summarization, such as relation triples (Cao et al., 2018), knowledge graphs (Zhu et al., 2021; Guan et al., 2021), and topics (Li et al., 2018, 2020; Aralikatte et al., 2021). However, these methods typically augment the source document with the extracted information and still learn to generate reference summaries from it in an *end-to-end* manner. By fully separating the modules during training, we can take a rewriter trained on a large dataset, and reuse it on a small target dataset while only training the content selector on as few as 1k examples.

We run experiments on Gigaword, DUC-2004 and Reddit-TIFU datasets and find that our approach produces summaries that are competitive to the end-to-end models in terms of automatic metrics. We also observe that a rewriter module trained on Gigaword, in the news domain, can be paired with a content selector trained on 1000 examples from Reddit-TIFU, a social media dataset, to produce high quality summaries, demonstrating the value of modularity in abstractive summarization.

Further, since our content planning is extractive in nature the summaries generated are also more faithful to the source as evidenced by a human evaluation comparing summaries from our modular approach and an end-to-end BART baseline. Lastly, We also observe that the rewriter module can be trained once on standalone text, which can enhance the controllability on the summary text generation style with minor changes of the training process.

2 Related Work

Knowledge-based Summarization Existing methods that use knowledge in summarization encodes it together with the input, e.g., Ribeiro et al. (2020) and Guan et al. (2021) introduce knowledge

[1]The codes are available on https://github.com/SeanG-325/ESR.

Proceedings of The 4th New Frontiers in Summarization Workshop, pages 41–48
December 6, 2023 ©2023 Association for Computational Linguistics

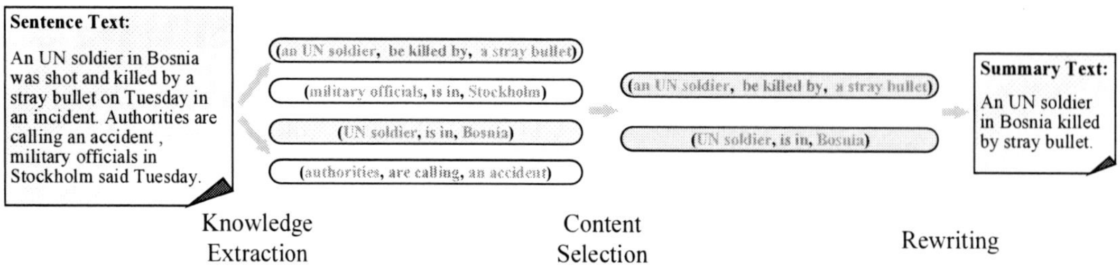

Figure 1: An overview of the three-phase summarization framework ESR.

graph encoding strategies for the graph-to-text generation model. Koncel-Kedziorski et al. (2019) and Wu et al. (2021) use a graph transformer encoder to consume knowledge and semantic graph. Huang et al. (2020) propose a model integrated with the GAT (Veličković et al., 2018) encoding knowledge graphs of the documents.

Modular Summarization Castro Ferreira et al. (2019) and Khot et al. (2021) showed the advantages of the modularity on text generation and question answering comparing to the end-to-end models. Pilault et al. (2020) and Chen and Bansal (2018) first extract sentences from the document and then perform abstractive summarization on them. Krishna et al. (2021) proposed a medical text generation method using modular summarization techniques based on clustering of utterances in sentences. However, the "modularity" in these methods rely on the neural networks to take in additional knowledge such as knowledge graphs, as opposed to splitting the model into different modules explicitly, which is where ESR differs.

3 Method

We divide the summarization task explicitly into three phases—Knowledge Extraction, Content Selection, and Rewriting, as shown in Figure 1.

Knowledge Extraction To enable fine-grained content selection and rewriting, we turn all documents into structured content representation. We adopt knowledge triples that can be extracted by off-the-shelf tools (Section 4.1). The knowledge triples are in the form of `<entity 1, relation, entity 2>`. The extractors usually generate a large number of redundant triples (i.e. triples with large overlap with each other.[2] To delete the overlapping things, we use the Jaccard distance on n-grams (J_{Uni}, J_{Bi}) of between any pairs of triples (x_1, x_2) to calculate their similarity:

$$\text{Sim}(x_i, x_j) \stackrel{\text{def}}{=} \lambda_1 \text{J}_{\text{Uni}}(x_i, x_j) + \lambda_2 \text{J}_{\text{Bi}}(x_i, x_j)$$

Here λ_1, λ_2 are hyperparameters determined on the validation data. We filter triples such that no pair of triples has a similarity score higher than the threshold. If the similarity between two tripes are larger than the threshold, the triple that has the larger length will be kept. The details of the threshold are in Section 4.1.

Content Selection The content selector selects the triples that are to be included in the summary out of the candidates. We train it as a sentence-pair classifier with two inputs, the *document* and the *candidate knowledge triple* extracted from it, and an output of whether to select the triple. If the triple is to be included in the summary of the document, the document-triple pair will be labeled positive, otherwise negative. We need to obtain supervised labels for the triples in the training set for training the content selector. For each triple in the training set, we use ROUGE (Lin, 2004) to measure the similarity to the corresponding summaries, if it is higher than a threshold then we label that triple as a positive example. Some representative examples of these sentence pairs and the details for selecting the threshold can be found in Section 4.1.

Rewriting The rewriter converts the selected triples into fluent summaries, where the triples serve as a content plan. We train a sequence-to-sequence text generation model, similar to converting meaning-representation to natural language text (Kedzie and McKeown, 2020). The train data for this phase contains the texts and the triples extracted from them. To train the generation model,

[2]For example, given the sentence "German chemical giant Hoechst Group announced plans wednesday to invest over a million dollars in China next year" our extractors might generate two candidates `<German chemical giant Hoechst Group, announced, plans>` and `<chemical giant Hoechst group, announced, plans>` which are clearly redundant.

	Ext.	Valid	Redun.	Pos/Neg
Train Articles	6.34	2.53	60.1%	0.91
Train Summaries	4.51	1.76	62.0%	-
Test Articles	6.19	2.42	60.9%	-

Table 1: Triple statistics in train and test sets. "*Ext.*" (Extracted) and "*Valid*" are the mean numbers of the the extracted and valid triplets (redundance removed). "*Redun.*" is the redundancy rate. "*Pos/Neg*" is the positive and negative sample ratio of the constructed data set in the content selection phase.

we concatenate the extracted triples from the document as the source sequence, and use the text as the target sequence. Note that training the rewriter only requires a piece of text and knowledge triples extracted from it. Therefore it can be potentially trained on much larger data (like Wiki text).

4 Experiments

4.1 Experiment Settings

Datasets Our main results are based on 2 news summarization datasets: (i) the Gigaword corpus (Rush et al., 2015), with around 3.8M summaries of single sentence news documents; (ii) DUC-2004, another test set in the news domain (Over et al., 2007)[3] To evaluate the modularity of our method, we reuse the rewriter trained on Gigaword and pair it with the content selector trained on another dataset from a different domain, Reddit TIFU (Kim et al., 2019); Gigaword contains news text while Reddit TIFU contains text from social media.

Training Details We used OLLIE (Mausam et al., 2012), two OpenIE tools (Angeli et al., 2015; Saha and Mausam, 2018) as the triple extractors. The triples from each of these are combined and then filtered for redundancy (Section 3). In order to ensure the quality of the triplet to the greatest extent, the methods such as co-reference resolution will be required. We fine-tuned the RoBERTa-large (Liu et al., 2019) as the content selector and fine-tuned the BART-large (Lewis et al., 2020) from `fairseq` (Ott et al., 2019) as the rewriter. All models are trained and fine-tuned on 2 NVIDIA RTX 2080 Ti GPUs. The detailed hyperparameters for three modules are in Appendix B.

4.2 Results

Intrinsic Evaluation of Each Module We first evaluate each of the three modules separately. Table 1 shows the detailed statistics of knowledge extraction based on Gigaword. The number of sentence-triple pairs is 400k, which are used to train the content selector. The accuracy of our fine-tuned RoBERTa content selector on this dataset is 88.9%. The details of the metrics are in Appendix Table 6. The size of the rewriting data set is 2M. We ablate the effect of the rewriting phase by comparing ROUGE scores before and after rewriting the triples in Appendix Table 7.

Model	R-1	R-2	R-L
BART (2020)	37.28	18.58	34.53
BART-RXF (2021)	40.45	20.69	36.56
PEGASUS+Dot (2021)	40.60	**21.00**	37.00
OFA (2022)	39.81	20.66	37.11
ESR	**40.63**	20.62	**37.14**

Table 2: ROUGE F1 on the Gigaword testset. It shows that ESR achieves or is competitive with the state-of-the-art on this dataset. **Bold** indicates the best score.

Model	R-1	R-2	R-L
RT+Conv (2018)	31.15	10.85	27.68
BART (2020)	31.36	11.40	28.02
ALONE (2020)	32.57	11.63	28.24
WDROP (2021)	33.06	11.45	28.51
ESR	**33.08**	**11.52**	**28.74**

Table 3: ROUGE F1 on DUC-2004 dataset. It shows ESR's performance achieved the SOTA on this dataset. **Bold** indicates the best score.

Automatic Evaluation Next, we evaluate the whole system on new summarization datasets. We report ROUGE score (Lin, 2004) on the Gigaword test set and the DUC-2004 dataset, containing 1951 and 500 samples respectively. We compare our ESR to a BART baseline that is fine-tuned in a single supervised step to generate the summary from the source documents. and some other strong models on the datasets.[4] The performance is shown in Table 2 and Table 3. On Gigaword and DUC2004, our approach outperforms the BART baseline and is within half the point of the SOTA results.[5]

Modularity One advantage of ESR is that training the rewriter does not require document-summary pairs and we can train it on any generic text. To test the modularity of ESR, we report the ROUGE on Reddit TIFU reusing a rewriter trained

[3]We use the DUC 2004 Task 1 which requires you to generate a sentence summary to a short article.

[4]These are typically modified variants of end-to-end models.We report the results from the PapersWithCode leaderboard and cite the corresponding works in the results table.

[5]State-of-the-art as of the date of submission per the leaderboard on PapersWithCode

Model	R-1	R-2	R-L
BART (2020)	24.19	8.12	21.31
PEGASUS+Sum (2022)	29.83	9.50	23.47
BART-R3F (2021)	30.31	**10.98**	24.74
ESR			
$S_R + R_G$	**30.63**	*10.82*	**24.78**
$S_R + R_R$	29.92	10.51	24.26
$S_{R1k} + R_{G1k}$	29.67	10.09	24.00
$S_{R1k} + R_{R1k}$	29.38	10.02	23.90
$S_{R1k} + R_G$	29.09	10.07	23.86

Table 4: ROUGE F1 on R-TIFU (Reddit-TIFU). S_R means the content selector was trained on R-TIFU, R_G and R_R mean rewriter trained on Gigaword and R-TIFU respectively. 1k means that the module is trained on 1k randomly sampled subset. The content selector can be trained with low-resourced data without large dropping. **Bold** means the best and *Italics* means the best in ESR.

on Gigaword in Table 4. The best ROUGE is obtained when using the Reddit TIFU content selector coupled with the Gigaword rewriter, highlighting the benefit of training the modules separately. One advantage of such decoupling is that we can train the rewriter on high resource domains and reuse it in low resource tasks. We further subsampled 1k samples from Reddit TIFU and Gigaword for training the modules to see how performance varies in the small data regime. We see that training a content selector on only 1k examples and reusing the rewriter from Gigaword is on-par with using the entire Reddit TIFU. Further, the modularity makes ESR able to control the text style, as in Figure 2.

Human Evaluation We conducted a user study on Amazon MTurk where annotators rated summaries of 100 randomly sampled texts from the Gigaword test set on faithfulness. We asked the annotators to rate summaries of our approach and BART, together with the results of the gold summaries of the data set. Each crowdworker was shown the source document and three summaries and asked to decide if each summary is individually supported by the text in the source. We collect three annotations for each example and decide the judgement via a majority vote. It is labeled inconclusive if there is no agreement. The results are in Table 5. We see that ESR is rated to be more faithful than the baseline and almost as good as the human-written summaries. A representative case is shown in Figure 2. It shows that ESR can eliminate the hallucination and control the summarization styles with different rewriter modules.

Summaries	Sup.	Unsup.	Incoh.	Inconc.
Human-Written	96	3	0	1
BART	90	6	2	2
ESR	94	3	2	1

Table 5: Human evaluation on faithfulness. The summaries from the dataset (Human-Written) and those from ESR and the BART are annotated by 3 annotators. Crowd workers find ESR to be more faithful than BART.

Case Study

ST: Zairean president Mobutu Sese Seko will stay at his French Riviera residence until at least the middle of the week because of an increase in diplomatic activity, a Mobutu aide said on Sunday.

Selected Triples:

(Zairean president Mobutu Sese Seko, will stay at, his French Riviera residence)

(Zairean president Mobutu Sese Seko, will stay until, the middle of the week)

Ref: Zairean president Mobutu to stay in France till mid-week

BART: Tanzania's Mobutu to stay at Riviera residence until middle of week

ESR (Gigaword content selector):

- **Gigaword rewriter:** Zairean president Mobutu will stay at his French Riviera residence until the middle of week
- **Reddit-TIFU rewriter:** Zairean Mobutu will stay at his French Riviera president residence... it's said that he will stay until the middle of week

Figure 2: A case on the Gigaword testset. **ST**: source text; **Ref**: reference summary; **Selected Triples**: triples selected by the content selector. With the rewriter module trained on different dataets, the text style of ESR can be controlled. The green shows the factual correctness and the red shows the error.

4.3 Analysis

The evaluations show that ESR can achieve or approach SOTA performance on multiple datasets and can enhance the faithfulness of summaries. We found ESR can limit the content of the generated summary in the content selection stage, and then rewrite only selected content. Therefore, text generation will introduce less hallucination. In addition, ESR has better modularity than other models, as the selector and rewriter can be trained separately on different data to enhance performance and controllability on summarization. This means that we can modify the modules to enhance performance rather than redesign the entire framework.

5 Conclusion

We propose ESR, a three-phase modular abstractive summarization method. It obtains competitive performance on automatic metrics while producing more faithful summaries, and its modularity makes it have a good controllability on summary generation, and maintains a good performance on low resource data. In the future, we are adapting the ESR method to multi-document summarization datasets.

Acknowledgement

We would like to appreciate Professor He He for her input and guidance at various stages of the project. This work is supported by the Samsung Advanced Institute of Technology (Next Generation Deep Learning: From Pattern Recognition to AI) and the National Science Foundation under Grant No.1922658. The computation resource of the work is supported by NYU Courant Institute of Mathematical Sciences.

Limitation

One limitation of our method is the reliance on off-the-shelf tools for the extraction phase. These tools are sometimes not able to successfully obtain triples from the source sentences, which results in empty summaries, and at others they returns multiple redundant candidates which makes selection challenging. We attempt to address the former by aggregating results from multiple extractors and the latter by filtering candidates through overlap based heuristics.

Ethical Consideration

One ethical consideration for the modular summarization method is that we are essentially using two different deep learning steps, content selection followed by text generation. There is a chance for model bias to have an impact at either stage. Additionally, we note that one of the features of modular summarization is that different applications can select different content to be relevant to a summary. Improper content selection here could exacerbate issues such as misinformation when used in real-world applications. We do however note that this is not isolated to our modular summarization approach, but is also the case even when the model is learned end-to-end.

References

Armen Aghajanyan, Akshat Shrivastava, Anchit Gupta, Naman Goyal, Luke Zettlemoyer, and Sonal Gupta. 2021. Better fine-tuning by reducing representational collapse. In *International Conference on Learning Representations*.

Gabor Angeli, Melvin Jose Johnson Premkumar, and Christopher D. Manning. 2015. Leveraging linguistic structure for open domain information extraction. In *Proceedings of the 53rd Annual Meeting of the Association for Computational Linguistics and the 7th International Joint Conference on Natural Language Processing (Volume 1: Long Papers)*, pages 344–354, Beijing, China. Association for Computational Linguistics.

Rahul Aralikatte, Shashi Narayan, Joshua Maynez, Sascha Rothe, and Ryan McDonald. 2021. Focus attention: Promoting faithfulness and diversity in summarization. In *Proceedings of the 59th Annual Meeting of the Association for Computational Linguistics and the 11th International Joint Conference on Natural Language Processing (Volume 1: Long Papers)*, pages 6078–6095, Online. Association for Computational Linguistics.

Ziqiang Cao, Furu Wei, Wenjie Li, and Sujian Li. 2018. Faithful to the original: Fact-aware neural abstractive summarization. In *Proceedings of the Thirty-Second AAAI Conference on Artificial Intelligence and Thirtieth Innovative Applications of Artificial Intelligence Conference and Eighth AAAI Symposium on Educational Advances in Artificial Intelligence*, AAAI'18/IAAI'18/EAAI'18. AAAI Press.

Thiago Castro Ferreira, Chris van der Lee, Emiel van Miltenburg, and Emiel Krahmer. 2019. Neural data-to-text generation: A comparison between pipeline and end-to-end architectures. In *Proceedings of the 2019 Conference on Empirical Methods in Natural Language Processing and the 9th International Joint Conference on Natural Language Processing (EMNLP-IJCNLP)*, pages 552–562, Hong Kong, China. Association for Computational Linguistics.

Yen-Chun Chen and Mohit Bansal. 2018. Fast abstractive summarization with reinforce-selected sentence rewriting. In *Proceedings of the 56th Annual Meeting of the Association for Computational Linguistics (Volume 1: Long Papers)*, pages 675–686, Melbourne, Australia. Association for Computational Linguistics.

Shuo Guan, Ping Zhu, and Zhihua Wei. 2021. Knowledge and keywords augmented abstractive sentence summarization. In *EMNLP 2021 Workshop on New Frontiers in Summarization*, pages 25–32, Online and in Dominican Republic. Association for Computational Linguistics.

Luyang Huang, Lingfei Wu, and Lu Wang. 2020. Knowledge graph-augmented abstractive summarization with semantic-driven cloze reward. In *Proceedings of the 58th Annual Meeting of the Association for Computational Linguistics*, pages 5094–5107, Online. Association for Computational Linguistics.

Akhil Kedia, Sai Chetan Chinthakindi, and Wonho Ryu. 2021. Beyond reptile: Meta-learned dot-product maximization between gradients for improved single-task regularization. In *Findings of the*

Association for Computational Linguistics: EMNLP 2021, pages 407–420, Punta Cana, Dominican Republic. Association for Computational Linguistics.

Chris Kedzie and Kathleen McKeown. 2020. Controllable meaning representation to text generation: Linearization and data augmentation strategies. In *Proceedings of the 2020 Conference on Empirical Methods in Natural Language Processing (EMNLP)*, pages 5160–5185, Online. Association for Computational Linguistics.

Tushar Khot, Daniel Khashabi, Kyle Richardson, Peter Clark, and Ashish Sabharwal. 2021. Text modular networks: Learning to decompose tasks in the language of existing models. In *Proceedings of the 2021 Conference of the North American Chapter of the Association for Computational Linguistics: Human Language Technologies*, pages 1264–1279, Online. Association for Computational Linguistics.

Byeongchang Kim, Hyunwoo Kim, and Gunhee Kim. 2019. Abstractive summarization of Reddit posts with multi-level memory networks. In *Proceedings of the 2019 Conference of the North American Chapter of the Association for Computational Linguistics: Human Language Technologies, Volume 1 (Long and Short Papers)*, pages 2519–2531, Minneapolis, Minnesota. Association for Computational Linguistics.

Rik Koncel-Kedziorski, Dhanush Bekal, Yi Luan, Mirella Lapata, and Hannaneh Hajishirzi. 2019. Text Generation from Knowledge Graphs with Graph Transformers. In *Proceedings of the 2019 Conference of the North American Chapter of the Association for Computational Linguistics: Human Language Technologies, Volume 1 (Long and Short Papers)*, pages 2284–2293, Minneapolis, Minnesota. Association for Computational Linguistics.

Kundan Krishna, Sopan Khosla, Jeffrey Bigham, and Zachary C. Lipton. 2021. Generating SOAP notes from doctor-patient conversations using modular summarization techniques. In *Proceedings of the 59th Annual Meeting of the Association for Computational Linguistics and the 11th International Joint Conference on Natural Language Processing (Volume 1: Long Papers)*, pages 4958–4972, Online. Association for Computational Linguistics.

Mike Lewis, Yinhan Liu, Naman Goyal, Marjan Ghazvininejad, Abdelrahman Mohamed, Omer Levy, Veselin Stoyanov, and Luke Zettlemoyer. 2020. BART: Denoising sequence-to-sequence pretraining for natural language generation, translation, and comprehension. In *Proceedings of the 58th Annual Meeting of the Association for Computational Linguistics*, pages 7871–7880, Online. Association for Computational Linguistics.

Chenliang Li, Weiran Xu, Si Li, and Sheng Gao. 2018. Guiding generation for abstractive text summarization based on key information guide network. In *Proceedings of the 2018 Conference of the North American Chapter of the Association for Computational Linguistics: Human Language Technologies, Volume 2 (Short Papers)*, pages 55–60, New Orleans, Louisiana. Association for Computational Linguistics.

Haoran Li, Junnan Zhu, Jiajun Zhang, Chengqing Zong, and Xiaodong He. 2020. Keywords-guided abstractive sentence summarization. In *Proceedings of the AAAI Conference on Artificial Intelligence*, volume 34, pages 8196–8203.

Chin-Yew Lin. 2004. ROUGE: A package for automatic evaluation of summaries. In *Text Summarization Branches Out*, pages 74–81, Barcelona, Spain. Association for Computational Linguistics.

Yinhan Liu, Myle Ott, Naman Goyal, Jingfei Du, Mandar Joshi, Danqi Chen, Omer Levy, Mike Lewis, Luke Zettlemoyer, and Veselin Stoyanov. 2019. Roberta: A robustly optimized bert pretraining approach. *arXiv e-prints*, arXiv:1907.11692.

Mausam, Michael Schmitz, Stephen Soderland, Robert Bart, and Oren Etzioni. 2012. Open language learning for information extraction. In *Proceedings of the 2012 Joint Conference on Empirical Methods in Natural Language Processing and Computational Natural Language Learning*, pages 523–534, Jeju Island, Korea. Association for Computational Linguistics.

Shashi Narayan, Gonçalo Simões, Yao Zhao, Joshua Maynez, Dipanjan Das, Michael Collins, and Mirella Lapata. 2022. A well-composed text is half done! composition sampling for diverse conditional generation. *arXiv preprint arXiv:2203.15108*.

Shashi Narayan, Yao Zhao, Joshua Maynez, Gonçalo Simões, Vitaly Nikolaev, and Ryan McDonald. 2021. Planning with learned entity prompts for abstractive summarization. *Transactions of the Association for Computational Linguistics*, 9:1475–1492.

Myle Ott, Sergey Edunov, Alexei Baevski, Angela Fan, Sam Gross, Nathan Ng, David Grangier, and Michael Auli. 2019. fairseq: A fast, extensible toolkit for sequence modeling. In *Proceedings of the 2019 Conference of the North American Chapter of the Association for Computational Linguistics (Demonstrations)*, pages 48–53, Minneapolis, Minnesota. Association for Computational Linguistics.

Paul Over, Hoa Dang, and Donna Harman. 2007. Duc in context. *Information Processing & Management*, 43(6):1506–1520.

Jonathan Pilault, Raymond Li, Sandeep Subramanian, and Chris Pal. 2020. On extractive and abstractive neural document summarization with transformer language models. In *Proceedings of the 2020 Conference on Empirical Methods in Natural Language Processing (EMNLP)*, pages 9308–9319, Online. Association for Computational Linguistics.

Mathieu Ravaut, Shafiq Joty, and Nancy Chen. 2022. SummaReranker: A multi-task mixture-of-experts re-ranking framework for abstractive summarization. In *Proceedings of the 60th Annual Meeting of the Association for Computational Linguistics (Volume 1: Long Papers)*, pages 4504–4524, Dublin, Ireland. Association for Computational Linguistics.

Leonardo F. R. Ribeiro, Yue Zhang, Claire Gardent, and Iryna Gurevych. 2020. Modeling global and local node contexts for text generation from knowledge graphs. *Transactions of the Association for Computational Linguistics*, 8:589–604.

Alexander M. Rush, Sumit Chopra, and Jason Weston. 2015. A neural attention model for abstractive sentence summarization. In *Proceedings of the 2015 Conference on Empirical Methods in Natural Language Processing*, pages 379–389, Lisbon, Portugal. Association for Computational Linguistics.

Swarnadeep Saha and Mausam. 2018. Open information extraction from conjunctive sentences. In *Proceedings of the 27th International Conference on Computational Linguistics*, pages 2288–2299, Santa Fe, New Mexico, USA. Association for Computational Linguistics.

Sho Takase, Shun Kiyono, and Sho Takase. 2021. Rethinking perturbations in encoder-decoders for fast training. In *Proceedings of the 2021 Conference of the North American Chapter of the Association for Computational Linguistics: Human Language Technologies*, pages 5767–5780, Online. Association for Computational Linguistics.

Sho Takase, Sosuke Kobayashi, and Sho Takase. 2020. All word embeddings from one embedding. In *Advances in Neural Information Processing Systems*, volume 33, pages 3775–3785. Curran Associates, Inc.

Petar Veličković, Guillem Cucurull, Arantxa Casanova, Adriana Romero, Pietro Lió, and Yoshua Bengio. 2018. Graph attention networks. In *International Conference on Learning Representations*.

Li Wang, Junlin Yao, Yunzhe Tao, Li Zhong, Wei Liu, and Qiang Du. 2018. A reinforced topic-aware convolutional sequence-to-sequence model for abstractive text summarization. In *Proceedings of the 27th International Joint Conference on Artificial Intelligence*, IJCAI'18, pages 4453–4460. AAAI Press.

Peng Wang, An Yang, Rui Men, Junyang Lin, Shuai Bai, Zhikang Li, Jianxin Ma, Chang Zhou, Jingren Zhou, and Hongxia Yang. 2022. Ofa: Unifying architectures, tasks, and modalities through a simple sequence-to-sequence learning framework. *CoRR*, abs/2202.03052.

Wenhao Wu, Wei Li, Xinyan Xiao, Jiachen Liu, Ziqiang Cao, Sujian Li, Hua Wu, and Haifeng Wang. 2021. BASS: Boosting abstractive summarization with unified semantic graph. In *Proceedings of the 59th Annual Meeting of the Association for Computational Linguistics and the 11th International Joint Conference on Natural Language Processing (Volume 1: Long Papers)*, pages 6052–6067, Online. Association for Computational Linguistics.

Chenguang Zhu, William Hinthorn, Ruochen Xu, Qingkai Zeng, Michael Zeng, Xuedong Huang, and Meng Jiang. 2021. Enhancing factual consistency of abstractive summarization. In *Proceedings of the 2021 Conference of the North American Chapter of the Association for Computational Linguistics: Human Language Technologies*, pages 718–733, Online. Association for Computational Linguistics.

Appendices

A Details of the Generated Summaries

The length statistics of the generated summaries of our model on Gigaword test set is showed in Table 8.

As mentioned in the paper, the summary generation of our model is based on triples extracted from the original text. Therefore, the quality of the extracted triples during inference will affect the quality of the generated abstracts to a certain extent. For example, the length of the final generated summaries will depend on the text length of the triples. In order to ensure the quality of the triplet to the greatest extent, methods such as co-reference resolution will be required.

	R-1	R-2	R-L
Concatenated Triples	38.98	18.12	35.76
Rewritten Summaries	40.63	20.62	36.71

Table 7: ROUGE comparing Concatenated Triples (aren't rewritten) and Rewritten Summaries (rewritten).

B Hyper Parameters

The hyper parameters for fine-tuning RoBERTa-large in content selection phase, and BART-large model in rewriting phase are listed.

B.1 Knowledge Extraction

The hyperparameters in Jaccard similarity are $\lambda_1 = 0.75$ and $\lambda_2 = 0.25$. The threshold for similarity is 0.7.

B.2 Content Selection

TOTAL_NUM_UPDATES=3000
WARMUP_UPDATES=500
LR=1e-05
NUM_CLASSES=2
MAX_SENTENCES=8

Acc.	Rec.	Prec.	F1
88.9%	88.6%	88.1%	88.4%

Table 6: Sentence-pair classification performance of the content selector.

Statistics	Articles	Ref.	Our Model
Avg Len	30.9	9.1	12.3

Table 8: Sentence-pair classification metrics of content selection phase.

B.3 Rewriting

TOTAL_NUM_UPDATES = 10000
WARMUP_UPDATES = 500
MAX_TOKENS = 256
UPDATE_FREQ = 2
LR = 3e-5

Summarization-based Data Augmentation for Document Classification

Yueguan Wang
The University of Tokyo
etsurin@iis.u-tokyo.ac.jp

Naoki Yoshinaga
Institute of Industrial Science,
The University of Tokyo
ynaga@iis.u-tokyo.ac.jp

Abstract

Despite the prevalence of pretrained language models in natural language understanding tasks, understanding lengthy text such as document is still challenging due to the data sparseness problem. Inspired by that humans develop their ability of understanding lengthy text form reading shorter text, we propose a simple yet effective summarization-based data augmentation, SUMMaug, for document classification. We first obtain easy-to-learn examples for the target document classification task by summarizing the input of the original training examples, while optionally merging the original labels to conform to the summarized input. We then use the generated pseudo examples to perform curriculum learning. Experimental results on two datasets confirmed the advantage of our method compared to existing baseline methods in terms of robustness and accuracy. We release our code and data at https://github.com/etsurin/summaug.

1 Introduction

Although the pretrained language models (Devlin et al., 2019; Liu et al., 2019; He et al., 2020) have boosted the accuracy of various natural language understanding tasks, the accuracy is still limited for complex tasks with lengthy input (Lin et al., 2023) and fine-grained output (Liu et al., 2021), such as document classification. These tasks require models to find a mapping between diverse input and output, which models are more likely to suffer from the data sparseness problem.

To address the data sparseness problem, researchers have studied data augmentation for text classification tasks. A basic approach is to generate pseudo training examples from gold examples by perturbing the inputs; those perturbation include back-and-forth translation (Shleifer, 2019) and minor editing of input text (Wei and Zou, 2019; Karimi et al., 2021) or its hidden representations (Chen et al., 2020, 2022; Wu et al., 2022).

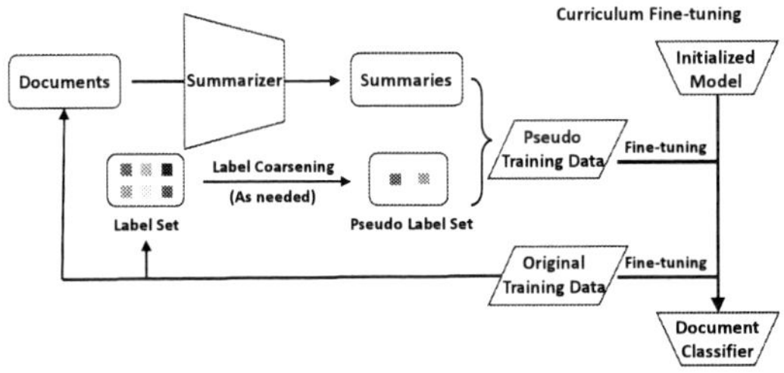

Figure 1: Curriculum fine-tuning for document classification using SUMMaug data augmentation: prior to the normal finetuning, it fine-tunes a model with easy-to-learn examples obtained by summarizing the original training examples.

These methods basically echo the information in the original training data, which will not help much the model learn to read lengthy inputs.

In this study, to effectively develop the model's ability to comprehend the content in document classification, we propose a simple yet effective summarization-based data augmentation, SUMMaug, to generate pseudo, abstractive training examples for document classification. Specifically, we apply text summarization to the input of gold examples in document classification task to obtain abstractive, easy-to-read examples, and merge fine-grained target labels as needed so that the labels conforms to the summarized input. Motivated by that we humans gradually develop the ability of understanding lengthy text from reading shorter text, we use the generated examples in the context of curriculum learning (surveyed in (Soviany et al., 2022)), namely, curriculum fine-tuning.

We compare our method to a baseline data augmentation (Karimi et al., 2021) on two versions of IMDb dataset with a different number of target labels. Experimental results confirm that curriculum fine-tuning with SUMMaug outperforms baseline methods on both accuracy and robustness.

Proceedings of The 4th New Frontiers in Summarization Workshop, pages 49–55

2 Related Work

In this section, we first review existing neural models for document classification, and next introduce existing data augmentation methods for text classification. We then mention other attempts to leverage summarization for text classification.

Document Classification In the literature, researchers explore a better neural architecture to comprehend the lengthy content in document classification; examples include a graph neural network (Zhang and Zhang, 2020; Zhang et al., 2022) and a convolutional attention network (Liu et al., 2021). Recently, Transformer (Vaswani et al., 2017)-based models have been revisited (Dai et al., 2022) and reported to outperform the task-specific networks. Since our work is model-agnostic and orthogonal to the model architecture, we adopt RoBERTa (Liu et al., 2019), a Transformer-based pre-trained model, as the target of evaluation.

Data Augmentation for Text Classification To address the data sparseness problem in text classification, researchers employ data augmentation, which generates pseudo training examples from the training examples. Shleifer (2019) leverages back-and-forth translation to paraphrase the inputs of training examples. Through translating the inputs into another language and then translating the resulting translation back to the source language, they obtain the input that are written in different ways but will have the same meanings conforming to the corresponding target labels. Xie et al. (2017) perturb the input by deleting and inserting words and replacing words with their synonyms. Karimi et al. (2021) propose a simple but more effective perturbation that randomly inserts punctuation marks. Rather than directly perturbing the input of training examples, some studies add noises in their continuous representations (Chen et al., 2020, 2022; Wu et al., 2022). However, these method predominantly echo existing training data, providing minimal assistance in understanding lengthy texts.

Use of Summarization in Text Classification Li and Zhou (2020) and Hartl and Kruschwitz (2022) utilize automatically generated summaries to retrieve fact for fake news detection. Whereas this approach uses summaries to retrieve knowledge for classification, our approach leverages summaries in training as easy-to-learn examples, which does not assume costly summarization in inference.

3 SUMMaug

Document classification requires a model to comprehend lengthy text with dozens of sentences, which is even difficult for humans, especially, children and second-language learners. Then, how do we humans develop an ability to comprehend lengthy text? In school, starting from reading short, concise text, we gradually read longer text.

In this study, we develop a summarization-based data augmentation method for document classification, SUMMaug, and use it to generate pseudo, abstractive training examples from gold examples to perform curriculum learning in document classification.

3.1 Summarization-based data augmentation

In SUMMaug, a summarization model M is used to generate pseduo, easy-to-learn examples for document classification. In this study, we apply an off-the-shelf summarization model, M, to each training pair $\{x, y\}$, where x denotes the document and y denotes the label, and then obtain a concise summary of x, namely, $\hat{x} = M(x)$.

An issue here is how to determine the label for the generated concise summary, $\hat{x}$. Since the summarization abstracts away detailed information for classification, the original target label y can be inappropriate especially when the target labels are fine-grained. We thus define a map function f to merge the fine-grained categories into a coarse-grained label group, and obtain the augmented training pair is $\{\hat{x}, f(y)\}$, as shown in Figure 1.

On summarization model To summarize diverse text handled in document classification, we assume an off-the-shelf summarization model that can handle documents with diverse topics. In this study, we choose an off-the-shelf BART (Lewis et al., 2020)-based summarization model fine-tuned on CNN-Dailymail (Hermann et al., 2015) dataset as an implementation of M,[1] since the writing style of news reports is suitable for most of the text in daily life. We should mention that the CNN-Dailymail dataset contains mostly extractive summaries, and the resulting summarization model will be less likely to suffer from hallucinations (Maynez et al., 2020) that have been reported for a summarization model trained on abstractive summarization datasets such as XSum (Narayan et al., 2018).

[1] https://huggingface.co/facebook/bart-large-cnn

I am Anthony Park, Glenn Park is my father. First off I want to say that the story behind this movie and the creation of the Amber Alert system is a good one. However the movie itself was poorly made and the acting was terrible. The major problem I had with the movie involved the second half with Nichole Timmons and father Glenn Park. The events surrounding that part of the story were not entirely correct. My father was suffering from psychological disorders at the time and picked up Nichole without any intent to harm her at all. He loved her like a daughter and was under the mindset that he was rescuing her from some sort of harm or neglect that he likely believed was coming from her mother who paid little attention to her over the 3 plus years that my father took care of her and summarily raised her so her mother could frolic about. The movie depicted my father in a manner that he was going to harm her in some way shape or form. The funny thing is that Nichole had spent many nights sometimes consecutively at my fathers place while Sharon would be working or doing whatever she was doing. The reason that my father was originally thought to be violent was because he had items that could be conceived to be weapons on his truck. My father was a landscaper. The items they deemed to be weapons were landscaping tools that he kept in his truck all the time for work. My recommendation is take this movie with a grain of salt, it is a good story and based on true events however the details of the movie (at least the Nichole Timmons - Glenn Park portion) are largely inaccurate and depict the failure of the director to discover the truth in telling the story. The funny thing is, that if the director would have interviewed any of Sharon's friends who knew the situation they would have stated exactly what I have posted here.
The movie itself was poorly made and the acting was terrible. The events surrounding that part of the story were not entirely correct. My recommendation is take this movie with a grain of salt, it is a good story and based on true events.

Table 1: An example of original text an generated summary on IMDb dataset. The first row is the original text while the second row is the generated summary. Red text are counterparts of summary in the original text.

Table 1 exemplifies a summary generated for IMDb datasets. While the original input (review) exhibits a mild negative sentiment, its compression into a summary intensifies this sentiment. This observation underscores the imperative to categorize labels of augmented data into coarser groups.

3.2 Learning a Classifier with augmented data

In the literature of data augmentation, the models are basically trained with the original and augmented training data, since both data are related to the target task. In our settings, however, the labels will be merged into fewer labels so that the labels conform to the generated summaries. We thus consider the following two strategies to utilize the pseudo abstractive training data.

Mixed fine-tuning We combine the original and pseudo training data to fine-tune a pre-trained model for classification. In this setting, we do not collapse labels, namely, $f(y) = y$.

Curriculum fine-tuning We first finetune a pre-trained model on the pseudo training data, and then finetune a pre-trained model on the original training data. This strategy is inspired by curriculum learning (Bengio et al., 2009). In this setting, we collapse labels as needed. When we collapse labels, we discard parameters for the collapsed labels in the fine-tuning with the original examples.

In the following experiments, we compare two strategies for datasets with different numbers of labels.

Dataset	train	val	test	C	L	L_M
IMDb-2	22500	2500	25000	2	279.5	51.3
IMDb-10	108670	13432	13567	10	394.2	50.2

Table 2: Details of the IMDb datasets: C denotes the number of classes. L and L_M denote the average length of the inputs and the generated summaries, respectively.

4 Experiments

We conduct experiments on two datasets to evaluate our method, thus demonstrating that: (1) our method shows better accuracy and robustness compared with baseline methods in both general setting and low-resource settings; and (2) curriculum fine-tuning plays an important role in achieving improvements.

4.1 Dataset

We use two versions of large-scale movie reviews dataset IMDb for evaluation. One contains 50,000 movie reviews with a positive or negative label (Maas et al., 2011), while the other involves 10 different labels from rating 1 to 10. For the IMDB-2 dataset, we split 10% of the training data for validation. For the IMDb-10 dataset, the same splitting as Adhikari et al. (2019) is used. The detailed information of the two datasets is shown in Table 2.

4.2 Methods

We use the following three models for evaluation. All models are based on RoBERTa (Liu et al., 2019) with a classification layer.

Model	The size of training data		
	200	1500	all
RoBERTa	$92.19_{1.21}$	$94.21_{0.62}$	$94.63_{0.56}$
+ AEDA (mixed)	$90.91_{1.44}$	$94.43_{0.49}$	$94.75_{0.66}$
+ AEDA (curriculum)	$\mathbf{93.59}_{1.16}$	$94.26_{0.74}$	$\mathbf{95.56}_{0.12}$
+ SUMMaug (mixed)	$92.94_{0.99}$	$94.61_{0.64}$	$94.85_{0.62}$
+ SUMMaug (curriculum)	$93.36_{0.97}$	$\mathbf{94.77}_{0.28}$	$95.45_{0.17}$

Table 3: Classification accuracy$_{\text{stdev.}}$ (%) on IMDb-2: mixed and curriculum denotes mixed and curriculum fine-tuning. All the results are averages over five runs. The best results are marked as **bold**.

Model	The size of training data	
	1500	all
RoBERTa	$39.99_{8.46}$	$56.58_{0.34}$
+ AEDA (mixed)	$36.58_{10.64}$	$51.23_{14.39}$
+ AEDA (curriculum)	$41.77_{3.01}$	$56.63_{1.65}$
+ SUMMaug (mixed)	$40.65_{2.71}$	$55.81_{2.00}$
+ SUMMaug (curriculum)	$\mathbf{42.14}_{1.48}$	$\mathbf{57.55}_{0.29}$

Table 4: Classification accuracy$_{\text{stdev.}}$ (%) on IMDb-10. All the results are averages over five runs. The notations follow Table 3.

RoBERTa We finetune a pre-trained RoBERTa[2] on the original training data as a baseline.

RoBERTa + AEDA We use AEDA (Karimi et al., 2021), a strong data augmentation method for text classification as another baseline. We apply AEDA[3] to the original documents, and then fine-tune a RoBERTa model on the augmented data and original data.

RoBERTa + SUMMaug We use BART-based summarizer trained on CNN-Dailymail to generate concise summaries, and fine-tune a RoBERTa model on the augmented data and original data.

To evaluate the performance of our method in low resource settings, we randomly select 200 and 1500 samples from the two datasets and train a model on these sub datasets. However, on the IMDb-10 dataset, we observe that all models diverge and perform randomly when training data is reduced to 200, likely due to the challenges of fine-grained classification with rather limited training data; we thereby do not report the results.

In order to reveal the effectiveness of curriculum fine-tuning, we apply curriculum fine-tuning not only to SUMMaug but also to AEDA. On the IMDb-10 dataset, we map the labels of the augmented data into coarse-grained ones, as mentioned in § 3.1. Specifically, labels between 0-4 are mapped into 0 (negative) while labels between 5-9 are mapped into 1 (positive).

4.3 Implementation Details

We set the model's hyperparameters as follows. For experiments on the IMDb-2 dataset, batch size is set to 64 and learning rate is set to 1e-5. For experiments on the IMDb-10 dataset, following Adhikari et al. (2019), batch size is set to 16, with learning rate set to 2e-5. Detailed information of training epochs can be found at Appendix A. All the experiments were conducted on four NVIDIA Quadro P6000 GPUs with 24GB memory.

The final model for evaluation is selected on the basis of the performance on validation set. To eliminate the effect of random factors, we report the average accuracy over five runs.

5 Results

Tables 3 and 4 list the results of baseline methods and our proposed method. Our method outperforms baseline methods in all experimental settings. We additionally confirm on both datasets that our data augmentation is effective even when the training data size is small.

How robustly does SUMMaug work? SUMMaug achieves higher classification accuracy across datasets while improving or maintaining robustness (low standard deviations), whereas the original AEDA, namely AEDA (mixed), reduces the accuracy on IMDb-2 when 200 training examples are used, and it leads to unstable results on IMDb-10 dataset.

Is curriculum fine-tuning effective? We use mixed fine-tuning with SUMMaug and curriculum fine-tuning with AEDA. We observe that under mixed fine-tuning method, the data augmented by SUMMaug exhibited less improvements and even turns to be harmful on the IMDb-10 dataset. Conversely, it turns out that curriculum learning helps the AEDA method achieve further improvements in some cases while addressing the low robustness issue. However, curriculum learning with AEDA does not consistently enhance results because the AEDA augmented data retains the same information as the original data, which offers limited benefits in improving text comprehension.

[2]https://huggingface.co/roberta-large

[3]https://github.com/akkarimi/aeda_nlp

N	f	Accuracy$_{\text{stdev.}}$
2	[0,0,0,0,0,1,1,1,1,1]	$57.55_{0.29}$
3	[0,0,0,1,1,1,1,2,2,2]	$57.47_{0.20}$
4	[0,0,0,1,1,2,2,3,3,3]	$57.66_{0.31}$
5	[0,0,1,1,2,2,3,3,4,4]	$57.32_{0.60}$
10	[0,1,2,3,4,5,6,7,8,9]	$57.20_{0.56}$

Table 5: Classification accuracy$_{\text{stdev.}}$ (%) on IMDb-10 with different label coarsening function under SUMMaug (curriculum) method. N denotes the number of merged label groups while f shows how the original label 0-9 is mapped into coarse-grained label. All the results are averages over five runs.

How label coarsening affects accuracy? Table 5 shows the results of SUMMaug (curriculum) under different map function f. The accuracy is comparable when $N \leq 4$, while there's a noticeable decline in accuracy, accompanied by decreased stability when label coarsening is insufficient or not adopted. This is probably because the summaries can filter out detailed content, which is essential for fine-grained classification. On the other hand, unlike mixed fine-tuning, in which potentially noisy augmented data is used throughout the training process, in the curriculum fine-tuning, the effect of noise diminishes after model turns to train on the original data. Consequently, it can still achieve improvement even without label coarsening.

6 Conclusion and Future Work

This study explores a novel application of a summarization model and proposes a simple yet effective data-augmentation method, SUMMaug, for document classification. It performs curriculum learning-style fine-tuning to first train a model on concise summaries prior to the fine-tuning on the original training data. This mirrors the human process of mastering lengthy text comprehension, through gradual exposure to longer text. Experimental results on two document classification datasets confirm that SUMMaug enhances both accuracy and training stability compared to the baseline data augmentation method. Meanwhile, our method shows effective in low-resource settings.

The future work will focus on searching for the optimal mapping function f and exploring the effect of different summarization models. We will also apply SUMMaug to other document classification tasks of various domains.

Limitations

One of the drawbacks of this study is that we do not consider the label coarsening function f as a hyper-parameter and just choose the simplest one for experiments. The effect of label coarsening function on accuracy is still insufficiently explored. For the datasets, despite the different numbers of labels, the documents used are originally from the same kind of domain, which is not convincing enough to show that SUMMaug is robust across diverse classification tasks in different domains.

Acknowledgements

This work was partially supported by the special fund of Institute of Industrial Science, The University of Tokyo, and by JSPS KAKENHI Grant Number JP21H03494.

References

Ashutosh Adhikari, Achyudh Ram, Raphael Tang, and Jimmy Lin. 2019. DocBERT: BERT for document classification. *arXiv preprint arXiv:1904.08398*.

Yoshua Bengio, Jérôme Louradour, Ronan Collobert, and Jason Weston. 2009. Curriculum learning. In *Proceedings of the 26th Annual International Conference on Machine Learning*, ICML '09, page 41–48, New York, NY, USA. Association for Computing Machinery.

Hui Chen, Wei Han, Diyi Yang, and Soujanya Poria. 2022. DoubleMix: Simple interpolation-based data augmentation for text classification. In *Proceedings of the 29th International Conference on Computational Linguistics*, pages 4622–4632, Gyeongju, Republic of Korea. International Committee on Computational Linguistics.

Jiaao Chen, Zichao Yang, and Diyi Yang. 2020. MixText: Linguistically-informed interpolation of hidden space for semi-supervised text classification. In *Proceedings of the 58th Annual Meeting of the Association for Computational Linguistics*, pages 2147–2157, Online. Association for Computational Linguistics.

Xiang Dai, Ilias Chalkidis, Sune Darkner, and Desmond Elliott. 2022. Revisiting transformer-based models for long document classification. In *Findings of the Association for Computational Linguistics: EMNLP 2022*, pages 7212–7230, Abu Dhabi, United Arab Emirates. Association for Computational Linguistics.

Jacob Devlin, Ming-Wei Chang, Kenton Lee, and Kristina Toutanova. 2019. BERT: Pre-training of deep bidirectional transformers for language understanding. In *Proceedings of the 2019 Conference of the North American Chapter of the Association for*

Computational Linguistics: Human Language Technologies, Volume 1 (Long and Short Papers), pages 4171–4186, Minneapolis, Minnesota. Association for Computational Linguistics.

Philipp Hartl and Udo Kruschwitz. 2022. Applying automatic text summarization for fake news detection. In *Proceedings of the Thirteenth Language Resources and Evaluation Conference*, pages 2702–2713, Marseille, France. European Language Resources Association.

Pengcheng He, Xiaodong Liu, Jianfeng Gao, and Weizhu Chen. 2020. Deberta: Decoding-enhanced BERT with disentangled attention.

Karl Moritz Hermann, Tomas Kocisky, Edward Grefenstette, Lasse Espeholt, Will Kay, Mustafa Suleyman, and Phil Blunsom. 2015. Teaching machines to read and comprehend. *Advances in neural information processing systems*, 28.

Akbar Karimi, Leonardo Rossi, and Andrea Prati. 2021. AEDA: An easier data augmentation technique for text classification. In *Findings of the Association for Computational Linguistics: EMNLP 2021*, pages 2748–2754, Punta Cana, Dominican Republic. Association for Computational Linguistics.

Mike Lewis, Yinhan Liu, Naman Goyal, Marjan Ghazvininejad, Abdelrahman Mohamed, Omer Levy, Veselin Stoyanov, and Luke Zettlemoyer. 2020. BART: Denoising sequence-to-sequence pre-training for natural language generation, translation, and comprehension. In *Proceedings of the 58th Annual Meeting of the Association for Computational Linguistics*, pages 7871–7880, Online. Association for Computational Linguistics.

Qifei Li and Wangchunshu Zhou. 2020. Connecting the dots between fact verification and fake news detection. In *Proceedings of the 28th International Conference on Computational Linguistics*, pages 1820–1825, Barcelona, Spain (Online). International Committee on Computational Linguistics.

Yu-Chen Lin, Si-An Chen, Jie-Jyun Liu, and Chih-Jen Lin. 2023. Linear classifier: An often-forgotten baseline for text classification. In *Proceedings of the 61st Annual Meeting of the Association for Computational Linguistics (Volume 2: Short Papers)*, pages 1876–1888, Toronto, Canada. Association for Computational Linguistics.

Yang Liu, Hua Cheng, Russell Klopfer, Matthew R. Gormley, and Thomas Schaaf. 2021. Effective convolutional attention network for multi-label clinical document classification. In *Proceedings of the 2021 Conference on Empirical Methods in Natural Language Processing*, pages 5941–5953, Online and Punta Cana, Dominican Republic. Association for Computational Linguistics.

Yinhan Liu, Myle Ott, Naman Goyal, Jingfei Du, Mandar Joshi, Danqi Chen, Omer Levy, Mike Lewis, Luke Zettlemoyer, and Veselin Stoyanov. 2019. RoBERTa: A robustly optimized bert pretraining approach. *arXiv preprint arXiv:1907.11692*.

Andrew L. Maas, Raymond E. Daly, Peter T. Pham, Dan Huang, Andrew Y. Ng, and Christopher Potts. 2011. Learning word vectors for sentiment analysis. In *Proceedings of the 49th Annual Meeting of the Association for Computational Linguistics: Human Language Technologies*, pages 142–150, Portland, Oregon, USA. Association for Computational Linguistics.

Joshua Maynez, Shashi Narayan, Bernd Bohnet, and Ryan McDonald. 2020. On faithfulness and factuality in abstractive summarization. In *Proceedings of the 58th Annual Meeting of the Association for Computational Linguistics*, pages 1906–1919, Online. Association for Computational Linguistics.

Shashi Narayan, Shay B. Cohen, and Mirella Lapata. 2018. Don't give me the details, just the summary! topic-aware convolutional neural networks for extreme summarization. In *Proceedings of the 2018 Conference on Empirical Methods in Natural Language Processing*, pages 1797–1807, Brussels, Belgium. Association for Computational Linguistics.

Sam Shleifer. 2019. Low resource text classification with ULMFit and backtranslation. *arXiv preprint arXiv:1903.09244*.

Petru Soviany, Radu Tudor Ionescu, Paolo Rota, and Nicu Sebe. 2022. Curriculum learning: A survey. *International Journal of Computer Vision*, 130(6):1526–1565.

Ashish Vaswani, Noam Shazeer, Niki Parmar, Jakob Uszkoreit, Llion Jones, Aidan N Gomez, Ł ukasz Kaiser, and Illia Polosukhin. 2017. Attention is all you need. In *Advances in Neural Information Processing Systems*, volume 30. Curran Associates, Inc.

Jason Wei and Kai Zou. 2019. EDA: Easy data augmentation techniques for boosting performance on text classification tasks. In *Proceedings of the 2019 Conference on Empirical Methods in Natural Language Processing and the 9th International Joint Conference on Natural Language Processing (EMNLP-IJCNLP)*, pages 6382–6388, Hong Kong, China. Association for Computational Linguistics.

Xing Wu, Chaochen Gao, Meng Lin, Liangjun Zang, and Songlin Hu. 2022. Text smoothing: Enhance various data augmentation methods on text classification tasks. In *Proceedings of the 60th Annual Meeting of the Association for Computational Linguistics (Volume 2: Short Papers)*, pages 871–875, Dublin, Ireland. Association for Computational Linguistics.

Ziang Xie, Sida I. Wang, Jiwei Li, Daniel Lévy, Aiming Nie, Dan Jurafsky, and Andrew Y. Ng. 2017. Data noising as smoothing in neural network language models. In *5th International Conference on Learning Representations, ICLR 2017, Toulon, France, April*

Dataset (fine-tuning method)	The size of training data		
	200	1500	all
IMDb-2 (w/o data augmentation)	70	18	2
IMDb-2 (mixed)	70	18	2
IMDb-2 (curriculum)	70/70	18/18	2/2
IMDb-10 (w/o data augmentation)	-	20	4
IMDb-10 (mixed)	-	20	4
IMDb-10 (curriculum)	-	5/20	2/6

Table 6: Detailed training epochs in our experiments. For curriculum fine-tuning method, x/y denotes that model is trained x epochs on augmented data and then y epochs on original data.

24-26, 2017, Conference Track Proceedings. OpenReview.net.

Chong Zhang, He Zhu, Xingyu Peng, Junran Wu, and Ke Xu. 2022. Hierarchical information matters: Text classification via tree based graph neural network. In *Proceedings of the 29th International Conference on Computational Linguistics*, pages 950–959, Gyeongju, Republic of Korea. International Committee on Computational Linguistics.

Haopeng Zhang and Jiawei Zhang. 2020. Text graph transformer for document classification. In *Proceedings of the 2020 Conference on Empirical Methods in Natural Language Processing (EMNLP)*, pages 8322–8327, Online. Association for Computational Linguistics.

A Detailed training epochs

Table 6 shows detailed training epochs in our experiments. We select training epochs based on the accuracy on the validation set.

In-context Learning of Large Language Models for Controlled Dialogue Summarization: A Holistic Benchmark and Empirical Analysis

Yuting Tang[†]*, **Ratish Puduppully**[§‡], **Zhengyuan Liu**[§‡], **Nancy F. Chen**[§‡]
[†]Nanyang Technological University, Singapore [§]CNRS@CREATE, Singapore
[‡]Institute for Infocomm Research (I^{2}R), A*STAR, Singapore

Abstract

Large Language Models (LLMs) have shown significant performance in numerous NLP tasks, including summarization and controlled text generation. A notable capability of LLMs is in-context learning (ICL), where the model learns new tasks using input-output pairs in the prompt without any parameter update. However, the performance of LLMs in the context of few-shot abstractive dialogue summarization remains underexplored. This study evaluates various state-of-the-art LLMs on the SAMSum dataset within a few-shot framework. We assess these models in both controlled (entity control, length control, and person-focused planning) and uncontrolled settings, establishing a comprehensive benchmark in few-shot dialogue summarization. Our findings provide insights into summary quality and model controllability, offering a crucial reference for future research in dialogue summarization.

1 Introduction

Abstractive dialogue summarization aims to distill human conversations into natural, concise, and informative text, and is a challenging and interesting task in text summarization (Chen and Yang, 2020; Liu et al., 2021). The major challenges come from several aspects: 1) it lacks large human-annotated datasets unlike document summarization (Feng et al., 2021), and 2) it requires responses to be not only fluent but also factually consistent (Liu and Chen, 2022; Wang et al., 2022). Moreover, in practical use cases, users may impose additional constraints on system outputs, and this task is known as controlled dialogue summarization, which requires models to be capable of coherent and flexible language generation.

In controlled dialogue summarization, users can specify desired attributes (i.e., control signals) to guide the response of language models. Previous works have explored to incorporate control signals during pre-training (Keskar et al., 2019), task-specific fine-tuning (Liu and Chen, 2021), and prompt tuning (Zhang et al., 2022b). Meanwhile, the advancements in LLMs have unveiled new paradigms. For instance, instruction tuning, which enables models to understand users' intent in natural language, is considered to be promising for conditional text generation (Zhang et al., 2023). Additionally, the emergence of in-context learning (ICL) in LLMs has recently gained attention. The ICL ability refers to learning from a few input-output pairs written in the natural language form (also called demonstrations) (Dong et al., 2023). Followed by demonstrations, a query question is appended at the end to form a complete prompt. Compared to the traditional supervised learning, ICL requires no training and only a few annotated samples. Motivated by the paradigm shift with LLMs and the challenges encountered in controlled dialogue summarization, this study answers the following two key questions:

- How is the quality of the dialogue summaries generated by LLMs via ICL?
- How is the controllability of LLMs in dialogue summarization?

We comprehensively evaluate a range of recent Large Language Models (LLMs) on the SAMSum dataset (Gliwa et al., 2019) using a few-shot framework. Our assessment covers several controlled scenarios, including entity control, length control, and person-focused planning, as well as uncontrolled settings. We establish a comprehensive benchmark for few-shot dialogue summarization in Section 2, and elaborate on the findings in Section 3. Specifically, in our experiments, we observe that LLMs can summarize dialogues reasonably given several demonstrations, and LLaMA and Alpaca achieve a factual consistency rate exceeding 90% in the automatic evaluation. Moreover, adding control

*Work done during internship at I^{2}R, A*STAR.

Proceedings of The 4th New Frontiers in Summarization Workshop, pages 56–67
December 6, 2023

Model	Architecture	Instruction-tuned	Training Data
OPT (Zhang et al., 2022a)	Decoder-only		RoBERTa + The Pile + Reddit
OPT-IML (Iyer et al., 2022)	Decoder-only	✓	OPT-IML Bench
mT5 (Xue et al., 2021)	Encoder-Decoder		mC4
CEREBRAS-GPT (Dey et al., 2023)	Decoder-only		The Pile
LLaMA (Touvron et al., 2023)	Decoder-only		CommonCrawl + C4 + Github, etc.
Alpaca (Taori et al., 2023)	Decoder-only	✓	Instruct dataset generated by GPT-3
BLOOM (BigScience Workshop, 2022)	Decoder-only		ROOTS

Table 1: Summary of the experimented LLMs.

Summary of SAMSum Dataset	
Training Set	14,732 samples
Validation Set	818 samples
Testing Set	819 samples
Language	English
Annotation Method	Manual

Table 2: Data details of the SAMSum dataset.

signals in prompts (particularly keywords) can effectively guide models to include key information in generated summaries.

2 Our Experimental Setting of ICL Dialogue Summarization

In this section, we describe how we establish the benchmark of evaluating LLMs' in-context learning for abstractive dialogue summarization.

2.1 Selected Models & Prompt Template

To conduct an extensive comparison, we evaluate various models that differ in architectures, training corpora, and paradigms. Previous work shows when LLMs reach a certain parameter size, their differences in performance on dialogue summarization become relatively small (Wang et al., 2023). Therefore, to balance the performance and inference latency, here we select models that are smaller than a 10B parameter size. Details of the experimented models are shown in Table 1. For a reproducible and fair comparison, consistent prompt templates are employed across all models, as detailed in Appendix A. Moreover, considering the encoder-decoder architecture of mT5, we follow the approach of Puduppully et al. (2023) for prompting bidirectional LLMs, specifically by adding control keywords and infilling text between them.

2.2 Experimental Dataset

All models are evaluated using SAMSum (Gliwa et al., 2019), a human-annotated dataset for abstractive multi-turn dialogue summarization. Table 2 lists some information about the dataset. We use samples from the test set for model evaluation. For

Control Signal Example: Length Control

Summarize the conversation with the defined length:
Kevin: Hi, will you come to the workshop?
Elena: I have to, I will present a paper.
Kevin: Nice, I can't wait!
Summary with the length of 8 words: Elena will present a paper at the workshop.

Summarize the conversation with the defined length:
Jamilla: remember that the audition starts at 19:30.
Kiki: which station?
Jamilla: Antena 3
Yoyo: roger that
Summary with the length of 9 words: <output>

the few-shot ICL inference, all demonstrations are randomly sampled from the training set.

2.3 ICL Inference Configuration

In this study, we consider two experiment settings: **uncontrolled** and **controlled** dialogue summarization. An uncontrolled setting is identical to a traditional summarization task without control signals. In contrast, a controlled setting involves user-provided control signals as constraints to LLMs' outputs. Here we focus on three types of control signals that are common and straightforward control aspects to users (He et al., 2022; Liu and Chen, 2021; Wang et al., 2023):

- **Entity control:** Given a set of user-specified keywords or entities, the generated summary should include them.
- **Length control:** In this case, the user determines the desired length for the summaries.
- **Personal named entity planning:** This is a specific form of entity control, where the user provides models with a sequence of personal named entities, indicating person-focused perspectives.

Control Signal Setup: To quantitatively evaluate the controllability of LLMs, we extract oracle control signals from human-annotated references (i.e.,

Model	Size	ROUGE-1	ROUGE-2	ROUGE-L	Perplexity	Factual Consistency(%)
OPT	1.3B	30.7	6.6	22.6	64.7	60.2
OPT-IML	1.3B	**34.6**	**9.9**	**27.8**	264.4	80.9
mT5-XL	3.7B	21.9	7.4	21.5	139.3	48.4
CEREBRAS-GPT	6.7B	31.5	7.4	22.4	**28.0**	66.6
LLaMA	7B	31.0	7.3	22.9	41.1	94.0
Alpaca	7B	32.0	7.1	23.7	90.8	**97.3**
BLOOM	7B	32.1	7.7	23.2	38.2	82.1
GPT3-davinci-003	175B	43.8	17.0	39.4	66.6	-

Table 3: Evaluation results in the **uncontrolled setting**. The ROUGE F-scores are reported. The optimal performance is highlighted in bold. GPT-3 serves as the factual consistency evaluator, so its factual consistency is excluded.

Model	Size	ROUGE-1	ROUGE-2	ROUGE-L	Perplexity	Success Rate(%)
OPT	1.3B	33.2	8.2	24.5	53.2	65.3 (↑ 14.8)
OPT-IML	1.3B	37.8	11.6	30.5	294.1	54.5 (↑ 9.5)
mT5-XL	3.7B	**39.8**	**15.2**	**34.6**	112.6	**100.0**
CEREBRAS-GPT	6.7B	36.0	9.7	26.0	**40.5**	73.0 (↑ 16.9)
LLaMA	7B	34.1	9.3	25.4	52.8	62.5 (↑ 14.0)
Alpaca	7B	35.9	9.6	27.1	111.9	63.4 (↑ 12.3)
BLOOM	7B	36.6	10.2	27.2	60.1	71.1 (↑ 17.0)
GPT3-davinci-003	175B	48.8	22.3	39.1	112.2	94.0 (↑ 18.8)

Table 4: Evaluation results in the **entity control setting** with 3 keywords. The ↑ symbol denotes the change of the appearance likelihood of keywords compared to the uncontrolled setting.

gold summaries), assuming the user provides the appropriate signals (He et al., 2022). For **entity control**, the top k words in every gold summary with the highest TF-IDF scores are extracted as keywords. Considering the shorter lengths of the dialogue summaries, the range of k is set as $\{1, 2, 3\}$. Table 8 shows several generated examples of entity control. For **length control**, the expected length is set equal to the length (number of words) of the gold summary. In **personal named entity planning**, the order of named entities[1] follows their occurrence in the gold summaries. The control signals are included in the prompt, and the prompt templates are shown in Appendix A.

Demonstration Selection: During few-shot inference, the prompt includes several input-output pairs followed by a query dialogue. We limit the number of demonstrations to $\{1, 2, 3\}$ due to computational constraints on the prompt's length. Demonstrations are randomly selected from the training set but are kept consistent across all models. Given the potential variance of ICL (Min et al., 2022), we repeat the generation process in 5 times using different demonstrations and report the average scores. The input-output pairs are concatenated with the query dialogue to compose the prompt.

[1]The personal named entities data is acquired from https://github.com/seq-to-mind/planning_dial_summ/tree/main/data (Liu and Chen, 2021).

Evaluation Metrics: Our evaluation has two primary objectives: 1) to assess the quality of the generated summaries, and 2) to measure the controllability of the models.

For assessing text-level quality automatically, we employ the **ROUGE** metric (Lin, 2004), which gauges the correspondence between the generated summaries and the reference (or gold) summaries. Following previous work (Fan et al., 2018), we also calculate the **perplexity** of model generations using GPT-2 (Radford et al., 2019), which serves as a measure of textual fluency.

Factual consistency represents another essential facet of quality. Since GPT-3 has demonstrated robust performance across various evaluation tasks (Luo et al., 2023; Fu et al., 2023; Chia et al., 2023), we utilize it as a binary natural language inference classifier. This classifier assesses **factual consistency** by determining if the generated summary aligns with the underlying dialogue. Further elaborations on this are provided in Appendix B.

Additionally, we perform automatic holistic evaluations of writing quality, focusing on **coherence** and **relevance**. Following previous work (Chia et al., 2023), where GPT-3 is used for automatic evaluations to benchmark instruction-tuned models, we instruct GPT-3 to score the generated summaries on a discrete scale of 1 to 5. To ensure comparability, we adopt the same prompt templates as in Chia et al. (2023). The average scores are pre-

Model	Size	ROUGE-1	ROUGE-2	ROUGE-L	Perplexity	Length Deviation
OPT	1.3B	30.7	6.5	22.2	54.2	12.4 (↓ 0.9)
OPT-IML	1.3B	**36.0**	**10.4**	**28.8**	252.0	11.7 (↓ 0.5)
mT5-XL	3.7B	21.1	5.6	18.4	102.4	10.7 (↑ 0.7)
CEREBRAS-GPT	6.7B	31.2	6.7	22.5	**31.8**	16.1 (↓ 1.4)
LLaMA	7B	33.7	8.2	24.8	57.8	12.3 (↓ 2.2)
Alpaca	7B	34.7	8.2	26.4	185.3	**7.2** (↓ 4.7)
BLOOM	7B	32.9	7.9	24.3	45.0	13.1 (↓ 1.3)
GPT3-davinci-003	175B	47.8	20.1	38.0	219.0	7.1 (↓ 12.6)

Table 5: Evaluation results in the **length control setting**. The ↑ and ↓ symbols denote the change of length deviations compared to the uncontrolled setting.

Model	Size	ROUGE-1	ROUGE-2	ROUGE-L	Perplexity	Success Rate (%)
OPT	1.3B	30.5	7.2	23.6	57.4	82.7 (↑ 4.1)
OPT-IML	1.3B	**36.5**	**11.1**	**29.5**	239.2	76.1 (↑ 4.2)
mT5-XL	3.7B	28.3	7.9	24.8	50.1	100
CEREBRAS-GPT	6.7B	32.8	8.8	24.2	**31.1**	88.0 (↑ 5.5)
LLaMA	7B	33.3	8.6	25.2	51.1	77.8 (↑ 7.1)
Alpaca	7B	33.8	8.5	25.8	102.4	76.6 (↑ 2.0)
BLOOM	7B	33.4	9.0	25.2	43.3	**89.2** (↑ 6.4)
GPT3-davinci-003	175B	47.3	21.6	36.7	65.7	96.8 (↑ 4.9)

Table 6: Evaluation results in the **person-focused planning setting**. The ↑ and ↓ symbols denote the change of length deviations compared to the uncontrolled setting.

Model	Size	Consistency (%)	Fluency	Coherence	Relevance
OPT	1.3B	60.2	64.7	**3.5**	3.2
OPT-IML	1.3B	80.9	264.4	3.4	3.2
mT5-XL	3.7B	48.4	139.3	3.3	3.0
CEREBRAS-GPT	6.7B	66.6	**28.0**	3.4	3.4
LLaMA	7B	94.0	41.1	3.4	**3.7**
Alpaca	7B	**97.3**	90.8	**3.5**	3.5
BLOOM	7B	82.1	38.2	3.4	3.5

Table 7: Holistic evaluations on the writing quality. For each aspect, the best score is in bold.

sented in Table 7, and a more detailed description is provided in Appendix C.

Regarding the model controllability, the **success rate of entity control** is determined by the proportion of specified keywords present in the generated summaries (He et al., 2022). This success rate metric is also applicable to personal named entity planning. Length controllability is evaluated by the mean absolute **length deviation**, formulated as $\frac{1}{N} \cdot \sum_{i=1}^{N} |l_{\text{generated}} - l_{\text{gold}}|$, where N represents the size of the test set, and l denotes the text length.

3 Our Findings

In this section, we analyze the experimental results by discussing about the two research problems.

3.1 How is the quality of the dialogue summaries generated by LLMs via ICL?

The experimented LLMs can generate reasonable summaries via ICL inference, but perform differently. In the uncontrolled setting, as shown in Table 3, OPT-IML 1.3B exhibits the highest ROUGE scores, despite having the fewest parameters. However, ROUGE scores cannot reflect factual correctness from the semantic view. In contrast, LLaMA and Alpaca tend to produce summaries that are the more factually consistent (i.e., their consistency in GPT3's assessment exceeds 90%). Considering other evaluation aspects, CEREBRAS-GPT consistently generates the most fluent sentences across all settings, and summaries generated by LLaMA obtain the highest score regarding relevance among all models (see Table 7).

In the controlled setting, as shown in Table 4, both entity control and person-focused planning improve ROUGE scores, and the former brings a substantial performance gain. Length control has a minor impact on ROUGE scores, especially for models without instruction-tuning. Moreover, mT5's performance is inferior to other models in non-entity control settings in terms of ROUGE scores and factual consistency. However, it achieves optimal ROUGE scores in entity control, as its architecture ensures the inclusion of keywords.

Gold Summary	Model	Uncontrolled setting	Entity control
The audition starts at 7.30 P.M. in Antena 3.	BLOOM-7b1	Jamilla and Yoyo are going to an audition for a TV show. They are waiting for the station to start broadcasting.	Jamilla and Kiki are going to an audition for a TV show. The station is Antena3.
Adam and Karen are worried that May suffers from depression. Karen will call her friend who is a psychologist and ask for advice.	mT5-XL	Melissa shows Brian what she bought and he finds it awesome.	Adam and karen talk to their friend about her depression. They talk to their friend's psychologist and she agrees to help.
Mike suspects he might have had an allergic reaction to something.	LLaMA-7B	Mike wakes up with a strange rash on his face. He has no clue what it is and asks his girlfriend Emma to help him figure it out.	Mike suspects that he is allergic to something, but he does not know what it is.
Flo cannot get an appointment at the salon until the 6th. Flo worries she's going to be gray. Flo will have to get a touch-up kit at Tesco.	CEREBRAS-6.7B	Gina and Flo are having a conversation about getting their hair done at the same time.	Flo is worried that she will be too late for her appointment at the hair salon. She will get a kit to get her hair touched up.

Table 8: Comparisons of generated summaries between controlled and uncontrolled settings. Underlined keywords are the control signals included in the prompts.

3.2 Can LLMs do controlled dialogue summarization?

Experimental results demonstrate that LLMs are capable of achieving controlled dialogue summarization via ICL. Evaluation details of LLMs in controlled settings are presented in Table 4 for entity control with 3 keywords, Table 5 for length control, and Table 6 for person-focused planning. Table 10 in Appendix provides a comprehensive evaluation with varying numbers of keywords.

In the entity control experiments, keywords are included in the prompts as constraints. All models exhibit improved ROUGE scores, and the likelihood of keywords appearing in the summaries is increased, indicating that LLMs effectively utilize the information from control signals. Notably, mT5 achieves a 100% success rate, benefiting from its bi-directional encoding architecture. Examples presented in Table 8 show how keywords can guide models to generate better summaries. Surprisingly, non-instruction-tuned models like CEREBRAS-GPT and BLOOM demonstrate better controllability than instruction-tuned models like Alpaca and OPT-IML in entity control.

The impact of length signals is relatively minor compared to keyword signals on ROUGE scores. However, the length distribution with length signals is more aligned with the actual length across models, except for mT5. Notably, Alpaca demonstrates the best length controllability. We also find that OPT-IML appears to have lower controllability compared to its foundation model, OPT.

Model	Success Rate (%)
OPT-IML-1.3B	19.0 (↑ 4.2)
LLaMA-7B	10.1 (↑ 4.7)
Alpaca-7B	7.8 (↑ 3.5)
BLOOM-7B	28.3 (↑ 17.0)

Table 9: The success rates of numerical keywords.

3.3 Further Analysis

Numerical keywords (e.g., time and quantity) tend to be left out by LLMs. Preliminary error analysis shows a large portion of the missing keywords in entity control contain numerical information. To verify that, the models are prompted with only numerical keywords (e.g., time, date, quantity, and percent) extracted from gold summaries using SpaCy (Honnibal et al., 2020). The results in Table 9 demonstrate a significant decrease in the success rates across all models. It implies that LLMs have some intrinsic bias toward non-numerical content, potentially causing them to overlook crucial numerical details within dialogues.

4 Conclusion

In this study, we have benchmarked the in-context learning performance of state-of-the-art LLMs in controlled and uncontrolled settings for abstractive dialogue summarization. We assessed their summarization quality, factual consistency, and controllability, while also conducting holistic evaluations and empirical analysis. We hope this study provides insights for the follow-up research about dialogue summarization using LLMs.

Limitations

One limitation of this study is that only LLMs with less than 10B parameters are experimented with due to hardware constraints. To address this issue, we release the evaluation codes, in order to facilitate the follow-up research.

Meanwhile, the control signals in this work are oracle, which means we assume the user provides indicative keywords to be included in the summary. There are automatic methods to extract keywords from dialogues (He et al., 2022), but it is not the focus and therefore not discussed in this study.

Due to time constraints, we adopted GPT-3 to conduct automatic qualitative evaluations. While GPT-based evaluations have proven to be competitive in some evaluation tasks, the necessity for human evaluations remains.

Acknowledgments

This research was supported by the Agency for Science, Technology and Research (A*STAR), Singapore under its Industry Alignment Pre-Positioning Fund (Grant No. H19/01/a0/023 - DCOF), and by the National Research Foundation, Prime Minister's Office, Singapore under its Campus for Research Excellence and Technological Enterprise (CREATE) programme. We also thank the anonymous reviewers for their precious feedback to help improve and extend this piece of work.

References

BigScience Workshop. 2022. BLOOM (revision 4ab0472).

Jiaao Chen and Diyi Yang. 2020. Multi-view sequence-to-sequence models with conversational structure for abstractive dialogue summarization. In *Proceedings of the 2020 Conference on Empirical Methods in Natural Language Processing (EMNLP)*, pages 4106–4118, Online. Association for Computational Linguistics.

Yew Ken Chia, Pengfei Hong, Lidong Bing, and Soujanya Poria. 2023. Instructeval: Towards holistic evaluation of instruction-tuned large language models. *arXiv preprint arXiv:2306.04757*.

Nolan Dey, Gurpreet Gosal, Zhiming, Chen, Hemant Khachane, William Marshall, Ribhu Pathria, Marvin Tom, and Joel Hestness. 2023. Cerebras-gpt: Open compute-optimal language models trained on the cerebras wafer-scale cluster.

Qingxiu Dong, Lei Li, Damai Dai, Ce Zheng, Zhiyong Wu, Baobao Chang, Xu Sun, Jingjing Xu, Lei Li, and Zhifang Sui. 2023. A survey on in-context learning.

Angela Fan, Mike Lewis, and Yann Dauphin. 2018. Hierarchical neural story generation. In *Proceedings of the 56th Annual Meeting of the Association for Computational Linguistics (Volume 1: Long Papers)*, pages 889–898, Melbourne, Australia. Association for Computational Linguistics.

Xiachong Feng, Xiaocheng Feng, and Bing Qin. 2021. A survey on dialogue summarization: Recent advances and new frontiers. *arXiv preprint arXiv:2107.03175*.

Jinlan Fu, See-Kiong Ng, Zhengbao Jiang, and Pengfei Liu. 2023. Gptscore: Evaluate as you desire.

Bogdan Gliwa, Iwona Mochol, Maciej Biesek, and Aleksander Wawer. 2019. SAMSum corpus: A human-annotated dialogue dataset for abstractive summarization. In *Proceedings of the 2nd Workshop on New Frontiers in Summarization*, pages 70–79, Hong Kong, China. Association for Computational Linguistics.

Junxian He, Wojciech Kryscinski, Bryan McCann, Nazneen Rajani, and Caiming Xiong. 2022. CTRLsum: Towards generic controllable text summarization. In *Proceedings of the 2022 Conference on Empirical Methods in Natural Language Processing*, pages 5879–5915, Abu Dhabi, United Arab Emirates. Association for Computational Linguistics.

Matthew Honnibal, Ines Montani, Sofie Van Landeghem, and Adriane Boyd. 2020. spaCy: Industrial-strength Natural Language Processing in Python.

Srinivasan Iyer, Xi Victoria Lin, Ramakanth Pasunuru, Todor Mihaylov, Dániel Simig, Ping Yu, Kurt Shuster, Tianlu Wang, Qing Liu, Punit Singh Koura, et al. 2022. Opt-iml: Scaling language model instruction meta learning through the lens of generalization.

Nitish Shirish Keskar, Bryan McCann, Lav R. Varshney, Caiming Xiong, and Richard Socher. 2019. Ctrl: A conditional transformer language model for controllable generation.

Chin-Yew Lin. 2004. ROUGE: A package for automatic evaluation of summaries. In *Text Summarization Branches Out*, pages 74–81, Barcelona, Spain. Association for Computational Linguistics.

Zhengyuan Liu and Nancy Chen. 2021. Controllable neural dialogue summarization with personal named entity planning. In *Proceedings of the 2021 Conference on Empirical Methods in Natural Language Processing*, pages 92–106, Online and Punta Cana, Dominican Republic. Association for Computational Linguistics.

Zhengyuan Liu and Nancy Chen. 2022. Entity-based denoising modeling for controllable dialogue summarization. In *Proceedings of the 23rd Annual Meeting of the Special Interest Group on Discourse and Dialogue*, pages 407–418, Edinburgh, UK. Association for Computational Linguistics.

Zhengyuan Liu, Ke Shi, and Nancy Chen. 2021. Coreference-aware dialogue summarization. In *Proceedings of the 22nd Annual Meeting of the Special Interest Group on Discourse and Dialogue*, pages 509–519, Singapore and Online. Association for Computational Linguistics.

Zheheng Luo, Qianqian Xie, and Sophia Ananiadou. 2023. Chatgpt as a factual inconsistency evaluator for text summarization.

Sewon Min, Xinxi Lyu, Ari Holtzman, Mikel Artetxe, Mike Lewis, Hannaneh Hajishirzi, and Luke Zettlemoyer. 2022. Rethinking the role of demonstrations: What makes in-context learning work?

Ratish Puduppully, Anoop Kunchukuttan, Raj Dabre, Ai Ti Aw, and Nancy F. Chen. 2023. Decomposed prompting for machine translation between related languages using large language models.

Alec Radford, Jeffrey Wu, Rewon Child, David Luan, Dario Amodei, Ilya Sutskever, et al. 2019. Language models are unsupervised multitask learners. *OpenAI blog*, 1(8):9.

Rohan Taori, Ishaan Gulrajani, Tianyi Zhang, Yann Dubois, Xuechen Li, Carlos Guestrin, Percy Liang, and Tatsunori B. Hashimoto. 2023. Stanford alpaca: An instruction-following llama model. `https://github.com/tatsu-lab/stanford_alpaca`.

Hugo Touvron, Thibaut Lavril, Gautier Izacard, Xavier Martinet, Marie-Anne Lachaux, Timothée Lacroix, Baptiste Rozière, Naman Goyal, Eric Hambro, Faisal Azhar, Aurelien Rodriguez, Armand Joulin, Edouard Grave, and Guillaume Lample. 2023. Llama: Open and efficient foundation language models.

Bin Wang, Zhengyuan Liu, and Nancy F Chen. 2023. Instructive dialogue summarization with query aggregations. *arXiv preprint arXiv:2310.10981*.

Bin Wang, Chen Zhang, Yan Zhang, Yiming Chen, and Haizhou Li. 2022. Analyzing and evaluating faithfulness in dialogue summarization. In *Proceedings of the 2022 Conference on Empirical Methods in Natural Language Processing*, pages 4897–4908.

Linting Xue, Noah Constant, Adam Roberts, Mihir Kale, Rami Al-Rfou, Aditya Siddhant, Aditya Barua, and Colin Raffel. 2021. mt5: A massively multilingual pre-trained text-to-text transformer.

Hanqing Zhang, Haolin Song, Shaoyu Li, Ming Zhou, and Dawei Song. 2023. A survey of controllable text generation using transformer-based pre-trained language models.

Susan Zhang, Stephen Roller, Naman Goyal, Mikel Artetxe, Moya Chen, Shuohui Chen, Christopher Dewan, Mona Diab, Xian Li, Xi Victoria Lin, Todor Mihaylov, Myle Ott, Sam Shleifer, Kurt Shuster, Daniel Simig, Punit Singh Koura, Anjali Sridhar, Tianlu Wang, and Luke Zettlemoyer. 2022a. Opt: Open pre-trained transformer language models.

Yubo Zhang, Xingxing Zhang, Xun Wang, Si qing Chen, and Furu Wei. 2022b. Latent prompt tuning for text summarization.

A Appendix: Prompt template

This section includes examples of the prompt templates, which remain consistent across models.

Uncontrolled Setting

Summarize the conversation:
Selby: anybody for indian?
Terri: yuo cooked?
Selby: yessir
Terri: sounds cool
Winslow: gr8. ill be there too
Summary: Selby invites Terri and Winslow for a home-cooked Indian meal.

Summarize the conversation:
Marta: <file_gif>
Marta: Sorry girls, I clicked something by accident :D
Agnieszka: No problem :p
Weronika: Hahaha
Agnieszka: Good thing you didn't send something from your gallery ;)
Summary:

(Last line of mT5)
Summary: <extra_id_0>

Length Control

Summarize the conversation with the defined length:
Kevin: Hi, will you come to the workshop?
Elena: I have to, I will present a paper.
Kevin: Nice, I can't wait!
Summary with the length of 8 words: Elena will present a paper at the workshop.

Summarize the conversation with the defined length:
Jamilla: remember that the audition starts at 7.30 P.M.
Kiki: which station?
Jamilla: Antena 3
Yoyo: roger that
Summary with the length of 9 words:

(Last line of mT5)
Summary with the length of 9 words: <extra_id_0>

Entity control (non-mT5)

Summarize the conversation with keywords:
Kevin: Hi, will you come to the workshop?
Elena: I have to, I will present a paper.
Kevin: Nice, I can't wait!
Summary with keywords ['Elena', 'workshop']: Elena will present a paper at the workshop.

Summarize the conversation with keywords:
Jamilla: remember that the audition starts at 19:30.
Kiki: which station?
Jamilla: Antena 3
Yoyo: roger that
Summary with keywords ['audition', 'antena']:

Entity Control / Person-focused Planning (mT5)

Summarize the conversation:
Selby: anybody for indian?
Terri: yuo cooked?
Selby: yessir
Terri: sounds cool
Winslow: gr8. ill be there too
Summary: Selby invites Terri and Winslow for a home-cooked Indian meal. Selby invites Terri and Winslow for a home-cooked Indian meal.</s>

Summarize the conversation:
Marta: <file_gif>
Marta: Sorry girls, I clicked something by accident :D
Agnieszka: No problem :p
Weronika: Hahaha
Agnieszka: Good thing you didn't send something from your gallery ;)
Summary: <extra_id_0> marta <extra_id_1> file <extra_id_2>

Person-focused Planning (non mT5)

Summarize the conversation with the focus perspectives provided:
Hugo: Im off to Mazagan (Morocco) this weekend
Lacey: Oh so nice!
Hugo: Where are you these days? In Spain already?
Lacey: No. In Poland all the time. I study here
Summary with the focus perspectives ['Hugo', 'Lacey']: Hugo is off to Mazagan in Morocco this weekend. Lacey studies in Poland.

Summarize the conversation with the focus perspectives provided:
Miley: don't want to go to work tomorrow!
Miley: wanna sleep!!!
Miley: need some rest :(
Aaron: know what u feelin
Aaron: really want some holiday already
Miley: :(
Aaron: fighting girl!
Summary with the focus perspectives ['Miley']:

B Appendix: Utilizing GPT-3 for factual consistency evaluation

This study employs text-davinci-003 model as the factual consistency evaluator. The prompt template adopts a zero-shot chain-of-thought style because it outperforms direct prompting and exhibits greater stability compared to the few-shot setup, as suggested in Luo et al. (2023).

An illustrative example of the prompt and GPT-3's response is provided below:

Prompt for factual consistency classification

Decide if the following summary is consistent with the corresponding dialogue. Note that consistency means all information in the summary is supported by the dialogue.
Dialogue:
Will: hey babe, what do you want for dinner tonight?
Emma: gah, don't even worry about it tonight
...
Will: Alright, love you.
Emma: love you too.
Summary: Emma doesn't want to cook for Will tonight.
Explain your reasoning step by step then answer (yes or no) the question:

GPT-3's response
Yes, the summary is consistent with the dialogue.
Step 1: Will asks Emma what she wants for dinner.
Step 2: Emma responds that she doesn't want to worry about it, implying that she does not want to cook.
Step 3: Will then asks what time she'll be HOME, and Emma says soon.
Step 4: Will then offers to pick her up to which Emma responds no, she'll tell him when she gets home.
Step 5: Will then tells her he loves her and she responds in kind.
Yes, the summary is consistent with the dialogue.

C Appendix: Holistic Evaluation

The holistic evaluation of writing quality utilizes GPT-3. We follow the evaluation templates as well as the rubrics in Chia et al. (2023). See details of the prompts for writing an evaluation of relevance and coherence on the next page.

Due to the API cost, each model is evaluated on 100 random samples from the test set.

D Appendix: Impact of the number of demonstrations

ICL's performance instability is influenced by the selection and quantity of demonstrations. This study employs a random selection strategy for efficiency and simplicity, with each test sample having five sets of demonstrations. The average values are reported.

Table 10 and Figure 1 show the metric trends for k demonstrations, indicating that an increase in demonstrations may degrade performance and increase instability in some models (e.g., Cerebras-GPT-6.7B, OPT-1.3B), possibly due to their small parameter sizes. Table 3 presents the optimal performance for k values in the set 1,2,3.

Writing evaluation on relevance

Text: Eric, Bella and Eric were talking about their boss and how he appreciated their decision of dismissing a potential client. Eric and Bella were discussing the reasons why they dismissed the client, while Eric was asking Bella about her reaction to his boss' reaction.

Prompt: Summarize the following dialogue:
Eric: Hey Bella, What happened today in boss's room?? Was he angry??
Bella: NO NO!!! He wasn't angry at all.. He actually appreciated on our brave deccision to dismiss the request of client..
Eric: REALLY!! He appreciated this decision.. Bella: Yeah he really did.. I too was astounded by his reaction...
Eric: What could possibly lead to this?? I mean , they were potential clients...
Bella: What he told me was that he was looking forward to bring in new clients which were our current client's competitor..
Eric: Oh that could possibly be the reason.Well anyways you got appreciation xD congo
Bella: hahaha Blessing in disguise xD

How relevant is the text to the prompt? Select a suitable option number between 1 and 5 based on the options below.

1. Inadequate: The text fails to provide any relevant information or insights related to the given prompt.
2. Limited: The text may contain some relevant information, but significant gaps exist, and key aspects of the prompt are not adequately covered.
3. Satisfactory: The text covers the main aspects of the prompt and provides relevant information, but it lacks depth and may not explore the topic in great detail.
4. Proficient: The text provides a comprehensive response by addressing the key aspects of the prompt, offering relevant and well-supported information or arguments.
5. Excellent: The text thoroughly and thoughtfully addresses the prompt, demonstrating a comprehensive understanding of the topic. It offers insightful and original ideas, supported by relevant arguments and information.

Writing evaluation on coherence

Text: Eric, Bella and Eric were talking about their boss and how he appreciated their decision of dismissing a potential client. Eric and Bella were discussing the reasons why they dismissed the client, while Eric was asking Bella about her reaction to his boss' reaction.
How coherent is the text? Select a suitable option number between 1 and 5 based on the options below.

1. Inadequate: The text lacks logical organization, making it difficult to follow. Ideas are disjointed and phrased awkwardly, requiring significant effort to understand.
2. Limited: The text demonstrates some attempt at organization, but there are significant gaps in coherence. Ideas may be loosely connected, and the arguments lack clarity.
3. Satisfactory: The text generally follows a logical organization, but occasional disruptions or awkward phrasing may occur. There is an acceptable level of readability and understanding.
4. Proficient: The text is clearly organized and easy to understand. Ideas and arguments flow smoothly, contributing to easy comprehension and a pleasant reading experience.
5. Excellent: The text presents exceptionally coherent writing with a fluent and engaging flow of ideas, ensuring effortless comprehension and a delightful reading experience.

Model	k	ROUGE-1	ROUGE-2	ROUGE-L	Succee Rate (%)
OPT-1.3B	1	30.0	6.4	22.1	71.7 (↑ 10.7)
	2	32.1	7.7	23.7	68.7 (↑ 14.1)
	3	33.2	8.2	24.5	65.3 (↑ 14.8)
OPT-IML-1.3B	1	36.5	11.0	30.0	61.9 (↑ 7.5)
	2	36.9	11.1	29.6	57.4 (↑ 8.7)
	3	37.8	11.6	30.5	54.5 (↑ 9.5)
mT5-XL	1	32.3	11.0	27.5	100.0
	2	36.3	13.0	31.4	100.0
	3	39.8	15.2	34.6	100.0
Cerebras-GPT-6.7B	1	32.6	7.7	23.2	79.6 (↑ 13.9)
	2	33.9	8.6	24.5	74.9 (↑ 15.1)
	3	36.0	9.7	26.0	73.0 (↑ 16.9)
LLaMA-7B	1	32.0	7.8	23.4	69.1 (↑ 12.6)
	2	33.6	8.8	24.8	65.2 (↑ 13.7)
	3	34.1	9.3	25.4	62.5 (↑ 14.0)
Alpaca-7B	1	33.3	7.6	24.7	67.6 (↑ 8.5)
	2	35.2	8.9	26.3	65.4 (↑ 11.5)
	3	35.9	9.6	27.1	63.4 (↑ 12.3)
BLOOM-7B	1	32.2	7.6	23.1	77.1 (↑ 12.2)
	2	34.9	9.2	25.7	73.0 (↑ 14.8)
	3	36.6	10.2	27.2	71.1 (↑ 17.0)

Table 10: Evaluation results in the entity control setting with k keywords.

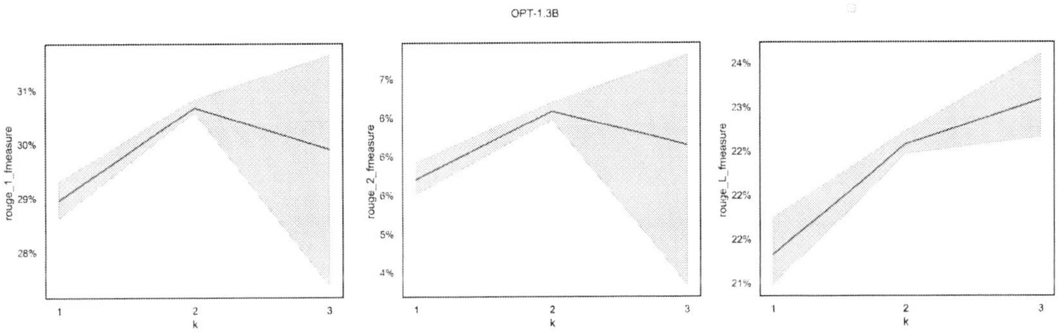

(a) OPT-1.3B

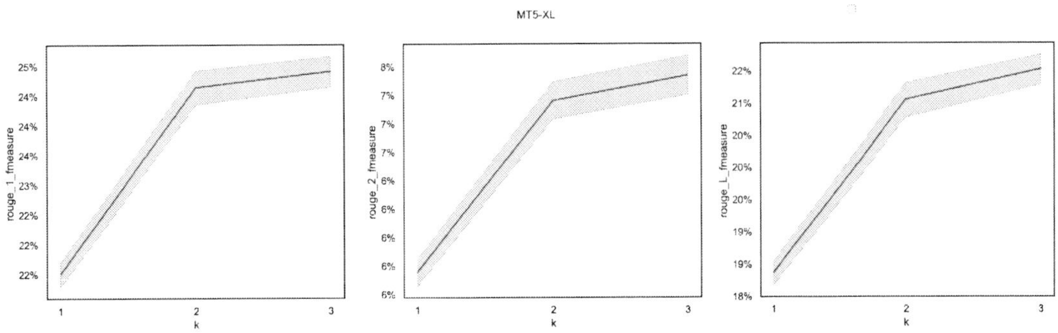

(b) mT5-XL

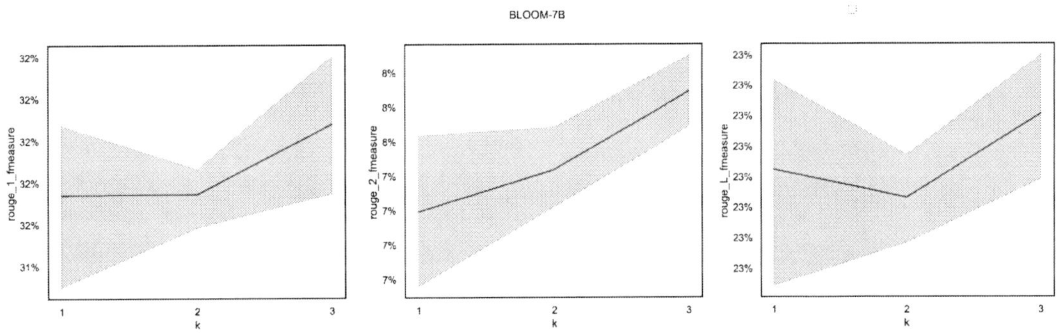

(c) BLOOM-7B

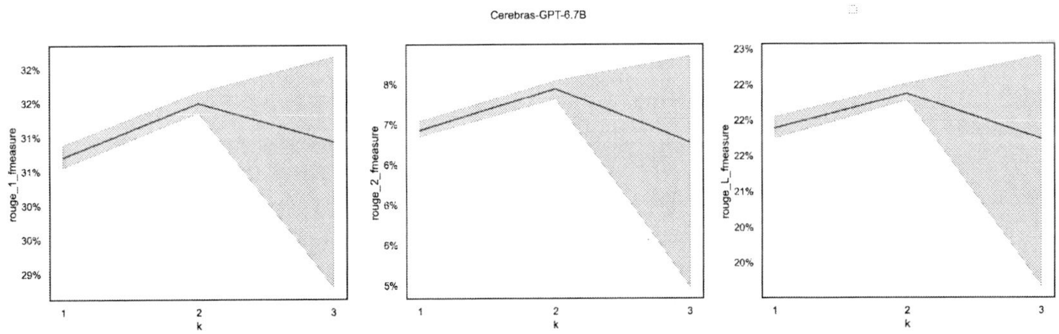

(d) CEREBRAS-GPT-6.7B

Figure 1: The line plots of evaluation metrics given k demonstrations in the uncontrolled setting. 95% confidence interval is highlighted within the plots.

From Sparse to Dense: GPT-4 Summarization with Chain of Density Prompting

Griffin Adams[♠,♣] griffin.adams@columbia.edu

Alexander R. Fabbri[◇] afabbri@salesforce.com

Faisal Ladhak[♠] faisal@cs.columbia.edu

Eric Lehman[♡] lehmer16@mit.edu

Noémie Elhadad[♠,♣] noemie.elhadad@columbia.edu

Columbia University: CS[♠]**, Biomedical Informatics**[♣] **Salesforce AI**[◇] **MIT**[♡]

Abstract

Selecting the "right" amount of information to include in a summary is a difficult task. A good summary should be detailed and entity-centric without being overly dense and hard to follow. To better understand this tradeoff, we solicit increasingly dense GPT-4 summaries with what we refer to as a "Chain of Density" (CoD) prompt. Specifically, GPT-4 generates an initial entity-sparse summary before iteratively incorporating missing salient entities without increasing the length. Summaries generated by CoD are more abstractive, exhibit more fusion, and have less of a lead bias than GPT-4 summaries generated by a vanilla prompt. We conduct a human preference study on 100 CNN DailyMail articles and find that humans prefer GPT-4 summaries that are more dense than those generated by a vanilla prompt and almost as dense as human written summaries. Qualitative analysis supports the notion that there exists a tradeoff between informativeness and readability. 500 annotated CoD summaries, as well as an extra 5,000 unannotated summaries, are freely available on HuggingFace[1].

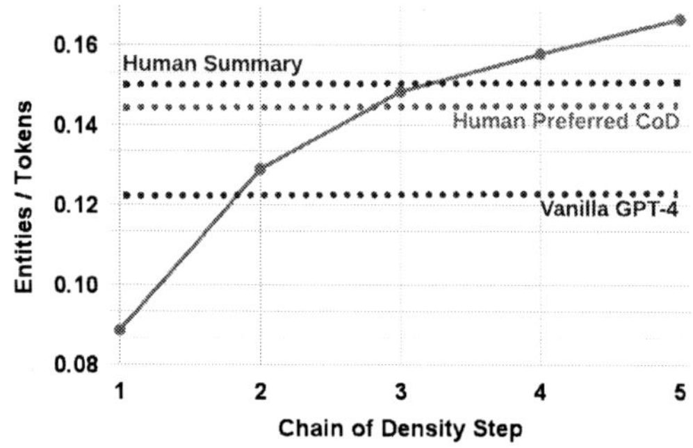

Figure 1: Chain of Density (**CoD**) summaries grow increasingly entity dense, starting off closer to vanilla GPT-4 summaries and eventually surpassing that of human written summaries. Human annotations suggest that a density similar to that of human-written summaries is preferable–striking the right balance between clarity (favors *less* dense) and informativeness (favors *more* dense).

1 Introduction

Automatic summarization has come a long way in the past few years, largely due to a paradigm shift away from supervised fine-tuning on labeled datasets to zero-shot prompting with Large Language Models (LLMs), such as GPT-4 (OpenAI, 2023). Without additional training, careful prompting can enable fine-grained control over summary characteristics, such as length (Goyal et al., 2022), topics (Bhaskar et al., 2023), and style (Pu and Demberg, 2023).

An overlooked aspect is the information density of an summary. In theory, as a compression of another text, a summary *should* be denser–containing a higher concentration of information–than the source document. Given the high latency of LLM decoding (Kaddour et al., 2023), covering more information in fewer words is a worthy goal, especially for real-time applications. Yet, how dense is an open question. A summary is uninformative if it contains insufficient detail. If it contains too much information, however, it can become difficult to follow without having to increase the overall length. Conveying more information subject to a fixed token budget requires a combination of abstraction, compression, and fusion. There is a limit to how much space can be made for additional information before becoming illegible or even factually incorrect.

In this paper, we seek to identify this limit by soliciting human preferences on a set of increasingly dense summaries produced by GPT-4. Treating entities, and, in particular, the average number of entities per token, as a proxy for density, we generate an initial, entity-sparse summary. Then, we iteratively identify and fuse 1-3 missing entities from the previous summary without increasing the overall length ($5x$ overall). Each summary has a higher ratio of entities to tokens than the previous one. Based on human preference data, we determine that humans prefer summaries that are almost as dense as human-written summaries and more

[1] https://huggingface.co/datasets/griffin/chain_of_density

Proceedings of The 4th New Frontiers in Summarization Workshop, pages 68–74
December 6, 2023 ©2023 Association for Computational Linguistics

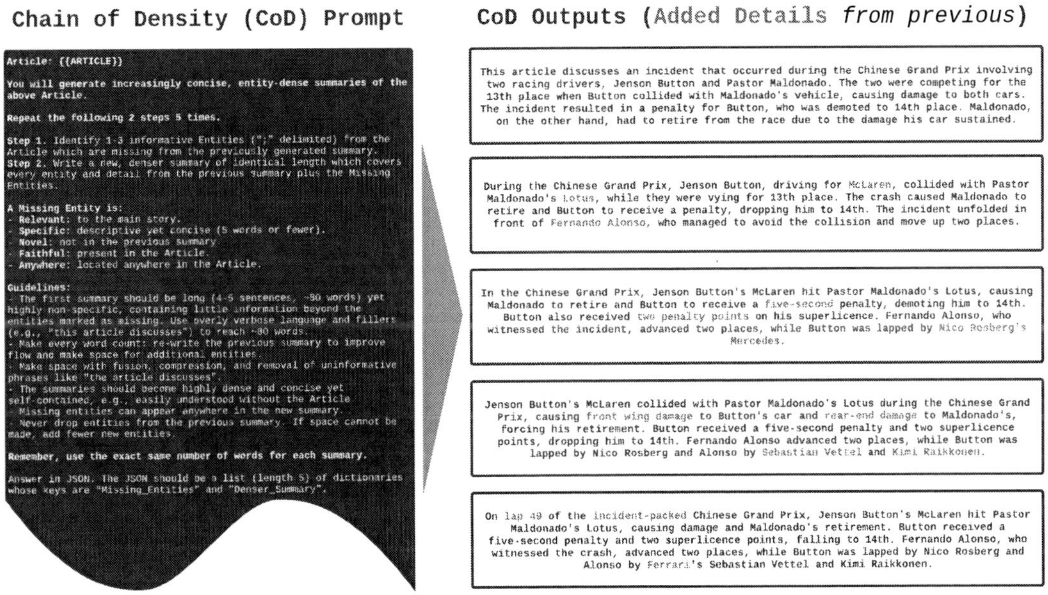

Figure 2: Chain of Density (CoD) Prompt and example output. At each step, 1-3 additional details (entities) are added to the previous summary without increasing the length. To make room for new entities, existing content is re-written (e.g., compression, fusion). Half the annotators (2/4) prefer the second to last summary, with the others preferring the final one.

dense than those generated by a vanilla GPT-4 prompt. Our primary contributions are to:

- Develop a prompt-based iterative method (CoD) for making summaries increasingly entity dense.
- Conduct both human and automatic evaluation of increasingly dense summaries on CNN/Dailymail articles to better understand the tradeoff between informativeness (favoring more entities) and clarity (favoring fewer entities).
- Open source GPT-4 summaries, annotations, and a set of 5,000 unannotated CoD summaries to be used for evaluation or distillation.

2 Chain of Density Prompting

Prompt. Our goal is to generate a set of summaries with GPT-4 with varying levels of information density, while controlling for length, which has proven to be a strong confounder when evaluating summaries (Fabbri et al., 2021; Liu et al., 2023b). To do this, we formulate a single Chain of Density (CoD) prompt, whereby an initial summary is generated and made increasingly entity dense. Specifically, for a fixed number of turns, a set of unique salient entities from the source text are identified and fused into the previous summary without increasing the length. The first summary is entity-sparse as it focuses on only 1-3 initial entities. To maintain the same length while increasing the number of entities covered, abstraction, fusion, and compression is explicitly encouraged, rather than dropping meaningful content from previous summaries.

Figure 2 displays the prompt along with an example output. Rather than be prescriptive about the types of entities, we simply define a Missing Entity as:

- **Relevant**: to the main story.
- **Specific**: descriptive yet concise (5 words or fewer).
- **Novel**: not in the previous summary.
- **Faithful**: present in the Article.
- **Anywhere**: located anywhere in the Article.

Data. We randomly sample 100 articles from the CNN/DailyMail summarization (Nallapati et al., 2016) test set for which to generate CoD summaries.

Reference Points. For frame of reference, we compare CoD summary statistics to human-written bullet-point style reference summaries as well as summaries generated by GPT-4 with a vanilla prompt: "Write a VERY short summary of the Article. Do not exceed 70 words." We set the desired token length to match that of CoD summaries (shown in Table 1).

3 Statistics

Direct statistics (tokens, entities, entity density) are ones directly controlled for by CoD, while Indirect

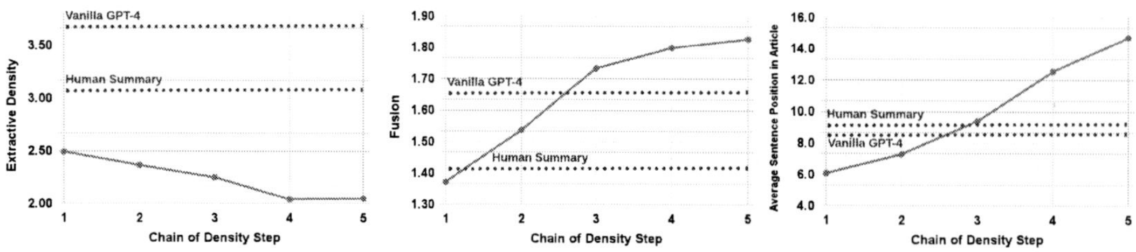

Figure 3: CoD-generated summaries grow increasingly abstractive while exhibiting more fusion and less of a lead bias.

statistics are expected byproducts of densification.

CoD Step	Tokens	Entities	Density (E/T)
1	72	6.4	0.089
2	67	8.7	0.129
3	67	9.9	0.148
4	69	10.8	0.158
5	72	12.1	0.167
Human	60	8.8	0.151
Vanilla GPT-4	70	8.5	0.122

Table 1: Explicit statistics for GPT-4 CoD summaries.

Direct Statistics. In Table 1, we compute tokens with NLTK (Loper and Bird, 2002), measure unique entities with Spacy[2], and compute entity density as the ratio. The CoD prompt largely adheres to a fixed token budget. In fact, the second step leads to an average 5-token (72 to 67) reduction in length as unnecessary words are removed from the initially verbose summary. The entity density rises–starting at 0.089, initially below Human and Vanilla GPT-4 (0.151 and 0.122)–to 0.167 after 5 steps of densification.

Indirect Statistics. ***Abstractiveness*** should increase with each CoD step because summaries are iteratively re-written to make space for each additional entity. We measure abstractiveness with extractive density: the average squared length of extractive fragments (Grusky et al., 2018). Similarly, the level of concept ***Fusion*** should increase monotonically as entities are added to a fixed-length summary. We proxy fusion as average number of source sentences aligned to each summary sentence. For alignment, we use the relative ROUGE gain method (Zhou et al., 2018), which aligns source sentences to a target sentence until the relative ROUGE gain of an additional sentence is no longer positive. We also expect the ***Content Distribution***–the position in the Article from which summary content is sourced–to shift. Specifically, we expect that CoD summaries initially exhibit a strong Lead Bias yet gradually start to pull in entities from the middle and end of the article. To measure this, we use our alignments from fusion and measure the average sentence rank of all aligned source sentences. Figure 3 confirms these hypotheses: abstractiveness increases with the number of re-writing steps (lower extractive density on the left), the rate of fusion rises (middle figure), and the summaries start to incorporate content from the middle and end of the article (right figure). Interestingly, all CoD summaries are more abstractive than both human written and baseline summaries.

[2] `https://spacy.io`.

4 Results

To better understand the tradeoffs present with CoD summaries, we conduct a preference-based human study and a rating-based evaluation with GPT-4.

CoD Step	% Share of First Place Votes				
	Individual Annotators				Aggregate
1	3.0	2.0	13.0	17.4	8.3
2	25.0	**28.0**	**43.0**	**31.4**	**30.8**
3	22.0	**28.0**	21.0	24.4	23.0
4	**29.0**	25.0	13.0	26.7	22.5
5	21.0	17.0	10.0	16.3	15.5

Table 2: Breakdown of first-place votes for CoD summaries by step. Based on aggregate preferences, the modal CoD step is **2**, median is **3**, and expected is **3.06**.

Human Preferences. We conduct a human evaluation to assess the impact of densification on human assessments of overall quality. Specifically, the first four authors of the paper were presented with randomly shuffled CoD summaries, along with the articles, for the same 100 articles (5 steps * 100 = 500 total summaries). Based on the definition of a "good summary" from Stiennon et al. (2020) (Table 6 from their paper), each annotator indicated their top preferred summary. Table 2 reports the breakdown of first place votes by CoD step across annotators–as well as aggregated across annotators. First, we report a low Fleiss' kappa (Fleiss, 1971) of 0.112, which points to the subtle differences between summaries and the subjective nature of the task. Recent work has

CoD Step	Entity Density	Informative	Quality	Coherence	Attributable	Overall	GPT-4 Eval Average
1	0.089	4.34	4.75	**4.96**	4.96	4.41	4.69
2	0.129	4.62	**4.79**	4.92	**5.00**	4.58	**4.78**
3	0.148	4.67	4.76	4.84	**5.00**	4.57	4.77
4	0.158	**4.74**	4.69	4.75	**5.00**	**4.61**	4.76
5	0.167	4.73	4.65	4.61	4.97	4.58	4.71

Table 3: GPT-4 Likert-scale (1-5) assessments of Chain of Density (CoD) Summaries by step.

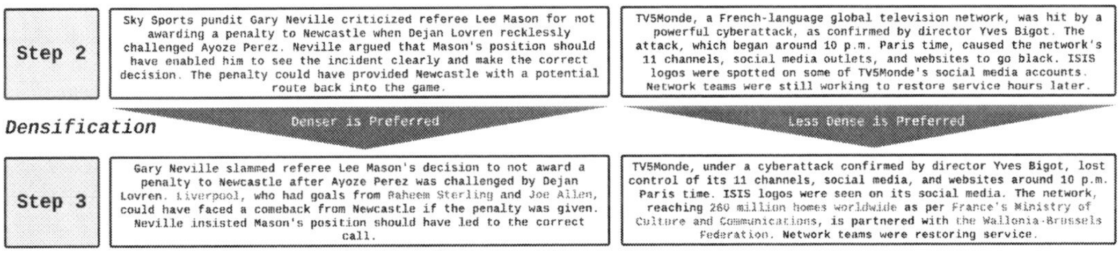

Figure 4: An example of a human-preferred densification step (left) and one which is not preferred. For the left, the bottom summary is preferred because the addition of "Liverpool" and the goal-scorers is relevant. The second summary makes room with sensible compressions, such as synthesizing "a potential route back into the game" into "a comeback". For the right, the addition of more details on "TVMonde" does not make up for the presence of an awkward fusion of entities ("cyberattack", and "Yves Bigot"), which was a direct result of having to tighten the previous summary.

similarly noted low instance-level agreement when judging GPT-based summaries (Goyal et al., 2022).

Yet, at the system level, some trends start to emerge. For 3 of the 4 annotators, CoD step 1 received the largest share of first-place votes across the 100 examples (28, 43, and 31.4%, respectively). Yet, in aggregate, 61% of first placed summaries (23.0+22.5+15.5) involved ≥ 3 densification steps. The median preferred CoD step is in the middle (3), and the expected step is 3.06.

Based on the average density of Step 3 summaries, we can roughly infer a preferred entity density of ~ 0.15 across the CoD candidates. From Table 1, we can see that this density aligns with human-written summaries (0.151), yet is noticeable higher than summaries produced with a vanilla GPT-4 prompt (0.122).

Automatic Metrics. As an evaluator, GPT-4 has been shown to adequately correlate to human judgments (Fu et al., 2023; Liu et al., 2023a), even potentially outperforming crowd-sourced workers on some annotation tasks (Gilardi et al., 2023). As a complement to our human evaluation (below), we prompt GPT-4 to rate CoD summaries (1-5) along 5 dimensions: **Informative**, **Quality**, **Coherence**, **Attributable**, and **Overall**. The definitions of **Informative**, **Quality**, and **Attributable** come from Aharoni et al. (2023), while **Coherence** comes from Fabbri et al. (2021)[3]. **Overall** aims to capture the qualities jointly. Please see Appendix A for the prompts used to solicit scores for each dimension. Table 3 suggests that densification is correlated with informativeness, yet there is a limit, with the score peaking at Step 4 (4.74). Article-free dimensions: **Quality** and **Coherence**, decline sooner (after 2 and 1 steps, respectively). All summaries are deemed **Attributable** to the source article. The **Overall** scores skew toward denser and more informative summaries, with **Step 4** having the highest score. On average across dimensions, the first and last CoD steps are *least* favored, while the middle three are close (4.78, 4.77, and 4.76, respectively).

In Appendix A, we report highest summary-level correlations of the **Overall** metric to human judgments (0.31 Pearson correlation), yet note low correlations overall–a phenomenon observed by Deutsch et al. (2022) when summaries are of similar quality.

Qualitative Analysis. There exists a clear trade-off between coherence / readability of summaries and informativeness. To illustrate, in Figure 4, we present two CoD steps: one for which the summary is improved with more detail, and one for which the summary is harmed. On average, intermediate CoD summaries best achieved this balance, yet we leave it to future work to precisely define and quantify this tradeoff.

5 Related Work

GPT Summarization. Goyal et al. (2022) benchmarked GPT-3 on news article summarization and found that humans preferred GPT-3 summaries over previous supervised baselines, which was

[3] **Quality** and **Coherence** are article-independent metrics.

not reflective of existing reference-based and reference-free metrics. Zhang et al. (2023) find that zeroshot GPT-3 summaries perform on par with humans by soliciting high-quality summaries from freelance writers. **Entity-Based Summarization.** Narayan et al. (2021) proposed generating entity chains as a planning step for supervised fine-tuning of summarization models, in contrast to keywords (Li et al., 2020; Dou et al., 2021) or purely extractive units (Dou et al., 2021; Adams et al., 2023a). Entities have also been incorporated for summarization as a form of control (Liu and Chen, 2021; He et al., 2022; Maddela et al., 2022), to improve faithfulness (Nan et al., 2021; Adams et al., 2022), and as a unit for evaluation (Cao et al., 2022; Adams et al., 2023b).

6 Conclusion

We study the impact of summary densification on human preferences of overall quality. We find that a degree of densification is preferred, yet, when summaries contain too many entities per token, it is very difficult maintain readability and coherence. We open-source annotated test set as well as a larger un-annotated training set for further research into the topic of fixed-length, variable density summarization.

7 Limitations

We only analyze `CoD` for a single domain, news summarization. Annotations did not show high summary-level agreement yet did start to show system-level trends, which is in line with previous work on LLM-based evaluation (Goyal et al., 2022). Finally, GPT-4 is a closed source model so we cannot share model weights. We do, however, publish all evaluation data, annotations, as well as $5,000$ un-annotated `CoD` to be used for downstream uses cases, e.g., density distillation into an open-sourced model such as LLAMA-2 (Touvron et al., 2023).

References

Griffin Adams, Alex Fabbri, Faisal Ladhak, Noémie Elhadad, and Kathleen McKeown. 2023a. Generating EDU extracts for plan-guided summary re-ranking. In *Proceedings of the 61st Annual Meeting of the Association for Computational Linguistics (Volume 1: Long Papers)*, pages 2680–2697, Toronto, Canada. Association for Computational Linguistics.

Griffin Adams, Han-Chin Shing, Qing Sun, Christopher Winestock, Kathleen McKeown, and Noémie Elhadad. 2022. Learning to revise references for faithful summarization. In *Findings of the Association for Computational Linguistics: EMNLP 2022*, pages 4009–4027, Abu Dhabi, United Arab Emirates. Association for Computational Linguistics.

Griffin Adams, Jason Zucker, and Noémie Elhadad. 2023b. A meta-evaluation of faithfulness metrics for long-form hospital-course summarization. *arXiv preprint arXiv:2303.03948*.

Roee Aharoni, Shashi Narayan, Joshua Maynez, Jonathan Herzig, Elizabeth Clark, and Mirella Lapata. 2023. Multilingual summarization with factual consistency evaluation. In *Findings of the Association for Computational Linguistics: ACL 2023*, pages 3562–3591, Toronto, Canada. Association for Computational Linguistics.

Adithya Bhaskar, Alex Fabbri, and Greg Durrett. 2023. Prompted opinion summarization with GPT-3.5. In *Findings of the Association for Computational Linguistics: ACL 2023*, pages 9282–9300, Toronto, Canada. Association for Computational Linguistics.

Meng Cao, Yue Dong, and Jackie Cheung. 2022. Hallucinated but factual! inspecting the factuality of hallucinations in abstractive summarization. In *Proceedings of the 60th Annual Meeting of the Association for Computational Linguistics (Volume 1: Long Papers)*, pages 3340–3354, Dublin, Ireland. Association for Computational Linguistics.

Daniel Deutsch, Rotem Dror, and Dan Roth. 2022. Re-examining system-level correlations of automatic summarization evaluation metrics. In *Proceedings of the 2022 Conference of the North American Chapter of the Association for Computational Linguistics: Human Language Technologies*, pages 6038–6052, Seattle, United States. Association for Computational Linguistics.

Zi-Yi Dou, Pengfei Liu, Hiroaki Hayashi, Zhengbao Jiang, and Graham Neubig. 2021. GSum: A general framework for guided neural abstractive summarization. In *Proceedings of the 2021 Conference of the North American Chapter of the Association for Computational Linguistics: Human Language Technologies*, pages 4830–4842, Online. Association for Computational Linguistics.

Alexander R. Fabbri, Wojciech Kryściński, Bryan McCann, Caiming Xiong, Richard Socher, and Dragomir Radev. 2021. SummEval: Re-evaluating summarization evaluation. *Transactions of the Association for Computational Linguistics*, 9:391–409.

Joseph L Fleiss. 1971. Measuring nominal scale agreement among many raters. *Psychological bulletin*, 76(5):378.

Jinlan Fu, See-Kiong Ng, Zhengbao Jiang, and Pengfei Liu. 2023. Gptscore: Evaluate as you desire. *arXiv preprint arXiv:2302.04166*.

Fabrizio Gilardi, Meysam Alizadeh, and Maël Kubli. 2023. Chatgpt outperforms crowd-workers for text-annotation tasks. *arXiv preprint arXiv:2303.15056*.

Tanya Goyal, Junyi Jessy Li, and Greg Durrett. 2022. News summarization and evaluation in the era of gpt-3. *arXiv preprint arXiv:2209.12356*.

Max Grusky, Mor Naaman, and Yoav Artzi. 2018. Newsroom: A dataset of 1.3 million summaries with diverse extractive strategies. In *Proceedings of the 2018 Conference of the North American Chapter of the Association for Computational Linguistics: Human Language Technologies, Volume 1 (Long Papers)*, pages 708–719, New Orleans, Louisiana. Association for Computational Linguistics.

Junxian He, Wojciech Kryscinski, Bryan McCann, Nazneen Rajani, and Caiming Xiong. 2022. CTRLsum: Towards generic controllable text summarization. In *Proceedings of the 2022 Conference on Empirical Methods in Natural Language Processing*, pages 5879–5915, Abu Dhabi, United Arab Emirates. Association for Computational Linguistics.

Jean Kaddour, Joshua Harris, Maximilian Mozes, Herbie Bradley, Roberta Raileanu, and Robert McHardy. 2023. Challenges and applications of large language models. *arXiv preprint arXiv:2307.10169*.

Haoran Li, Junnan Zhu, Jiajun Zhang, Chengqing Zong, and Xiaodong He. 2020. Keywords-guided abstractive sentence summarization. In *Proceedings of the AAAI conference on artificial intelligence*, volume 34, pages 8196–8203.

Yang Liu, Dan Iter, Yichong Xu, Shuohang Wang, Ruochen Xu, and Chenguang Zhu. 2023a. Gpteval: Nlg evaluation using gpt-4 with better human alignment. *arXiv preprint arXiv:2303.16634*.

Yixin Liu, Alex Fabbri, Pengfei Liu, Yilun Zhao, Linyong Nan, Ruilin Han, Simeng Han, Shafiq Joty, Chien-Sheng Wu, Caiming Xiong, and Dragomir Radev. 2023b. Revisiting the gold standard: Grounding summarization evaluation with robust human evaluation. In *Proceedings of the 61st Annual Meeting of the Association for Computational Linguistics (Volume 1: Long Papers)*, pages 4140–4170, Toronto, Canada. Association for Computational Linguistics.

Zhengyuan Liu and Nancy Chen. 2021. Controllable neural dialogue summarization with personal named entity planning. In *Proceedings of the 2021 Conference on Empirical Methods in Natural Language Processing*, pages 92–106, Online and Punta Cana, Dominican Republic. Association for Computational Linguistics.

Edward Loper and Steven Bird. 2002. Nltk: The natural language toolkit. *arXiv preprint cs/0205028*.

Mounica Maddela, Mayank Kulkarni, and Daniel Preotiuc-Pietro. 2022. EntSUM: A data set for entity-centric extractive summarization. In *Proceedings of the 60th Annual Meeting of the Association for Computational Linguistics (Volume 1: Long Papers)*, pages 3355–3366, Dublin, Ireland. Association for Computational Linguistics.

Ramesh Nallapati, Bowen Zhou, Cicero dos Santos, Çağlar Gulçehre, and Bing Xiang. 2016. Abstractive text summarization using sequence-to-sequence RNNs and beyond. In *Proceedings of the 20th SIGNLL Conference on Computational Natural Language Learning*, pages 280–290, Berlin, Germany. Association for Computational Linguistics.

Feng Nan, Ramesh Nallapati, Zhiguo Wang, Cicero Nogueira dos Santos, Henghui Zhu, Dejiao Zhang, Kathleen McKeown, and Bing Xiang. 2021. Entity-level factual consistency of abstractive text summarization. In *Proceedings of the 16th Conference of the European Chapter of the Association for Computational Linguistics: Main Volume*, pages 2727–2733, Online. Association for Computational Linguistics.

Shashi Narayan, Yao Zhao, Joshua Maynez, Gonçalo Simões, Vitaly Nikolaev, and Ryan McDonald. 2021. Planning with learned entity prompts for abstractive summarization. *Transactions of the Association for Computational Linguistics*, 9:1475–1492.

OpenAI. 2023. Gpt-4 technical report. *ArXiv*, abs/2303.08774.

Dongqi Pu and Vera Demberg. 2023. ChatGPT vs human-authored text: Insights into controllable text summarization and sentence style transfer. In *Proceedings of the 61st Annual Meeting of the Association for Computational Linguistics (Volume 4: Student Research Workshop)*, pages 1–18, Toronto, Canada. Association for Computational Linguistics.

Nisan Stiennon, Long Ouyang, Jeffrey Wu, Daniel Ziegler, Ryan Lowe, Chelsea Voss, Alec Radford, Dario Amodei, and Paul F Christiano. 2020. Learning to summarize with human feedback. *Advances in Neural Information Processing Systems*, 33:3008–3021.

Hugo Touvron, Louis Martin, Kevin Stone, Peter Albert, Amjad Almahairi, Yasmine Babaei, Nikolay Bashlykov, Soumya Batra, Prajjwal Bhargava, Shruti Bhosale, et al. 2023. Llama 2: Open foundation and fine-tuned chat models. *arXiv preprint arXiv:2307.09288*.

Tianyi Zhang, Faisal Ladhak, Esin Durmus, Percy Liang, Kathleen McKeown, and Tatsunori B Hashimoto. 2023. Benchmarking large language models for news summarization. *arXiv preprint arXiv:2301.13848*.

Qingyu Zhou, Nan Yang, Furu Wei, Shaohan Huang, Ming Zhou, and Tiejun Zhao. 2018. Neural document summarization by jointly learning to score and select sentences. In *Proceedings of the 56th Annual Meeting of the Association for Computational Linguistics (Volume 1: Long Papers)*, pages 654–663, Melbourne, Australia. Association for Computational Linguistics.

A GPT-4 Metrics

For the GPT-4 Likert-style evaluation, we use the following prompt template.

```
Article: {{Article}}

Summary: {{Summary}}
```

```
Please rate the summary
(1=worst to 5=best) with
respect to {{Dimension}}.

{{Definition}}
```

Below, we present the definitions provided for each quality metric.

- **Informative**: An informative summary captures the important information in the article and presents it accurately and concisely.
- **Quality**: A high quality summary is comprehensible and understandable.
- **Coherence**: A coherent summary is well-structured and well-organized.
- **Attributable**: Is all the information in the summary fully attributable to the Article?
- **Overall Preference**: A good summary should convey the main ideas in the Article in a concise, logical, and coherent fashion.

The **Quality** and **Coherence** prompts do not include the Article in the prompt. These definitions were paraphrased from previous summarization annotation efforts: (Fabbri et al., 2021; Aharoni et al., 2023).

Dimension	Correlation
Informative	0.215
Quality	0.120
Coherence	0.178
Attributable	0.245
Overall	**0.311**

Table 4: Summary-Level Pearson Correlation coefficient between human preferences and GPT-4 Likert ratings.

Meta-Evaluation. To compute the summary-level correlation, we first turned the preference data into a vector representing the number of times that summary received a first-placed vote. Table 4 demonstrates, unsurprisingly, that a prompt designed to capture overall summary rating has the highest summary-level Pearson correlation to overall preferences (31), yet overall correlations are still low.

Generating Extractive and Abstractive Summaries in Parallel from Scientific Articles Incorporating Citing Statements

Sudipta Singha Roy
The University of Western Ontario
London, ON, Canada
ssinghar@uwo.ca

Robert E. Mercer
The University of Western Ontario
London, ON, Canada
mercer@csd.uwo.ca

Abstract

Summarization of scientific articles often overlooks insights from citing papers, focusing solely on the document's content. To incorporate citation contexts, we develop a model to summarize a scientific document using the information in the source and citing documents. It concurrently generates abstractive and extractive summaries, each enhancing the other. The extractive summarizer utilizes a blend of heterogeneous graph-based neural networks and graph attention networks, while the abstractive summarizer employs an autoregressive decoder. These modules exchange control signals through the loss function, ensuring the creation of high-quality summaries in both styles.

1 Introduction

Text summarization automates condensing documents while preserving key information. Most neural summarization models, like those by Nallapati et al. (2016); Zhong et al. (2019), are designed for shorter texts, e.g., the CNN/Daily Mail dataset (Hermann et al., 2015). However, applying these models to longer documents, such as scientific research papers, remains limited. In scientific document summarization, it is common to focus solely on abstracts, introductions, and conclusions, as demonstrated in Yasunaga et al. (2019)'s work.

Summarizing scientific publications presents unique challenges due to their length, complex concepts, technical jargon, structured organization, and citations. These complexities make it a more daunting task compared to summarizing other types of documents. Additionally, the long-term impact of a scientific article may not be fully evident when it is first published, as its significance can evolve over time. While an abstract provides an initial overview from the authors' perspective, it may not capture the full extent of the paper's influence on the research community and its evolving impact (Yasunaga et al., 2019). As an example, we can consider the abstract from Bergsma and Lin (2006):

> We present an approach to pronoun resolution based on syntactic paths. ... we learn the likelihood of coreference between a pronoun and a candidate noun based on the path in the parse tree between the two entities. ... Highly coreferent paths also allow mining of precise probabilistic gender/number information. We combine statistical knowledge with well known features in a Support Vector Machine pronoun resolution classifier. Significant gains in performance are observed on several datasets.

This abstract gives insight into the methods the authors used. But the citations emphasize the corpus it presents. For example:

> We use the approach of Bergsma and Lin (2006), both because it achieves state-ofthe-art gender classification performance, and because a database of the obtained noun genders is available online. (Bergsma, 2005)

> For the gender task that we study in our experiments, we acquire class instances by filtering the dataset of nouns and their genders created by Bergsma and Lin (2006). (Bergsma and Van Durme, 2013)

Jaidka et al. (Jaidka et al., 2016, 2019) have identified this missing aspect in scientific document summarization and addressed it by introducing a shared task. This task aims to create summaries that take into account not only the information in the body of the documents but also the research community's overview of the documents over time. The work described here continues in this direction.

With the advancement of neural networks, there have been a few prominent research works in recent years for generating extractive (Yasunaga et al., 2019) and abstractive (Yu et al., 2020; Zhang et al.,

Proceedings of The 4th New Frontiers in Summarization Workshop, pages 75–86
December 6, 2023 ©2023 Association for Computational Linguistics

2019) summaries from scientific documents (Cohan et al., 2018; Zhang et al., 2022). Extractive summarization recognizes key sentences from the source document as the summary but lack the flow of information, whereas the abstractive summarization technique generates new phrases using language models while preserving the semantics of the input document but may miss some important aspects of the text. This is a motivation for designing a model to generate both summaries in parallel and help the counterpart to achieve a performance boost with additional guidance.

A key step in extracting brief synopsis sentences from a manuscript is to map the cross-sentence correlations. A lot of recent prominent works (Nallapati et al., 2017) have tried to do so using recurrent neural networks (RNNs). However, because of using RNNs, these models fail to capture long-distance sentence-level dependencies. Another approach to preserve sentence-level dependencies from long documents is using graph-based neural networks. A few recent works (e.g., (Cohan and Goharian, 2018; Yasunaga et al., 2017)) have utilized discourse information in the article along with inter-sentence correlations for constructing graphs and summarizing document. Another approach is to construct a sentence-level fully connected graph. Zhong et al. (Zhong et al., 2019) and Liu et al. (Liu and Lapata, 2019) used transformer (Vaswani et al., 2017) encoders to determine how sentences interact with each other. Wang et al. (Wang et al., 2020) introduced an heterogeneous graph neural network for extractive summarization which used additional semantic units (words) as intermediate nodes to construct relationships between sentences.

Abstractive summarizers focus heavily on form, with the goal of producing a generalized summary, which tends to necessitate complex language-generating models. These models are typically based on sequence-to-sequence (seq2seq) architectures, in which a source document is seen as one sequence whereas its summary as another. The majority of previous research on neural abstractive summarization depended on large-scale, high-quality datasets of supervised document-summarization pairings (See et al., 2017). Recently, state-of-the-art solutions on abstractive summarization are built upon the transformer (Vaswani et al., 2017) and BERT (Devlin et al., 2019) models. These attention-based abstractive models are being used in different fields like clinical note summarization (Kanwal and Rizzo, 2022), scientific document summarization (Zhang et al., 2022), and lay-abstract generation (Yu et al., 2020).

In this paper, addressing the above-mentioned issues, we have built a standalone summarization model which can generate both extractive and abstractive summaries from scientific documents incorporating the citation network. Analyzing the citation network, citing statements from the citing articles are accumulated with the original text document to incorporate the research community's observation on that particular cited manuscript. These summaries are the abstracts of the original papers with additional information reflecting the research community's view. After that, we run the LongFormer (Beltagy et al., 2020) encoder to generate sentence and word representations and train extractive and abstractive summarizers together. For the extractive summarizer, an heterogeneous graph neural network (Wang et al., 2020) is used as it has the ability to preserve sentence-level dependencies utilizing additional semantic units as intermediate nodes in the graph representation. Abstractive summaries are generated by the autoregressive decoder. The loss function is defined in such a way that both summarizers can achieve better ROUGE and METEOR scores. Furthermore, we have developed a corpus containing 10K research articles along with their corresponding citation statements and is a subset of the Semantic Scholar Network (SSN) corpus. The citation statements are collected utilizing the citation graph used in the SSN corpus. In short, the contributions of this work are:

- We have built a stand-alone summarizer model which can produce both extractive and abstractive summaries and each counterpart helps the other to generate better summaries.
- The summarizer model can work with long scientific text articles
- This model considers research communities' observations while generating the summaries
- We have proposed a new corpus containing 10K research articles along with the corresponding citing statements to incorporate the research communities' view.

2 Related Work

Text summarization aims to distill a document's essence efficiently. Recent NLP research has yielded effective neural summarization models, particularly those using transformer and BERT-based architectures. Work summarizing lengthy scientific documents often focuses on specific sections rather than the entire text (Yu et al., 2020) or citation statements (An et al., 2021).

2.1 Extractive Text Summarization

Extractive text summarization models classify sentences in a document using labels that indicate whether or not a sentence ought to be included in the summary. Originally, these models were designed based on the encoder-decoder architecture using RNNs (Nallapati et al., 2017). Since transformer and BERT-based models provide a more enriched sentence encoding, they have become the foundation for the majority of extractive summarizer models in recent years. Liu and Lapata (2019) fine-tuned BERT with stacked layers of transformer to obtain the sentence vectors and then used a sigmoid classifier for identifying the sentences that would be included in the summary. Zhang et al. (2019) fine-tuned an hierarchical transformer (HIBERT) for the extractive summarization task. Another prominent approach for extractive summarization is using graph representations which can preserve sentence-level correlations. Later, the graph convolutional network (GCN) (Welling and Kipf, 2016) has been espoused for building different inter-sentence correlation graphs (Yasunaga et al., 2017) for this task. Wang et al. (2020) built an heterogeneous graph neural network for extractive summarization (HeterSumGraph) which takes into account additional semantic units at the word level for building the sentence-level correlation graph.

2.2 Abstractive Text Summarization

Abstractive text summarization models, unlike the extractive summarizers which work like classifiers, are intended to generate summaries comprising new sentences which may or may not be present in the body of the document. These models are mostly based on the encoder-decoder architecture of the sequence-to-sequence models and language models like BART (Lewis et al., 2020), BigBird (Zaheer et al., 2020), and T5 (Raffel et al., 2020). Aksenov et al. (2020) applied BERT-windowing to overcome the length limitation of the BERT model and summarize long documents. Gidiotis and Tsoumakas (2020) trained the summarizer model to generate separate abstractive summaries for small parts of the document. Pilault et al. (2020) combined both the extractive and abstractive summarization using a transformer language model and built an hybrid summarizer model. Yu et al. (2020) fine-tuned pretrained BERT as the abstractive summarizer for generating a lay summary from the document.

2.3 Scientific Article Summarization

Existing scientific article summarizers, in most cases, are extractive models designed on the idea of sentence selection (Cohan and Goharian, 2018). Cohan et al. (2018) developed the first abstractive summarizer for long scientific articles using an hierarchical encoder and discourse-aware attentive decoder. Mishra et al. (2022) applied citation contextualization to extract unique relevant sentences from the document and final summaries are generated using a multi-objective clustering approach. Gupta et al. (2022) applied BERT and graph-based approaches for biomedical document summarization. Li et al. (2020) fine tuned T5 for generating summaries from long scientific documents and implemented an extractive summarizer using GCN. Yasunaga et al. (2019) built a corpus (Scisumm-Net) that includes a citation network for scientific document summarization and extracted the summary-candidate sentences using a GCN. An et al. (2021) introduced a large corpus (SSN) with 141K research papers connected with a citation graph. They also proposed a graph-based summarization model (CGSUM) for extractive document summarization. This model can draw information from both the source and the citing texts.

3 Methodology

This section defines the problem of scientific document summarization using a citation graph. Then, the two benchmark datasets used for the scientific article summarization experiments are discussed along with the pre-processing procedures. Finally, the proposed deep learning model is explained.

3.1 Problem Formulation: Summarization Using Citation Graph

Scientific articles possess distinctive attributes, including citation linkages, that establish profound connections between their contents. These studies may also yield unforeseen impacts and evolve in importance as research progresses. In such cases, ideal summaries should encompass both the authors' key points and the perspectives of the scientific community, as reflected in citations (Yasunaga et al., 2019). To serve this intent we have utilized two resources: the citation graph provided in the Semantic Scholar Network (SSN) corpus (An et al., 2021), and the ScisummNet/CL-SciSumm-2020 (CL-SciSumm-2020) corpus (Chandrasekaran et al., 2020; Yasunaga et al., 2019) which supplies documents and their corresponding citing statements.

3.2 Description of the Datasets

As this work is focused on generating summaries from scientific articles that incorporate the research community's views, we have considered two benchmark datasets: ScisummNet/CL-SciSumm (Chandrasekaran et al., 2020; Yasunaga et al., 2019), and Semantic Scholar Network (SSN) (An et al., 2021) for the experiments done here. To the best of our knowledge, these are the only datasets for the summarization task that also provide citation information. The ScisummNet corpus consists of abstracts of the 1000 most cited research articles from the ACL Anthology Network (Radev et al., 2013) along with 15 citing statements per article. The gold standard summaries for these 1000 documents are manually summarized by domain experts. The CL-SciSumm-2020 corpus (Chandrasekaran et al., 2020) extends the ScisummNet corpus with 40 extra documents and human-generated summaries thereby providing 1040 documents, citation sentences, and summaries. For testing, we have used the test set comprising 200 scientific articles from the CL-SciSumm-2020 corpus. The other benchmark dataset used for this task is the SSN corpus. It includes 140,799 research articles culled from the Semantic Scholar Open Research Corpus (S20RC) (Lo et al., 2020) together with a large citation graph. This citation graph has each article as a node and 660,908 edges indicating the citations. This corpus covers research articles from three domains: physics, mathematics and computer science.

The primary objective of this study is to develop a deep learning model capable of generating summaries for lengthy scientific documents while incorporating insights from other researchers citing the document. While the ScisummNet/CL-SciSumm dataset provides citation statements, the SSN corpus lacks this information. Originally, the SSN corpus consisted of documents and their references, but for our purpose of including citing statements, modifications were necessary. We leveraged the citation graph to identify citing papers and manually extracted the statements referring to the cited articles. Given the substantial size of the SSN corpus, containing nearly 141K articles, we randomly selected 10K papers for summarization. These papers have body lengths ranging from 1000 to 3500 words (with background/related work sections removed), aligning with the capacity of the LongFormer model (as described in Section 4), which can handle a maximum of 4096 tokens at a time. The dataset was divided into training (8000), validation (1000), and testing (1000) articles to facilitate model development and evaluation.

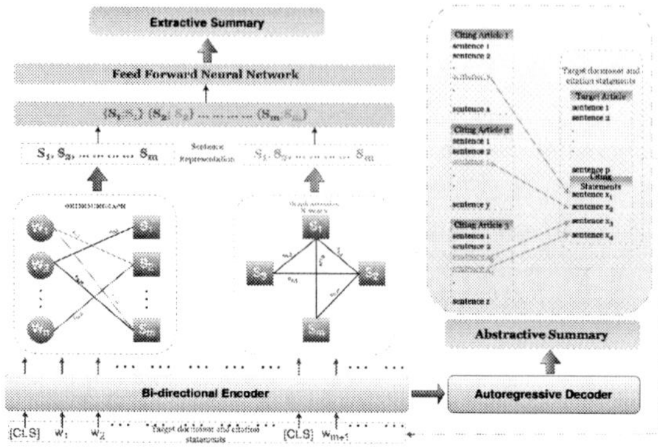

Figure 1: System architecture of the proposed model

Citations can convey positive, neutral, or negative intentions. To capture this diversity, we systematically categorized citing statements into these three classes after gathering them from citing articles. In cases where a paper had limited negative citations, we balanced the selection by including more neutral and positive citation statements. To classify these citation statements, we have employed RoBERTa trained on Athar (2014) following the approach used by Kundu (2023).

In the SSN corpus, the summaries are limited to the authors' perspectives as they consist of the paper abstracts. To create more comprehensive summaries, we employed a two-step approach. First, we used a fine-tuned T5 model (Raffel et al., 2020), trained on the CL-SciSumm-2020 corpus, to generate five summaries per document by inputting both the abstracts and corresponding citation statements. Then, we have employed a pre-trained RoBERTa architecture to obtain five vector representations for these summaries. The most similar summary to the reference summary, determined by cosine similarity, was selected as our T5-Generated Summary.

3.3 Model Overview

The investigated summarization model has two units: an extractive and an abstractive summarizer. The overall architecture of the model is portrayed in Figure 1. This section discusses the architecture and working principle of these two units.

While designing the extractive summarizer, we have considered two issues: how the sentences are connected to each other and how semantic units like words affect the sentence level correlations. To fulfill these purposes, we have utilized two different graph-based neural networks: an heterogeneous graph neural network (HeterSumGraph) (Wang et al., 2020) and a graph attention network (GAT) (Velickovic et al., 2018).

For any graph $G = \{V, E\}$, V denotes the nodes and E, the edges between them. HeterSumGraph defines $V = V_w \cup V_s$, V_w is the set of unique words and V_s is the set of sentences in the document. For a document with n unique words and m sentences, E is the edge weight matrix, where $e_{i,j}$ represents word i in sentence j, $(i \in \{1:n\}, j \in \{1:m\})$ (Wang et al., 2020). The nodes that represent the sentences are initialized with LongFormer [CLS] tokens. Because LogFormer generates a contextualized word embedding for each occurrence of the word in the document, all of the word embeddings for a word are averaged to initialize that particular word-representing node in the graph. The edges between the words and sentences are initialized with the corresponding TF-IDF values.

After the graph G is constructed, a graph attention network (GAT) is used to update the node feature values. Considering $h_i \in \mathbb{R}^{d_h}$ where $i \in \{1:(n+m)\}$ as the hidden states of the word and sentence nodes, the GAT layer is designed as:

$$\mathcal{T}_{i,j} = \mathit{LeakyReLU}(\omega_a[\omega_q h_i; \omega_k h_j; e_{i,j}]) \quad (1)$$

$$\alpha_{i,j} = \frac{\exp(\mathcal{T}_{i,j})}{\sum_{l \in \mathcal{N}_i} \exp(\mathcal{T}_{i,l})} \quad (2)$$

$$u_i = \sigma(\sum_{j \in \mathcal{N}_i} \alpha_{i,j}\omega_v h_j) \quad (3)$$

where ω_a, ω_q, ω_k and ω_v are learnable weight matrices. $\mathcal{N}_i$ denotes the list of the neighbor nodes. The attention value between h_i and h_j is denoted by $\alpha_{i,j}$. The GAT with multi-head attention (considering $\mathcal{K}$ attention heads) is designed as:

$$u_i = ||_{k=1}^{\mathcal{K}} \sigma(\sum_{j \in \mathcal{N}_i} \alpha_{i,j}^k \omega^k h_i) \quad (4)$$

To prevent the gradient from vanishing, HeterSumGraph incorporates a residual connection and the final hidden state representation becomes:

$$h_i = u_i + h_i \quad (5)$$

Through the aforementioned GAT and position-wise feed-forward network (FFN) layer comprising two linear transformations (Wang et al., 2020), the sentence nodes are updated with their adjacent word nodes:

$$\mathcal{U}_{w \to s}^1 = \mathit{GAT}(\mathcal{H}_s^0, \mathcal{H}_w^0, \mathcal{H}_w^0) \quad (6)$$

$$\mathcal{H}_s^1 = \mathit{FFN}(\mathcal{U}_{w \to s}^1 + \mathcal{H}_s^0) \quad (7)$$

where $\mathcal{U}_{w \to s}^1 \in \mathbb{R}^{n \times d_h}$ $\mathcal{H}_w^1 = \mathcal{H}_w^0 = V_w$, and $\mathcal{H}_s^0 = V_s$. In Eq. 6, $\mathcal{H}_s^0$ is employed as the attention query and for both the attention key and value $\mathcal{H}_w^0$ is used. Then, the revised sentence nodes are used to generate new representations for the individual word nodes and continue to refine the revised sentence nodes in an iterative fashion. At each iteration, sentence-to-word and word-to-sentence updates continue to be processed. The process can be depicted as follows for the t-th iteration:

$$\mathcal{U}_{s \to w}^{t+1} = \mathit{GAT}(\mathcal{H}_w^t, \mathcal{H}_s^t, \mathcal{H}_s^t) \quad (8)$$

$$\mathcal{H}_w^{t+1} = \mathit{FFN}(\mathcal{U}_{s \to w}^{t+1} + \mathcal{H}_w^t) \quad (9)$$

$$\mathcal{U}_{w \to s}^{t+1} = \mathit{GAT}(\mathcal{H}_s^t, \mathcal{H}_w^{t+1}, \mathcal{H}_w^{t+1}) \quad (10)$$

$$\mathcal{H}_s^{t+1} = \mathit{FFN}(\mathcal{U}_{w \to s}^{t+1} + \mathcal{H}_s^t) \quad (11)$$

Once the model training is done, the sentence nodes' representations are used as the sentence vector representations.

For direct sentence-level interactions, we have also used a graph attention neural network (GAT). Here, for the graph $G = \{V, E\}$, $V = V_s$ where V_s is the set of all the sentences in the document. The edge weight matrix E preserves the semantic similarity values between sentences. The nodes are initialized in the same manner as the sentence nodes in HeterSumGraph. For initializing the edges between nodes, at first we have acquired the vector representations of the sentences using pre-trained LongFormer and then computed the cosine similarity between the sentences. The edges are initialized with the corresponding similarity values between sentences. However, as scientific documents come with many sentences, working with a fully connected graph is not computationally cost effective. To reduce the burden of computational overhead, we have dropped the edge connections between nodes whose cosine similarity values are below a certain cut-off value. Throughout the conducted experiments, we have found that if we set the cut-off value below 0.3, the performance of the summarizer model remains the same.

Considering node features $h = \{h_1, h_n, ..., h_m\}$ as the input, GAT applies a self attention on the nodes and computes the attention coefficients as follows:

$$\mathcal{T}_{i,j} = a(\omega h_i, \omega h_j) \tag{12}$$

where a is a single-layer feed forward neural network with the *LeakyReLU* activation function, and ω is a learnable parameter. This attention coefficient shows node j's importance on node i and it is computed only for the corresponding one-hop neighbour nodes ($j \in \mathcal{N}_i$). This attention coefficient value is normalized to compute the attention values as follows:

$$\alpha_{i,j} = \frac{\exp(\mathcal{T}_{i,j})}{\sum_{l \in \mathcal{N}_i} \exp(\mathcal{T}_{i,l})} \tag{13}$$

The multi-head attention is computed in the same way it has been done for HeterSumGraph (Eq. 4).

Once the sentence representations from both the HeterSumGraph and GAT are computed, they are concatenated and fed to the feed-forward neural network layer. This is a two-layer position-wise feed-forward layer (Wang et al., 2020) for labeling the sentences with 1 or 0; 1 indicates that particular sentence is included in the extractive summary.

The abstractive summary is generated by the LongFormer decoder. To train the summarizer units in parallel, the training mechanism in Yu et al. (2020) is used. The overall loss L of the model is:

$$L = L_{ext} + L_{abs} \tag{14}$$

where L_{ext} and L_{abs} represent the cross-entropy losses of the extractive and abstractive summarizers, respectively.

4 Experimental Results and Analysis

This section gives a brief description of the model parameters used in the experiments as well as the results achieved on CL-SciSumm-2020 and the customized SSN datasets.

4.1 Model Parameters and Training Details

We have trained our model on a 48GB NVIDIA RTX A6000 GPU. The batch size has been set to 1 as the length of input documents plus the citation statements is large. Since all the experiments are done on a small batch-size, we have followed the training procedure of Sefid and Giles (2022) and accumulated gradients for 10 steps and updated the parameters. The NOAM scheduler has been utilized to adjust the learning rate and gradients are clipped so that exploding gradients during training can be prevented. The model has been trained for 20,000 epochs. The extractive summarizer is initialized with the LongFormer embeddings. Following that, the LongFormer encoder-decoder architecture for the abstractive summarizer and the extractive summarizer units' forward passes are trained separately. Once both of the forward passes are done for each iteration and the individual losses are calculated, the model's overall loss is calculated. If either of the two unit's validation loss continues to go down for 5 epochs, the parameter settings for that particular unit are saved and that unit's training is postponed for the next 10 epochs. The number of attention-heads for multi-head attention has been set to 8. The stop words and punctuation have been filtered out when pre-processing the word nodes in the graph. Following Wang et al. (2020), 10% of the words in the vocabulary having low TF-IDF values have been further filtered out. The word and sentence nodes have been initialized with 768-dimensional vectors. And the sentence representations from both the HeterSumGraph and GAT are 512-dimensional vectors. So, the final sentence vectors after the concatenation step are 1024-dimensional vectors. The Feed Forward Network hidden layer size is 512.

4.2 Performance Analysis of the Model

We have performed experiments on two datasets: modified SSN and CL-SciSumm-2020. The results achieved by our models are reported as overlapping unigrams, bigrams, and the longest common sequence between the generated summaries and the reference summaries by means of R-1, R-2, and R-L metrics; and semantic compatibility between the reference and generated summaries by means of METEOR metric, respectively, for the modified SSN corpus. R-1, and R-2 show the informativeness, and R-L shows the fluency of the generated summary. The metrics used for analyzing the model performance on CL-SciSumm-2020 are R-2 and R-SU4, which indicate the proportion of bigram overlap and unigram plus skipgram of

Table 1: Results on the modified SSN corpus. The results consider both the abstracts and the T5-generated summaries incorporating citation statements as the reference summaries. The best results are boldfaced.

Models	On Abstracts as Summaries				On T5-Generated Summaries			
	R-1	R-2	R-L	METEOR	R-1	R-2	R-L	METEOR
Extractive								
BERTSumExt	42.92	14.19	39.01	33.09	43.11	14.21	39.12	33.07
HeterSumGraph	44.27	14.52	39.73	33.18	44.30	14.53	39.74	33.18
GRETEL	**45.22**	**15.19**	**40.23**	**36.87**	**45.23**	15.19	**40.24**	**36.88**
Proposed Model (Extractive)	45.19	15.18	40.21	36.83	45.19	**15.21**	40.23	36.85
Abstractive								
PTGen+Cov	41.66	13.08	36.95	32.44	41.60	13.10	36.72	32.40
BERTSumAbs	42.06	14.52	38.17	32.49	42.04	14.56	38.17	32.49
BERT+CopyTransformer	42.43	15.01	39.03	32.88	42.44	15.05	39.04	32.91
Proposed Model (Abstractive)	**44.82**	**15.19**	**39.31**	**36.50**	**44.83**	**15.19**	**39.30**	**36.51**

4 tokens overlap, respectively, between the reference and generated summaries. The performance here is also analyzed with the METEOR metric. As the Bi-directional encoder and autoregressive decoder we have also experimented with BigBird. However, the better performance was found with LongFormer. That is why in the final model, we have used LongFormer in all the cases for initial encoding and generating abstractive summaries.

4.3 Results: Modified SSN Corpus

To compare the performance of our model with the existing extractive models, we train and test the following extractive summarizer models on our modified corpus: (1) BERTSumEXT (Liu and Lapata, 2019): a BERT-based model; (2) HeterSumGraph (Wang et al., 2020): a heterogeneous graph-based approach that considers the cross-sentence correlations using additional semantic units; and (3) GRETEL: fuses semantic information from the document context and gold summary using a hierarchical transformer encoder and graph contrastive learning. For the abstractive summarization baseline, we have experimented with: (1) PTGen+Cov (See et al., 2017): based on a hybrid pointer generator network to copy words from the source text, (2) BERTSumAbs (Liu and Lapata, 2019): a BERT-based model; and (3) BERT+CopyTransformer (Aksenov et al., 2020): applies BERT-windowing for processing data longer than the BERT window.

The performance of the existing models and our proposed models are shown in Table 1. As reference summaries, we have considered both the paper abstracts as well as the summaries we have generated from the abstracts plus the citing statements using T5.

Although BERTSumExt and BERTSumAbs perform very well with short documents, their performance metrics are not at that level when summarizing scientific documents. The main reason for this is their limitation to working with a maximum 512 input tokens, but scientific documents are much longer. For this, they have applied the greedy algorithm introduced by Nallapati et al. (2016). HeterSumGraph considers direct relationships between words and sentences on texts with a 50-sentence maximum, whereas our proposed model considers direct cross-sentence correlations, as well, and can deal with longer text spans (up to 3500 words). These additional features, together with LongFormer's enriched word and sentence features, gives our model a performance boost, but our model requires more computational time and resources. Our model performs better by a good margin compared to the other models apart from GRETEL. Our extractive summarizer shows slightly lower performance compared to GRETEL which is a more complex model. Still, because of the parallel training approach, our model has achieved comparable results. Our abstractive summarizer model outperforms the other experimental abstractive summarizers by large margins: PTGen+Cov by 2.36, BertSumAbs by 1.14, and BERT+CopyTransformer by 0.28 R-L scores. The METEOR scores achieved by our model are 36.83 and 36.50 for extractive and abstractive summaries, respectively, when tested over the T5-generated summaries. In the experiment with the abstracts as summaries, the METEOR scores are 36.51 and 36.85 for the abstractive and extractive summaries, respectively. Looking at the METEOR scores achieved by the other models (see Table 1), it is clearly visible that both the extractive and abstractive summarizer units of our model have outper-

Table 2: Model performance analysis on two CL-SciSumm-2020 summary categories. All values are F-1 scores.

Models	Abstracts as Summaries			Human-created Summaries		
	R-2	**R-SU4**	**METEOR**	**R-2**	**R-SU4**	**METEOR**
Jaccard-focused GCN	0.19931	0.09956	-	0.2042	0.14162	-
Clustering	0.1959	0.0962	-	0.1749	0.1169	-
MMR2	0.15067	0.07851	-	0.15073	0.10237	-
LSTM+BabelNet	0.329	0.172	-	0.241	0.171	-
Proposed Model						
Extractive Summarizer	0.43	0.266	31.12	0.42	0.249	30.18
Abstractive Summarizer	0.43	0.250	30.98	0.41	0.234	30.06

formed them by at least 3. This observation indicates that the summaries generated by our proposed model are more semantically similar to the reference summaries. To see the importance of the individual units, please check the ablation study in the appendix.

4.4 Results: CL-SciSumm-2020 Corpus

For analyzing our proposed model's performances on CL-SciSumm-2020 Corpus, we have used R-2 and R-SU4 F-1 scores (as the other comparable models are reported with these metrics) We have experimented to generate abstract and human summaries. As benchmarks, we have selected the research works submitted to CL-SciSumm-2019/2020: (1) Jaccard-focused GCN (Umapathy et al., 2020): an extractive summarizer utilizing cross-sentence graph and graph attention networks, (2) Clustering (Mishra et al., 2020): based on different clustering algorithms followed by sentence-scoring functions, (3) MMR2 (Reddy et al., 2020): based on the maximal marginal relevance technique, and (4) LSTM+BabelNet (Chiruzzo et al., 2019): BabelNet vectors were used to train the LSTM. The CL-SciSumm task provides a performance metric evaluation script which is used to calculate the R-2 and R-SU4 values for the model-generated summaries against the test set.

Results on CL-SciSumm-2020 are reported in Table 2. Looking at the results, it is clear that our model outperforms the other existing extractive models on every measure. The R-2 and R-SU4 achieved for both of our model-generated extractive and abstractive summaries are very high compared to the other existing extractive models. And this is the case for both the original abstracts and the human-created summaries as reference summaries. For the human-created reference summaries, our extractive and abstractive summarizers have achieved 0.078 and 0.063 R-SU4 F-1 score gains, respectively, compared to the LSTM+BabelNet model, which comes with the best result among the other considered models. While considering the abstracts of the papers as reference summaries, these gains are 0.094 and 0.078, respectively. For the abstractive summaries, the METEOR score achieved by our model is 30.18 whereas for the extractive summaries, it has achieved a 30.06 METEOR score on the human-generated summaries. Over the abstracts of the papers, these scores are 31.12 and 30.98, respectively.

5 Conclusion and Future Work

In this paper, we have introduced a summarizer model considering two intentions: first, summarize scientific documents incorporating citation contexts, and second, build a summarizer model which can generate both extractive and abstractive summaries by means of parallel training so that both counterparts can gain a performance boost. For this, we have utilized both the sentence-sentence and sentence-word correlations. Furthermore, we have constructed a corpus comprising 10K scientific articles with their corresponding citation statements for the summarization task. The experimental results show that our model performs well compared to other well-known methods. Though this work considers the research community's observations (citing statements), it doesn't consider the background information (references presented in the target article). In our future work, we are planning to use both sides of the citation graph (references as the background knowledge and the citing statements as the research community's views) while summarizing a scientific article.

Acknowledgements

We would like to thank all reviewers for their comments. This research is partially funded by The Natural Sciences and Engineering Research Council of Canada (NSERC) through a Discovery Grant to R. E. Mercer.

Limitations

Our experiments are limited to summarize long scientific texts only. We have not conducted any experiments with short target texts, consequently we are not sure how well the model may perform while summarizing short texts. We are also unsure how well this model may perform for extreme summary generation like TLDR (Cachola et al., 2020). Moreover, we have trained both the extractive and abstractive summarizer units for a large number of epochs. Though to prevent any unit from being over-fitted we have checked the curve of validation loss after every 5 epochs. This is very computationally expensive and demands a longer period of time for model training. Furthermore, no tests have been performed to see how the abstractive summarizer unit suffers from hallucination.

Ethics Statement

We do not see any ethics issue here in this paper.

References

Dmitrii Aksenov, Julian Moreno Schneider, Peter Bourgonje, Robert Schwarzenberg, Leonhard Hennig, and Georg Rehm. 2020. Abstractive text summarization based on language model conditioning and locality modeling. In *Proceedings of the 12th Language Resources and Evaluation Conference*, pages 6680–6689.

Chenxin An, Ming Zhong, Yiran Chen, Danqing Wang, Xipeng Qiu, and Xuanjing Huang. 2021. Enhancing scientific papers summarization with citation graph. In *Proceedings of the AAAI Conference on Artificial Intelligence*, volume 35, pages 12498–12506.

Awais Athar. 2014. Sentiment analysis of scientific citations. university of cambridge. *Computer Laboratory, Stroudsburg, PA, USA*.

Iz Beltagy, Matthew E Peters, and Arman Cohan. 2020. Longformer: The long-document transformer. *arXiv preprint arXiv:2004.05150*.

Shane Bergsma. 2005. Automatic acquisition of gender information for anaphora resolution. In *Proceedings of the 18th Conference of the Canadian Society for Computational Studies of Intelligence*, pages 342–353.

Shane Bergsma and Dekang Lin. 2006. Bootstrapping path-based pronoun resolution. In *Proceedings of the 21st International Conference on Computational Linguistics and 44th Annual Meeting of the Association for Computational Linguistics*, pages 33–40.

Shane Bergsma and Benjamin Van Durme. 2013. Using conceptual class attributes to characterize social media users. In *Proceedings of the 51st Annual Meeting of the Association for Computational Linguistics (Volume 1: Long Papers)*, pages 710–720.

Isabel Cachola, Kyle Lo, Arman Cohan, and Daniel S Weld. 2020. Tldr: Extreme summarization of scientific documents. *arXiv preprint arXiv:2004.15011*.

Muthu Kumar Chandrasekaran, Guy Feigenblat, Eduard Hovy, Abhilasha Ravichander, Michal Shmueli-Scheuer, and Anita De Waard. 2020. Overview and insights from scientific document summarization shared tasks 2020: CL-SciSumm, LaySumm and LongSumm. In *Proceedings of the First Workshop on Scholarly Document Processing (SDP 2020)*.

Luis Chiruzzo, Àlex Bravo, Horacio Saggion, et al. 2019. Lastus-taln+ inco@ cl-scisumm 2019. In *BIRNDL@ SIGIR*.

Arman Cohan, Franck Dernoncourt, Doo Soon Kim, Trung Bui, Seokhwan Kim, Walter Chang, and Nazli Goharian. 2018. A discourse-aware attention model for abstractive summarization of long documents. In *Proceedings of the 2018 Conference of the North American Chapter of the Association for Computational Linguistics: Human Language Technologies, Volume 2 (Short Papers)*, pages 615–621.

Arman Cohan and Nazli Goharian. 2018. Scientific document summarization via citation contextualization and scientific discourse. *International Journal on Digital Libraries*, 19(2):287–303.

Jacob Devlin, Ming-Wei Chang, Kenton Lee, and Kristina Toutanova. 2019. BERT: pre-training of deep bidirectional transformers for language understanding. In *Proceedings of the 2019 Conference of the North American Chapter of the Association for Computational Linguistics: Human Language Technologies, NAACL-HLT Volume 1 (Long and Short Papers)*, pages 4171–4186.

Alexios Gidiotis and Grigorios Tsoumakas. 2020. A divide-and-conquer approach to the summarization of long documents. *IEEE/ACM Transactions on Audio, Speech, and Language Processing*, 28:3029–3040.

Supriya Gupta, Aakanksha Sharaff, and Naresh Kumar Nagwani. 2022. Biomedical text summarization: a graph-based ranking approach. In *Applied Information Processing Systems*, pages 147–156. Springer.

Karl Moritz Hermann, Tomas Kocisky, Edward Grefenstette, Lasse Espeholt, Will Kay, Mustafa Suleyman, and Phil Blunsom. 2015. Teaching machines to read and comprehend. *Advances in neural information processing systems*, 28.

Kokil Jaidka, Muthu Kumar Chandrasekaran, Sajal Rustagi, and Min-Yen Kan. 2016. Overview of the CL-SciSumm 2016 shared task. In *Proceedings of the Joint Workshop on Bibliometric-enhanced Information Retrieval and Natural Language Processing for Digital Libraries (BIRNDL)*, pages 93–102.

Kokil Jaidka, Michihiro Yasunaga, Muthu Kumar Chandrasekaran, Dragomir Radev, and Min-Yen Kan. 2019. The CL-SciSumm shared task 2018: Results and key insights. In *CEUR Proceedings*, volume 2132.

Neel Kanwal and Giuseppe Rizzo. 2022. Attention-based clinical note summarization. In *Proceedings of the 37th ACM/SIGAPP Symposium on Applied Computing*, pages 813–820.

Souvik Kundu. 2023. Citation polarity identification from scientific articles using deep learning methods. Master's thesis, The University of Western Ontario.

Mike Lewis, Yinhan Liu, Naman Goyal, Marjan Ghazvininejad, Abdelrahman Mohamed, Omer Levy, Veselin Stoyanov, and Luke Zettlemoyer. 2020. Bart: Denoising sequence-to-sequence pre-training for natural language generation, translation, and comprehension. In *Proceedings of the 58th Annual Meeting of the Association for Computational Linguistics*, pages 7871–7880.

Lei Li, Yang Xie, Wei Liu, Yinan Liu, Yafei Jiang, Siya Qi, and Xingyuan Li. 2020. Cist@ cl-scisumm 2020, longsumm 2020: Automatic scientific document summarization. In *Proceedings of the First Workshop on Scholarly Document Processing*, pages 225–234.

Yang Liu and Mirella Lapata. 2019. Text summarization with pretrained encoders. In *Proceedings of the 2019 Conference on Empirical Methods in Natural Language Processing and the 9th International Joint Conference on Natural Language Processing (EMNLP-IJCNLP)*, pages 3730–3740.

Kyle Lo, Lucy Lu Wang, Mark Neumann, Rodney Kinney, and Daniel S Weld. 2020. S2orc: The semantic scholar open research corpus. In *Proceedings of the 58th Annual Meeting of the Association for Computational Linguistics*, pages 4969–4983.

Santosh Kumar Mishra, Harshavardhan Kundarapu, Naveen Saini, Sriparna Saha, and Pushpak Bhattacharyya. 2020. Iitp-ai-nlp-ml@ cl-scisumm 2020, cl-laysumm 2020, longsumm 2020. In *Proceedings of the First Workshop on Scholarly Document Processing*, pages 270–276.

Santosh Kumar Mishra, Naveen Saini, Sriparna Saha, and Pushpak Bhattacharyya. 2022. Scientific document summarization in multi-objective clustering framework. *Applied Intelligence*, 52(2):1520–1543.

Ramesh Nallapati, Feifei Zhai, and Bowen Zhou. 2017. Summarunner: A recurrent neural network based sequence model for extractive summarization of documents. In *Thirty-first AAAI conference on artificial intelligence*.

Ramesh Nallapati, Bowen Zhou, Caglar Gulcehre, Bing Xiang, et al. 2016. Abstractive text summarization using sequence-to-sequence rnns and beyond. *arXiv preprint arXiv:1602.06023*.

Jonathan Pilault, Raymond Li, Sandeep Subramanian, and Christopher Pal. 2020. On extractive and abstractive neural document summarization with transformer language models. In *Proceedings of the 2020 Conference on Empirical Methods in Natural Language Processing (EMNLP)*, pages 9308–9319.

Dragomir R Radev, Pradeep Muthukrishnan, Vahed Qazvinian, and Amjad Abu-Jbara. 2013. The ACL anthology network corpus. *Language Resources and Evaluation*, 47(4):919–944.

Colin Raffel, Noam Shazeer, Adam Roberts, Katherine Lee, Sharan Narang, Michael Matena, Yanqi Zhou, Wei Li, Peter J Liu, et al. 2020. Exploring the limits of transfer learning with a unified text-to-text transformer. *Journal of Machine Learning Research*, 21(140):1–67.

Saichethan Reddy, Naveen Saini, Sriparna Saha, and Pushpak Bhattacharyya. 2020. Iiitbh-iitp@ cl-scisumm20, cl-laysumm20, longsumm20. In *Proceedings of the First Workshop on Scholarly Document Processing*, pages 242–250.

Abigail See, Peter J Liu, and Christopher D Manning. 2017. Get to the point: Summarization with pointer-generator networks. In *Proceedings of the 55th Annual Meeting of the Association for Computational Linguistics (Volume 1: Long Papers)*, pages 1073–1083.

Athar Sefid and C Lee Giles. 2022. Scibertsum: Extractive summarization for scientific documents. In *International Workshop on Document Analysis Systems*, pages 688–701. Springer.

Anjana Umapathy, Karthik Radhakrishnan, Kinjal Jain, and Rahul Singh. 2020. Citeqa@ clscisumm 2020. In *Proceedings of the First Workshop on Scholarly Document Processing*, pages 297–302.

Ashish Vaswani, Noam Shazeer, Niki Parmar, Jakob Uszkoreit, Llion Jones, Aidan N Gomez, Łukasz Kaiser, and Illia Polosukhin. 2017. Attention is all you need. *Advances in neural information processing systems*, 30.

Petar Velickovic, Guillem Cucurull, Arantxa Casanova, Adriana Romero, Pietro Liò, and Yoshua Bengio. 2018. Graph attention networks. In *Proceedings of the 6th International Conference on Learning Representations, ICLR*.

Danqing Wang, Pengfei Liu, Yining Zheng, Xipeng Qiu, and Xuanjing Huang. 2020. Heterogeneous graph neural networks for extractive document summarization. In *Proceedings of the 58th Annual Meeting of the Association for Computational Linguistics*, pages 6209–6219.

Max Welling and Thomas N Kipf. 2016. Semi-supervised classification with graph convolutional networks. In *J. International Conference on Learning Representations (ICLR 2017)*.

Michihiro Yasunaga, Jungo Kasai, Rui Zhang, Alexander R Fabbri, Irene Li, Dan Friedman, and Dragomir R Radev. 2019. ScisummNet: A large annotated corpus and content-impact models for scientific paper summarization with citation networks. In *Proceedings of the AAAI Conference on Artificial Intelligence*, volume 33, pages 7386–7393.

Michihiro Yasunaga, Rui Zhang, Kshitijh Meelu, Ayush Pareek, Krishnan Srinivasan, and Dragomir Radev. 2017. Graph-based neural multi-document summarization. In *Proceedings of the 21st Conference on Computational Natural Language Learning (CoNLL 2017)*, pages 452–462.

Tiezheng Yu, Dan Su, Wenliang Dai, and Pascale Fung. 2020. Dimsum@ laysumm 20: Bart-based approach for scientific document summarization. In *Proceedings of the First Workshop on Scholarly Document Processing*, pages 303–309.

Manzil Zaheer, Guru Guruganesh, Kumar Avinava Dubey, Joshua Ainslie, Chris Alberti, Santiago Ontanon, Philip Pham, Anirudh Ravula, Qifan Wang, Li Yang, et al. 2020. Big bird: Transformers for longer sequences. *Advances in Neural Information Processing Systems*, 33:17283–17297.

Haopeng Zhang, Semih Yavuz, Wojciech Kryscinski, Kazuma Hashimoto, and Yingbo Zhou. 2022. Improving the faithfulness of abstractive summarization via entity coverage control. *arXiv preprint arXiv:2207.02263*.

Xingxing Zhang, Furu Wei, and Ming Zhou. 2019. Hibert: Document level pre-training of hierarchical bidirectional transformers for document summarization. In *Proceedings of the 57th Annual Meeting of the Association for Computational Linguistics*, pages 5059–5069.

Ming Zhong, Pengfei Liu, Danqing Wang, Xipeng Qiu, and Xuanjing Huang. 2019. Searching for effective neural extractive summarization: What works and what's next. *arXiv preprint arXiv:1907.03491*.

A Appendix

A.1 Ablation Study

Table 3: Ablation Study: Rows labeled with † indicate the extractive summaries and rows labeled with ∗ indicate abstractive summaries.

Discarded Unit	On T5-Generated Summaries			
	R-1	R-2	R-L	METEOR
GAT†	44.86	14.9	39.96	36.52
HeterSumGraph†	44.78	14.81	39.84.	36.49
Extractive Summarizer∗	43.01	15.02	38.99	35.92
Abstractive Summarizer†	44.91	14.95	39.96	36.50

To portray a better grasp of each component's contribution in our suggested model, we have experimented with different units of our model separately and the results are reported in Table 3. All of these experiments are performed on the T5-generated corpus which combines the abstract of the paper along with the citation statements.

In our first experiment, we have discarded the GAT unit which works with cross-sentence relationships and kept only the HeterSumGraph for extractive summary generation. This time the performances of the model are lower than the reported results in Tables 1 (R-1: 44.86, R-2: 14.91, R-L: 39.96, and METEOR: 36.52) for our generated extractive summaries. Still, these results are higher compared to the original HeterSumGraph model. It shows, using the LongFormer encoder in the beginning and using the collective loss function for both the abstractive and extractive summarizer units play a significant role in the performance boost. And it also indicates that taking direct cross-sentence correlations into consideration provides some additional features to enrich the model which helps the model's performance to improve.

In the second experiment, we have discarded the HeterSumGraph unit and used only GAT in the extractive summarization unit. This time the performance metrics for extractive summaries are R-1: 44.78, R-2: 14.81, R-L: 39.84,and METEOR: 36.4. These values are comparably lower than we gained in the last experiment. The reason behind this incident is, though no direct cross-sentence relationships are present, HeterSumGraph, by 2-hop distance, considers the correlations between sentences.

The third experiment discards the extractive summarizer unit. The LongFormer abstractive summarizer unit achieves very poor R-1: 43.01, R-2: 15.02, R-L: 38.99, and METEOR: 35.92 scores compared to the proposed model. This poor performance demonstrates the importance of the information that the extractive summarizer provides the abstractive summarizer through the combined loss function.

Finally, we have discarded the abstract summarizer unit and used the combination of HeterSumGraph and GAT for extractive summary generation. During this experiment, the achieved R-1, R-2 R-L, and METEOR scores are 44.91, 14.95, 39.96, and 36.50, respectively, which are more than the cases for the three above-mentioned ablation experiments. It indicates the significance of training the abstractive summarization unit in parallel as well as using the cross-sentence and semantic unit-sentence correlations at the same time.

A.2 Validity Check of the Proposed Corpus

To ascertain the corpus's quality, a rigorous analysis was conducted on a statistically significant subset of the dataset, with a confidence level of 95% and a margin of error of 3%, aided by three human annotators. Within the vast pool of 10,000 summarization samples, a random selection of 400 was subject to annotation for this statistical inquiry.

Each annotator was tasked with evaluating whether the summaries generated by the T5 model effectively encapsulated the same information as the combination of the abstract and the citing statements. The first annotator affirmed that 374 samples achieved this concurrence, the second annotator concurred with 368, and the third annotator with 371.

When comparing the assessments of the first and second annotators, it was determined they agreed that 368 samples were appropriately summarized, while 16 were not, resulting in a substantial Cohen's κ of 0.89. In the comparison between the second and third annotators, a significant concurrence emerged for 396 samples, where 368 were accurately summarized, and 28 were not, yielding κ value of 0.93. Similarly, when examining the assessments of the first and third annotators, agreement was established for 398 summaries, with 370 being correctly summarized and 27 not, resulting in κ of 0.94.

Supervising the Centroid Baseline for Extractive Multi-Document Summarization

Simão Gonçalves[ᵖ] **Gonçalo Correia**[ᵖ] **Diogo Pernes**[ᵖ,ᶠ] **Afonso Mendes**[ᵖ]
[ᵖ]Priberam Labs, Alameda D. Afonso Henriques, 41, 2°, 1000-123 Lisboa, Portugal
[ᶠ]Faculdade de Engenharia da Universidade do Porto, Porto, Portugal
{simao.goncalves, goncalo.correia, diogo.pernes, amm}@priberam.pt

Abstract

The centroid method is a simple approach for extractive multi-document summarization and many improvements to its pipeline have been proposed. We further refine it by adding a beam search process to the sentence selection and also a centroid estimation attention model that leads to improved results. We demonstrate this in several multi-document summarization datasets, including in a multilingual scenario.

1 Introduction

Multi-document summarization (MDS) addresses the need to condense content from multiple source documents into concise and coherent summaries while preserving the essential context and meaning. Abstractive techniques, which involve generating novel text to summarize source documents, have gained traction in recent years (Liu and Lapata, 2019; Jin et al., 2020; Xiao et al., 2022), following the advent of large pre-trained generative transformers. However, their effectiveness in summarizing multiple documents remains challenged. This is attributed not only to the long input context imposed by multiple documents but also to a notable susceptibility to factual inconsistencies. In abstractive methods, this is more pronounced when compared to their extractive counterparts due to the hallucination-proneness of large language models.

Extractive approaches, on the other hand, tackle this problem by identifying and selecting the most important sentences or passages from the given documents to construct a coherent summary. Extractive MDS usually involves a sentence importance estimation step (Hong and Nenkova, 2014; Cao et al., 2015; Cho et al., 2019), in which sentences from the source document are scored according to their relevance and redundancy with respect to the remaining sentences. Then, the summary is built by selecting a set of sentences achieving high relevance and low redundancy. The centroid-based method (Radev et al., 2000) is a cheap unsupervised solution in which each cluster of documents is represented by a centroid that consists of the sum of the TF-IDF representations of all the sentences within the cluster and the sentences are ranked by their cosine similarity to the centroid vector. While the original method is a baseline that can be easily surpassed, subsequent enhancements have been introduced to make it a more competitive yet simple approach (Rossiello et al., 2017; Gholipour Ghalandari, 2017; Lamsiyah et al., 2021).

In this work, we refine the centroid method even further: i) we utilize multilingual sentence embeddings to enable summarization of clusters of documents in various languages; ii) we employ beam search for sentence selection, leading to a more exhaustive exploration of the candidate space and ultimately enhancing summary quality; iii) we leverage recently proposed large datasets for multi-document summarization by adding supervision to the centroid estimation process. To achieve this, we train an attention-based model to approximate the oracle centroid obtained from the ground-truth target summary, leading to significant ROUGE-score improvements in mono and multilingual settings. To the best of our knowledge, we are the first to tackle the problem within a truly multilingual framework, enabling the summarization of a cluster of documents in different languages.[1]

2 Related Work

Typical supervised methods for extractive summarization involve training a model to predict sentence saliency, i.e. a model learns to score sentences in a document with respect to the target summary, either by direct match in case an extractive target is available or constructed (Svore et al., 2007; Woodsend and Lapata, 2012; Mendes et al., 2019) or by maximizing a similarity score (*e.g.*, ROUGE)

[1] https://github.com/Priberam/cera-summ

Proceedings of The 4th New Frontiers in Summarization Workshop, pages 87–96
December 6, 2023 ©2023 Association for Computational Linguistics

with respect to the abstractive target summaries (Narayan et al., 2018). Attempts to reduce redundancy exploit the notion of maximum marginal relevance (MMR; Carbonell and Goldstein, 1998; McDonald, 2007) or are coverage-based (Gillick et al., 2008; Almeida and Martins, 2013), seeking a set of sentences that cover as many concepts as possible while respecting a predefined budget. During inference, the model is then able to classify the sentences with respect to their salience, selecting the highest-scored sentences for the predicted summary. Rather than training a model that predicts salience for each individual sentence, we employ a supervised model that directly predicts an overarching summary representation, specifically predicting the centroid vector of the desired summary. Training this model can thus be more direct when training with abstractive summaries (as is the case in most summarization datasets), since computing the reference summary centroid is independent of whether the target is extractive or abstractive.

Regarding enhancements to the centroid method for extractive MDS, Rossiello et al. (2017) refined it by substituting the TF-IDF representations with word2vec embeddings (Mikolov et al., 2013), and further incorporated a redundancy filter into the algorithm. Gholipour Ghalandari (2017), on the other hand, retained the utilization of TF-IDF sentence representations but improved the sentence selection process. Recently, Lamsiyah et al. (2021) introduced modifications to the sentence scoring mechanism, incorporating novelty and position scores, and evaluated a diverse array of sentence embeddings with the proposed methodology, including contextual embeddings provided by ELMo (Peters et al., 2018) and BERT (Devlin et al., 2019).

While there have been initiatives to foster research in multilingual extractive MDS (Giannakopoulos, 2013; Giannakopoulos et al., 2015), the proposed approaches (Litvak and Vanetik, 2013; Aries et al., 2015; Huang et al., 2016) are only language-agnostic, requiring all the documents within each cluster to be in the same language. In contrast, we address extractive MDS in a scenario where each cluster is multilingual.

3 Methodology

The pipeline of our proposed model is divided into two stages. In the first stage, we use an attention model to obtain a cluster representation that replaces the naive centroid obtained by averaging sentence embeddings of the documents in a cluster. The rationale behind this approach is that the contribution of each sentence to the cluster centroid should depend on its relevance to the cluster summary. In order to capture the whole cluster context, a sentence-level attention model is employed, assigning variable weights to each sentence embedding so as to approximate the resulting average to the centroid that would be obtained by averaging the sentence embeddings of the target summary. In the second stage, an adapted version of the greedy sentence selection algorithm from Gholipour Ghalandari (2017) for extractive MDS is used to select the sentences included in the predicted summary. This adapted version uses our proposed supervised centroid and also includes a beam search algorithm to better explore the space of candidate summaries.

3.1 Centroid Estimation

Gholipour Ghalandari (2017) builds a centroid by summing TF-IDF sentence representations of all the sentences that compose the cluster to summarize. In our research, we compute the centroid from a learnable weighted average of the contextual sentence embeddings, via an attention model.

Attention Model In our centroid estimation procedure, we use a pre-trained multilingual sentence transformer from Yang et al. (2020) to encode the sentences from the news articles, obtaining contextual embeddings $\boldsymbol{e}_k \in \mathbb{R}^d$, $k \in \{1, \dots, N\}$, for each of the N sentences in a cluster. Since it is often the case that the first sentences of a document are especially important for news summarization tasks, we add sentence-level learnable positional embeddings to the contextual embeddings at the input of the attention model. Specifically, given a cluster D comprising N sentences, we compute:

$$\boldsymbol{e}_{\text{pos},k} = \boldsymbol{e}_k + \boldsymbol{p}_{\text{pos}(k)}, \qquad (1)$$

where $\text{pos}(k)$ is the position within the respective document of the k-th sentence in the cluster and $\boldsymbol{p}_{\text{pos}(k)} \in \mathbb{R}^d$ is the corresponding learnable positional embedding. Each $\boldsymbol{e}_{\text{pos},k} \in \mathbb{R}^d$ is then concatenated with the mean-pool vector of the cluster,[2] denoted by $\overline{\boldsymbol{e}_{\text{pos}}} \in \mathbb{R}^d$, resulting in $\boldsymbol{e}'_{\text{pos},k} = \text{concat}(\boldsymbol{e}_{\text{pos},k}, \overline{\boldsymbol{e}_{\text{pos}}})$ for each sentence. This concatenation ensures that the computation of

[2]This is calculated by averaging the sentence embeddings within each document and then computing the mean of these individual document averages.

the attention weight for each position uses information from all the remaining positions. The vector $\boldsymbol{\beta} \in \mathbb{R}^N$ of attention weights is obtained as:

$$\boldsymbol{\beta} = \mathrm{softmax}\left(\mathrm{MLP}(\boldsymbol{e}'_{\mathrm{pos},1}), \ldots, \mathrm{MLP}(\boldsymbol{e}'_{\mathrm{pos},N})\right), \tag{2}$$

where MLP is a two-layer perceptron shared by all the positions. It has a single output neuron and a hidden layer with d units and a tanh activation.

After computing the attention weights for the cluster, we take the original sentence embeddings $\boldsymbol{e}_k$, $k \in \{1, \ldots, N\}$, and compute a weighted sum of these representations:

$$\boldsymbol{h} = \sum_{k=1}^{N} \beta_k \boldsymbol{e}_k. \tag{3}$$

Consequently, the resultant vector $\boldsymbol{h} \in \mathbb{R}^d$ is a convex combination of the input sentence embeddings. Since it is not guaranteed that the target centroid lies within this space, $\boldsymbol{h}$ is subsequently mapped to the output space through a linear layer, yielding an estimate $\hat{\boldsymbol{c}}_{\mathrm{attn}} \in \mathbb{R}^d$ of the centroid. Hereafter we refer to this attention model as **Ce**ntroid **R**egression **A**ttention (CeRA).

Interpolation The original (unsupervised) approach involves estimating the centroid by computing the average of all sentence representations $\boldsymbol{e}_k$ within a cluster, which has consistently demonstrated strong performance. Let $\overline{\boldsymbol{e}}_D$ represent this centroid for cluster D. To leverage the advantages of this effective technique, we introduce $\overline{\boldsymbol{e}}_D$ as a residual component to enhance the estimate produced by the attention model. Thus, our final centroid estimate is computed as:

$$\hat{\boldsymbol{c}} = \boldsymbol{\alpha} \odot \hat{\boldsymbol{c}}_{\mathrm{attn}} + (1 - \boldsymbol{\alpha}) \odot \overline{\boldsymbol{e}}_D, \tag{4}$$

where $\boldsymbol{\alpha} \in [0, 1]^d$ is a vector of interpolation weights and $\odot$ denotes elementwise multiplication. The interpolation weights are obtained from concatenating $\hat{\boldsymbol{c}}_{\mathrm{attn}}$ and $\overline{\boldsymbol{e}}_D$ and mapping it through an MLP of two linear linear layers with d units each. The two layers are interleaved with a ReLU activation and a sigmoid is applied at the output. We call the model with interpolation CeRAI.

Training Objective Finally, we minimize the cosine distance between the model predictions $\hat{\boldsymbol{c}}$ and the mean-pool of the sentence embeddings of the target summary $\boldsymbol{c}_{\mathrm{gold}}$.

3.2 Sentence Selection

Considering the cluster D and a set S with the current sentences in the summary. at each iteration of greedy sentence selection (Gholipour Ghalandari, 2017), we have

$$\boldsymbol{e}_{S\cup\{s\}} = \sum_{s'\in S} \boldsymbol{e}_{s'} + \boldsymbol{e}_s \tag{5}$$

for each sentence $s \in D \setminus S$. Then, the new sentence s^* to be included in the summary is

$$s^* = \arg\max_{s\in D\setminus S} \cos\mathrm{sim}(\boldsymbol{e}_{S\cup\{s\}}, \overline{\boldsymbol{e}}_D), \tag{6}$$

where $\cos\mathrm{sim}$ is the cosine similarity. The algorithm stops when the summary length reaches the specified budget.[3] As demonstrated in that work, redundancy is mitigated since the centroid is compared to the whole candidate summary $S \cup \{s\}$ at each iteration and not only to the new sentence s.

In our version of the algorithm, we not only estimate the cluster centroids as explained in §3.1, replacing $\overline{\boldsymbol{e}}_D$ by $\hat{\boldsymbol{c}}$ in equation (6), but also employ a beam search (BS) algorithm so that the space of candidate summaries is explored more thoroughly. Moreover, in order to exhaust the chosen budget, we add a final greedy search to do further improvements to the extracted summary. The procedure is defined in Algorithm 1, shown in Appendix A, and we describe it less formally below.

Beam Search The process begins by preselecting sentences, retaining only the first n sentences from each document. Beam search initiates by selecting the top B sentences with the highest similarity scores with the centroid, where B represents the beam size. In each subsequent iteration, the algorithm finds the highest-scoring B sentences on each beam, generating a total of B^2 candidates. Among these candidates, only the highest-ranked B sentences are retained. Suppose any of these sentences exceed the specified budget length for the summary. In that case, we preserve the corresponding previous state, and no further exploration is conducted on that beam. The beam search concludes when all candidate beams have exceeded the budget or when no more sentences are available.

Greedy Search To exhaust the specified budget and improve results, we add a greedy search of

[3] While the original algorithm would stop after the first sentence that exceeded the budget, we stop before it is exceeded, and thus we do not need truncation to respect the budget.

Method	Multi-News	WCEP-10	TAC2008	DUC2004
Oracle centroid	21.72 ± 0.33	28.54 ± 1.21	11.99 ± 1.32	10.29 ± 1.01
Gholipour Ghalandari	16.07 ± 0.26	15.09 ± 0.92	7.36 ± 1.15	6.82 ± 0.76
Lamsiyah et al.	13.92 ± 0.22	16.10 ± 0.96	7.91 ± 1.31	**7.80** ± 0.78
BS (*Ours*)	16.22 ± 0.25	15.64 ± 0.97	8.10 ± 1.32	7.03 ± 0.64
BS+GS (*Ours*)	16.70 ± 0.26	16.41 ± 0.91	8.16 ± 1.25	7.46 ± 0.83
CeRA (*Ours*)	17.98 ± 0.23	**17.46** ± 0.98	8.27 ± 1.26	7.31 ± 0.74
CeRAI (*Ours*)	**17.99** ± 0.27	17.24 ± 0.93	**8.37** ± 1.24	7.72 ± 0.77

Table 1: ROUGE-2 recall with 95% bootstrap confidence intervals of different extractive methods on the considered test sets. CeRA and CeRAI were only trained on the Multi-News training dataset.

sentences that are allowed within the word limit. The top-scoring B states from the beam search are used as starting points for this greedy search. Then, for each state, we greedily select the highest-scoring sentence that does not exceed the budget among the top T ranked sentences. This process iterates until either all of the top T ranked sentences would exceed the budget or there are no further sentences left for consideration.

4 Experimental Setup

Herein, we outline the methods, datasets, and evaluation metrics employed in our experiments.

Methods We compare our approaches with the centroid-based methods from Gholipour Ghalandari (2017) and Lamsiyah et al. (2021), described in §2. To be consistent with the remaining methods, the approach by Gholipour Ghalandari (2017) was implemented on top of contextual sentence embeddings instead of TF-IDF. Additionally, we perform ablation evaluations in three scenarios: i) a scenario (BS) where we do not use the centroid estimation model (§3.1) and rely solely on the beam search for the sentence selection step (§3.2); ii) a scenario (BS+GS) identical to the previous one, except that we perform the greedy search step after the beam search; iii) two scenarios (CeRAI and CeRA) where we utilize the centroid estimation model with and without incorporating interpolation, and apply the BS+GS algorithm on the predicted centroid. The "Oracle centroid" upperbounds our approaches, since it results from applying BS+GS on the mean-pool of the sentence embeddings of the target summary, $\mathbf{c}_{\text{gold}}$, as the cluster centroid. Appendix C provides additional details about data processing and hyperparameters.

Datasets We used four English datasets, Multi-News (Fabbri et al., 2019), WCEP-10 (Ghalandari et al., 2020; Xiao et al., 2022), TAC2008, and DUC2004, and one multilingual dataset, CrossSum (Bhattacharjee et al., 2023), in our experiments. We used the centroid-estimation models trained on Multi-News to evaluate CeRA and CeRAI on WCEP-10, TAC2008, and DUC2004 since these datasets do not provide training splits. CrossSum was conceived for single-document cross-lingual summarization, so we had to adapt it for multilingual MDS. This adaptation results in clusters that encompass documents in multiple languages, with each cluster being associated with a single reference summary containing sentences in various languages. We explain this procedure and provide further details about each dataset in Appendix B.

Evaluation Metrics We evaluate ROUGE scores (Lin, 2004) in all the experiments. When evaluating models in the multilingual setting, we translated both the reference summaries and the extracted summaries into English prior to ROUGE computation. As we optimized for R2-R on the validation sets, we report it as our main metric in Tables 1 and 2. The remaining scores are shown in Appendix D.

5 Results

Monolingual Setting The ROUGE-2 recall (R2-R) of all the methods in the monolingual datasets are presented in Table 1. F1 scores and results for the other ROUGE variants are presented in Table 4, in Appendix D. The first observation is that BS alone outperforms Gholipour Ghalandari (2017) in all datasets, with additional improvements obtained when the greedy search step is also performed (BS+GD). This was expected since our approach explores the candidate space more thoroughly. The motivation for using a supervised centroid estimation model arose from the excellent ROUGE results obtained when using the target summaries to build the centroid ("Oracle centroid" in the tables), showing that an enhanced centroid estimation procedure could improve the results substantially. This is con-

Method	CrossSum	CrossSum-ZS
Oracle centroid	11.74 $\pm$ 0.55	14.91 $\pm$ 0.49
Gholipour Ghalandari	7.72 $\pm$ 0.43	10.03 $\pm$ 0.40
Lamsiyah et al.	8.01 $\pm$ 0.52	10.45 $\pm$ 0.46
BS (*Ours*)	7.74 $\pm$ 0.44	10.16 $\pm$ 0.40
BS+GS (*Ours*)	8.23 $\pm$ 0.43	10.85 $\pm$ 0.41
CeRA (*Ours*)	**9.65** $\pm$ 0.49	11.67 $\pm$ 0.41
CeRAI (*Ours*)	9.38 $\pm$ 0.50	**11.73** $\pm$ 0.43

Table 2: ROUGE-2 recall results with 95% bootstrap confidence intervals of different extractive methods on the multilingual test sets. The CrossSum set contains the same languages used for training the centroid estimation model, whereas CrossSum-ZS (*zero-shot*) consists of languages that were not present in the training data.

firmed by the two methods using the centroid estimation model (CeRA and CeRAI), which improve R2-R significantly in Multi-News and WCEP-10 and perform at least on par with Lamsiyah et al. (2021) in TAC2008 and DUC2004. It's also worth noting that CeRA and CeRAI were only trained on the Multi-News training set and nevertheless performed better or on par with the remaining baselines on the test sets of the remaining corpora. Incorporating the interpolation step (CeRAI) appears to yield supplementary enhancements compared to the non-interpolated version (CeRA) across various settings, which we attribute to this method adding regularization to the estimation process, improving results on harder scenarios.

Multilingual Setting The R2-R scores of all the methods in CrossSum can be found in Table 2, while additional results are in Table 5 of Appendix D. Once again, we observe the superiority of the centroid estimation models, CeRA and CeRAI, in comparison to all the remaining methods, with the variants with and without interpolation performing on par with each other. Most notably, these models prove to be useful even when tested with languages unseen during the training phase, underscoring their robustness and applicability in a zero-shot setting.

6 Conclusions

We enhanced the centroid method for multi-document summarization by extending a previous approach with a beam search followed by a greedy search. Additionally, we introduced a novel attention-based regression model for better centroid prediction. These improvements outperform existing methods across various datasets, including a multilingual setting, offering a robust solution for this challenging scenario. Regarding future work, we believe an interesting research direction would be to further explore using the supervised centroids obtained by the CeRA and CeRAI models, by having them as a proxy objective to obtain improved abstractive summaries.

Limitations

While we believe that our approach possesses merits, it is equally important to recognize its inherent limitations. Diverging from conventional centroid methods that operate entirely in an unsupervised manner, our centroid estimation model necessitates training with reference summaries. Nevertheless, its robustness to dataset shifts was demonstrated: the model trained on Multi-News consistently yielded strong results when assessed on different English datasets, and the model trained on a subset of languages from CrossSum displayed successful generalization to other languages.

Finally, our method introduces increased computational complexity. This arises from both the forward pass through the attention model and the proposed beam search algorithm, which incurs a greater computational cost compared to the original, simpler greedy approach proposed by Gholipour Ghalandari (2017).

Acknowledgements

This work is supported by the EU H2020 SELMA project (grant agreement No. 957017).

References

Miguel Almeida and André Martins. 2013. Fast and robust compressive summarization with dual decomposition and multi-task learning. In *Proceedings of the 51st Annual Meeting of the Association for Computational Linguistics (Volume 1: Long Papers)*, pages 196–206, Sofia, Bulgaria. Association for Computational Linguistics.

Abdelkrime Aries, Djamel Eddine Zegour, and Khaled Walid Hidouci. 2015. AllSummarizer system at MultiLing 2015: Multilingual single and multi-document summarization. In *Proceedings of the 16th Annual Meeting of the Special Interest Group on Discourse and Dialogue*, pages 237–244, Prague, Czech Republic. Association for Computational Linguistics.

Jimmy Lei Ba, Jamie Ryan Kiros, and Geoffrey E. Hinton. 2016. Layer normalization. *preprint arXiv:1607.06450*.

Abhik Bhattacharjee, Tahmid Hasan, Wasi Uddin Ahmad, Yuan-Fang Li, Yong-Bin Kang, and Rifat Shahriyar. 2023. CrossSum: Beyond English-centric cross-lingual summarization for 1,500+ language pairs. In *Proceedings of the 61st Annual Meeting of the Association for Computational Linguistics (Volume 1: Long Papers)*, pages 2541–2564, Toronto, Canada. Association for Computational Linguistics.

Steven Bird, Ewan Klein, and Edward Loper. 2009. *Natural language processing with Python: analyzing text with the natural language toolkit*. "O'Reilly Media, Inc.".

Ziqiang Cao, Furu Wei, Li Dong, Sujian Li, and Ming Zhou. 2015. Ranking with recursive neural networks and its application to multi-document summarization. In *Proceedings of the AAAI conference on artificial intelligence*, volume 29.

Jaime Carbonell and Jade Goldstein. 1998. The use of MMR, diversity-based reranking for reordering documents and producing summaries. In *Proceedings of the 21st annual international ACM SIGIR conference on Research and development in information retrieval*, pages 335–336.

Sangwoo Cho, Chen Li, Dong Yu, Hassan Foroosh, and Fei Liu. 2019. Multi-document summarization with determinantal point processes and contextualized representations. In *Proceedings of the 2nd Workshop on New Frontiers in Summarization*, pages 98–103, Hong Kong, China. Association for Computational Linguistics.

Jacob Devlin, Ming-Wei Chang, Kenton Lee, and Kristina Toutanova. 2019. BERT: Pre-training of deep bidirectional transformers for language understanding. In *Proceedings of the 2019 Conference of the North American Chapter of the Association for Computational Linguistics: Human Language Technologies, Volume 1 (Long and Short Papers)*, pages 4171–4186, Minneapolis, Minnesota. Association for Computational Linguistics.

Alexander Fabbri, Irene Li, Tianwei She, Suyi Li, and Dragomir Radev. 2019. Multi-news: A large-scale multi-document summarization dataset and abstractive hierarchical model. In *Proceedings of the 57th Annual Meeting of the Association for Computational Linguistics*, pages 1074–1084, Florence, Italy. Association for Computational Linguistics.

Angela Fan, Shruti Bhosale, Holger Schwenk, Zhiyi Ma, Ahmed El-Kishky, Siddharth Goyal, Mandeep Baines, Onur Celebi, Guillaume Wenzek, Vishrav Chaudhary, et al. 2021. Beyond english-centric multilingual machine translation. *The Journal of Machine Learning Research*, 22(1):4839–4886.

Demian Gholipour Ghalandari, Chris Hokamp, Nghia The Pham, John Glover, and Georgiana Ifrim. 2020. A large-scale multi-document summarization dataset from the wikipedia current events portal. *preprint arXiv:2005.10070.*

Demian Gholipour Ghalandari. 2017. Revisiting the centroid-based method: A strong baseline for multi-document summarization. In *Proceedings of the Workshop on New Frontiers in Summarization*, pages 85–90, Copenhagen, Denmark. Association for Computational Linguistics.

George Giannakopoulos. 2013. Multi-document multilingual summarization and evaluation tracks in ACL 2013 MultiLing workshop. In *Proceedings of the MultiLing 2013 Workshop on Multilingual Multi-document Summarization*, pages 20–28, Sofia, Bulgaria. Association for Computational Linguistics.

George Giannakopoulos, Jeff Kubina, John Conroy, Josef Steinberger, Benoit Favre, Mijail Kabadjov, Udo Kruschwitz, and Massimo Poesio. 2015. MultiLing 2015: Multilingual summarization of single and multi-documents, on-line fora, and call-center conversations. In *Proceedings of the 16th Annual Meeting of the Special Interest Group on Discourse and Dialogue*, pages 270–274, Prague, Czech Republic. Association for Computational Linguistics.

Daniel Gillick, Benoit Favre, and Dilek Hakkani-Tür. 2008. The ICSI summarization system at TAC 2008. In *Proceedings of Text Understanding Conference*.

Tahmid Hasan, Abhik Bhattacharjee, Md. Saiful Islam, Kazi Mubasshir, Yuan-Fang Li, Yong-Bin Kang, M. Sohel Rahman, and Rifat Shahriyar. 2021. XL-sum: Large-scale multilingual abstractive summarization for 44 languages. In *Findings of the Association for Computational Linguistics: ACL-IJCNLP 2021*, pages 4693–4703, Online. Association for Computational Linguistics.

Kai Hong and Ani Nenkova. 2014. Improving the estimation of word importance for news multi-document summarization. In *Proceedings of the 14th Conference of the European Chapter of the Association for Computational Linguistics*, pages 712–721, Gothenburg, Sweden. Association for Computational Linguistics.

Taiwen Huang, Lei Li, and Yazhao Zhang. 2016. Multilingual multi-document summarization with enhanced hlda features. In *Chinese Computational Linguistics and Natural Language Processing Based on Naturally Annotated Big Data*, pages 299–312, Cham. Springer International Publishing.

Hanqi Jin, Tianming Wang, and Xiaojun Wan. 2020. Multi-granularity interaction network for extractive and abstractive multi-document summarization. In *Proceedings of the 58th Annual Meeting of the Association for Computational Linguistics*, pages 6244–6254, Online. Association for Computational Linguistics.

Salima Lamsiyah, Abdelkader El Mahdaouy, Bernard Espinasse, and Saïd El Alaoui Ouatik. 2021. An unsupervised method for extractive multi-document summarization based on centroid approach and sentence embeddings. *Expert Systems with Applications*, 167:114152.

Chin-Yew Lin. 2004. ROUGE: A package for automatic evaluation of summaries. In *Text Summarization Branches Out*, pages 74–81, Barcelona, Spain. Association for Computational Linguistics.

Marina Litvak and Natalia Vanetik. 2013. Multilingual multi-document summarization with POLY2. In *Proceedings of the MultiLing 2013 Workshop on Multilingual Multi-document Summarization*, pages 45–49, Sofia, Bulgaria. Association for Computational Linguistics.

Yang Liu and Mirella Lapata. 2019. Hierarchical transformers for multi-document summarization. In *Proceedings of the 57th Annual Meeting of the Association for Computational Linguistics*, pages 5070–5081, Florence, Italy. Association for Computational Linguistics.

Ryan McDonald. 2007. A study of global inference algorithms in multi-document summarization. In *European Conference on Information Retrieval*, pages 557–564. Springer.

Afonso Mendes, Shashi Narayan, Sebastião Miranda, Zita Marinho, André F. T. Martins, and Shay B. Cohen. 2019. Jointly extracting and compressing documents with summary state representations. In *Proceedings of the 2019 Conference of the North American Chapter of the Association for Computational Linguistics: Human Language Technologies, Volume 1 (Long and Short Papers)*, pages 3955–3966, Minneapolis, Minnesota. Association for Computational Linguistics.

Tomas Mikolov, Ilya Sutskever, Kai Chen, Greg S Corrado, and Jeff Dean. 2013. Distributed representations of words and phrases and their compositionality. In *Advances in Neural Information Processing Systems*, volume 26. Curran Associates, Inc.

Shashi Narayan, Shay B. Cohen, and Mirella Lapata. 2018. Ranking sentences for extractive summarization with reinforcement learning. In *Proceedings of the 2018 Conference of the North American Chapter of the Association for Computational Linguistics: Human Language Technologies, Volume 1 (Long Papers)*, pages 1747–1759, New Orleans, Louisiana. Association for Computational Linguistics.

Matthew E. Peters, Mark Neumann, Mohit Iyyer, Matt Gardner, Christopher Clark, Kenton Lee, and Luke Zettlemoyer. 2018. Deep contextualized word representations. In *Proceedings of the 2018 Conference of the North American Chapter of the Association for Computational Linguistics: Human Language Technologies, Volume 1 (Long Papers)*, pages 2227–2237, New Orleans, Louisiana. Association for Computational Linguistics.

Dragomir R. Radev, Hongyan Jing, and Malgorzata Budzikowska. 2000. Centroid-based summarization of multiple documents: sentence extraction, utility-based evaluation, and user studies. In *NAACL-ANLP 2000 Workshop: Automatic Summarization*.

Gaetano Rossiello, Pierpaolo Basile, and Giovanni Semeraro. 2017. Centroid-based text summarization through compositionality of word embeddings. In *Proceedings of the MultiLing 2017 Workshop on Summarization and Summary Evaluation Across Source Types and Genres*, pages 12–21, Valencia, Spain. Association for Computational Linguistics.

Krysta Svore, Lucy Vanderwende, and Christopher Burges. 2007. Enhancing single-document summarization by combining RankNet and third-party sources. In *Proceedings of the 2007 Joint Conference on Empirical Methods in Natural Language Processing and Computational Natural Language Learning (EMNLP-CoNLL)*, pages 448–457, Prague, Czech Republic. Association for Computational Linguistics.

Kristian Woodsend and Mirella Lapata. 2012. Multiple aspect summarization using integer linear programming. In *Proceedings of the 2012 Joint Conference on Empirical Methods in Natural Language Processing and Computational Natural Language Learning*, pages 233–243, Jeju Island, Korea. Association for Computational Linguistics.

Wen Xiao, Iz Beltagy, Giuseppe Carenini, and Arman Cohan. 2022. PRIMERA: Pyramid-based masked sentence pre-training for multi-document summarization. In *Proceedings of the 60th Annual Meeting of the Association for Computational Linguistics (Volume 1: Long Papers)*, pages 5245–5263, Dublin, Ireland. Association for Computational Linguistics.

Yinfei Yang, Daniel Cer, Amin Ahmad, Mandy Guo, Jax Law, Noah Constant, Gustavo Hernandez Abrego, Steve Yuan, Chris Tar, Yun-hsuan Sung, Brian Strope, and Ray Kurzweil. 2020. Multilingual universal sentence encoder for semantic retrieval. In *Proceedings of the 58th Annual Meeting of the Association for Computational Linguistics: System Demonstrations*, pages 87–94, Online. Association for Computational Linguistics.

A Sentence Selection Algorithm

Algorithm 1 Sentence Selection

Require: Cluster D, centroid $\hat{\mathbf{c}}$, summary budget ℓ, number of sentences n to pre-select, beam size B, number of candidates T for greedy search.

$D_n \leftarrow$ select-first(D, n)
$\pi, \pi_{\text{next}}, \pi_{\text{bs}} \leftarrow$ empty list
while $\exists b$: length$(\pi_{\text{next}}[b]) < \ell$ **do**: ▷ Beam Search
    $\pi_{\text{next}} \leftarrow \text{BS}_{\text{step}}(\pi, D_n, B, \hat{\mathbf{c}})$ [4]
    if $\exists b$: length$(\pi_{\text{next}}[b]) > \ell$ **then**
        π_{bs}.append(π)
    end if
    $\pi \leftarrow \forall \pi_{\text{next}}[b]$: length$(\pi_{\text{next}}[b]) \leq \ell$
end while
$\pi_{\text{best}} \leftarrow$ highest-scored B states in π_{bs} (sorted)
for $b = 1, 2, \ldots, B$ **do**: ▷ Greedy Search
    $t \leftarrow 0$
    $D'_n \leftarrow D_n \setminus \pi_{\text{best}}[b]$
    while $t < T$ **do**:
        $s^* \leftarrow \arg\max_{s \in D'_n} \cos\text{sim}(\boldsymbol{e}_{\pi_{\text{best}}[b] \cup \{s\}}, \hat{\mathbf{c}})$
        $\pi'_{\text{best}}[b] \leftarrow \pi_{\text{best}}[b] \cup \{s^*\}$
        if length$(\pi'_{\text{best}}[b]) \leq \ell$ **then**:
            $\pi_{\text{best}}[b] \leftarrow \pi'_{\text{best}}[b]$
            $t \leftarrow 0$
        else:
            $t \leftarrow t + 1$
        end if
        $D'_n \leftarrow D'_n \setminus \{s^*\}$
    end while
end for
return $S \leftarrow$ highest-scored state in π_{best}

B Datasets

We now describe each of the datasets used for evaluation and explain how we have adapted CrossSum for the task of MDS.

Multi-News The Multi-News dataset (Fabbri et al., 2019) is a large-scale dataset for MDS of news articles. It contains up to 10 documents per cluster and more than 50 thousand clusters divided into training, validation, and test splits. There is a single human-written reference summary for each cluster.

WCEP-10 This dataset (Ghalandari et al., 2020; Xiao et al., 2022) consists of short human-written target summaries extracted from the Wikipedia Current Events Portal (WCEP). Each news cluster associated with a certain event is paired with a single reference summary, and there are at most 10 documents per cluster. The dataset comprises 1022 clusters, all of which are used for testing.

TAC2008 This is a multi-reference dataset introduced by the Text Analysis Conference (TAC)[5]. It provides no training nor validation sets and the test set consists of 48 news clusters, each with 10 related documents and 4 human-written summaries as references.

DUC2004 Another multi-reference news summarization dataset[6] designed and used for testing only. It contains 50 clusters with 10 documents and 4 human-written reference summaries each.

CrossSum To assess the performance of the models in a multilingual context, we have adapted the CrossSum dataset (Bhattacharjee et al., 2023) for the task of MDS. Initially designed for cross-lingual summarization, this dataset offers document-summary pairs for more than 1500 language directions. The dataset is derived from pairs of articles sourced from the multilingual summarization dataset XL-Sum (Hasan et al., 2021). Notably, these pairings were established using an automatic similarity metric, resulting in many pairs covering similar topics rather than the exact same stories, rendering it well-suited MDS.

To tailor this dataset for our specific task, we began by selecting the data from a predefined subset of the languages. Subsequently, we aggregated the documents into clusters, taking into account their pairings. For instance, if document A was paired with document B and document B was paired with document C, then A, B, and C would belong to the same cluster. Clusters containing only one document were discarded. For obtaining multilingual reference summaries for each cluster, we interleaved the sentences from the individual summaries until we reached a predefined limit of 100 words. We have built training, validation, and test sets using data in English, Spanish, and French, and another test set using data in Portuguese, Russian, and Turkish to evaluate our model in a zero-shot

[4] BS_{step} denotes a step of the usual beam search algorithm. Details omitted for brevity.

[5] https://tac.nist.gov

[6] https://duc.nist.gov

setting. Statistics about each split are presented in Table 3.

C Experimental Details

Data Processing To ensure a fair comparison, all the models we evaluated used the same sentence representations, specifically, sentence embeddings obtained from the `distiluse-base-multilingual-cased-v2`[7] sentence encoder (Yang et al., 2020).

For monolingual datasets, the documents were split into sentences using `sent_tokenize` from the NLTK library (Bird et al., 2009). For CrossSum, we used `SentSplitter` from the multilingual ICU-tokenizer.[8] Regular expressions were applied to replace redundant white spaces and excessive paragraphs and empty sentences were excluded. Before sentence selection (Algorithm 1), the data goes through a second processing step, during which duplicate sentences and sentences that individually exceed the summary budget are eliminated.

When evaluating models in CrossSum, we translated both the reference summaries and the extracted summaries into English prior to ROUGE computation. All the translations were performed using the M2M-100 12-billion-parameter model (Fan et al., 2021).

The following word-limit budgets were used by all models: 230 words for the Multi-News dataset, 100 words for TAC2008, DUC2004 and CrossSum, and 50 words for WCEP-10.[9]

Hyperparameters The hyperparameters for the beam search-based methods were tuned by running a grid search on the BS+GS approach on the Multi-News validation set. For the number of sentences n, odd numbers from 1 to 9 were tested. For the beam width B values 1,5, and 9 were examined, and regarding the number of candidates T, values 1,5, and 9 were considered. The values that maximized R2-R on this validation set were n = 9, B=5, and T=9. In all of our experiments, these were the values we considered for the parameters. Note that for the BS method only n and B are relevant.

The hyperparameters of the centroid estimation model used in CeRA were obtained by random search on Multi-News. The hyperparameters yielding the highest R2-R score on the validation set for the produced summaries were kept. The CeRAI model was trained using the optimal hyperparameters found for CeRA. The optimal parameters were: *batch size* = 2, *learning rate* = 5×10^{-4}, and *number of positional encodings* = 35. We utilized the Adam optimizer with a multi-step learning rate scheduler configured with *step size* = 3 and $\gamma = 0.1$.

Implementation Details Our CeRA and CeRAI models used early stopping, where the stopping criteria metric was based on R2-R. Layer normalization (Ba et al., 2016) was applied on the input data before adding the positional information to it and before passing the data through the last linear layer that transforms $\boldsymbol{h}$ (equation (3)) into $\hat{c}_{\text{attn}}$ in the CeRA and CeRAI models. We have also normalized the input data to have a unit L2 norm.

D Additional Results

The ROUGE-1/2/L recall and F1 scores obtained by all the methods in the monolingual datasets are shown in Table 4. Table 5 presents the same quantities for the multilingual case.

[7] `https://huggingface.co/sentence-transformers/distiluse-base-multilingual-cased-v2`

[8] `https://pypi.org/project/icu-tokenizer`

[9] We used ROUGE 1.5.5 toolkit with the following arguments: `-n 4 -m -2 4 -l budget -u -c 95 -r 1000 -f A -p 0.5 -t 0 -a`

Split	Languages	#Clusters	#Docs per cluster	Avg #sentences per doc	Avg #words per summary
Train	en, es, fr	6541	2–10	38.5 ± 28.8	52.5 ± 16.1
Val	en, es, fr	889	2–6	34.4 ± 27.4	52.3 ± 15.5
Test	en, es, fr	853	2–6	36.6 ± 35.4	52.2 ± 16.2
Test-ZS	pt, ru, tr	933	2–5	23.4 ± 21.1	60.2 ± 20.8

Table 3: CrossSum: statistics of each split. Averages are indicated with standard deviations.

Test set	Method	R1-R	R1-F	R2-R	R2-F	RL-R	RL-F
Multi-News	Oracle centroid	54.26	50.36	21.72	20.02	24.33	22.42
	Gholipour Ghalandari	47.91	45.64	16.07	15.16	21.41	20.24
	Lamsiyah et al.	44.91	43.02	13.93	13.18	20.56	19.53
	BS (*Ours*)	48.34	45.81	16.22	15.24	21.34	20.08
	BS+GS (*Ours*)	49.54	45.98	16.70	15.36	21.81	20.08
	CeRA (*Ours*)	50.75	47.07	17.98	16.52	**22.69**	20.86
	CeRAI (*Ours*)	**50.76**	**47.08**	**17.99**	**16.53**	**22.69**	**20.87**
WCEP-10	Oracle centroid	58.72	44.94	28.54	21.50	42.38	31.94
	Gholipour Ghalandari	41.26	35.09	15.09	12.61	29.42	24.86
	Lamsiyah et al.	41.65	**35.62**	16.10	**13.38**	30.53	**25.75**
	BS (*Ours*)	43.48	35.07	15.64	12.42	30.49	24.44
	BS+GS (*Ours*)	46.23	34.72	16.41	12.05	31.85	23.60
	CeRA (*Ours*)	**47.14**	35.23	**17.46**	12.65	**33.03**	24.28
	CeRAI (*Ours*)	46.85	35.17	17.24	12.59	32.81	24.24
TAC2008	Oracle centroid	41.07	42.02	11.99	12.26	20.66	21.11
	Gholipour Ghalandari	32.00	34.38	7.36	7.91	16.64	17.87
	Lamsiyah et al.	31.00	33.75	7.91	**8.65**	16.65	18.16
	BS (*Ours*)	33.93	35.62	8.10	8.53	17.62	**18.50**
	BS+GS (*Ours*)	**35.12**	**35.98**	8.16	8.34	**17.99**	18.40
	CeRA (*Ours*)	34.43	35.07	8.27	8.42	17.35	17.66
	CeRAI (*Ours*)	34.44	35.11	**8.37**	8.52	17.73	18.06
DUC2004	Oracle centroid	39.93	41.10	10.29	10.60	19.48	20.05
	Gholipour Ghalandari	32.82	35.86	6.82	7.48	16.00	17.51
	Lamsiyah et al.	32.81	36.03	**7.80**	**8.61**	16.66	**18.34**
	BS (*Ours*)	34.01	36.20	7.03	7.51	16.35	17.41
	BS+GS (*Ours*)	35.11	36.37	7.46	7.74	**16.98**	17.60
	CeRA (*Ours*)	34.88	36.06	7.31	7.56	16.67	17.23
	CeRAI (*Ours*)	**35.16**	**36.38**	7.72	7.99	16.89	17.48

Table 4: ROUGE-1/2/L recall and F1 results of different extractive methods on the considered monolingual test sets.

Test set	Method	R1-R	R1-F	R2-R	R2-F	RL-R	RL-F
CrossSum	Oracle centroid	46.86	31.85	11.74	7.93	27.64	18.57
	Gholipour Ghalandari	38.64	27.88	7.72	5.56	23.30	16.65
	Lamsiyah et al.	37.89	27.53	8.01	5.77	23.81	17.13
	BS (*Ours*)	39.24	27.83	7.74	5.48	23.60	16.53
	BS+GS (*Ours*)	40.78	27.71	8.23	5.57	24.42	16.39
	CeRA (*Ours*)	**42.45**	**28.89**	**9.65**	**6.52**	**25.64**	**17.27**
	CeRAI (*Ours*)	42.31	28.73	9.38	6.31	25.55	17.15
CrossSum-ZS	Oracle centroid	50.55	37.30	14.91	11.00	28.90	21.08
	Gholipour Ghalandari	41.70	32.65	10.03	7.82	24.52	19.02
	Lamsiyah et al.	41.14	32.39	10.45	8.17	24.81	19.31
	BS (*Ours*)	42.53	32.65	10.16	7.81	24.87	18.90
	BS+GS (*Ours*)	44.36	32.65	10.85	7.99	25.74	18.74
	CeRA (*Ours*)	**45.44**	**33.43**	11.67	8.57	**26.52**	**19.30**
	CeRAI (*Ours*)	45.37	33.38	**11.73**	**8.62**	26.51	19.26

Table 5: ROUGE-1/2/L recall and F1 results of different extractive methods on the considered multilingual test sets.

DebateKG – Automatic Policy Debate Case Creation with Semantic Knowledge Graphs

Allen Roush
Plailabs
allen@plailabs.com

David Mezzetti
NeuML
david.mezzetti@neuml.com

Abstract

Recent work within the Argument Mining community has shown the applicability of Natural Language Processing systems for solving problems found within competitive debate. One of the most important tasks within competitive debate is for debaters to create high quality debate cases. We show that effective debate cases can be constructed using constrained shortest path traversals on Argumentative Semantic Knowledge Graphs. We study this potential in the context of a type of American Competitive Debate, called "Policy Debate", which already has a large scale dataset targeting it called "DebateSum". We significantly improve upon DebateSum by introducing 53180 new examples, as well as further useful metadata for every example, to the dataset. We leverage the txtai semantic search and knowledge graph toolchain to produce and contribute 9 semantic knowledge graphs built on this dataset. We create a unique method for evaluating which knowledge graphs are better in the context of producing policy debate cases. A demo which automatically generates debate cases, along with all other code and the Knowledge Graphs, are open-sourced and made available to the public here: https://huggingface.co/spaces/Hellisotherpeople/DebateKG

1 Introduction

1.1 Policy Debate

Persuasion has been of interest to humans since we first began communicating with each other. The formal process of using argumentation and rhetoric to convince others to see in one's own way is known as "debate". With varying levels of formality and intensity, these debates happen all around us every day.

More formalized, competitive forms of debate are both highly educational and integral to the formation of a lawful and just society. There is a long and time-honored tradition of academic institutions and news organizations facilitating competitive debate. Many organizations and associations organize debate tournaments according to their differing traditions and rule sets.

Some types of debate are more suited to be assisted with Natural Language Processing systems than others. A popular form of competitive debate done predominantly within United States high schools and universities is called "Policy Debate". Policy Debate maintains one extremely broad and open-ended topic over a whole year, and challenges teams to be ready to either affirm any plan which implements the topic, or to be ready to explain why the opposing teams plan is a bad idea.

Policy Debate is a highly technical form of debate, which puts relatively little emphasis on the aesthetic quality of the speech act, and correspondingly strong emphasis on the quality of the delivered evidence and the delivered argumentation around it. For this reason, Policy Debate rewards teams who can present the maximum amount of evidence possible during their limited speaking time. This leads to a peculiar phenomenon known as "speed reading" or "spreading" which is normalized among most serious competitors. While Policy Debate idiosyncrasies may end up making it less amicable for the general public to watch than other forms, those very same traits make it a uniquely good source of data for NLP systems which generate high quality debate cases.

Proceedings of The 4th New Frontiers in Summarization Workshop, pages 97–104
December 6, 2023 ©2023 Association for Computational Linguistics

1.2 Policy Debate Cases

Luckily, a large-scale dataset of Policy Debate evidence called DebateSum (Roush and Ballaji., 2020) exists. DebateSum includes all publically available Policy Debate evidence gathered from 2013-2019, which totals to over 180,000 pieces of evidence with corresponding abstractive and extractive summaries alongside rich metadata such as the citation author and word counts.

Beyond its original targeted task of queryable word-level extractive summarization, DebateSum is an excellent dataset for the task of constructing Policy Debate cases. This is because most Policy Debate cases are highly standardized. In almost every Policy Debate round, each debater carefully reads a set of around 3-12 pieces of evidence, starting first with slowly reading the abstractive summary of the evidence (the "argument"), then formulaically reading the evidence citation, and then finally speed reading the extractive summary of the evidence that supports the argument. Moving from each piece of evidence to the next can sometimes be so imperceptible that debaters are instructed to add a slow verbal "next" to their speeches in-between each piece of evidence. Each piece of evidence is likely to be highly related to the previous piece, as they are being chained together to advance the larger narrative of the debate case. This extractive format for debate case construction can be naturally performed by NLP systems which leverage ideas from the Information Retrieval, Graph Analysis, and Distributional Semantics communities.

1.3 Semantic Knowledge Graphs

Knowledge Graphs are systems which store information about entities and relates them to each other using (often weighted) edges which show the relationships between each entity. We denote Knowledge Graphs, where each entity consists of documents or sentences, and where weighted edges are constructed between each based on their semantic similarity to each other as "Semantic Knowledge Graphs".

1.4 txtai

Computing the semantic similarity between each entity and every other entity is an ideal place to leverage a large scale language model. Approximate Nearest Neighbor (ANN) Systems unlock viable semantic search of these entities, and storing and querying these is a natural place to leverage a database. We are fortunate in that software which does all of these things already exists, and it is called "txtai".

Txtai is a python software package for building AI powered semantic search applications. Txtai features support for a wide variety of backends to power its aforementioned components. Txtai is a natural choice for building Semantic Knowledge Graphs.

2 Innovations Introduced

In this work, we introduce several innovations related to automatic Policy Debate case generation.

2.1 DebateSum

We significantly improve the existing DebateSum dataset by adding the most recent three additional years of evidence (2020-2022) using the same preprocessing tools as discussed in Roush and Ballaji (2020). This totals to an addition of 53,180 number of documents, bringing the total number of documents within DebateSum to 240,566.

We also add further metadata columns, indicating the source DebateCamp, the broad type of argument, and the topic-year, for all documents within DebateSum. The type of the argument, designated as the "tag", This metadata was extracted from the "openCaselist[1]" project. Figure 1 shows how this metadata was represented on openCaselist.

The additional metadata is particularly useful for more fine-grained information retrieval (e.g. "Give me all evidence about the environment from Gonzaga debate camp in 2013") as well as for leveraging information about the type of debate argument (e.g. "Give me an argument about why individual states should do the plan from the arguments labeled as counterplans").

2.2 Contributed Semantic Graphs

We use txtai to build 9 Semantic Knowledge Graphs, which differ based on which column of DebateSum was indexed semantically, and on the language model underlying language model used

[1] openCaselist is a continuation of the Open Evidence project and it can be accessed here: https://opencaselist.com/

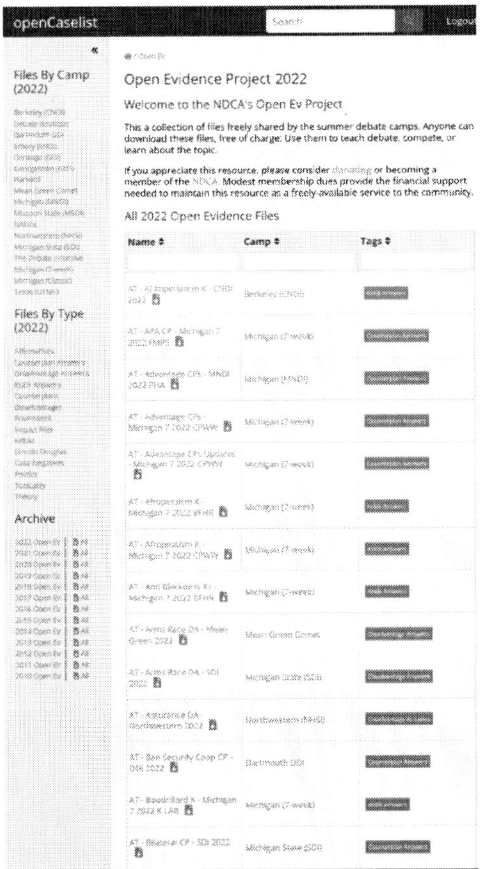

Figure 1: The added metadata to DebateSum was parsed from tables on openCaselist, which associates each debate document with its camp, its tag (argument types), and its year.

for similarity calculations. We leave all settings at their defaults during graph construction, which means that networkx is used for the graph backend, huggingface for the language models, faiss for the ANN index, and sqlite for the database. A table of these contributed models is presented in Appendix 1.

Txtai automatically does topic modeling on each graph using the Louvain (Blondel et al, 2008) community detection algorithm. This data is stored as further information within the graph and unlocks a powerful way to constrain the topics of the generated arguments.

2.3 DebateKG

The system that we demonstrate is called "DebateKG". DebateKG is a huggingface "space" webapp which leverages the contributed Semantic Knowledge Graphs to build Policy Debate cases. Users can specify a starting, an ending, and any

1. Warming is real and the product of anthropogenic carbon emissions.
2. Continuing consumption and growth kills the warming
3. Warming prevents drought and famine
4. Warming leads to marine life extinction
5. Extinction – oxygen depletion and food chains
6. Economic growth depletes water resources – recent studies
7. Economic development causes resource depletion
8. Air pollution causes extinction

Figure 2: A Policy Debate Case created with DebateKG. Arguments are shown. The citation, read-aloud extracts, and evidence are omitted for brevity. The first and final argument are the inputs supplied by the user. The highlighted portions show the tokens with the highest similarity to the previous argument, and functions as interpretability.

number of middle arguments. They can also specify any additional constraints, like on the topic, or on the contents of each piece of evidence. DebateKG extracts the evidence closest to the given arguments which meets the given constraints, and then connects these evidence examples together by calculating the constrained weighted shortest path between each evidence example. The portions of each extracted piece of evidence which match the previous portions are highlighted, which functions as a kind of interpretability.

Since there are usually many paths which connect the given pieces of evidence together, there are also many viable debate cases which can be generated. We allow users to generate all possible connected paths (all debate cases), and we enable users to manually display any possible debate case and to interpret the connections between the evidence within them. Besides the automatic case construction functionality, users can also individually query for evidence using txtai's built in semantic SQL language, which helps in the construction of input arguments. Figure 2 shows a sample generated debate case from DebateKG.

2.4 Summarization

This work on constructing policy debate cases from semantic knowledge graphs has important implications for summarization tasks. The abstractive and extractive summaries associated with each piece of evidence in DebateSum provide a rich source of training data for abstractive and extractive summarizers. The ability to find constrained shortest paths between evidence examples based on their semantic similarity is analogous to how multi-document summarization aims to find common themes and topics across documents. Additionally, the choice of which text columns to index semantically in the knowledge graphs parallels decisions made in query-focused summarization on what aspects of the text are most relevant to the query. The DebateKG demo itself extracts and concatenates relevant passages into coherent arguments, functioning as an extractive summarization system. The semantic knowledge graph techniques introduced in this work are highly relevant for developing more robust summarization systems. More broadly, the semantic knowledge graph approach introduced here offers representational and algorithmic tools for identifying salient semantics within text collections

3 Prior Work

Many others have looked at the relationships between Graph Methods and Argumentation.

The closest prior work to our own comes from IBM Project Debater (Slonim et al., 2021). They created a full debating system which they prominently pitted against champion parliamentary debaters. They defined a custom tailored, "simplified version" of the Parliamentary Debate style. Parliamentary Debate has dramatic differences compared to Policy Debate, namely that the topics are only known to each side 15 minutes ahead of time. As a result, Parliamentary Debate relies far less on evidence, usually only including small snippets as part of a larger speech. In Policy Debate, the vast majority of most of the opening speeches is recitation of extractive summaries of evidence for or against a position. This dramatically simplifies the required system for Policy Debate case generation. Project Debater utilizes many closed source models models, a massive but generalized corpus and requires significantly more compute resources than DebateKG to run.

Finally, Policy Debate is considered to be a more "rigorous style" of debate at its highest level than Parliamentary Debate, which requires dramatically more effort to participate in. An example of this can be found in the 2014-2015 National Parliamentary Tournament of Excellence (NPDA) tournament, the largest American college level parliamentary debate tournament, where the winning team had no prior Parliamentary Debate experience and was otherwise a good but not champion Policy Debate team [2]. Their defeated opponents had been undefeated for the prior 3 years that they competed in the national tournament.

Further work coming from IBM exists about Knowledge Graphs directly being used for Argument Generation (Khatib et al., 2021). Their work explores how to utilize KG encoded knowledge to fine-tune GPT-2 to generate arguments. Our system is extractive in nature, as it creates debate cases by chaining together evidence from DebateSum utilizing graph traversals. Extractive systems are far more appropriate for Policy Debate.

There is fascinating work that applies the idea of Graph Neural Networks for predicting the way that each member of a legislative branch will vote on an input motion (Sawhney et al., 2020). Our work does not try to predict how judges will vote based on any inputs, but instead generates debate cases given input arguments. Their work is in the context of elected officials, whereas ours is in the context high school and collegic competitive debate. There is also work related to trying to understand the arguments made within these legislative Parliamentary Debates (Tamper et al., 2022)

Knowledge Graphs have been utilized for fact checked arguments. ClaimsKG (Tchechmedjiev et al., 2019) is an example, which indexes a wide variety of fact checking websites and annotates them. DebateSum and its contributed KGs do not have fact checking information directly since it is considered the debaters job to convince the judge of the truth of each presented piece of evidence. DebateSum and DebateKG are also significantly larger in size than ClaimsKG and its training corpus.

Work related to automatically evaluating the quality of arguments using Knowledge Graphs exists (Dolz et al., 2022). In their work, they leverage a dataset of debate, the VivesDebate corpus, to identify if an argument is likely to "win". They also recognized the potential for graph

[2] A recording of that final debate round and results can be found here: https://www.youtube.com/watch?v=l9HJ6Iq6Vas

traversals to form arguments, or whole debate cases (see figures 2 and 3 from their work). VivesDebate is significantly smaller and less encompassing than DebateSum, and DebateSum does not have information about how successful the arguments within it are.

Other work, which recognizes the potential for paths within knowledge graphs to form arguments, exists (Das et al., 2017). The idea of using "debate dynamics" to present evidence for graph classification has been extensively explored (Hildebrandt et al., 2020). They imagine triple classification and link prediction in graphs as a figurative "debate game" between two reinforcement learning agents who extract "arguments" (paths) which support or oppose a hypothesis. A final binary classifier "judge" votes based on the presented "arguments". They show parallels within Graph Analysis algorithm development to the ideas that we present, but they evaluate this algorithm on non-argumentative datasets. To our knowledge, we are the first work to explore "arguments" (constrained paths) within Knowledge Graphs on an argumentative dataset.

4 Details

The DebateKG demo is hosted on huggingface[3]. In this section, we describe the details of DebateKG and its underlying Semantic Knowledge Graphs.

4.1 Underlying Language Models

Txtai supports several language modeling backends, the most modern of which is sentence transformers (Reimers and Gurevych., 2019). Besides having many pre-trained language models which are designed for Semantic Textual Similarity or for Sentence Modeling, any Transformer model can be transformed into a "sentence transformer" model with nothing more than a pooling layer added.

We choose three language models for building the Knowledge Graphs. The first is the recommended model from the sentence transformers documentation [4], "all-mpnet-base-v2". We are also curious about the potential usefulness of language models which are fine-tuned in a domain similar to DebateSum, such as the legal domain. We choose "legal-bert-base-uncased" (Chalkidis et al., 2020) for this reason, as it is trained on a diverse legal corpus. Finally, we are curious about language models which can model long sequences. We choose "allenai/longformer-base-4096" (Beltagy et al., 2020) due to its potential to model sequences up to 4096 tokens long directly.

4.2 Importance of Granularity

For each piece of evidence in DebateSum, there is an associated abstractive summary and biased extractive summary. Since at the time of writing, txtai and DebateKG can only semantically index one text column at a time, the choice of which column and at what granularity is highly important. There are merits and drawbacks to each approach. For this reason, we construct Graphs which index two of these columns (denoted with the prefixes "DebateKG-ext", and "DebateKG-abs"). We also construct graphs which index each individual sentence of the full document (denoted as "DebateKG-sent"). These graphs are significantly larger, but are potentially far more potent since the sentence transformers recommended models are designed for the sentence granularity and because the other two models are average pooled and subsequently long sequences dilute their embeddings.

4.3 Importance of Settings

DebateKG computes the semantic similarity between each entity, and connects the entities whose similarity is greater than a user-defined threshold. We use the default threshold of 0.10, and each entity has a limit of no more than 100 edges. Changes in these settings, such as lowering the threshold and increasing the entity limit, will result in more highly connected and correspondingly larger graphs.

4.4 Policy Debate Case Construction

The shortest paths, which minimizes the semantic distance between each input argument, are also

[3] The link to that demo is here: https://huggingface.co/spaces/Hellisotherpeople/DebateKG

[4] An analysis of the pretrained models can be found here: https://www.sbert.net/docs/pretrained_models.html

Policy Debate Arguments[5]. One or more of these Arguments can be concatenated to form Policy Debate Cases. The ideal Policy Debate Argument uses the minimum amount of spoken words. This enables competitors to make more arguments, and to make broader and stronger cases.

Beyond a naïve shortest path calculation on the whole graph, we can control how Debate Case are constructed by choosing to run these calculations on subgraphs. These subgraphs include only entities which fulfil a particular constraint – enabling things like arguments where all of the evidence stays on a particular topic, or which always includes a keyword, or even where the evidence isn't longer than a certain number of words.

Related to the idea of minimizing the number of words spoken out loud within each debate case, we can also modify the scoring function used within the shortest path calculations to account for and try to minimize the length of the evidences extracts. This has the advantage over selecting subgraphs of allowing for inclusion of long documents within the argument if they are actually the most appropriate.

4.5 Value of Knowledge Graphs

While an exhaustive analysis of these Knowledge Graphs is beyond the scope of this paper, it is important to recognize that techniques and algorithms from the Graph Analysis literature can be particularly illuminating. Centrality algorithms, like Pagerank (Page et al., 1998), will find evidence which is highly applicable to many arguments. Community detection, also known as clustering – finds evidence which is highly related to each other. A treasure trove of insights into DebateSum are unlocked for those willing to explore the Semantic Knowledge Graphs.

4.6 Connection to the Legal Domain

Policy debate focuses extensively on legal topics, as debaters must argue matters of policy frequently connected to the law. As such, the DebateSum dataset provides a trove of legal text spanning diverse issues. The constrained shortest path approach introduced mirrors legal research in finding related precedents and documents to build a broader argument. The graph structure encodes

Model	**Average Words in Case**
Mpnet-DebateKG-abs	406
Mpnet-DebateKG-ext	305
Mpnet-DebateKG-sent	760
legalbert-DebateKG-abs	502
legalbert-DebateKG-ext	**230**
legalbert-DebateKG-sent	709
longformer-DebateKG-abs	500
longformer-DebateKG-ext	457
longformer-DebateKG-sent	301

Table 1: Results of experiment on sample 10 arguments

useful semantics for legal information retrieval, while segmentation by sentence allows fine-grained modeling of argument components within judicial opinions.

Further, the legal-domain language model explores domain adaptation of BERT models, an important avenue in legal NLP. The interpretable paths can explain how fragments are related, promoting model transparency important for legal applications. Graph-based representation and algorithms for semantic similarity offer techniques to push forward core legal NLP tasks. With rich legal data and domain-specific modeling, this work makes both methodological and data contributions highly relevant for legal NLP. The techniques could further applications like legal search, summarization of contracts or cases, and argument mining over caselaw.

5 Evaluation

DebateSum does not include any data indicating if an argument is "strong", or if it is likely to win or not. It also does not have similarity labels between each example or even between pairs of samples. This means that it is challenging to compare the

[5] And in fact, any path on this graph can be an Argument

argumentation quality of each graph. Fortunately, it is simple to look at the lengths of the spoken aloud extracts. Since Policy Debaters are trying to minimize the time spent on each argument, they will prefer Graphs that extract evidence chains with shorter extracts.

Thus, we evaluate each graph based on how long the created Debate Cases extracts are. We choose 10 input argument pairs (a table of which is included within the github repo) and rank each graph based on the average length of the read aloud extracts from the generated debate cases across all 10 of these argument pairs. Table 1 shows the results of this experiment.

Due to the unique and small-scale nature of our evaluation, we hope that future work can find more effective ways to evaluate Semantic Knowledge Graphs in an argumentative context.

6 Conclusion

In this paper, we significantly expanded and improved an existing large scale argument mining dataset called "DebateSum". We created 9 Semantic Knowledge Graphs using the "txtai" Semantic AI toolkit. We showed how constrained shortest path traversals on these graphs can be used to create Policy Debate Cases. We created a System Demonstration of this called DebateKG which is a "space" webapp hosted on huggingface. We discuss implementation details of this system. We propose a way for Policy Debaters to decide which graph is better for their needs, and evaluate our systems using this technique. We open source all data, code, and graphs.

Limitations

The largest of the contributed Semantic Graphs, denoted "DebateKG-sent", can require as much as 100gb of free-space on disk when uncompressed (which is required to leverage them). All training and creation of these graphs was performed on a personal computer with an RTX 3080ti GPU, an I7 8700K CPU, and 32gigs of ram.

American Policy Debate, is almost always performed in English, and it is unlikely that suitable training data targeting it outside of English will be created in the near future.

DebateSum is crowd sourced from high school and college Policy Debate camp attendees. The evidence found within DebateSum, as well as the additions included within this paper, may have some annotation and/or parsing errors. This is because while the general layout of evidence is agreed upon by all, there is much variance in the formatting.

Ethics Statement

Philosophy, Law, Politics, Economics, and other Social Sciences are particularly well represented within DebateSum due to its nature as an argumentative dataset. The Policy Debate community has strong norms and supervision related to the included content which make the risk of hurtful or harmful content being included to be low. Still, the possibility of problematic content being included cannot be fully eliminated.

DebateKG is an extractive system. While extractive systems have far lower abuse potential compared to generative systems, the risk of abuse is also not totally eliminated. A "dialectic", according to the ancient philosopher Plato, is a dialogue held between two or more people for the purposes of finding truth. By contrast, a "debate", as far as competitors are concerned, is nothing more than a game of rhetorical persuasion played with real life evidence and situations. While most evidence within DebateSum is fully cited and is generally high quality, the way that that the evidence is summarized is biased towards the targeted argument that the competitor was trying to craft.

We also point out that DebateSum is not necessarily factual or "truthful". While the evidence within it should have almost no direct "lies", "fabrications" or "fake-news", the evidence can still be misleading or without important context.

References

Allen Roush and Arvind Balaji. 2020. DebateSum: A large-scale argument mining and summarization dataset. In *Proceedings of the 7th Workshop on Argument Mining*, pages 1–7, Online. Association for Computational Linguistics.

Vincent D. Blondel, Jean-Loup Guillaume, Renaud Lambiotte, Etienne Lefebvre. 2008. Fast unfolding of communities in large networks. In Journal of Statistical Mechanics, pages 1-8

Slonim, N., Bilu, Y., Alzate, C. et al. 2021. An autonomous debating system. In *Nature*, pages 379–384.

Khalid Al Khatib, Lukas Trautner, Henning Wachsmuth, Yufang Hou, and Benno Stein. 2021.

Employing Argumentation Knowledge Graphs for Neural Argument Generation. In *Proceedings of the 59th Annual Meeting of the Association for Computational Linguistics and the 11th International Joint Conference on Natural Language Processing (Volume 1: Long Papers)*, pages 4744–4754, Online. Association for Computational Linguistics.

Ramit Sawhney, Arnav Wadhwa, Shivam Agarwal, and Rajiv Ratn Shah. 2020. GPolS: A Contextual Graph-Based Language Model for Analyzing Parliamentary Debates and Political Cohesion. In *Proceedings of the 28th International Conference on Computational Linguistics*, pages 4847–4859, Barcelona, Spain (Online). International Committee on Computational Linguistics.

Minna Tamper, Rafael Leal, Laura Sinikallio, Petri Leskinen, Jouni Tuominen, and Eero Hyvonen. 2022. Extracting Knowledge from Parliamentary Debates for Studying Political Culture and Language. Online

Tchechmedjiev, A., Fafalios, P., Boland, K., Gasquet, M., Zloch, M., Zapilko, B., Dietze, S., Todorov, K., ClaimsKG: A Live Knowledge Graph of Fact-Checked Claims. 2019. In *18th International Semantic Web Conference (ISWC19)*, Auckland, New Zealand,

Ruiz-Dolz, R., Heras, S., & García-Fornes, A. 2022. Automatic Debate Evaluation with Argumentation Semantics and Natural Language Argument Graph Networks. *arXiv preprint arXiv:2203.14647*.

Rajarshi Das, Arvind Neelakantan, David Belanger, and Andrew McCallum. 2017. Chains of Reasoning over Entities, Relations, and Text using Recurrent Neural Networks. In *Proceedings of the 15th Conference of the European Chapter of the Association for Computational Linguistics: Volume 1, Long Papers*, pages 132–141, Valencia, Spain. Association for Computational Linguistics.

Hildebrandt, Marcel & Serna, Jorge & Ma, Yunpu & Ringsquandl, Martin & Joblin, Mitchell & Tresp, Volker. 2020. Debate Dynamics for Human-comprehensible Fact-checking on Knowledge Graphs. *In AAAI 2019 Fall Symposium Series*

Nils Reimers and Iryna Gurevych. 2019. Sentence-BERT: Sentence Embeddings using Siamese BERT-Networks. In *Proceedings of the 2019 Conference on Empirical Methods in Natural Language Processing and the 9th International Joint Conference on Natural Language Processing (EMNLP-IJCNLP)*, pages 3982–3992, Hong Kong, China. Association for Computational Linguistics.

Ilias Chalkidis, Manos Fergadiotis, Prodromos Malakasiotis, Nikolaos Aletras, and Ion Androutsopoulos. 2020. LEGAL-BERT: The Muppets straight out of Law School. In *Findings of the Association for Computational Linguistics: EMNLP 2020*, pages 2898–2904, Online. Association for Computational Linguistics.

Iz Beltagy, Matthew E. Peters, Arman Cohan. 2020. Longformer: The Long-Document Transformer, *arXiv*.

Page, Lawrence and Brin, Sergey and Motwani, Rajeev and Winograd, Terry. 1999. The PageRank Citation Ranking: Bringing Order to the Web. Technical Report. *Stanford InfoLab*.

A Appendix 1: Table of Contributed Models

Model Name	Number of Vertices	Number of Edges	Average Degree
Mpnet-abs	240566	1876918	7.80
Mpnet-ext	240566	2133792	8.86
Mpnet-sent	2546059	68305930	19.3
Legalbert-abs	240566	3006572	11.16
Legalbert-ext	240566	2685362	12.49
Legalbert-sent	2546059	48352931	21.5
Longformer-abs	240566	3685467	6.56
Longformer-ext	240566	5507938	8.89
Longformer-sent	2546059	59743621	22.4

Unsupervised Opinion Summarization Using Approximate Geodesics

Somnath Basu Roy Chowdhury[†,1] **Nicholas Monath**[2] **Avinava Dubey**[3]
Amr Ahmed[3] **Snigdha Chaturvedi**[1]
[1]UNC Chapel Hill, [2]Google DeepMind, [3] Google Research
{somnath, snigdha}@cs.unc.edu
{nmonath, avinavadubey, amra}@google.com

Abstract

Opinion summarization is the task of creating summaries capturing popular opinions from user reviews. In this paper, we introduce Geodesic Summarizer (GeoSumm), a novel system to perform unsupervised extractive opinion summarization. GeoSumm consists of an encoder-decoder based representation learning model that generates topical representations of texts. These representations capture the underlying semantics of the text as a distribution over learnable latent units. GeoSumm generates these topical representations by performing dictionary learning over pre-trained text representations at multiple layers of the decoder. We then use these topical representations to quantify the importance of review sentences using a novel approximate geodesic distance-based scoring mechanism. We use the importance scores to identify popular opinions in order to compose general and aspect-specific summaries. Our proposed model, GeoSumm, achieves strong performance on three opinion summarization datasets. We perform additional experiments to analyze the functioning of our model and showcase the generalization ability of GeoSumm across different domains.

1 Introduction

As more and more human interaction takes place online, consumers find themselves wading through an ever-increasing number of documents (e.g., customer reviews) when trying to make informed purchasing decisions. As this body of information grows, so does the need for automatic systems that can summarize it in an unsupervised manner. Opinion summarization is the task of automatically generating concise summaries from online user reviews (Hu and Liu, 2004; Pang, 2008; Medhat et al., 2014). For instance, opinion summaries allow a consumer to understand product reviews without reading all of them. Opinion summaries are also useful for sellers to receive feedback, and compare different products. The recent success of deep learning techniques has led to a significant improvement in summarization (Rush et al., 2015; Nallapati et al., 2016; Cheng and Lapata, 2016; See et al., 2017; Narayan et al., 2018; Liu et al., 2018) in supervised settings. However, it is difficult to leverage these techniques for opinion summarization due to the scarcity of annotated data. It is expensive to collect good-quality opinion summaries as human annotators need to read hundreds of reviews to write a single summary (Moussa et al., 2018). Therefore, most works on opinion summarization tackle the problem in an unsupervised setting.

Recent works (Bražinskas et al., 2021; Amplayo et al., 2021a) focus on abstractive summarization, where fluent summaries are generated using novel phrases. However, these approaches suffer from issues like text hallucination (Rohrbach et al., 2018) that affect the faithfulness of generated summaries (Maynez et al., 2020). Extractive summaries are less prone to these problems presenting the user with a representative subset of the original reviews.

We focus on the task of unsupervised extractive opinion summarization, where the system selects sentences representative of the user opinions. Inspired by previous works (Chowdhury et al., 2022; Angelidis et al., 2021a), we propose a novel encoder-decoder architecture along with objectives for (1) learning sentence representations that capture the underlying semantics, and (2) a sentence selection algorithm to compose a summary.

One of the challenges in extractive summarization is quantifying the importance of opinions. An opinion is considered to be important if it is semantically similar to opinions from other users. Using off-the-shelf pre-trained representations to obtain semantic similarity scores has known issues (Timkey and van Schijndel, 2021). These similarity scores can behave counterintuitively due to the high anisotropy of the representation space

[†] Work done during an internship at Google Research.

Proceedings of The 4th New Frontiers in Summarization Workshop, pages 105–120
December 6, 2023

(a few dimensions dominate the cosine similarity scores). Therefore, we use topical representations (Blei et al., 2003), which capture the semantics of text as a distribution over latent semantic units. These semantic units encode underlying concepts or topics. The semantic units can be captured using a learnable dictionary (Engan et al., 1999; Mairal et al., 2009; Aharon et al., 2006; Lee et al., 2006). Topical representations enable us to effectively measure semantic similarity between text representations as they are distributions over the same support. Text representations from reviews lie on a high-dimensional manifold. It is important to consider the underlying manifold while computing the importance score of a review. Therefore, we use the approximate geodesic distance between topical text representations to quantify the importance scores of reviews.

In this paper, we present **Geo**desic **Summ**arizer (GeoSumm) that learns topical text representations in an unsupervised manner from distributed representations (Hinton, 1984). We also present a novel sentence selection scheme that compares topical sentence representations in high-dimensions using approximate geodesics. Empirical evaluations show that GeoSumm achieves strong performance on three opinion summarization datasets – OPOSUM+ (Amplayo et al., 2021a), AMAZON (He and McAuley, 2016) and SPACE (Angelidis et al., 2021b). Our primary contributions are:

- We present an extractive opinion summarization system, GeoSumm. It consists of an unsupervised representation learning system and a sentence selection algorithm (Section 3).
- We present a novel representation learning model that learns topical text representations from distributed representations using dictionary learning (Section 3.1).
- We present a novel sentence selection algorithm that computes the importance of text using approximate geodesic distance (Section 3.2).
- GeoSumm achieves strong performance on 3 opinion summarization datasets (Section 4.4).

2 Task Setup

In extractive opinion summarization, the objective is to select representative sentences from a review set. Specifically, each dataset consists of a set of entities $\mathbf{E}$ and their corresponding review set $\mathcal{R}$. For each entity $e \in \mathbf{E}$ (e.g., a particular hotel such as the Holiday Inn in Redwood City, CA), a review set $\mathcal{R}_e = \{r_1, r_2, \ldots\}$ is provided, where each review is an ordered set of sentences $r_i = \{s_1^{(i)}, s_2^{(i)}, \ldots\}$. For simplicity of notation, we will represent the set of review sentences corresponding to an entity e as $\mathcal{S}_e = \bigcup_{r_i \in \mathcal{R}_e} r_i$. For each entity, reviews encompass a set of aspects $\mathcal{A}_e = \{a_1, a_2, \ldots\}$ (e.g., service, food of a hotel). In this work, we consider two forms of extractive summarization: (a) *general summarization*, where the system selects a subset of sentences $\mathcal{O}_e \subset \mathcal{S}_e$, that best represents popular opinions in the review set $\mathcal{R}_e$; (b) *aspect summarization*, where the system selects a representative sentence subset $\mathcal{O}_e^{(a)} \subset \mathcal{S}_e$, about a specific aspect a (e.g., service) of an entity e (e.g., hotel).

3 Geodesic Summarizer (GeoSumm)

In this section, we present our proposed approach Geodesic Summarizer (GeoSumm). GeoSumm has two parts: (a) an unsupervised model to learn topical representations of review sentences, and (b) a sentence selection algorithm that uses the approximate geodesic distance between topical representations, to compose the extractive summary.

3.1 Unsupervised Representation Learning

The goal of the representation learning model is to learn topical representations of review sentences. Topical representations model text as a distribution over underlying concepts or topics. This is useful for unsupervised extractive summarization because we want to capture the aggregate semantic distribution and quantify the importance of individual review sentences with respect to the aggregate distribution. Topical representations allow us to achieve both. Being a distribution over latent units, topical representations can be combined to form an aggregate (mean) representation, enabling compositionality. Also, it is convenient to measure the similarity between representations using conventional metrics (like cosine similarity).

We propose to model topical representations by decomposing pre-trained representations using dictionary learning (Tillmann, 2015; Lotfi and Vidyasagar, 2018). In this setup, the various components of the dictionary capture latent semantic units and we consider the representation over dictionary elements as the topical representation. Unlike conventional dictionary learning algorithms, we use a sentence reconstruction objective for learning the dictionary. We use an encoder-decoder architecture to achieve this. We retrieve word embeddings

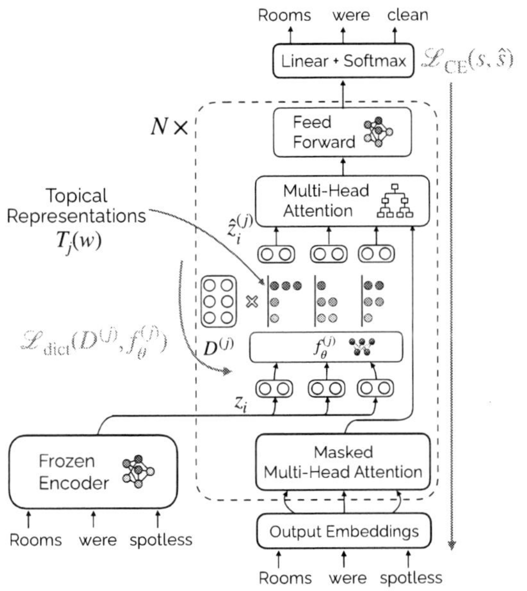

Figure 1: Architecture of Geodesic Summarizer. Sparse representations of words are formed via the kernel function $f_\theta^{(j)}$. The representations are trained to reconstruct the output embeddings of the encoder layer. Alongside the dictionary learning objective, we use an unsupervised sentence reconstruction cross-entropy loss. N indicates the number of decoder layers.

from a pre-trained encoder. We modify the architecture of a standard Transformer decoder by introducing a dictionary learning component at each decoder layer. The pre-trained word embeddings obtained from the encoder are decomposed using these dictionary learning components to obtain topical representations. Then, we combine the topical word representations at different decoder layers to form a sentence representation. The schematic diagram of the model is shown in Figure 1. Next, we will discuss each of the components in detail.

Encoder. We obtain contextual word embeddings from a pre-trained BART (Lewis et al., 2020) encoder. We keep the weights of the encoder frozen during training. In Section 5, we discuss why frozen representations are important for our model. Given an input sentence $s = \{w_1, \ldots, w_L\}$, we retrieve contextual word embeddings z_i's from the BART encoder:

$$z_i = \mathrm{sg}(\mathrm{enc}(\mathrm{w}_i)) \in \mathbb{R}^d \tag{1}$$

where $\mathrm{sg}(\cdot)$ denotes the stop gradient operator.

Dictionary Learning. We describe the dictionary learning component within each decoder layer. We use dictionary learning to decompose pre-trained word representations from the encoder to obtain a sparse representation for each word. We want word representations to be sparse because each word can capture only a small number of semantics. We forward word representations from the encoder to the decoder layers. For the j-th decoder layer, we use a dictionary, $\mathbf{D}^{(j)} \in \mathbb{R}^{m \times d}$, and kernel function, $k_j(\cdot, \cdot)$, where $j \in \{1, \ldots, N\}$ (N is the number of decoder layers). The dictionary captures the underlying semantics in the text by enabling us to model text representations as a combination of dictionary elements. Specifically, we learn a topical word representation $T_j(w_i)$ over the dictionary $\mathbf{D}^{(j)}$ as:

$$\begin{aligned} \hat{z}_i^{(j)} &= \mathbf{D}^{(j)^T} T_j(w_i) \\ T_j(w_i) &= k_j(z_i, \mathbf{D}^{(j)}) \in \mathbb{R}^m, \end{aligned} \tag{2}$$

where $\hat{z}_i^{(j)}$ is the reconstructed word embedding, and $k_j(\cdot, \cdot) \in \mathbb{R}^m$ is the kernel function that measures the similarity between z_i and individual dictionary elements. In practice, since the dictionary is common for all word embeddings z_i's, the kernel function can be implemented as:

$$k_j(\mathrm{z}_i, \mathbf{D}^{(j)}) = f_\theta^{(j)}(\mathrm{z}_i) \in \mathbb{R}^m, \tag{3}$$

where $f_\theta^{(j)}$ is a feed-forward neural network with ReLU non-linearity. ReLU non-linearity ensures that the kernel coefficients are positive and also encourages sparsity.

Following conventional dictionary learning algorithms (Beck and Teboulle, 2009), the dictionary $\mathbf{D}^{(j)}$ and kernel layer $f_\theta^{(j)}$ are updated iteratively. We ensure the sparsity of the word representations $f_\theta^{(j)}(z)$ by adding an L1-penalty to the loss. Overall, this can be achieved by using the loss function:

$$\begin{aligned} \mathcal{L}_{\mathrm{dict}}(\mathbf{D}^{(j)}, f_\theta^{(j)}) = &\|\mathrm{z}_i - \mathrm{sg}(\mathbf{D}^{(j)^T}) f_\theta^{(j)}(\mathrm{z}_i)\|_2 \\ &+ \|\mathrm{z}_i - \mathbf{D}^{(j)^T} \mathrm{sg}(f_\theta^{(j)}(\mathrm{z}_i))\|_2 \\ &+ \left| f_\theta^{(j)}(z_i) - \mathbb{E}\left[f_\theta^{(j)}(z_i) \right] \right|_1, \end{aligned}$$

where the gradient update of the dictionary $\mathbf{D}^{(j)}$ and kernel layer $f_\theta^{(j)}$ are performed independently.

Decoder. We build on the decoder architecture introduced by Vaswani et al. (2017). A decoder layer consists of 3 sub-layers (a) masked multi-head attention layer that takes as input decoder token embeddings, (b) multi-head attention that performs cross-attention between decoder tokens and encoder stack output, and (c) feed-forward network. We modify the cross attention multi-head sub-layer to attend over the reconstructed word embeddings $\hat{z}_i^{(j)}$ (Equation 2), instead of the encoder stack output (shown in Figure 1). Finally, the decoder autoregressively generates the reconstructed sentence $\hat{s} = \{\hat{w_1}, \ldots, \hat{w_L}\}$.

Training. The system is trained using the sentence reconstruction objective. The overall objective function is shown below:

$$\mathcal{L}_{\text{CE}}(s, \hat{s}) + \sum_{j=1}^{N} \mathcal{L}_{\text{dict}}(\mathbf{D}^{(j)}, f_\theta^{(j)}), \quad (4)$$

where $\mathcal{L}_{\text{CE}}$ is the cross-entropy loss, and $f_\theta^{(j)}$ is the implementation of the kernel function $k_j(\cdot,\cdot)$ corresponding to the j-th decoder layer. The above loss function is used to update the decoder, the dictionary elements, and the kernel parameters while keeping the encoder weights frozen.

Sentence Representations. We combine topical word representations from different decoder layers to form a sentence representation. First, we obtain a word representation, $T_j(w) \in \mathbb{R}^m$ from each decoder layer. We compose the final word representation $\mathbf{x}_w$ by concatenating representations from all decoder layers.

$$\mathbf{x}_w = [T_1(w), \ldots, T_N(w)] \in \mathbb{R}^{mN}, \quad (5)$$

where m is the dictionary dimension and N is the number of decoder layers. We use max-pooling over the dimensions of word representations to form a sentence representation $\mathbf{x}_s$ as shown below.

$$\begin{aligned} \mathbf{x}_n^s &= \max_{w \in \{w_1, \ldots, w_L\}} \mathbf{x}_w\big|_n \\ \bar{\mathbf{x}}_s &= \{\mathbf{x}_n^s\}_{n=1}^{mN}, \mathbf{x}_s = \bar{\mathbf{x}}_s / \|\bar{\mathbf{x}}_s\|_1 \in \mathbb{R}^{mN}, \end{aligned} \quad (6)$$

where $\mathbf{x}_w\big|_n$ is the n-th entry of the vector $\mathbf{x}_w$. The sentence representation $\mathbf{x}_s$ is normalized to a unit vector. Next, we discuss how we leverage these topical sentence representations to compute importance scores using approximate geodesics. We use the importance scores to compose the final extractive summary for a given entity.

3.2 General Summarization

We use representations retrieved from GeoSumm to select sentences representative of popular opinions in the review set. For an entity e, the set of sentence representations is denoted as $\mathcal{X}_e = \{\mathbf{x}_s | s \in \mathcal{S}_e\}$. For a summary budget q, we select a subset of

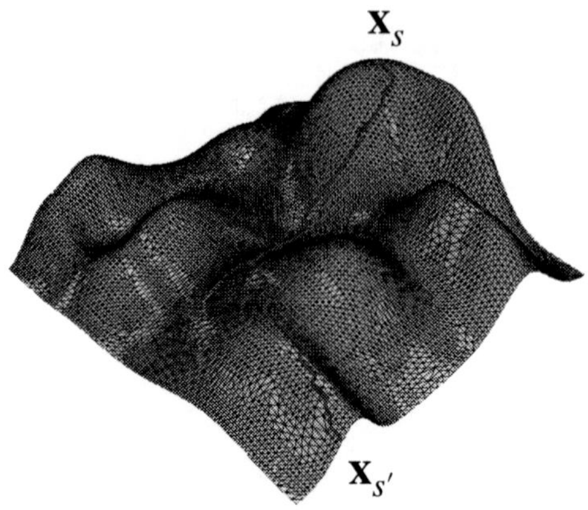

Figure 2: Illustration of the geodesic shortest path (shown in **blue**) between two sentence representations $\mathbf{x}_s$ and $\mathbf{x}_{s'}$ on a three-dimensional manifold.

sentences $\mathcal{O}_e \subset \mathcal{S}_e$ according to their importance scores, such that $|\mathcal{O}_e| = q$. First, we compute a mean representation as shown: $\mu_e = \mathbb{E}_{s \sim \mathcal{S}_e}[\mathbf{x}_s]$. Secondly, we define the importance of a sentence s, as the distance from the mean representation $d(\mathbf{x}_s, \mu_e)$. However, we do not directly evaluate $d(\cdot,\cdot)$ using a similarity metric. Representations in $\mathcal{X}_e$ lie in a high-dimensional manifold, and we aim to measure the geodesic distance (Jost and Jost, 2008) between two points along that manifold. An illustration of the geodesic distance between two points is shown in Figure 2. Computing the exact geodesic distance is difficult without explicit knowledge of the manifold structure (Surazhsky et al., 2005). We approximate the manifold structure using a k-NN graph. Each sentence representation forms a node in this graph. A directed edge exists between two nodes if the target node is among the k-nearest neighbours of the source node. The edge weight between two nodes (s, s') is defined using their cosine similarity distance, $d(s, s') = 1 - \mathbf{x}_s \mathbf{x}_{s'}^T$. The geodesic distance between two sentence representations is computed using the shortest path distance along the weighted graph. Therefore, the importance score $I(s)$ for a sentence s, is defined as:

$$I(s) = 1/\text{ShortestPath}(\mathbf{x}_s, \mu_e), \quad (7)$$

where the shortest path distance is computed using Dijkstra's algorithm (Dijkstra et al., 1959). We select the top-q sentences according to their importance scores $I(s)$ to form the final general extractive summary. The overall sentence selection routine is shown in Algorithm 1.

Algorithm 1 General Summarization Routine

```
Input: A set of sentence representations 𝒳_e = {x_s | s ∈ 𝒮_e} are review sentences for entity e.
μ_e ← E_{s∼𝒮_e}[x_s]
A ← knn(𝒳_e ∪ μ_e) ∈ ℝ^{l×l}        ▷ adjacency matrix of k-NN graph, l = |S_e| + 1.
d ← Dijkstra(A, μ_e)   ▷ shortest distances of all nodes from μ_e
I ← {1/d(s) | s ∈ 𝒮_e}      ▷ importance scores
t_q ← min top-q(I)          ▷ top-q threshold
𝒪_e ← {s | I(s) ≥ t_q, s ∈ 𝒮_e}
return 𝒪_e
```

3.3 Aspect Summarization

In aspect summarization, the goal is to select representative sentences to form a summary specific to an aspect (e.g., durability) of an entity (e.g., bag). To perform aspect summarization, we compute the mean representation of aspect-specific sentences as shown: $\mu_e^{(a)} = \mathbb{E}_{s \sim \mathcal{S}_e^{(a)}}[\mathbf{x}_s]$, where $\mathcal{S}_e^{(a)}$ is the set of sentences mentioning aspect a. We identify $\mathcal{S}_e^{(a)}$ by detecting the presence of aspect-specific keywords available with the dataset. To ensure the selected sentences are aspect-specific, we introduce a measure of *informativeness* (Chowdhury et al., 2022; Peyrard, 2019). Informativeness penalizes a sentence for being close to the overall mean μ_e. Therefore, we model the aspect-specific importance score $I_a(s)$ as:

$$I_a(s) = 1/\text{ShortestPath}(\mathbf{x}_s, \mu_e^{(a)}) - \gamma I(s), \quad (8)$$

where γ is a hyperparameter, $I(s)$ is the overall importance score (obtained from Eqn. 7). Aspect summary $\mathcal{O}_e^{(a)}$ is composed using the top-q sentences according to the aspect-specific scores, $I_a(s)$.

4 Experiments

We evaluate the performance of GeoSumm on extractive summarization. Given a set of user reviews the system needs to select a subset of the sentences as the summary. This summary is then compared with human-written summaries. In this section, we discuss the experimental setup in detail.

4.1 Datasets & Metrics

We evaluate GeoSumm on three publicly available opinion summarization datasets:

(a) OPOSUM+ (Amplayo et al., 2021b) is an extended version of the original OPOSUM dataset (Angelidis and Lapata, 2018a). This dataset contains Amazon reviews from six product categories (like laptops, bags, etc.), with 3 human-written summaries in the test set. The extended version contains additional product reviews and aspect-specific human annotations.

(b) AMAZON (He and McAuley, 2016; Bražinskas et al., 2020a) has product reviews of 4 different categories (like electronics, clothing, etc.) from Amazon, with 3 human summaries per entity.

(c) SPACE (Angelidis et al., 2021a) contains reviews for hotels from Tripadvisor. SPACE provides three human-written abstractive summaries and six aspect-specific summaries per hotel entity.

Dataset	Reviews	Train / Test Ent.	Rev./Ent.
OPOSUM+	4.13M	95K / 60	10
AMAZON	4.75M	183K / 60	8
SPACE	1.14M	11.4K / 50	100

Table 1: Dataset statistics for OPOSUM+, AMAZON and SPACE datasets. (Train/Test Ent.: Number of entities in the *training* and *test* set; Rev./Ent.: Number of reviews per entity in the *test* set.)

Statistics of the datasets are provided in Table 1. We observe that SPACE dataset has significantly more reviews per entity compared to other datasets.

4.2 Implementation Details

Our experiments are implemented using the TensorFlow (Abadi et al., 2015) framework. We use $\text{BART}_{\text{base}}$ (Lewis et al., 2020) architecture as our encoder-decoder model. We initialize the encoder with pre-trained weights from BART, while the decoder is trained from scratch. In our experiments, we use dictionary dimension $m = 8192$, number of decoder layers $N = 6$, and hidden dimension $d = 768$. GeoSumm was trained for 15K steps on 16 TPUs in all setups. We optimize our model using Adam (Kingma and Ba, 2014) optimizer with a learning rate of 10^{-5}. We set aspect-summarization parameter $\gamma = 0.5$ for OPOSUM+ and $\gamma = 0.7$ for SPACE (Equation 8). All hyperparameters were tuned using grid-search on the development set. We will make our code publicly available.

4.3 Baselines

We compare GeoSumm with several summarization systems (including the current state-of-the-art) that can be classified into three broad categories:

• *Single Review* systems select a single review as the summary. We compare with the following systems: (a) *Random* samples a review randomly from

	Method	OpoSum+ R1	OpoSum+ R2	OpoSum+ RL	Amazon R1	Amazon R2	Amazon RL	Space R1	Space R2	Space RL
Single Rev.	Random	29.88	5.64	17.19	27.66	4.72	16.95	26.24	3.58	14.72
	$\text{Centroid}_{\text{BERT}}$	33.44	11.00	20.54	29.94	5.19	17.70	31.29	4.91	16.43
	Oracle	32.89	23.20	28.73	31.69	6.47	19.25	33.21	8.33	18.02
Abstractive	Opinosis (Ganesan et al., 2010)	-	-	-	28.42	4.57	15.50	28.76	4.57	15.96
	MeanSum (Chu and Liu, 2019)	34.95	7.49	19.92	29.20	4.70	18.15	34.95	7.49	19.92
	Copycat (Bražinskas et al., 2020b)	36.66	8.87	20.90	31.97	5.81	20.16	36.66	8.87	20.90
	PlanSum (Amplayo et al., 2021c)	-	-	-	32.87	6.12	19.05	-	-	-
	TranSum (Wang and Wan, 2021)	-	-	-	34.23	7.24	20.49	-	-	-
	CoOP (Iso et al., 2021)	-	-	-	36.57	7.23	21.24	-	-	-
	AceSum (Amplayo et al., 2021c)	32.98	10.72	20.27	-	-	-	40.37	11.51	23.23
Extractive	$\text{LexRank}_{\text{BERT}}$ (Erkan and Radev, 2004)	35.42	10.22	20.92	31.47	5.07	16.81	31.41	5.05	18.12
	QT (Angelidis et al., 2021a)	37.72	14.65	21.69	31.27	5.03	16.42	38.66	10.22	21.90
	$\text{AceSum}_{\text{EXT}}$ (Amplayo et al., 2021b)	38.48	15.17	22.82	-	-	-	35.50	7.82	20.09
	SemAE (Chowdhury et al., 2022)	39.16	16.85	23.61	32.03	5.38	16.47	**42.48**	**13.48**	**26.40**
	Geodesic Summarizer (GeoSumm)	**41.55**	**20.77**	**25.19**	**33.75**	**7.15**	**18.79**	42.36	12.44	24.80

Table 2: Evaluation results of GeoSumm and baseline approaches on general summarization. We observe that GeoSumm achieves strong performance on all datasets. We report the ROUGE-F scores denoted as – R1: ROUGE-1, R2: ROUGE-2, RL: ROUGE-L. We highlight the best performance achieved by an extractive summarization system in **bold** and the best abstractive summarization performance in underline.

	Method	OpoSum+ R1	OpoSum+ R2	OpoSum+ RL	Space R1	Space R2	Space RL
Abstract	MeanSum	24.63	3.47	17.53	23.24	3.72	17.02
	CopyCat	26.17	4.30	18.20	24.95	4.82	17.53
	AceSum	29.53	6.79	21.06	**32.41**	9.47	**25.46**
Extractive	LexRank	22.51	3.35	17.27	27.72	7.54	20.82
	QT	23.99	4.36	16.61	28.95	8.34	21.77
	SemAE	25.30	5.08	17.62	31.24	**10.43**	24.14
	$\text{AceSum}_{\text{EXT}}$	26.16	5.75	18.55	30.91	8.77	23.61
	GeoSumm	**30.84**	**8.98**	**21.64**	26.61	5.82	19.37

Table 3: Evaluation results on aspect summarization. The best scores for each metric is highlighted in **bold**. GeoSumm achieves the state-of-the-art performance on OpoSum+, while achieving competitive performance with other extractive methods on Space.

the review set; (b) *Centroid* selects a review closest to the centroid of the review set. The centroid is computed using BERT (Devlin et al., 2019) embeddings; (c) *Oracle* selects the best review based on ROUGE overlap with the human-written summary.

• *Abstractive* systems generate summaries using novel phrasing. We compare GeoSumm with the following systems: MeanSum (Chu and Liu, 2019), Copycat (Bražinskas et al., 2020b), PlanSum (Amplayo et al., 2021c), TranSum (Wang and Wan, 2021), CoOP (Iso et al., 2021), and AceSum (Amplayo et al., 2021b).

• *Extractive* systems select text phrases from the review set to form the summary. We compare with

General	Inform.	Coherence	Redund.
SemAE	-7.3	-10.0	-51.3
QT	**8.0**	-4.7	12.7
GeoSumm	-0.7	**14.7***	**38.7***

Table 4: Human evaluation results of general summarization for Space dataset. (*): statistically significant difference with all baselines ($p < 0.05$, using paired bootstrap resampling Koehn (2004)).

the following systems: LexRank (Erkan and Radev, 2004) using BERT embeddings, QT (Angelidis et al., 2021a), $\text{AceSum}_{\text{EXT}}$ (Amplayo et al., 2021b), and SemAE (Chowdhury et al., 2022).

4.4 Results

We discuss the performance of GeoSumm on general and aspect-specific summarization. We evaluate the quality of the extracted summaries using the automatic metric – ROUGE F-scores (Lin, 2004), which measures the n-gram overlap with the human-written summaries.

General Summarization. We present the results of GeoSumm and baseline approaches on general summarization in Table 2. We observe that GeoSumm achieves strong performance across all datasets. For OpoSum+ and Amazon datasets, GeoSumm achieves significant improvement over baselines achieving the best performance among extractive summarization systems. For the Space dataset, it is competitive with baselines falling

Aspect	Exclusive	Partial	None
SemAE	22.1	43.8	34.1
QT	22.2	41.9	35.9
GeoSumm	**46.4***	**45.6**	**8.0***

Table 5: Human evaluation results of aspect summarization for OPOSUM+ dataset. GeoSumm generates more aspect-specific summaries compared to baselines.

Dataset	R1	R2	RL
OPOSUM+	35.7 (↓5.9)	13.9 (↓6.9)	21.1 (↓4.1)
AMAZON	32.2 (↓1.6)	6.2 (↓1.0)	17.3 (↓1.5)
SPACE	33.5 (↓8.9)	6.9 (↓5.5)	19.5 (↓5.3)

Table 6: Evaluation results when GeoSumm's encoder is fine-tuned during training. We observe a significant drop in performance when the encoder is fine-tuned.

slightly short of the state-of-the-art model, SemAE. However, we observe that GeoSumm's summaries are much more diverse leading to significantly better human evaluation scores compared to SemAE.

Aspect Summarization. We report the performance on different approaches on aspect summarization in Table 3 on OPOSUM+ and SPACE. We observe that GeoSumm achieves the state-of-the-art performance for all metrics on the OPOSUM+ dataset. On SPACE dataset, it achieves comparable scores to other extractive approaches.

Human Evaluation. We perform a human evaluation to compare the summaries from GeoSumm with the state-of-the-art extractive summarization systems SemAE and QT. General summaries were judged based on the following criteria: *informativeness*, *coherence*, and *redundancy*. We present human evaluators with summaries in a pairwise fashion and ask them to select which one was better/worse/similar according to the criteria. The final scores for each system reported in Table 4 were computed using Best-Worst Scaling (Louviere et al., 2015). We observe that GeoSumm outperforms the baselines in coherence and redundancy. GeoSumm performs slightly worse than QT in informativeness. This is expected as GeoSumm greedily select sentences (that are often similar), while QT performs sampling leading to more coherent summaries (compromising on informativeness).

For aspect summaries, we ask annotators to judge whether a summary discusses a specific aspect *exclusively*, *partially*, or *does not mention* it at all. In Table 5, we report the human evaluation results for aspect summaries on OPOSUM+ dataset. We observe that GeoSumm generates summaries that are significantly more aspect-specific compared to baselines. We provide further details about human evaluation in Appendix A.1.

5 Analysis

Thawed Encoder. In this experiment, we compare the performance of GeoSumm when the encoder is allowed to be fine-tuned with the original setup, where the encoder weights are frozen. In Table 6, we observe that there is a significant drop in performance when the encoder is fine-tuned. We hypothesize that this happens because the model overfits shallow word-level semantics, and is unable to capture more abstract semantics. This showcases the utility of pre-trained representations that helps GeoSumm perform well in an unsupervised setting.

Next, we investigate the efficacy of the representation learning and sentence selection modules by replacing each of them with a competitive variant.

Dataset	R1	R2	RL
OPOSUM+	28.1 (↓13.5)	6.2 (↓14.6)	15.8 (↓9.4)
AMAZON	32.6 (↓1.2)	6.1 (↓1.1)	17.9 (↓0.8)
SPACE	41.4 (↓1.0)	11.5 (↓0.9)	24.0 (↓0.8)

Table 7: Evaluation results of GeoSumm with a modified score $I(s) = -\|\mathbf{x}_s - \mu_e\|_2^2$. We observe a significant drop in performance across all three datasets.

Euclidean-based Importance Score. We investigate the utility of geodesic-based importance scoring over Euclidean-based scoring. In this experiment, instead of $I(s)$ (defined in Equation 7) we compute the importance score of a sentence, s, as the Euclidean distance from the mean representation, μ_e ($I(s) = -\|\mathbf{x}_s - \mu_e\|_2^2$). We report the results of this setup in Table 7 (relative performance to GeoSumm is shown in brackets). We observe that performing sentence selection using Euclidean distance results in a significant drop in performance across all datasets. We believe that leveraging the kNN graph provides us with a better approximation of the underlying representation manifold, which results in better summarization performance.

Distributed vs. Topical Representations. In this experiment, we investigate the relative efficacy of topical representations compared to distributed representations. We retrieve distributed sentence representations from RoBERTa (Liu et al., 2019) (`[CLS]` token feature) and SimCSE (Gao et al., 2021) model. Then, we use these representations in our sentence selection algorithm (Section 3.2) to compose the summary. In Table 8, we observe that topical representations (obtained from GeoSumm) outperform distributed representations by a

Dataset	Model	R1	R2	RL
OpoSum+	RBT	35.1 (↓6.5)	13.0 (↓7.8)	21.2 (↓4.0)
	SCS	33.5 (↓8.1)	6.9 (↓13.9)	19.5 (↓5.7)
Amazon	RBT	29.4 (↓4.4)	4.7 (↓2.4)	15.3 (↓3.5)
	SCS	31.0 (↓2.8)	5.2 (↓1.9)	16.4 (↓2.4)
Space	RBT	26.8 (↓15.6)	3.7 (↓8.7)	15.4 (↓9.4)
	SCS	30.1 (↓12.3)	4.8 (↓7.6)	17.3 (↓7.5)

Table 8: Evaluation results of GeoSumm using RoBERTa (RBT) and SimCSE's (SCS) representations. We observe that opinion summarization using topical representations from GeoSumm outperforms distributed representations across all datasets.

Perplexity (PPL) ↓	Space	Amazon
QT	33.46	63.70
SemAE	15.95	55.46
GeoSumm	**14.95**	**45.55**

Table 9: Perplexity of the summaries generated by different extractive summarization systems. We observe that GeoSumm achieves the best perplexity scores, indicating more coherent summaries.

significant margin across all setups. This shows the utility of topical representations over distributed representations for unsupervised summarization.

Summary Coherence. In this experiment, we evaluate the coherence of the generated extractive summaries using automatic measures. Specifically, we measure the perplexity scores (from HuggingFace (Wolf et al., 2020) Evaluate API) using the GPT-Neo model (Black et al., 2021). The perplexity scores are indicative of the coherence of the generated text. In Table 9, we report the perplexity scores on Space and Amazon datasets for extractive systems QT, SemAE, and GeoSumm. We observe that GeoSumm achieves the best perplexity scores showcasing that it is able to generate superior-quality summaries in terms of coherence. We believe that the greedy aggregation of sentences in GeoSumm often results in the selection of semantically similar sentences thereby leading to more coherent summaries with fewer context switches.

Cluster Interpretation. In this experiment, we investigate whether different parts of the representation space capture distinct semantics. We partition the space by performing agglomerative clustering with Ward's linkage (Ward Jr, 1963) on the representation set for a particular entity. In Table 10, we report example sentences within different clusters. We observe that sentences belonging to the same cluster share a common theme. The underlying semantics of a cluster can vary from being coarse, like the presence of the phrase 'Calistoga', to more nuanced concepts like pillows & beds in the room, flowers in the hotel's garden, etc.

Theme	Sentences
Flowers	• The gardens are lovely with wide varieties of flowering plants and shrubs, koi ponds and hummingbird feeders. • Pots of tulips and daffodils in full bloom; other plantings well cared for; pathways clean and swept.
Location 'Calistoga'	• Calistoga is a beautiful historic town with good restaurants and beautiful old houses –a fun place to walk. • The Roman Spa and Calistoga is our favorite spot in the Wine Country.
Pillows & Beds	• The rooms were in great shape, very clean, comfortable beds with lots of pillows. • The pillows and bed coverings were of very good quality There was also a mini-refrigerator and coffeemaker.
Phrase 'every year'	• We return every year to the Roman Space after the holidays and brought Seattle friends this January. • Every year for the past 15 years we have met at the Roman Spa ...

Table 10: Sentences within a cluster produced from agglomerate clustering. Sentences in a row belong to the same cluster. We highlight the dominant theme of a cluster in green.

Generated Summaries. In Table 11, we report the summaries generated by GeoSumm, and other comparable extractive summarization systems like SemAE and QT. We observe that GeoSumm is able to generate a comprehensive summary that reflects the main considerations mentioned in the human summary. Compared to SemAE, we see more specific adjectival descriptions; SemAE indicates that many of the hotel characteristics are simply 'great'. Compared to QT, we see a review that seems to more accurately reflect the human-written summary.

We perform additional ablations experiments to investigate the domain transfer capabilities, sparsity of representations, among others in Appendix A.2.

6 Related Work

Most work on opinion summarization focuses on generating summaries in an unsupervised setup due to the scarcity of labeled data. These works are broadly classified into two categories based on the type of summaries being generated: *abstractive* (Ganesan et al., 2010; Carenini et al., 2006; Di Fabbrizio et al., 2014) or *extractive* (Erkan and Radev, 2004; Nenkova and Vanderwende, 2005;

Human	GeoSumm	SemAE	QT
All staff members were friendly, accommodating, and helpful. The hotel and room were very clean. The room had modern charm and was nicely remodeled. The beds are extremely comfortable. The rooms are quite with wonderful beach views. The food at Hash, the restaurant in lobby, was fabulous. The location is great, very close to the beach. It's a longish walk to Santa Monica. The price is very affordable.	Overall we had a nice stay at the hotel. Our room was very clean and comfortable. The atmosphere is stylish and the service was great. We ate breakfast at the hotel and it was great. I appreciate the location and the security in the hotel. The food and service at the restaurant was awesome. The Hotel is classy and has a rooftop bar. The restaurant is cozy but they have good healthy food. Great hotel.	The staff is great. The Hotel Erwin is a great place to stay. The staff were friendly and helpful. The location is perfect. We ate breakfast at the hotel and it was great. The hotel itself is in a great location. The service was wonderful. It was great. The rooms are great. The rooftop bar HIGH was the icing on the cake. The food and service at the restaurant was awesome. The service was excellent.	Great hotel. We liked our room with an ocean view. The staff were friendly and helpful. There was no balcony. The location is perfect. Our room was very quiet. I would definitely stay here again. You're one block from the beach. So it must be good! Filthy hallways. Unvacuumed room. Pricy, but well worth it.

Table 11: Human-written and generated summaries from GeoSumm, SemAE, and QT. For a fair comparison, we present the summary for the instance reported in previous works. GeoSumm generates a comprehensive review with a relatively logical ordering that starts with a clear topic sentence and then proceeds to details. Compared to SemAE, we see more descriptive sentences selected. Compared to QT, we see a summary that more closely matches the human-written summary.

Zhao et al., 2022; Li et al., 2023). Abstractive systems, in an unsupervised setup (Chu and Liu, 2019; Bražinskas et al., 2020b; Iso et al., 2021; Wang and Wan, 2021; Amplayo et al., 2021a) train an encoder-decoder setup using a self-supervised objective and generate the summary by leveraging the aggregate opinion representation. On the other hand, extractive opinion systems (Kim et al., 2011), select sentences using an importance score that quantifies their salience. Salience has been computed using frequency-based approaches (Nenkova and Vanderwende, 2005), distance from mean (Radev et al., 2004), or graph-based techniques (Erkan and Radev, 2004). Few approaches focus on aspect specificity and sentiment polarity for sentence selection (Angelidis and Lapata, 2018b; Zhao and Chaturvedi, 2020).

Our work is most similar to extractive summarization systems SemAE (Chowdhury et al., 2022), and QT (Angelidis et al., 2021a). Similar to these systems, Geodesic Summarizer has two components: a representation learning system, and a sentence selection routine. However, unlike these approaches, we leverage pre-trained models to learn topical representations over a latent dictionary and propose a sentence selection mechanism using approximate geodesics to perform summarization.

Approaches in our work resemble prior works in deep clustering, which considers a similar combination of unsupervised representation learning and sparse structures (Yang et al., 2016; Jiang et al., 2016; Law et al., 2017; Caron et al., 2020; Zhao et al., 2020). In a similar fashion, dictionary learning-like approaches have been combined with deep networks (Liang et al., 2021; Zheng et al., 2021) for various tasks.

7 Conclusion

We present Geodesic Summarizer, a novel framework for extractive opinion summarization. GeoSumm uses a representation learning model to convert distributed representations from a pre-trained model into topical text representations. GeoSumm uses these representations to compute the importance of a sentence using approximate geodesics. We show that GeoSumm achieves strong performance on several opinion summarization datasets. However, there are a lot of open questions about the inductive biases of representation learning that are needed for unsupervised summarization. In this work, we show the efficacy of topical representations. However, are there better approaches to capturing language semantics that help us quantify the importance of an opinion? Our analysis shows that representations from GeoSumm span the high-dimensional space in a manner that different parts of it capture distinct semantics. This opens up the possibility of leveraging the representation geometry to capture different forms of semantics. Future work can explore ways to leverage topical representations from GeoSumm for tasks where there is a scarcity of labeled data.

8 Acknowledgement

The authors are thankful to Anneliese Brei, Haoyuan Li, Anvesh Rao Vijjini, and Chao Zhao for helpful feedback on an earlier version of this paper. This work is supported in part by the National Science Foundation under award DRL-2112635.

9 Limitations

We propose GeoSumm, a novel system that learns topical representations of text and uses them to compute the importance of opinion reviews for extractive summarization. One of the limitations of GeoSumm is that it requires pre-training of the representation learning module using reviews sentences from a similar domain. For this, GeoSumm requires access to a large collection of review data from the target domain, thereby limiting its applicability in zero-shot or few-shot setups. This can be alleviated by future research on developing foundational models that learn topical representations on large-scale datasets and generalize across different opinion summarization domains.

Ethical Considerations

We do not foresee any ethical issues from the technology introduced in this paper. However, we would like to mention certain limitations of extractive summarization systems in general. As extractive systems select review sentences from the input, it can produce undesirable output when the input reviews have foul or offensive language. Therefore, it is important to remove foul language from the input in order to ensure the end user is not affected. In general, we use public datasets and do not annotate any data manually. All datasets used in this paper have customer reviews in the English language. Human evaluations for summarization were performed on Amazon Mechanical Turks (AMT) platform. Human judges were based in the United States. Human judges were compensated at a rate of at least $15 USD per hour.

References

Martín Abadi, Ashish Agarwal, Paul Barham, Eugene Brevdo, Zhifeng Chen, Craig Citro, Greg S. Corrado, Andy Davis, Jeffrey Dean, Matthieu Devin, Sanjay Ghemawat, Ian Goodfellow, Andrew Harp, Geoffrey Irving, Michael Isard, Yangqing Jia, Rafal Jozefowicz, Lukasz Kaiser, Manjunath Kudlur, Josh Levenberg, Dandelion Mané, Rajat Monga, Sherry Moore, Derek Murray, Chris Olah, Mike Schuster, Jonathon Shlens, Benoit Steiner, Ilya Sutskever, Kunal Talwar, Paul Tucker, Vincent Vanhoucke, Vijay Vasudevan, Fernanda Viégas, Oriol Vinyals, Pete Warden, Martin Wattenberg, Martin Wicke, Yuan Yu, and Xiaoqiang Zheng. 2015. TensorFlow: Large-scale machine learning on heterogeneous systems. Software available from tensorflow.org.

Michal Aharon, Michael Elad, and Alfred Bruckstein. 2006. K-svd: An algorithm for designing overcomplete dictionaries for sparse representation. IEEE Transactions on signal processing.

Reinald Kim Amplayo, Stefanos Angelidis, and Mirella Lapata. 2021a. Aspect-controllable opinion summarization. In Proceedings of the 2021 Conference on Empirical Methods in Natural Language Processing, pages 6578–6593, Online and Punta Cana, Dominican Republic. Association for Computational Linguistics.

Reinald Kim Amplayo, Stefanos Angelidis, and Mirella Lapata. 2021b. Aspect-controllable opinion summarization. In Proceedings of the 2021 Conference on Empirical Methods in Natural Language Processing, pages 6578–6593.

Reinald Kim Amplayo, Stefanos Angelidis, and Mirella Lapata. 2021c. Unsupervised opinion summarization with content planning. In Proceedings of the AAAI Conference on Artificial Intelligence, volume 35, pages 12489–12497.

Stefanos Angelidis, Reinald Kim Amplayo, Yoshihiko Suhara, Xiaolan Wang, and Mirella Lapata. 2021a. Extractive opinion summarization in quantized transformer spaces. Transactions of the Association for Computational Linguistics, 9:277–293.

Stefanos Angelidis, Reinald Kim Amplayo, Yoshihiko Suhara, Xiaolan Wang, and Mirella Lapata. 2021b. Extractive opinion summarization in quantized transformer spaces. Transactions of the Association for Computational Linguistics, 9:277–293.

Stefanos Angelidis and Mirella Lapata. 2018a. Summarizing opinions: Aspect extraction meets sentiment prediction and they are both weakly supervised. In Proceedings of the 2018 Conference on Empirical Methods in Natural Language Processing, pages 3675–3686, Brussels, Belgium. Association for Computational Linguistics.

Stefanos Angelidis and Mirella Lapata. 2018b. Summarizing opinions: Aspect extraction meets sentiment prediction and they are both weakly supervised. In Proceedings of the 2018 Conference on Empirical Methods in Natural Language Processing, pages 3675–3686, Brussels, Belgium. Association for Computational Linguistics.

Amir Beck and Marc Teboulle. 2009. A fast iterative shrinkage-thresholding algorithm for linear inverse problems. SIAM journal on imaging sciences, 2(1):183–202.

Federico Bianchi, Silvia Terragni, Dirk Hovy, Debora Nozza, and Elisabetta Fersini. 2021. Cross-lingual contextualized topic models with zero-shot learning. In Proceedings of the 16th Conference of the European Chapter of the Association for Computational Linguistics: Main Volume, pages 1676–1683, Online. Association for Computational Linguistics.

Sid Black, Leo Gao, Phil Wang, Connor Leahy, and Stella Biderman. 2021. GPT-Neo: Large Scale Autoregressive Language Modeling with Mesh-Tensorflow.

David M Blei, Andrew Y Ng, and Michael I Jordan. 2003. Latent dirichlet allocation. Journal of machine Learning research, 3(Jan):993–1022.

Arthur Bražinskas, Mirella Lapata, and Ivan Titov. 2020a. Unsupervised opinion summarization as copycat-review generation. In Proceedings of the 58th Annual Meeting of the Association for Computational Linguistics, pages 5151–5169, Online. Association for Computational Linguistics.

Arthur Bražinskas, Mirella Lapata, and Ivan Titov. 2020b. Unsupervised opinion summarization as copycat-review generation. In Proceedings of the 58th Annual Meeting of the Association for Computational Linguistics, pages 5151–5169, Online. Association for Computational Linguistics.

Arthur Bražinskas, Mirella Lapata, and Ivan Titov. 2021. Learning opinion summarizers by selecting informative reviews. In Proceedings of the 2021 Conference on Empirical Methods in Natural Language Processing, pages 9424–9442, Online and Punta Cana, Dominican Republic. Association for Computational Linguistics.

Giuseppe Carenini, Raymond Ng, and Adam Pauls. 2006. Multi-document summarization of evaluative text. In 11th Conference of the European Chapter of the Association for Computational Linguistics, pages 305–312.

Mathilde Caron, Ishan Misra, Julien Mairal, Priya Goyal, Piotr Bojanowski, and Armand Joulin. 2020. Unsupervised learning of visual features by contrasting cluster assignments. Advances in Neural Information Processing Systems, 33:9912–9924.

Jianpeng Cheng and Mirella Lapata. 2016. Neural summarization by extracting sentences and words. In Proceedings of the 54th Annual Meeting of the Association for Computational Linguistics (Volume 1: Long Papers), pages 484–494, Berlin, Germany. Association for Computational Linguistics.

Somnath Basu Roy Chowdhury, Chao Zhao, and Snigdha Chaturvedi. 2022. Unsupervised extractive opinion summarization using sparse coding. In Proceedings of the 60th Annual Meeting of the Association for Computational Linguistics (Volume 1: Long Papers), pages 1209–1225, Dublin, Ireland. Association for Computational Linguistics.

Eric Chu and Peter J. Liu. 2019. Meansum: A neural model for unsupervised multi-document abstractive summarization. In Proceedings of the 36th International Conference on Machine Learning, ICML 2019, 9-15 June 2019, Long Beach, California, USA, volume 97 of Proceedings of Machine Learning Research, pages 1223–1232. PMLR.

Jacob Devlin, Ming-Wei Chang, Kenton Lee, and Kristina Toutanova. 2019. BERT: Pre-training of deep bidirectional transformers for language understanding. In Proceedings of the 2019 Conference of the North American Chapter of the Association for Computational Linguistics: Human Language Technologies, Volume 1 (Long and Short Papers), pages 4171–4186, Minneapolis, Minnesota. Association for Computational Linguistics.

Giuseppe Di Fabbrizio, Amanda Stent, and Robert Gaizauskas. 2014. A hybrid approach to multi-document summarization of opinions in reviews. In Proceedings of the 8th International Natural Language Generation Conference (INLG), pages 54–63, Philadelphia, Pennsylvania, U.S.A. Association for Computational Linguistics.

Edsger W Dijkstra et al. 1959. A note on two problems in connexion with graphs. Numerische mathematik, 1(1):269–271.

Susan T Dumais et al. 2004. Latent semantic analysis. Annu. Rev. Inf. Sci. Technol., 38(1):188–230.

Kjersti Engan, Sven Ole Aase, and John Håkon Husøy. 1999. Method of optimal directions for frame design. International Conference on Acoustics, Speech, and Signal Processing. Proceedings. (ICASSP).

Günes Erkan and Dragomir R Radev. 2004. Lexrank: Graph-based lexical centrality as salience in text summarization. Journal of artificial intelligence research, 22:457–479.

Kavita Ganesan, ChengXiang Zhai, and Jiawei Han. 2010. Opinosis: A graph based approach to abstractive summarization of highly redundant opinions. In Proceedings of the 23rd International Conference on Computational Linguistics (Coling 2010), pages 340–348, Beijing, China. Coling 2010 Organizing Committee.

Tianyu Gao, Xingcheng Yao, and Danqi Chen. 2021. SimCSE: Simple contrastive learning of sentence embeddings. In Proceedings of the 2021 Conference on Empirical Methods in Natural Language Processing, pages 6894–6910, Online and Punta Cana, Dominican Republic. Association for Computational Linguistics.

Ruining He and Julian McAuley. 2016. Ups and downs: Modeling the visual evolution of fashion trends with one-class collaborative filtering. In proceedings of the 25th international conference on world wide web, pages 507–517.

Geoffrey E Hinton. 1984. Distributed representations.

Minqing Hu and Bing Liu. 2004. Mining and summarizing customer reviews. In Proceedings of the tenth ACM SIGKDD international conference on Knowledge discovery and data mining, pages 168–177.

Hayate Iso, Xiaolan Wang, Yoshihiko Suhara, Stefanos Angelidis, and Wang-Chiew Tan. 2021. Convex Aggregation for Opinion Summarization. In Findings of the Association for Computational Linguistics: EMNLP 2021, pages 3885–3903, Punta Cana, Dominican Republic. Association for Computational Linguistics.

Zhuxi Jiang, Yin Zheng, Huachun Tan, Bangsheng Tang, and Hanning Zhou. 2016. Variational deep embedding: An unsupervised and generative approach to clustering. arXiv preprint arXiv:1611.05148.

Jürgen Jost and Jeurgen Jost. 2008. Riemannian geometry and geometric analysis, volume 42005. Springer.

Hyun Duk Kim, Kavita Ganesan, Parikshit Sondhi, and ChengXiang Zhai. 2011. Comprehensive review of opinion summarization.

Diederik P Kingma and Jimmy Ba. 2014. Adam: A method for stochastic optimization. arXiv preprint arXiv:1412.6980.

Philipp Koehn. 2004. Statistical significance tests for machine translation evaluation. In Proceedings of the 2004 Conference on Empirical Methods in Natural Language Processing, pages 388–395, Barcelona, Spain. Association for Computational Linguistics.

Marc T Law, Raquel Urtasun, and Richard S Zemel. 2017. Deep spectral clustering learning. In International conference on machine learning, pages 1985–1994. PMLR.

Daniel Lee and H Sebastian Seung. 2000. Algorithms for non-negative matrix factorization. Advances in neural information processing systems, 13.

Honglak Lee, Alexis Battle, Rajat Raina, and Andrew Ng. 2006. Efficient sparse coding algorithms. Advances in neural information processing systems, 19.

Mike Lewis, Yinhan Liu, Naman Goyal, Marjan Ghazvininejad, Abdelrahman Mohamed, Omer Levy, Veselin Stoyanov, and Luke Zettlemoyer. 2020. BART: Denoising sequence-to-sequence pre-training for natural language generation, translation, and comprehension. In Proceedings of the 58th Annual Meeting of the Association for Computational Linguistics, pages 7871–7880, Online. Association for Computational Linguistics.

Haoyuan Li, Somnath Basu Roy Chowdhury, and Snigdha Chaturvedi. 2023. Aspect-aware unsupervised extractive opinion summarization. In Findings of the Association for Computational Linguistics: ACL 2023, pages 12662–12678.

Paul Pu Liang, Manzil Zaheer, Yuan Wang, and Amr Ahmed. 2021. Anchor & transform: Learning sparse embeddings for large vocabularies. International Conference on Learning Representations (ICLR).

Chin-Yew Lin. 2004. ROUGE: A package for automatic evaluation of summaries. In Text Summarization Branches Out, pages 74–81, Barcelona, Spain. Association for Computational Linguistics.

Peter J. Liu, Mohammad Saleh, Etienne Pot, Ben Goodrich, Ryan Sepassi, Lukasz Kaiser, and Noam Shazeer. 2018. Generating wikipedia by summarizing long sequences. In 6th International Conference on Learning Representations, ICLR 2018, Vancouver, BC, Canada, April 30 - May 3, 2018, Conference Track Proceedings. OpenReview.net.

Yinhan Liu, Myle Ott, Naman Goyal, Jingfei Du, Mandar Joshi, Danqi Chen, Omer Levy, Mike Lewis, Luke Zettlemoyer, and Veselin Stoyanov. 2019. Roberta: A robustly optimized bert pretraining approach. arXiv preprint arXiv:1907.11692.

Mahsa Lotfi and Mathukumalli Vidyasagar. 2018. A fast noniterative algorithm for compressive sensing using binary measurement matrices. IEEE Transactions on Signal Processing, 66(15):4079–4089.

Jordan J Louviere, Terry N Flynn, and Anthony Alfred John Marley. 2015. Best-worst scaling: Theory, methods and applications. Cambridge University Press.

Julien Mairal, Francis Bach, Jean Ponce, and Guillermo Sapiro. 2009. Online dictionary learning for sparse coding. In International Conference on Machine Learning (ICML).

Joshua Maynez, Shashi Narayan, Bernd Bohnet, and Ryan McDonald. 2020. On faithfulness and factuality in abstractive summarization. In Proceedings of the 58th Annual Meeting of the Association for Computational Linguistics, pages 1906–1919, Online. Association for Computational Linguistics.

Walaa Medhat, Ahmed Hassan, and Hoda Korashy. 2014. Sentiment analysis algorithms and applications: A survey. Ain Shams engineering journal, 5(4):1093–1113.

Mohammed Elsaid Moussa, Ensaf Hussein Mohamed, and Mohamed Hassan Haggag. 2018. A survey on opinion summarization techniques for social media. Future Computing and Informatics Journal, 3(1):82–109.

Ramesh Nallapati, Bowen Zhou, Cicero dos Santos, Caglar Gulcehree, and Bing Xiang. 2016. Abstractive text summarization using sequence-to-sequence RNNs and beyond. In Proceedings of The 20th SIGNLL Conference on Computational Natural Language Learning, pages 280–290, Berlin, Germany. Association for Computational Linguistics.

Shashi Narayan, Shay B. Cohen, and Mirella Lapata. 2018. Ranking sentences for extractive summarization with reinforcement learning. In Proceedings of the 2018 Conference of the North American Chapter of the Association for Computational Linguistics: Human Language Technologies, Volume 1 (Long Papers), pages 1747–1759, New Orleans, Louisiana. Association for Computational Linguistics.

Ani Nenkova and Lucy Vanderwende. 2005. The impact of frequency on summarization. Microsoft Research, Redmond, Washington, Tech. Rep. MSR-TR-2005, 101.

Bo Pang. 2008. lee, l.(2008). opinion mining and sentiment analysis. Foundations and trends in information retrieval, 2(1-2):1–135.

Maxime Peyrard. 2019. A simple theoretical model of importance for summarization. In Proceedings of the 57th Annual Meeting of the Association for Computational Linguistics, pages 1059–1073, Florence, Italy. Association for Computational Linguistics.

Dragomir R Radev, Hongyan Jing, Małgorzata Styś, and Daniel Tam. 2004. Centroid-based summarization of multiple documents. Information Processing & Management, 40(6):919–938.

Colin Raffel, Noam Shazeer, Adam Roberts, Katherine Lee, Sharan Narang, Michael Matena, Yanqi Zhou, Wei Li, Peter J Liu, et al. 2020. Exploring the limits of transfer learning with a unified text-to-text transformer. J. Mach. Learn. Res., 21(140):1–67.

Anna Rohrbach, Lisa Anne Hendricks, Kaylee Burns, Trevor Darrell, and Kate Saenko. 2018. Object hallucination in image captioning. In Proceedings of the 2018 Conference on Empirical Methods in Natural Language Processing, pages 4035–4045, Brussels, Belgium. Association for Computational Linguistics.

Alexander M. Rush, Sumit Chopra, and Jason Weston. 2015. A neural attention model for abstractive sentence summarization. In Proceedings of the 2015 Conference on Empirical Methods in Natural Language Processing, pages 379–389, Lisbon, Portugal. Association for Computational Linguistics.

Abigail See, Peter J. Liu, and Christopher D. Manning. 2017. Get to the point: Summarization with pointer-generator networks. In Proceedings of the 55th Annual Meeting of the Association for Computational Linguistics (Volume 1: Long Papers), pages 1073–1083, Vancouver, Canada. Association for Computational Linguistics.

Vitaly Surazhsky, Tatiana Surazhsky, Danil Kirsanov, Steven J Gortler, and Hugues Hoppe. 2005. Fast exact and approximate geodesics on meshes. ACM transactions on graphics (TOG), 24(3):553–560.

Yee Teh, Michael Jordan, Matthew Beal, and David Blei. 2004. Sharing clusters among related groups: Hierarchical dirichlet processes. Advances in neural information processing systems, 17.

Andreas M. Tillmann. 2015. On the computational intractability of exact and approximate dictionary learning. IEEE Signal Processing Letters, 22(1):45–49.

William Timkey and Marten van Schijndel. 2021. All bark and no bite: Rogue dimensions in transformer language models obscure representational quality. In Proceedings of the 2021 Conference on Empirical Methods in Natural Language Processing, pages 4527–4546, Online and Punta Cana, Dominican Republic. Association for Computational Linguistics.

Ashish Vaswani, Noam Shazeer, Niki Parmar, Jakob Uszkoreit, Llion Jones, Aidan N. Gomez, Lukasz Kaiser, and Illia Polosukhin. 2017. Attention is all you need. In Advances in Neural Information Processing Systems 30: Annual Conference on Neural Information Processing Systems 2017, December 4-9, 2017, Long Beach, CA, USA, pages 5998–6008.

Ke Wang and Xiaojun Wan. 2021. TransSum: Translating aspect and sentiment embeddings for self-supervised opinion summarization. In Findings of the Association for Computational Linguistics: ACL-IJCNLP 2021, pages 729–742, Online. Association for Computational Linguistics.

Joe H Ward Jr. 1963. Hierarchical grouping to optimize an objective function. Journal of the American statistical association, 58(301):236–244.

Thomas Wolf, Lysandre Debut, Victor Sanh, Julien Chaumond, Clement Delangue, Anthony Moi, Pierric Cistac, Tim Rault, Remi Louf, Morgan Funtowicz, Joe Davison, Sam Shleifer, Patrick von Platen, Clara Ma, Yacine Jernite, Julien Plu, Canwen Xu, Teven Le Scao, Sylvain Gugger, Mariama Drame, Quentin Lhoest, and Alexander Rush. 2020. Transformers: State-of-the-art natural language processing. In Proceedings of the 2020 Conference on Empirical Methods in Natural Language Processing: System Demonstrations, pages 38–45, Online. Association for Computational Linguistics.

Jianwei Yang, Devi Parikh, and Dhruv Batra. 2016. Joint unsupervised learning of deep representations and image clusters. In Proceedings of the IEEE conference on computer vision and pattern recognition, pages 5147–5156.

Chao Zhao and Snigdha Chaturvedi. 2020. Weakly-supervised opinion summarization by leveraging external information. In Proceedings of the AAAI

Conference on Artificial Intelligence, volume 34, pages 9644–9651.

Chao Zhao, Tenghao Huang, Somnath Basu Roy Chowdhury, Muthu Kumar Chandrasekaran, Kathleen Mckeown, and Snigdha Chaturvedi. 2022. Read top news first: A document reordering approach for multi-document news summarization. In Findings of the Association for Computational Linguistics: ACL 2022, pages 613–621.

Jinyu Zhao, Yi Hao, and Cyrus Rashtchian. 2020. Unsupervised embedding of hierarchical structure in euclidean space. arXiv preprint arXiv:2010.16055.

Hongyi Zheng, Hongwei Yong, and Lei Zhang. 2021. Deep convolutional dictionary learning for image denoising. In Proceedings of the IEEE/CVF Conference on Computer Vision and Pattern Recognition (CVPR).

A Appendix

A.1 Human Evaluation

We perform the human evaluation on the Amazon Mechanical Turk (AMT) platform. We designed the payment rate per Human Intelligence Task (HIT) in a manner to ensure that judges were compensated at a rate of at least $15 USD per hour. In all tasks, each HIT was evaluated by three human judges.

For general summarization, we performed a pairwise evaluation of two summarization systems. Specifically, we were given two system summaries the human judges were asked to judge each pair as better, worse, or similar. We asked the judges to evaluate the pair based on the following criteria – *informativeness*, *redundancy*, and *coherence*, in independent tasks. For informativeness, we also provide the judges with a human-written summary. The judges annotate a summary as more informative only if the information is consistent with the human-written summaries. The reported scores (-100 to +100) were computed using Best-worst scaling (Louviere et al., 2015). For a fair comparison, we consider the version of SemAE that does not use additional aspect-related information.

For aspect summarization, we provide human judges with a system-generated aspect summary and the corresponding aspect. Judges were asked to annotate whether the system summary discusses the mentioned aspect *exclusively*, *partially*, or *does not mention* the aspect at all.

A.2 Analysis

Dictionary Size Ablation. In this experiment, we vary the number of elements in each dictionary (m) and observe the summarization performance on SPACE dataset. We conduct these experiments on the SPACE dataset. In Table 12, we observe GeoSumm achieves comparable performance with significantly smaller dictionary sizes. In fact, for the smallest dictionary sizes GeoSumm achieves the best ROUGE-1 and ROUGE-L scores.

Sparsity.

We examine the sparsity of sentence representations from GeoSumm. For each sentence representation, we sort the dimensions by magnitude, from smallest to largest. This enables us to compare magnitudes across sentences for a specific sorted rank position. We then plot the mean magnitude (and two standard deviations) for each sorted rank position, as illustrated in Figure 3. Our observations indicate that most sentences possess only a few dimensions with high magnitude, while the remaining dimensions have magnitudes of zero or close to zero.

m	R1	R2	RL
512	**43.36**	11.53	24.10
1024	42.76	**12.66**	24.28
4096	42.77	11.47	24.11
8192	42.36	12.44	**24.80**
16384	41.24	10.92	23.92

Table 12: Evaluation results with a varying number of dictionary elements on SPACE dataset. We observe that there is only a small drop in performance of GeoSumm, when the dictionary sizes are reduced.

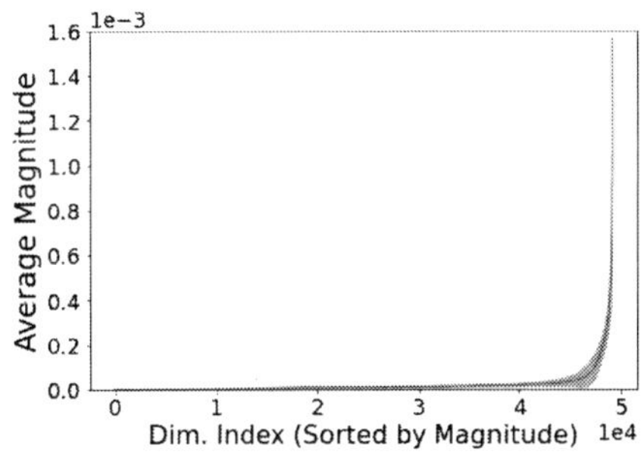

Figure 3: Plot depicting the sparsity of sentence representations retrieved from GeoSumm. We sort, individually for each sentence, the dimensions from the smallest to the largest magnitude and report the mean magnitude for each sorted position (and two standard deviations). Most sentences seem to have only a few large magnitude dimensions and many close to zero.

Domain Transfer capability. In this experiment, we investigate the domain transfer capability of GeoSumm. Specifically, we evaluate how GeoSumm trained on one dataset, performs on others. We also evaluate GeoSumm when it is trained on C4 dataset (Raffel et al., 2020). In Table 14, we report the results of this experiment. We observe that when training on the non-domain specific C4 corpus, performance is nearly that of in-domain training. The largest degradation of performance occurs when training on OPOSUM+ or AMAZON and evaluating on SPACE. We hypothesize that this happens due to a domain shift, where both AMAZON and OPOSUM+ are product review datasets, while SPACE has reviews for hotel entities. When evaluated on OPOSUM+ or AMAZON, we observe that GeoSumm is generalizing well, and out-of-domain performance is not much worse than in-domain performance (highlighted in gray).

Method	OpoSum+			Amazon			Space		
	R1	R2	RL	R1	R2	RL	R1	R2	RL
NMF (Lee and Seung, 2000)	32.85	10.44	18.96	30.33	5.07	16.10	34.88	6.14	18.87
LDA (Blei et al., 2003)	32.70	10.85	19.60	31.31	5.27	16.51	26.57	3.46	14.81
LSA (Dumais et al., 2004)	32.41	10.33	19.66	31.71	6.11	17.79	31.64	5.57	17.72
HDP (Teh et al., 2004)	34.60	11.29	19.39	30.60	4.91	16.20	29.77	4.44	16.49
NTM_{BERT} (Bianchi et al., 2021)	33.00	11.01	19.01	31.62	5.29	16.54	26.12	2.74	15.29
Geodesic Summarizer (GeoSumm)	**41.55**	**20.77**	**25.19**	**33.75**	**7.15**	**18.79**	**42.36**	**12.44**	**24.80**

Table 13: Comparison of Geodesic Summarizer's performance with other unsupervised topic modeling techniques on general summarization. In this experiment, we modify the representation learning module of Geodesic Summarizer while keeping the sentence selection approach same. We observe that Geodesic Summarizer's topic modeling approach achieves the best performance across all datasets.

Train→Predict	R1	R2	RL
Space→OpoSum+	38.94	16.80	22.60
Amazon→OpoSum+	40.14	18.97	24.91
C4→OpoSum+	37.96	15.97	21.93
OpoSum+→OpoSum+	**41.55**	**20.77**	**25.19**
Space→Amazon	32.29	6.36	17.22
OpoSum+→Amazon	33.57	6.46	17.86
C4→Amazon	32.03	6.35	17.04
Amazon→Amazon	**33.75**	**7.15**	**18.79**
OpoSum+→Space	27.85	4.93	16.03
Amazon→Space	25.14	2.95	14.98
C4→Space	41.81	11.61	24.28
Space→Space	**42.36**	**12.44**	**24.80**

Table 14: Evaluation results when the representation learning system is trained on a different dataset. In-domain performance is highlighted in gray. GeoSumm shows decent domain transfer performance for OpoSum+ and Amazon datasets.

Unsupervised Topic Modeling Ablations In this setup, we experiment with different unsupervised topic modeling approaches – latent Dirichlet allocation (LDA) (Blei et al., 2003), linear semantic analysis (LSA) (Dumais et al., 2004), non-negative matrix factorization (NMF) (Lee and Seung, 2000), hierarchical Dirichlet process (HDP) (Teh et al., 2004), and neural topic model (NTM) using contextual embeddings (Bianchi et al., 2021). Most of these approaches focus on factorizing sentence representations into topical representations over a set of learned topics. We set the sentence representation dimension $d = 100$ for all approaches. Specifically, we replace the representation learning module from GeoSumm while keeping the sentence selection algorithm the same. In Table 13, we report the performance on general summarization of different methods. We observe that most of the other topical approaches perform significantly worse than GeoSumm. These approaches use significantly fewer parameters compared to a Transformer decoder used in GeoSumm. We believe that leveraging more parameters helps the unsupervised model to capture latent semantics better leading to better summarization performance.

Analyzing Multi-Sentence Aggregation in Abstractive Summarization via the Shapley Value

Jingyi He[1*] **Meng Cao**[2] **Jackie Chi Kit Cheung**[2]

Cohere AI[1] Mila / McGill University[2]

{jingyi.he@mail, meng.cao@mail, jcheung@cs}.mcgill.ca

Abstract

Abstractive summarization systems aim to write concise summaries capturing the most essential information of the input document in their own words. One of the ways to achieve this is to gather and combine multiple pieces of information from the source document, a process we call *aggregation*. Despite its importance, the extent to which both reference summaries in benchmark datasets and system-generated summaries require aggregation is yet unknown. In this work, we propose **AGGSHAP**, a measure of the degree of aggregation in a summary sentence. We show that AGGSHAP distinguishes multi-sentence aggregation from single-sentence extraction or paraphrasing through automatic and human evaluations. We find that few reference or model-generated summary sentences have a high degree of aggregation measured by the proposed metric. We also demonstrate negative correlations between AGGSHAP and other quality scores of system summaries. These findings suggest the need to develop new tasks and datasets to encourage multi-sentence aggregation in summarization.

1 Introduction

Abstractive summarization aims to gather important information from some source text and to synthesize this information into a brief, informative, and factually correct summary. Summary-worthy information on a topic can be located in multiple parts of the document or even in different documents in the multi-document summarization case. They may appear in multiple sentences with either overlapping content or complementary information that is related in discourse. Therefore, *aggregation*, the process of combining multiple related pieces of information, is necessary to generate more useful and concise abstractive summaries.

Multi-sentence aggregation or fusion has been studied as a way to perform abstractive summarization (Barzilay and McKeown, 2005; Thadani and McKeown, 2013; Brook Weiss et al., 2022). A good summary can be written by fusing a set of salient sentences on the same topic. Therefore, the capability of aggregating information is extremely important in many summarization settings, such as long document summarization, multi-document summarization and timeline summarization. Moreover, from the theoretical perspective, multi-sentence aggregation motivates future studies of more fine-grained semantic operations (e.g. modelling contradictions and synthesizing common information across texts).

Previous studies compute proxies of abstractiveness that are closely related to the aggregation of a summary. They quantify how a summary uses words and phrases that are not found in the document, such as the percentage of novel n-grams as one of the ways to achieve highly condensed and abstractive summaries. Note that higher abstractiveness can be achieved by a broader set of rewriting operations (e.g. paraphrasing, sentence fusion, synthesizing and external knowledge). In this paper, we are particularly interested in measuring summary sentences formed by multi-sentence aggregation.

As an illustration of the difference between aggregation and abstractiveness, all three summary sentences in Table 1 contain a similar percentage of novel uni-, bi- and tri-grams, but they are formed by using different types of rewriting techniques. Novel n-grams are not able to distinguish instances that require information from multiple sentences, or that require external knowledge to infer the summary sentence, from those only formed by single-sentence compression and paraphrasing.

Another reason that aggregation is under-explored is that some popular summarization benchmark datasets are nearly extractive. As a

*Work done at Mila/McGill University

Proceedings of The 4th New Frontiers in Summarization Workshop, pages 121–134
December 6, 2023

Rewriting Type	Source Document	Summary Sentence Novel [uni-, bi- tri-]grams	AGGSHAP [LM, ROUGE]
Paraphrase	(1) (CNN)Recently, a New York judge issued an opinion authorizing service of divorce papers on a husband completely via Facebook.	A court allowed a wife to serve divorce papers via Facebook . [0.25, 0.72, 0.9]	[0.449, 0.651]
Multi-sentence Fusion	(1) (CNN) Five years ago , Rebecca Francis posed for a photo while lying next to a dead giraffe . (2) The trouble started Monday , when comedian Ricky Gervais tweeted the photo with a question .	Rebecca Francis' photo with a giraffe was shared by Ricky Gervais. [0.153, 0.666, 0.909]	[0.823, 0.856]
External Knowledge	(1)The Masters 2015 is almost here. (2) To help get you in the mood for the first major of the year, [golfers' names] give the lowdown on every hole at the world-famous Augusta National Golf Club. (3) Click on the graphic below to get a closer look at what the biggest names in the game will face when they tee off on Thursday.	The 79th Masters Tournament gets underway at Augusta National on Thursday . [0.33,0.72,0.93]	[0.951, 0.896]

Table 1: Examples from CNN/DM test set show summary sentences formed by diverse types of rewriting techniques with a similar level of novel n-grams. The source sentences are highlighted based on the magnitude of their Shapley values from AGGSHAP-LM. We use three shades to indicate the relative contributions of the individual source sentence, namely [40%, 100%] , [20%, 40%) and [0, 20%) .

result, systems are not rewarded for performing aggregation. For example, Lebanoff et al. (2019b) show that only 30% of the summary sentences in the CNN/DM (Nallapati et al., 2016) are generated by fusing two or more sentences. Only relatively recently have datasets been proposed which are less extractive in terms of novel n-grams (Hermann et al., 2015; Narayan et al., 2018; Grusky et al., 2018; Koupaee and Wang, 2018; Fabbri et al., 2019). Some specifically encourage multi-sentence aggregation with summary-worthy content evenly distributed in the source (Sharma et al., 2019b). These datasets are designed to encourage systems to learn information aggregation in dispersed source document sentences, but automatically measuring this property is not yet available.

In this work, we propose a novel measure of aggregation AGGSHAP by computing a measure of many-to-one dependency between source and summary sentences. Specifically, we focus on multi-sentence aggregation where supporting information is present in the source document. Our measure uses the Shapley value (Shapley, 1953) from co-operative game theory by treating the coverage of information in a summary sentence as a coalition game played by source sentences. We compute the contribution of each source sentence using the Shapley value. Finally, the degree of aggregation of a summary sentence is characterized by the dispersion of their contributions. This measure helps us quantify intuitions about summarization datasets and the types of semantic operations that we can hope to train systems to perform using them. It also allows us to examine the phenomenon of aggregation in existing abstractive summarizers.

We validate the proposed AGGSHAP by using it to distinguish between sentences that require fusing information from multiple sentences and sentences that do not. More importantly, we show that AGGSHAP has a stronger correlation with direct human ratings of aggregation than other abstractiveness measures such as novel n-grams. Next, we apply our measure to examine the need for aggregation in existing summarization datasets and in the output of recent neural abstractive summarization models trained on these datasets. Finally, we demonstrate a negative correlation between the degree of aggregation and existing summary quality measures. This suggests that multi-sentence aggregation remains largely beyond the capability of current abstractive summarizers.

2 Related Work

2.1 Aggregation in Text Summarization

Aggregation, broadly defined, has long been a research area in NLG (Reape and Mellish, 1999; Dalianis and Hovy, 1996; Di Eugenio et al., 2005). In summarization, Jing and McKeown (1999) showed some human-written summary sentences are formed by aggregating information from multiple text spans through manual inspection. Sentence fusion is one of the most studied aggregation behaviors in the literature (Barzilay and McKeown, 2005; Elsner and Santhanam, 2011; Cheung and Penn, 2014; Yuan et al., 2021; Brook Weiss et al., 2022). Lebanoff et al. (2019a, 2020) studied sentence fusion by leveraging the syntactic cues. Much work in sentence fusion literature focuses on the syntactic dependency between similar sentences without understanding the semantic dependency between disparate sentences. As a step towards understanding semantic abstraction, Jumel et al. (2020) introduced a task of generalization and semantic aggregations of entities which is useful for performing higher-level aggregation across sentences. Ernst et al. (2021) proposed a task of aligning summary sentences and document sentences in summarization, where aligned document sentences can be viewed as the source of aggregation.

Humans write summaries at different levels of granularity using aggregation operations beyond sentence fusion. For example, in the news domain (Hermann et al., 2015; Grusky et al., 2018), summaries are usually formed by copying and are affected by strong layout biases (Grenander et al., 2019). On the other hand, salient content may be distributed evenly throughout the text in scientific documents (Sharma et al., 2019b). Datasets for summarizing dialog (Chen et al., 2021), fiction (Kryściński et al., 2021) and meetings (Liu and Liu, 2013) show varying types of aggregation and amount of reused text (Song et al., 2020).

2.2 Measuring Aggregation

Previous work reported the percentage of novel n-grams or the notion of *Coverage* (Grusky et al., 2018) as a proxy for abstractiveness. These metrics have been adopted in other areas such as dialog (Dziri et al., 2022) to inspect the qualities and characteristics of datasets. Despite being convenient, these measures do not enable fine-grained analyses of multi-sentence aggregation.

Cheung and Penn (2013) proposed a quantitative measure of the degree of sentence aggregation at the shallow semantic level of caseframes. However, their method only accounts for limited types of aggregation and cannot be used to analyze aggregation in sentences with substantial rewriting. Wolhandler et al. (2022) proposed a metric to measure how information in a summary is dispersed in source documents in the multi-document summarization setting. They found that most summaries in certain datasets can be generated using information from only one source document.

The aggregation metric proposed in this work is inspired by the Shapley value, which is used to measure the contributions of individual players in a cooperative game (Shapley, 1953). Shapley values have been applied to settings such as feature attribution (Lundberg and Lee, 2017; Dhamdhere et al., 2019) and explaining training data contribution (Parvez and Chang, 2021).

3 Method

In this section, we propose **AGGSHAP**, an automatic metric to quantify the degree of aggregation of a summary sentence using the Shapley value. Shapley value is a concept from cooperative game theory used to determine the contributions of individual players to the outcome of a coalition game. We consider how much information in a summary sentence is covered as a coalition game in which source sentences are players. The Shapley value of a source sentence can be interpreted as its contribution to covering information in the summary sentence. The AGGSHAP score of a summary sentence captures the dispersion of source sentences' Shapley values. The degree of aggregation of a multi-sentence summary is the mean AGGSHAP scores of summary sentences.

3.1 Shapley Value Formulation

Let $D = \{d^1, ..., d^{|D|}\}$ denote a source document with $|D|$ source sentences and $S = \{s^1, ..., s^{|S|}\}$ denote a corresponding summary with $|S|$ summary sentences.

We formulate the contribution of a source sentence d_i to a summary sentence s using the Shapley value. We first define a score function $v(s, C)$ that maps a subset of source sentences $C \subseteq D$ and a summary sentence s to a real value. This represents how much information in a summary sentence is covered by the subset of source sentences. We will specify different possible instantiations of the score function $v(s, C)$ in Section 3.2 using ROUGE scores or probabilities from a conditional language model.

The Shapley value of source sentence d_i with respect to the summary sentence s is defined as

$$\phi_i(v(s, \cdot)) = \sum_{C \subset D \setminus \{i\}} \frac{|C|!(|D| - |C| - 1)!}{|D|!} [v(s, C \cup \{i\}) - v(s, C)] \tag{1}$$

where $\frac{1}{|D|!}$ is a normalization factor equal to the number of all permutations formed by $|D|$ source sentences. Given a source sentence subset C, $|C|!(|D| - |C| - 1)!$ is the number of orders in which sentences in C appear before d_i and sentences in $D \setminus (C \cup \{i\})$ can appear after d_i. We multiply the marginal gain of d_i entering into C by this factor because the marginal gains are the same for all such orders. We present a working example in the Appendix.

The time complexity for computing exact Shapley values is exponential in the number of source sentences. Therefore, we use a Monte-Carlo method to sample subsets of source sentences and get an unbiased estimator of $\tilde{\phi}_i(v(s,\cdot))$

Measure Aggregation as Information Dispersion We define the final AGGSHAP score based on the dispersion of source sentences' Shapley values. We choose the **coefficient of variation**[1] ($\mathrm{CV}(s) := \frac{\sigma(\phi_i(v(\cdot))}{\mu(\phi_i(v(\cdot)))}$) as the dispersion metric as it is scale-invariant. Next, we normalize the CV such that AGGSHAP $\in [0,1]$.[2]

$$\text{AGGSHAP}(s) := -\frac{\mathrm{CV}(s)}{\sqrt{k-1}} + 1 \in [0,1] \quad (2)$$

The AGGSHAP of a summary sentence is maximized when only one of the source sentences has a non-negative Shapley value. Conversely, AGGSHAP is minimized when source sentences' Shapley values are at the same level (i.e. variance is close to 0).

3.2 Score Function Instantiations

We experimented with two methods of specifying $v(s, C)$, one based on lexical overlaps and another based on language model probabilities.

Measuring support using lexical overlap. Lexical overlap between a source and a summary sentence is one way to measure the information of s covered by a subset of source sentences C: $v^{\text{ROUGE}}(s, C) = \text{avg}(\text{ROUGE}_1(s, C) + \text{ROUGE}_2(s, C) + \text{ROUGE}_L(s, C))$. We use ROUGE recall scores in these calculations. One potential issue with lexical overlap is that it is a crude proxy of semantic relatedness, and does not account for issues such as paraphrasing.

Measuring support using LM predictions. Given a sequence-to-sequence (seq2seq) conditional text generation model, $\mathcal{M}$, parametrized by $\theta_\mathcal{M}$, the probability of a target sequence of n tokens $s = (s_1, ..., s_n)$ conditioning on the source text with m tokens $d = (d_1, ..., d_m)$ reflects how likely the target sequence s is to be generated. The log-likelihood of the target sequence is:

$$\mathcal{L}(s|d;\theta_\mathcal{M}) = \sum_{i=1}^{n} \log p(s_i|s_{<i}, d; \theta_\mathcal{M}) \quad (3)$$

[1] σ and μ are standard deviation and mean. The coefficient of variation goes to infinity when the mean is close to zero. To avoid this, we take $\phi_i(v(\cdot) = \max(\phi_i(v(\cdot)), 0)$.

[2] Proof in the Appendix.

We use the normalized log probability of the summary sentence as the value function:

$$v^{\text{LM}}(s, C) = \frac{1}{n}\mathcal{L}(s|d;\theta_\mathcal{M}) \quad (4)$$

$v^{\text{LM}}(\emptyset, s)$ is the (unconditional) score from a language model with no input document.

We call the two versions of the metric AGGSHAP-ROUGE and AGGSHAP-LM, respectively.

4 Evaluations of AGGSHAP

We validate the effectiveness of AGGSHAP through two experiments. First, we show fusional sentences can be distinguished from extractive ones. Next, we compute correlations between AGGSHAP or word overlap metrics on the one hand and direct assessment of aggregation on the other.

4.1 Validating AGGSHAP in Sentence Fusion

In this section, we will show that AGGSHAP effectively distinguishes instances that are a fusion of a pair of source sentences from sentences that do not require aggregation. Our assumption is that fusional instances require a higher level of aggregation and thus should be ranked higher in terms of a measure of aggregation compared to extractive instances.

Dataset. The PoC (Points of Correspondence) dataset introduced by Lebanoff et al. (2019a) consists of 1,599 summary sentences and their supporting source sentence pairs from the validation and test set of the CNN/DM. The data points are deemed fusional by human annotators. The fusional instances are constructed as follows: first, the two source sentences most similar to the summary sentence based on ROUGE are selected as candidate sentences. Next, human annotators judge if the summary sentence is the fusion of these two sentences. Additionally, we extract 1,599 highly extractive summary sentences that are unlikely to require aggregation from the CNN/DM test set. These sentences are those that have at least 90% trigram overlap with a source sentence. We call this CNN/DM-EXTRACTIVE.

AGGSHAP Implementation. For all experiments and analyses in this work, we take the 30 most similar source sentences, based on ROUGE-1 F-score, to the summary sentence as the source document. We use NLTK for sentence tokenization

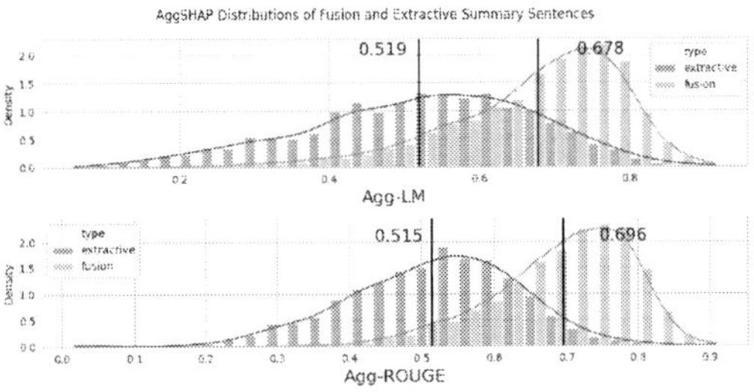

Figure 1: AGGSHAP score distributions of CNN/DM extractive and PoC fusional instances using the two variants. Gaussian kernel density estimators are fitted for each group. Mean AGGSHAP scores are annotated.

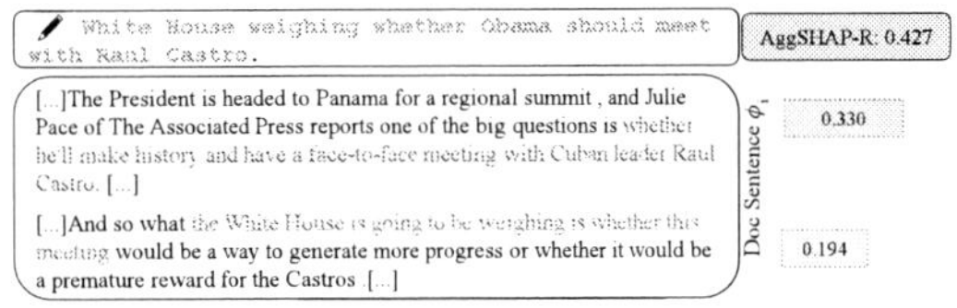

(a) Multi-sentence Fusion

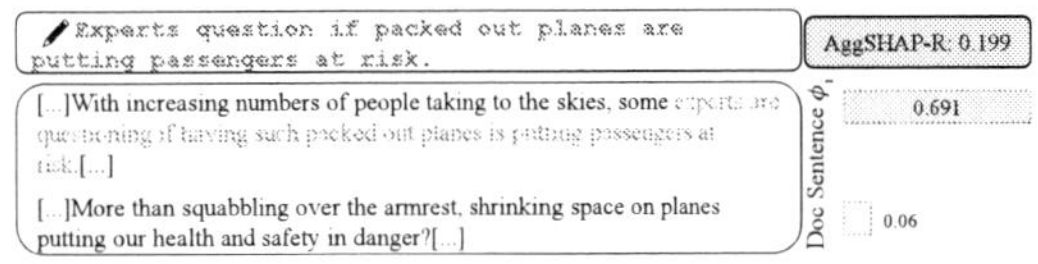

(b) Single-sentence Simplification

Figure 2: Eamples of multi-sentence fusion and single-sentence simplification from PoC. Document sentences with the two highest Shapley values are shown.

unless they are provided in the dataset. We use PEGASUS (Zhang et al., 2019)[3], a state-of-the-art encoder-decoder model for abstractive summarization, for computing AGGSHAP-LM. We sample 15 subsets of source sentences to compute the source sentence's Shapley value. For this particular experiment, we use PEGASUS fine-tuned on CNN/DM.[4]

Results. Figure 1 shows the distributions of AGGSHAP of fusional and extractive sentences measured by AGGSHAP-ROUGE and AGGSHAP-LM. Extractive instances and fusional instances have mean AGGSHAP-LM 0.519 and 0.678, respectively and mean AGGSHAP-ROUGE 0.515 and 0.696. The two groups are statistically significantly different with $p < 0.05$ according to the Student's t-test. AGGSHAP are effective automatic metrics capturing the difference between sentence fusion and single sentence extraction.

It is expected that novel n-grams can also separate the two groups of sentences because they are used as selection criteria for the dataset curation. Therefore they have an unfair advantage in this dataset in particular. As a strong baseline, the novel bigrams are 0.143 for fusional instances and 0.579 for extractive instances. Moreover, one should note that novel n-grams only offer an overview of how different the summary is written compared to the document. They do not provide information about the source of the supporting information.

AGGSHAP on the other hand allows fine-grained analysis of the contributions from each source sentence, which is not trivial for novel n-grams. Since computing Shapley values of source sentences is an intermediate step of AGGSHAP, we can see if the magnitude of a source sentence's Shapley value aligns with human judgments. That is, whether sentences with higher Shapley values are indeed supporting sentences. We find for 95% $(1{,}520/1{,}599)$ of the fusional summary sentences, the highest Shapley value is assigned to one of the PoC supporting source sentences. For 50% $(802/1{,}599)$ of the fusional sentences, the sentences with the top-2 highest Shapley values are the same as the pair of supporting sentences in PoC. In Figure 2, the sentence fusion example shows that the distribution of source sentences' Shapley values is flatter. In contrast, the extractive case results in a distribution with a narrow spike.

4.2 Human Evaluation of AGGSHAP

To the best of our knowledge, there is no direct assessment of multi-sentence aggregation. In order to measure how AGGSHAP aligns with human intuition about aggregation, we compute the correlations between human ratings of aggregation and AGGSHAP.

We designed the annotation procedure to directly quantify the degree of aggregation as the number of source sentences which cover all information in a summary sentence. Specifically, two of the authors of the paper are presented with 100 instances randomly sampled from the CNN/DM test set. To avoid trivial extractive cases, we filtered out summary sentences that have less than 0.3 novel bi-grams. Each instance consists of a summary sentence and the 10 most similar source sentences sorted in the decreasing order of the percentage of extractive bi-grams. We asked annotators to select the source sentence if it covers information in the summary sentence and does not cover the same

[3]google/pegasus-cnn_dailymail from huggingface (Wolf et al., 2020).

[4]In fact, AGGSHAP is flexible in the choice of similarity measure and language model.

piece of information as previously chosen source sentences. Finally, the number of supporting source sentences is the human rating of aggregation. We include the detailed protocol and additional analysis in the appendix.

The inter-annotator agreement measured by Krippendorff's alpha (Krippendorff, 2011) is 0.604. We used bootstrapping method with bootstrap sample size of 50 to get the 95% confidence interval of $[0.431, 0.743]$.

We compare AGGSHAP to other metrics quantifying the level of abstractiveness in summarization. **Novel n-grams** is the percentage of novel words or n-grams in a summary that is not present in the source document. **Abstractivity** (Bommasani and Cardie, 2020) derives from the notion of *coverage*, a measure of extractiveness, proposed by Grusky et al. (2018). $\text{ABS}(D, S) = 1 - \frac{\sum_{f \in \mathcal{F}(D,S)} |f|}{|S|}$, where $\mathcal{F}(D, S)$ is the set of extractive fragments in a summary extracted by greedily matching text spans shared between D and S. $|f|$ is the number of tokens in extractive fragment f.

NN-2	Abs.	AggSHAP-LM	AggSHAP-R
0.354	0.360	0.375	0.554

Table 2: Spearman correlation of various metrics and human ratings of aggregation. Abs. stands for abstractivity. All correlations have p-value $< 1.0 \times 10^{-5}$.

Table 2 presents the Spearman correlation between measures of aggregation and abstractivity and direct measure of aggregation by human annotators. AGGSHAP-ROUGE demonstrates the strongest correlation with human judgment among all measures whereas AGGSHAP-LM shows a similar level of correlation to novel n-grams and abstractivity. We speculate that the CNN/DM dataset is more extractive, thus quantifying supporting information with lexical overlaps in AGGSHAP-ROUGE is more effective than that using language model prediction.

5 Analysis

Given our automatic tool for measuring aggregation, we can use it to investigate the current state of multi-sentence aggregation in abstractive summarization. First, we study whether widely used datasets have sufficient signals to train summarization systems to perform multi-sentence aggregation (Sec. 5.1). Next, Sec. 5.2 presents how well summarizers that are trained or fine-tuned on one of these datasets (CNN/DM) perform aggregation. Finally, we are interested in whether the quality of a summary is affected by its degree of aggregation. (Sec. 5.3)

5.1 Aggregation in Summarization Datasets

In this section, we first apply AGGSHAP to measure the degree of aggregation in datasets from various genres. We are interested in the following questions in frequently used datasets: **Q1.** What is the level of aggregation exhibited by reference summaries in abstractive summarization datasets? **Q2.** Previous work reported word overlaps as intrinsic characteristics of a dataset. What is the relationship between aggregation and lexical overlaps? We answer these questions based on observation of the Table 3.

The implementation of AGGSHAP is described in Sec. 4.1. We use PEGASUS (Zhang et al., 2019) fine-tuned on corresponding datasets for AGGSHAP-LM.

Datasets. We conduct analysis on aggregation in human-written summaries of six abstractive summarization datasets. From the news domain, we analyze single-document summarization datasets CNN/Dailymail (Hermann et al., 2015), XSUM (Narayan et al., 2018), Newsroom (Grusky et al., 2018) and a multi-document summarization dataset Multinews (Fabbri et al., 2019). We also report results on PubMed (Cohan et al., 2018), a long-document dataset of scientific papers, and WikiHow (Koupaee and Wang, 2018), a dataset of articles describing a procedural task.

A1. Datasets examined show a different level of aggregation as measured by AGGSHAP, but datasets in the news domain share a similarly low level of aggregation except XSUM, as expected. Kryscinski et al. (2020) characterize CNN/DM as a benchmark dataset for the field. We show that CNN/DM has a rather low level of aggregation, novel n-grams and abstractivity. Multi-News and Newsroom display a similar level of aggregation and percentage of novel words as CNN/DM. Despite being a multi-document summarization dataset, we find that there is a substantial portion of summaries that rely on extraction from only one of the source documents in Multi-News.

The XSUM dataset has significantly higher AGGSHAP scores and novel n-grams compared to other datasets. Models that are trained on this

	CNN/DM	XSUM	Multi-News	Newsroom	PubMed	Wikihow	PoC (Fus.)	CNN/DM (Ext.)
AGGSHAP-LM	0.677	**0.800**	0.588	0.557	0.688	0.732	0.678	0.519
AGGSHAP-R	0.678	**0.828**	0.674	0.560	0.737	0.686	0.696	0.515
ABS	0.217	**0.319**	0.173	0.176	0.109	0.211	0.117	0.036
NN-1	0.203	0.356	0.277	0.202	0.171	**0.359**	0.143	0.044
NN-2	0.548	**0.816**	0.604	0.499	0.494	0.723	0.571	0.143
NN-3	0.738	**0.956**	0.764	0.615	0.696	0.908	0.802	0.254

Table 3: **Top section**: Mean aggregation scores in the test sets. **Bottom section**: Measures based on lexical overlap. Higher Novel n-grams (NN) and Abstractivity (ABS) suggest more novel phrases are used in summaries, which potentially indicates aggregation. Datasets that have the **highest** value on the measured dimension are boldfaced and the lowest values are underlined. The right section shows statistics of the PoC dataset.

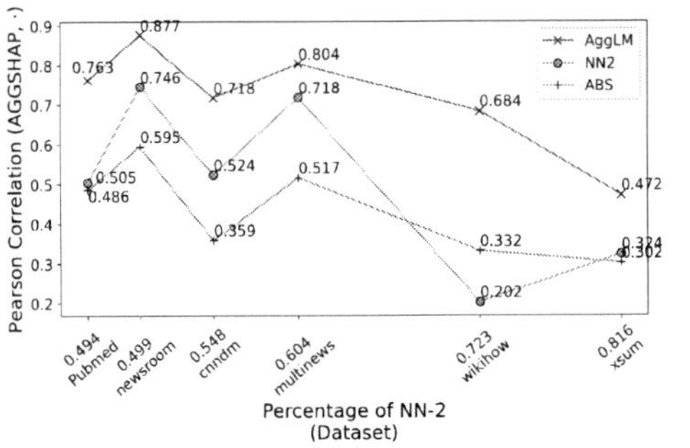

Figure 3: Pearson correlations between AGGSHAP-ROUGE and other measures as a function of dataset's percentage of novel bigrams.

dataset may be more likely to perform abstraction, multi-sentence aggregation, and utilize external knowledge. We inspected examples from the XSUM dataset with high AGGSHAP scores and their source sentences' Shapley values. We find that contributions to the summary sentence are shared among multiple source sentences.

A2. AGGSHAP and abstractiveness show strong correlations in the near-extractive datasets. The correlation between the two decreases in more abstractive datasets. We observe from Figure 3 that correlations between AGGSHAP-ROUGE and lexical overlap-based abstractiveness measures and AGGSHAP-LM decrease for datasets that have a higher proportion of novel bigrams. Since AGGSHAP-ROUGE has a moderately strong Spearman correlation with human ratings of aggregation (Table 2), decreases in correlations between AGGSHAP-ROUGE and other measures suggest that using semantic similarity measures beyond lexical overlap is necessary for investigating higher-level aggregation in more abstractive datasets.

We also notice that low novel n-gram does not necessarily imply the dataset is extractive. For example, PubMed summaries have a low proportion of novel n-grams, but they display a similarly high level of aggregation in terms of AGGSHAP as Wikihow. We speculate that mentioning proper nouns of studies in summaries is common in scientific papers, which contributes to low level of novel n-grams.

5.2 Aggregation in Current Models

We analyze the level of aggregation of summaries generated by recent abstractive summarization models trained or fine-tuned on the CNN/DM dataset. Similar analysis can be conducted on other datasets, but we focus on CNN/DM as it is one of the most frequently used datasets by models proposed over the years. We can then analyze how systems improve in aggregation. The systems-generated summaries are provided by the authors of the model and collected by Fabbri et al. (2021) under the MIT License. We follow the implementation details described in Section 4.1.

Table 4 shows the performance of summaries according to ROUGE and various measures of aggregation level and abstractiveness[5]. Overall, we find that recent abstractive summarizers display a lower level of aggregation and novel n-grams than human-written summaries across the board. Some recent models such as BART and PEGASUS use fewer novel words on average to achieve higher ROUGE scores compared to previous models, and they display a wider range of AGGSHAP scores.

We manually inspected some summaries from systems with high AGGSHAP scores. We find that BART and PEGASUS summaries often involve simple rewriting operations such as paraphrasing and concatenating text spans from multiple sentences, which may explain how they achieve higher AGGSHAP scores despite a lower proportion of

[5]Full results in the Appendix.

	ROUGE-1/2/3/L	AGGSHAP-LM	AGGSHAP-R	NN-1	NN-2	NN-3	ABS
Reference	-	**0.678**	**0.677**	**0.203**	**0.548**	**0.738**	**0.217**
M10 - **Bottom-Up**	0.412 / 0.187 / 0.106 / 0.382	0.553	**0.579**	0.155	**0.355**	**0.497**	0.019
M11 - **Improve-abs**	0.399 / 0.172 / 0.093 / 0.373	0.527	**0.580**	0.153	0.328	0.458	**0.025**
M17 - **T5**	0.448 / 0.221 / 0.134 / 0.417	0.543	0.557	**0.171**	**0.364**	**0.486**	0.011
M18 - **NeuralTD**	0.400 / 0.176 / 0.100 / 0.372	0.520	0.540	**0.173**	**0.369**	**0.497**	0.018
M21 - **UniLM**	0.431 / 0.204 / 0.122 / 0.401	0.554	0.559	0.032	0.164	0.284	**0.023**
M22 - **BART**	0.442 / 0.213 / 0.129 / 0.410	**0.555**	0.554	0.022	0.125	0.225	0.015
M23 - **Pegasus** (huge news)	0.441 / 0.215 / 0.130 / 0.410	**0.580**	0.570	0.029	0.176	0.303	0.018

Table 4: Models' ROUGE scores (partial, adapted from SummEval (Fabbri et al., 2021)) and aggregation statistics. The highest aggregation scores and percentages of novel n-grams are bolded.

novel n-grams. Bottom-Up (M10) and Improve-abs(M11) have aggregation scores on par with PEGASUS and BART. However, the quality of the generated text is significantly lower as shown by ROUGE. Enabling multi-sentence aggregation in abstractive summarization is a promising open research area, since there is still a large gap in aggregation between system-generated summaries and reference summaries.

5.3 Aggregation Versus Summary Quality

We are interested in whether systems can perform aggregation as well as generate high-quality summaries. Kryściński et al. (2018) reported a negative result where novel n-grams negatively correlate with ROUGE scores. Inspired by this, we inspect if there is a similar trade-off between aggregation and summaries' quality.

We use the human annotations from SummEval (Fabbri et al., 2019) (11 abstractive models evaluated on *Coherence*, *Factuality*, *Fluency* and *Relevance*) and NeR18 (Grusky et al., 2018) (7 systems evaluated on *Coherence*, *Fluency*, *Informativeness*, *Relevance*). We compute system-level correlations between AGGSHAP and human judgement scores. We follow the definition of system-level correlation in (Louis and Nenkova, 2013), as follows: first, we compute a system-level score of the system by averaging the scores of interest over all instances in the dataset. Next, we compute Kendall's τ between the rankings of the systems.

	SummEval				Newsroom			
	COH	FAC	FLU	REL	COH	FLU	INF	REL
NN-1	0.090	-0.310	-0.270	-0.240	-0.520	-0.520	-0.520	-0.430
NN-2	-0.050	-0.380	-0.270	-0.310	-0.900	-0.900	-0.710	-0.810
NN-3	-0.020	-0.420	-0.310	-0.350	-0.810	-0.810	-0.620	-0.710
ABS	0.050	-0.490	-0.160	-0.270	-0.330	-0.330	-0.330	-0.240
AGG-LM	-0.117	-0.450	-0.243	-0.283	-0.810	-0.810	-0.619	-0.714
AGG-R	-0.133	-0.467	-0.259	-0.267	-0.714	-0.714	-0.714	-0.619

Table 5: System-level Kendall's tau correlation coefficients between metrics of interest (AGGSHAP and novel n-grams) and human judgments. AGG are the abbreviated version of AGGSHAP.

Table 5 shows the results of these correlation computations. Both AGGSHAP and abstractiveness measures have consistent negative correlations with human ratings of quality. AGGSHAP show moderate negative correlations in factuality and weak negative correlations in relevance, indicating systems that attempt to aggregate are likely to introduce factual error into the summary. Weak correlations are shown in coherence and fluency dimensions because neither abstractiveness metrics nor AGGSHAP measure the inter-sentence connections of a summary.

One of the findings from SummEval is that reference summaries have lower scores than extractive systems (e.g. lead-3) across all four dimensions. This indicates that human judges prefer nearly extractive summaries in this dataset. Therefore, systems that are able to perform multi-sentence aggregation might not be rewarded by current evaluation schemes. To track the progress of aggregation in summarization systems, human annotators should directly assess the degree of aggregation.

6 Conclusion

In this paper, we propose AGGSHAP to quantify aggregation operations in abstractive summarization. Our metric effectively distinguishes sentences that require multiple points of dependencies from those that do not in a dataset containing fusional summary sentences. Moreover, it has a stronger correlation with human ratings of aggregation than existing n-grams overlap measures. We use AGGSHAP to compare the levels of aggregation in summarization datasets and conclude that most recent summarization datasets from the news domain contain limited instances of reference summaries that require aggregation. We show that abstractive summarization models rarely perform semantic aggregation beyond simple concatenation of text units. Finally, we find improvements in the dimension of aggregation may not be rewarded by current evaluation schemes of general summarization qualities. Future evaluations should thus focus specifically on the issue of aggregation, ideally in a domain or setting whether aggregation is necessary to derive a reference summary or a useful conclusion.

Acknowledgements The authors acknowledge the material support of NVIDIA in the form of computational resources. The first author is supported by the Fonds de recherche du Quebec – Nature et technologies. The last author is supported in part by the Canada CIFAR AI Chair program.

Limitations

Computation Efficiency. As noted in the method section 3.2, computation of the Shapley value has exponential time complexity. We address this issue by using Monte-Carlo sampling method but it is still computationally expensive to conduct analysis of aggregation at a large scale. For each sentence evaluated, it requires (#Number of source sentences × #Shapley value sample) times of forward pass to compute the estimated Shapley values of source sentences. We only conducted analysis on the test set of the datasets and, for example, it took 24 hours on a single V100 GPU with 16GB of memory to evaluate AGGSHAP-LM of CNN/DM (11490 summaries with 3 sentences per summary on average).

Interpretation. In this work, we mainly focused on analyzing how summary sentences aggregate information that is faithful to the source document, and we did not address cases where information has to be drawn from external knowledge. AGGSHAP is not suitable for interpreting low-quality examples as the fundamental assumption of AGGSHAP is to quantify the degree of aggregation by how well the summary sentence is supported by the source. AGGSHAP may fail to find any supporting information from the source and consider the low-quality example to have a high level of aggregation.

Potential Risks. All scientific artifacts in this study have been made publicly available and consistent with their intended use and access conditions.

References

Regina Barzilay and Kathleen R. McKeown. 2005. Sentence Fusion for Multidocument News Summarization. *Computational Linguistics*, 31(3):297–328.

Florian Böhm, Yang Gao, Christian M. Meyer, Ori Shapira, Ido Dagan, and Iryna Gurevych. 2019. Better rewards yield better summaries: Learning to summarise without references. In *Proceedings of the 2019 Conference on Empirical Methods in Natural Language Processing and the 9th International Joint Conference on Natural Language Processing (EMNLP-IJCNLP)*, pages 3110–3120, Hong Kong, China. Association for Computational Linguistics.

Rishi Bommasani and Claire Cardie. 2020. Intrinsic evaluation of summarization datasets. In *Proceedings of the 2020 Conference on Empirical Methods in Natural Language Processing (EMNLP)*, pages 8075–8096, Online. Association for Computational Linguistics.

Daniela Brook Weiss, Paul Roit, Ori Ernst, and Ido Dagan. 2022. Extending multi-text sentence fusion resources via pyramid annotations. In *Proceedings of the 2022 Conference of the North American Chapter of the Association for Computational Linguistics: Human Language Technologies*, pages 1854–1860, Seattle, United States. Association for Computational Linguistics.

Yen-Chun Chen and Mohit Bansal. 2018. Fast abstractive summarization with reinforce-selected sentence rewriting. In *Proceedings of ACL*.

Yulong Chen, Yang Liu, Liang Chen, and Yue Zhang. 2021. DialogSum: A real-life scenario dialogue summarization dataset. In *Findings of the Association for Computational Linguistics: ACL-IJCNLP 2021*, pages 5062–5074, Online. Association for Computational Linguistics.

Jackie Chi Kit Cheung and Gerald Penn. 2013. Towards robust abstractive multi-document summarization: A caseframe analysis of centrality and domain. In *Proceedings of the 51st Annual Meeting of the Association for Computational Linguistics (Volume 1: Long Papers)*, pages 1233–1242, Sofia, Bulgaria. Association for Computational Linguistics.

Jackie Chi Kit Cheung and Gerald Penn. 2014. Unsupervised sentence enhancement for automatic summarization. In *Proceedings of the 2014 Conference on Empirical Methods in Natural Language Processing (EMNLP)*, pages 775–786, Doha, Qatar. Association for Computational Linguistics.

Arman Cohan, Franck Dernoncourt, Doo Soon Kim, Trung Bui, Seokhwan Kim, Walter Chang, and Nazli Goharian. 2018. A discourse-aware attention model for abstractive summarization of long documents. In *Proceedings of the 2018 Conference of the North American Chapter of the Association for Computational Linguistics: Human Language Technologies,*

Volume 2 (Short Papers), pages 615–621, New Orleans, Louisiana. Association for Computational Linguistics.

Hercules Dalianis and Eduard Hovy. 1996. On lexical aggregation and ordering. In *Eighth International Natural Language Generation Workshop (Posters and Demonstrations)*.

Kedar Dhamdhere, Ashish Agarwal, and Mukund Sundararajan. 2019. The shapley taylor interaction index.

Barbara Di Eugenio, Davide Fossati, Dan Yu, Susan Haller, and Michael Glass. 2005. Aggregation improves learning: Experiments in natural language generation for intelligent tutoring systems. In *Proceedings of the 43rd Annual Meeting of the Association for Computational Linguistics (ACL'05)*, pages 50–57, Ann Arbor, Michigan. Association for Computational Linguistics.

Li Dong, Nan Yang, Wenhui Wang, Furu Wei, Xiaodong Liu, Yu Wang, Jianfeng Gao, Ming Zhou, and Hsiao-Wuen Hon. 2019. Unified language model pre-training for natural language understanding and generation. In *Advances in Neural Information Processing Systems*, volume 32. Curran Associates, Inc.

Nouha Dziri, Ehsan Kamalloo, Sivan Milton, Osmar Zaiane, Mo Yu, Edoardo Ponti, and Siva Reddy. 2022. Faithdial: A faithful benchmark for information-seeking dialogue. *arXiv preprint, arXiv:2204.10757*.

Micha Elsner and Deepak Santhanam. 2011. Learning to fuse disparate sentences. In *Proceedings of the Workshop on Monolingual Text-To-Text Generation*, pages 54–63, Portland, Oregon. Association for Computational Linguistics.

Ori Ernst, Ori Shapira, Ramakanth Pasunuru, Michael Lepioshkin, Jacob Goldberger, Mohit Bansal, and Ido Dagan. 2021. Summary-source proposition-level alignment: Task, datasets and supervised baseline. In *Proceedings of the 25th Conference on Computational Natural Language Learning*, pages 310–322. Association for Computational Linguistics.

Alexander Fabbri, Irene Li, Tianwei She, Suyi Li, and Dragomir Radev. 2019. Multi-news: A large-scale multi-document summarization dataset and abstractive hierarchical model. In *Proceedings of the 57th Annual Meeting of the Association for Computational Linguistics*, pages 1074–1084, Florence, Italy. Association for Computational Linguistics.

Alexander R. Fabbri, Wojciech Kryściński, Bryan McCann, Caiming Xiong, Richard Socher, and Dragomir Radev. 2021. SummEval: Re-evaluating Summarization Evaluation. *Transactions of the Association for Computational Linguistics*, 9:391–409.

Sebastian Gehrmann, Yuntian Deng, and Alexander Rush. 2018. Bottom-up abstractive summarization. In *Proceedings of the 2018 Conference on Empirical Methods in Natural Language Processing*, pages 4098–4109, Brussels, Belgium. Association for Computational Linguistics.

Matt Grenander, Yue Dong, Jackie Chi Kit Cheung, and Annie Louis. 2019. Countering the effects of lead bias in news summarization via multi-stage training and auxiliary losses. In *Proceedings of the 2019 Conference on Empirical Methods in Natural Language Processing and the 9th International Joint Conference on Natural Language Processing (EMNLP-IJCNLP)*, pages 6019–6024, Hong Kong, China. Association for Computational Linguistics.

Max Grusky, Mor Naaman, and Yoav Artzi. 2018. Newsroom: A dataset of 1.3 million summaries with diverse extractive strategies. In *Proceedings of the 2018 Conference of the North American Chapter of the Association for Computational Linguistics: Human Language Technologies, Volume 1 (Long Papers)*, pages 708–719, New Orleans, Louisiana. Association for Computational Linguistics.

Han Guo, Ramakanth Pasunuru, and Mohit Bansal. 2018. Soft layer-specific multi-task summarization with entailment and question generation. In *Proceedings of the 56th Annual Meeting of the Association for Computational Linguistics (Volume 1: Long Papers)*, pages 687–697, Melbourne, Australia. Association for Computational Linguistics.

Karl Moritz Hermann, Tomas Kocisky, Edward Grefenstette, Lasse Espeholt, Will Kay, Mustafa Suleyman, and Phil Blunsom. 2015. Teaching machines to read and comprehend. In *Advances in Neural Information Processing Systems*, volume 28. Curran Associates, Inc.

Wan-Ting Hsu, Chieh-Kai Lin, Ming-Ying Lee, Kerui Min, Jing Tang, and Min Sun. 2018. A unified model for extractive and abstractive summarization using inconsistency loss. In *Proceedings of the 56th Annual Meeting of the Association for Computational Linguistics (Volume 1: Long Papers)*, pages 132–141, Melbourne, Australia. Association for Computational Linguistics.

Yichen Jiang and Mohit Bansal. 2018. Closed-book training to improve summarization encoder memory. In *Proceedings of the 2018 Conference on Empirical Methods in Natural Language Processing*, pages 4067–4077, Brussels, Belgium. Association for Computational Linguistics.

Hongyan Jing and Kathleen R. McKeown. 1999. The decomposition of human-written summary sentences. In *Proceedings of the 22nd Annual International ACM SIGIR Conference on Research and Development in Information Retrieval*, SIGIR '99, page 129–136, New York, NY, USA. Association for Computing Machinery.

Clément Jumel, Annie Louis, and Jackie Chi Kit Cheung. 2020. TESA: A Task in Entity Semantic Aggregation for abstractive summarization. In *Proceedings of the 2020 Conference on Empirical Methods in Natural Language Processing (EMNLP)*, pages 8031–8050, Online. Association for Computational Linguistics.

Mahnaz Koupaee and William Yang Wang. 2018. Wikihow: A large scale text summarization dataset. *CoRR*, abs/1810.09305.

Klaus Krippendorff. 2011. Computing krippendorff's alpha-reliability.

Wojciech Kryscinski, Bryan McCann, Caiming Xiong, and Richard Socher. 2020. Evaluating the factual consistency of abstractive text summarization. In *Proceedings of the 2020 Conference on Empirical Methods in Natural Language Processing (EMNLP)*, pages 9332–9346, Online. Association for Computational Linguistics.

Wojciech Kryściński, Romain Paulus, Caiming Xiong, and Richard Socher. 2018. Improving abstraction in text summarization. In *Proceedings of the 2018 Conference on Empirical Methods in Natural Language Processing*, pages 1808–1817, Brussels, Belgium. Association for Computational Linguistics.

Wojciech Kryściński, Nazneen Rajani, Divyansh Agarwal, Caiming Xiong, and Dragomir Radev. 2021. Booksum: A collection of datasets for long-form narrative summarization.

Logan Lebanoff, Franck Dernoncourt, Doo Soon Kim, Lidan Wang, Walter Chang, and Fei Liu. 2020. Learning to fuse sentences with transformers for summarization. In *Proceedings of the 2020 Conference on Empirical Methods in Natural Language Processing (EMNLP)*, pages 4136–4142, Online. Association for Computational Linguistics.

Logan Lebanoff, John Muchovej, Franck Dernoncourt, Doo Soon Kim, Seokhwan Kim, Walter Chang, and Fei Liu. 2019a. Analyzing sentence fusion in abstractive summarization. In *Proceedings of the 2nd Workshop on New Frontiers in Summarization*, pages 104–110, Hong Kong, China. Association for Computational Linguistics.

Logan Lebanoff, Kaiqiang Song, Franck Dernoncourt, Doo Soon Kim, Seokhwan Kim, Walter Chang, and Fei Liu. 2019b. Scoring sentence singletons and pairs for abstractive summarization. In *Proceedings of the 57th Annual Meeting of the Association for Computational Linguistics*, pages 2175–2189, Florence, Italy. Association for Computational Linguistics.

Mike Lewis, Yinhan Liu, Naman Goyal, Marjan Ghazvininejad, Abdelrahman Mohamed, Omer Levy, Veselin Stoyanov, and Luke Zettlemoyer. 2020. BART: Denoising sequence-to-sequence pre-training for natural language generation, translation, and comprehension. In *Proceedings of the 58th Annual Meeting of the Association for Computational Linguistics*, pages 7871–7880, Online. Association for Computational Linguistics.

Fei Liu and Yang Liu. 2013. Towards abstractive speech summarization: Exploring unsupervised and supervised approaches for spoken utterance compression. *IEEE Transactions on Audio, Speech, and Language Processing*, 21(7):1469–1480.

Annie Louis and Ani Nenkova. 2013. Automatically Assessing Machine Summary Content Without a Gold Standard. *Computational Linguistics*, 39(2):267–300.

Scott M Lundberg and Su-In Lee. 2017. A unified approach to interpreting model predictions. In I. Guyon, U. V. Luxburg, S. Bengio, H. Wallach, R. Fergus, S. Vishwanathan, and R. Garnett, editors, *Advances in Neural Information Processing Systems 30*, pages 4765–4774. Curran Associates, Inc.

Ramesh Nallapati, Bowen Zhou, Cicero dos Santos, Caglar Gulcehre, and Bing Xiang. 2016. Abstractive text summarization using sequence-to-sequence RNNs and beyond. In *Proceedings of The 20th SIGNLL Conference on Computational Natural Language Learning*, pages 280–290, Berlin, Germany. Association for Computational Linguistics.

Shashi Narayan, Shay B. Cohen, and Mirella Lapata. 2018. Don't give me the details, just the summary! topic-aware convolutional neural networks for extreme summarization. In *Proceedings of the 2018 Conference on Empirical Methods in Natural Language Processing*, pages 1797–1807, Brussels, Belgium. Association for Computational Linguistics.

Md Rizwan Parvez and Kai-Wei Chang. 2021. Evaluating the values of sources in transfer learning. In *Proceedings of the 2021 Conference of the North American Chapter of the Association for Computational Linguistics: Human Language Technologies*, pages 5084–5116, Online. Association for Computational Linguistics.

Ramakanth Pasunuru and Mohit Bansal. 2018. Multi-reward reinforced summarization with saliency and entailment. In *Proceedings of the 2018 Conference of the North American Chapter of the Association for Computational Linguistics: Human Language Technologies, Volume 2 (Short Papers)*, pages 646–653, New Orleans, Louisiana. Association for Computational Linguistics.

Colin Raffel, Noam Shazeer, Adam Roberts, Katherine Lee, Sharan Narang, Michael Matena, Yanqi Zhou, Wei Li, and Peter J. Liu. 2020. Exploring the limits of transfer learning with a unified text-to-text transformer. *Journal of Machine Learning Research*, 21(140):1–67.

Mike Reape and Chris Mellish. 1999. Just what is aggregation anyway? In *ENLG 1999)*, pages 20–29.

Abigail See, Peter J. Liu, and Christopher D. Manning. 2017. Get to the point: Summarization with pointer-generator networks. In *Proceedings of the 55th Annual Meeting of the Association for Computational Linguistics (Volume 1: Long Papers)*, pages 1073–1083, Vancouver, Canada. Association for Computational Linguistics.

L. S. Shapley. 1953. *17. A Value for n-Person Games*, pages 307–318. Princeton University Press.

Eva Sharma, Luyang Huang, Zhe Hu, and Lu Wang. 2019a. An entity-driven framework for abstractive summarization. In *Proceedings of the 2019 Conference on Empirical Methods in Natural Language Processing and the 9th International Joint Conference on Natural Language Processing (EMNLP-IJCNLP)*, pages 3280–3291, Hong Kong, China. Association for Computational Linguistics.

Eva Sharma, Chen Li, and Lu Wang. 2019b. BIGPATENT: A large-scale dataset for abstractive and coherent summarization. In *Proceedings of the 57th Annual Meeting of the Association for Computational Linguistics*, pages 2204–2213, Florence, Italy. Association for Computational Linguistics.

Kaiqiang Song, Bingqing Wang, Zhe Feng, Liu Ren, and Fei Liu. 2020. Controlling the amount of verbatim copying in abstractive summarization. In *Proceedings of the AAAI Conference on Artificial Intelligence*.

Kapil Thadani and Kathleen McKeown. 2013. Supervised sentence fusion with single-stage inference. In *Proceedings of the Sixth International Joint Conference on Natural Language Processing*, pages 1410–1418, Nagoya, Japan. Asian Federation of Natural Language Processing.

Thomas Wolf, Lysandre Debut, Victor Sanh, Julien Chaumond, Clement Delangue, Anthony Moi, Pierric Cistac, Tim Rault, Remi Louf, Morgan Funtowicz, Joe Davison, Sam Shleifer, Patrick von Platen, Clara Ma, Yacine Jernite, Julien Plu, Canwen Xu, Teven Le Scao, Sylvain Gugger, Mariama Drame, Quentin Lhoest, and Alexander Rush. 2020. Transformers: State-of-the-art natural language processing. In *Proceedings of the 2020 Conference on Empirical Methods in Natural Language Processing: System Demonstrations*, pages 38–45, Online. Association for Computational Linguistics.

Ruben Wolhandler, Arie Cattan, Ori Ernst, and Ido Dagan. 2022. How "multi" is multi-document summarization? *ArXiv*, abs/2210.12688.

Ruifeng Yuan, Zili Wang, and Wenjie Li. 2021. Event graph based sentence fusion. In *Proceedings of the 2021 Conference on Empirical Methods in Natural Language Processing*, pages 4075–4084, Online and Punta Cana, Dominican Republic. Association for Computational Linguistics.

Jingqing Zhang, Yao Zhao, Mohammad Saleh, and Peter J. Liu. 2019. Pegasus: Pre-training with extracted gap-sentences for abstractive summarization.

Daniel M. Ziegler, Nisan Stiennon, Jeffrey Wu, Tom B. Brown, Alec Radford, Dario Amodei, Paul Christiano, and Geoffrey Irving. 2019. Fine-tuning language models from human preferences.

A Appendix

A.1 Human Annotation Details

We give the following instructions to the annotators:

1. Read the summary sentence
2. Read the supporting sentences in the order presented in the spreadsheet (supporting sentence_0 to supporting sentence_9)
    - If the supporting sentence covers the information in the summary sentence and this piece of information has not been covered by previous supporting sentences then highlight it.
    - If two sentences are identical or very similar in content, highlight both.
    - If no single supporting sentence covers information in the summary sentence, enter *missing*

To evaluate the inter-annotator agreement of the selected supporting sentence (i.e. how well annotators agree on which source sentences are supporting sentences), we computed the Krippendorff alpha of annotated instances. The Krippendorff alpha is 0.714 with a 95% confidence interval of $[0.579, 0.835]$ from bootstrapping with bootstrap sample size of 100.

We manually inspected some instances where two annotators do not agree on the number of supporting sentences. We found that most ambiguities came from judging whether two supporting sentences are very similar in content or not.

A.2 Full results of Table 4

See Table 6.

A.3 Examples of Human-written Summaries

Table 7-10 shows randomly sampled reference summary sentences from the six datasets we evaluated. We sampled examples that are extractive AGGSHAP-LM < 0.45 and are of higher level of aggregation AGGSHAP-LM > 0.7

A.4 Examples of System-generated Summaries

Table 11 shows an example in which the reference summary contains aggregations of information from multiple points in the source text. The summary generated by PEGASUS (Zhang et al.,

	ROUGE-1/2/3/L	AGGSHAP-LM	AGGSHAP-R	NN-1	NN-2	NN-3	ABS
Reference	-	**0.678**	**0.677**	**0.203**	**0.548**	**0.738**	**0.217**
M8 - **Pointer Generator**	0.392 / 0.172 / 0.100 / 0.360	0.486	0.517	0.129	0.250	0.344	0.002
M9 - **Fast-abs-rl**	0.406 / 0.177 / 0.098 / 0.381	0.515	0.524	0.149	0.347	0.482	0.014
M10 - **Bottom-Up**	0.412 / 0.187 / 0.106 / 0.382	0.553	**0.579**	0.155	**0.355**	**0.497**	0.019
M11 - **Improve-abs**	0.399 / 0.172 / 0.093 / 0.373	0.527	**0.580**	0.153	0.328	0.458	**0.025**
M12 - **Unified-ext-abs**	0.404 / 0.179 / 0.104 / 0.368	0.470	0.502	0.138	0.258	0.351	0.013
M13 - **ROUGESal**	0.402 / 0.180 / 0.105 / 0.368	0.488	0.515	0.149	0.285	0.387	0.018
M14 - **Multi-task (Ent + QG)**	0.395 / 0.176 / 0.104 / 0.363	0.492	0.520	0.141	0.275	0.373	0.015
M15 - **Closed book decoder**	0.398 / 0.176 / 0.103 / 0.364	0.484	0.512	0.137	0.261	0.355	0.013
M16 - **SENECA**	0.415 / 0.184 / 0.105 / 0.381	0.521	0.568	0.161	0.340	0.453	0.013
M17 - **T5**	0.448 / 0.221 / 0.134 / 0.417	0.543	0.557	**0.171**	**0.364**	**0.486**	0.011
M18 - **NeuralTD**	0.400 / 0.176 / 0.100 / 0.372	0.520	0.540	**0.173**	**0.369**	**0.497**	0.018
M20 - **GPT-2** (supervised)	0.398 / 0.176 / 0.099 / 0.367	0.470	0.506	0.010	0.043	0.063	0.010
M21 - **UniLM**	0.431 / 0.204 / 0.122 / 0.401	**0.554**	0.559	0.032	0.164	0.284	**0.023**
M22 - **BART**	0.442 / 0.213 / 0.129 / 0.410	**0.555**	0.554	0.022	0.125	0.225	0.015
M23 - **Pegasus** (huge news)	0.441 / 0.215 / 0.130 / 0.410	0.580	0.570	0.029	0.176	0.303	0.018

Table 6: Models' ROUGE scores (Adapted from SummEval (Fabbri et al., 2021)) and aggregation statistics. The highest aggregation scores and percentages of novel N-grams are bolded. We remove M19 BertSum-abs from the analysis as no punctuation at the end of sentences resulting in misleadingly high aggregation scores.

Aggregation Candidate	Summary [Agg-LM, Agg-ROUGE]
Example 1: (1) Investigators found that a number of flavors were labeled 'healthy' - brimming with fiber, protein and antioxidants, while being low in fat and sodium.	FDA Investigators found that a number of flavors were labeled 'healthy' - brimming with fiber and antioxidants, while being low in fat and sodium . [0.431, 0.414]
Example 2: (1) '(CNN) Five years ago , Rebecca Francis posed for a photo while lying next to a dead giraffe . (2) The trouble started Monday , when comedian Ricky Gervais tweeted the photo with a question .	Rebecca Francis ' photo with a giraffe was shared by Ricky Gervais . [0.759, 0.801]

Table 7: CNN/DM extractive (Top) and higher-level aggregation (Bottom)

2019) contains aggregations from three source sentences, as does the human summary, while the summary generated by improve-abs (Kryściński et al., 2018) is produced by compressing a single sentence.

A.5 Abstractive Models in Section 5.2

Here we cite the list of abstractive summarization models we evaluated for aggregation. We evaluated the summaries generated by the following systems: (M8) Pointer Generator (See et al., 2017), (M9) Fast-abs-rl (Chen and Bansal, 2018), (M10) Bottom-up (Gehrmann et al., 2018), (M11) Improve-abs (Kryściński et al., 2018), (M12) Unified-ext-abs (Hsu et al., 2018), (M13) ROUGE-Sal (Pasunuru and Bansal, 2018), (M14) Multi-task(Ent+QG) (Guo et al., 2018), (M15) Closed book decoder (Jiang and Bansal, 2018), (M16) SENECA (Sharma et al., 2019a), (M17) T5 (Raffel et al., 2020), (M18) NeuralTD (Böhm et al., 2019), (M20) GPT-2 (supervised) (Ziegler et al., 2019), (M21) UniLM (Dong et al., 2019), (M22) BART (Lewis et al., 2020) and (M23) PEGASUS (Zhang et al., 2019).

Aggregation Candidate	Summary [Agg-LM, Agg-ROUGE]
Example 1: (1) Joseph Fox photographed the mudlarkers who comb the shore of London's River Thames.	All photographs taken by Joseph Fox. [0.192, 0.300]
Example 2: (1) <n> Protesters allege Edir Frederico Da Costa, 25, was "brutally beaten" by Met Police officers earlier this month. (2) <n> The Independent Police Complaints Commission (IPCC) is investigating the treatment of Mr Da Costa, who died six days after he was stopped by police. (3) <n> Mr Da Costa, known by friends as Edson, died on 21 June, six days after being stopped in a car in Woodcocks, Beckton, in Newham, east London.	Protesters have faced off with police in a demonstration over the death of a man after a traffic stop. [0.799, 0.854]

Table 8: XSUM extractive (Top) and higher-level aggregation (Bottom) instances

Aggregation Candidate	Summary [Agg-LM, Agg-ROUGE]
Example 1: (1) source sent: (PHOTOS: Scenes from Eric Cantor HQ) Asked about his future plans, Cantor replied: "That's probably between my wife and me." Addressing his colleagues earlier, Cantor's words drove Speaker John Boehner (R-Ohio) to tears.	"That's probably between my wife and me," he said. [0.182, 0.382]
Example 2: (1) More than 90% of the parts needed to restore a 1967 Mustang convertible are available new as Ford-licensed reproduction components, allowing enthusiasts to basically build from scratch a new Mustang of that era. (2) To build up a Mustang using the body shell, the powertrain, suspension and brakes, the electrical systems, the interior and trim can either be bought new or transferred from an existing car to the new body.	Just in time for classic car buffs' Christmas, Ford has added a brand-new shell for the '67 Mustang convertible to its Ford Restoration Parts line, giving enthusiasts a chance to build their own from scratch, the Los Angeles Times reports. [0.818, 0.834]

Table 9: Multi-news extractive (Top) and higher-level aggregation (Bottom) instances

Aggregation Candidate	Summary [Agg-LM, Agg-ROUGE]
Example 1: (1) source sent: If you don't have a water bottle or hot compress pad, you can pour warm water (104-108 degrees Fahrenheit) into a basin and immerse the injured area in the water for 30-45 minutes.It's normal to feel severe pain as the tissue begins to warm up, so do not be alarmed about this.	Pour warm water into a basin. [0.323, 0.306]
Example 2: (1) Disney Parks park maps aren't just written in English and Spanish. (2) , (3) Parade routes differ between the different parks. (4) The parade route will be marked on the map by some type of dotted or broken line.	Visit the Disney Park that the parade will be shown in. [0.818, 0.856]

Table 10: WikiHow extractive (Top) and higher-level aggregation (Bottom) instances

Source:
British jihadis have posted pictures of junk food and drinks such as Burger King, Pringles and mojitos which they have had carried across the Turkish border into Syria. [...] It's not the first time ISIS fighters have been caught with fast food sneaked across the border. Last month a delighted fighter known only as Ghareeb posted a picture of a McDonalds bag on his social media page.
Reference summary:
ISIS fighters have posted pictures on social media of Western junk food .
Pegasus generated:
ISIS fighters have been posting pictures of food and drinks smuggled in .
Improve-abs generated: british jihadis have posted pictures of junk food and mojitos .

Table 11: Example of summary sentences aggregating information from three source sentences in CNN/DM dataset. Human editor aggregates *British jihadis* and *a delighted fighter know as Ghareeb* as *ISIS fighters*, and aggregates *junk food such as Burger King, Pringles* and *McDonalds* as *Western junk food.*

Improving Multi-Stage Long Document Summarization with Enhanced Coarse Summarizer

Jinhyeong Lim and Hyun-Je Song
Department of Computer Science and Artificial Intelligence
Jeonbuk National University
Jeonju, 54896, Korea
{dlawlsgud, hyunje.song}@jbnu.ac.kr

Abstract

Multi-stage long document summarization, which splits a long document as multiple segments and each of which is used to generate a coarse summary in multiple stage, and then the final summary is produced using the last coarse summary, is a flexible approach to capture salient information from the long document. Even if the coarse summary affects the final summary, however, the coarse summarizer in the existing multi-stage summarization is coarsely trained using data segments that are not useful to generate the final summary. In this paper, we propose a novel method for multi-stage long document summarization. The proposed method first generates new segment pairs, ensuring that all of them are relevant to generating the final summary. We then incorporate contrastive learning into the training of the coarse summarizer, which tries to maximize the similarities between source segments and the target summary during training. Through extensive experiments on six long document summarization datasets, we demonstrate that our proposed method not only enhances the existing multi-stage long document summarization approach, but also achieves performance comparable to state-of-the-art methods, including those utilizing large language models for long document summarization.

1 Introduction

Long document summarization aims to compress a long document, such as meeting minutes, reports, and scientific articles, into a concise text that captures salient information. Since the number of tokens in a long document usually exceeds the limit of the summarization models, various summarization approaches (Mao et al., 2022; Beltagy et al., 2020; Tay et al., 2020; Rohde et al., 2021; Pu et al., 2023a; Xie et al., 2022) to deal with long document has proposed. One promising approach among the long document summarization approaches is the multi-stage split-then-summarization approach (Zhang et al., 2022). It first splits the long document into source segments and each of which is used to generate a coarse summary. After splitting into source segments and generating a coarse summary in multiple stages, it produces the final summary using the last coarse summaries. This approach offers flexibility in processing documents of arbitrary length by adjusting the number of stages and has achieved state-of-the-art performance on several long document summarization benchmark datasets. However, there is still room for improvement in terms of the quality of the coarse summary.

It should be noted that the quality of the final summary depends on the quality of the coarse summaries. In the previous multi-stage split-then-summarization approach, Zhang et al. (2022) construct the training data using pairs of long documents and target summaries for the coarse summarizer because there is no official data for the coarse summarizer. That is, it first splits the long document and the target summary into segments, respectively. Each document segment is then aligned with a subset of the target segments, maximizing the ROUGE-1 score between the document segment and the subset. The resulting aligned pairs are used to train the coarse summarizer. Even though some document segments may be irrelevant to the target summary, aligned pairs derived from these segments are employed to train the coarse summarizer. It results in the generation of coarse summaries that may contain some noise. Figure 1 shows an example of the construction of the training data for the coarse summarizer, where the dotted line indicates the alignment of one document segment with a subset of the target segments. As all document segments are aligned and used to train the coarse summarizer, the coarse summarizer may generate low quality and excessively verbose summaries.

In this paper, we propose a novel approach suitable for multi-stage summarization. The proposed

Proceedings of The 4th New Frontiers in Summarization Workshop, pages 135–144
December 6, 2023 ©2023 Association for Computational Linguistics

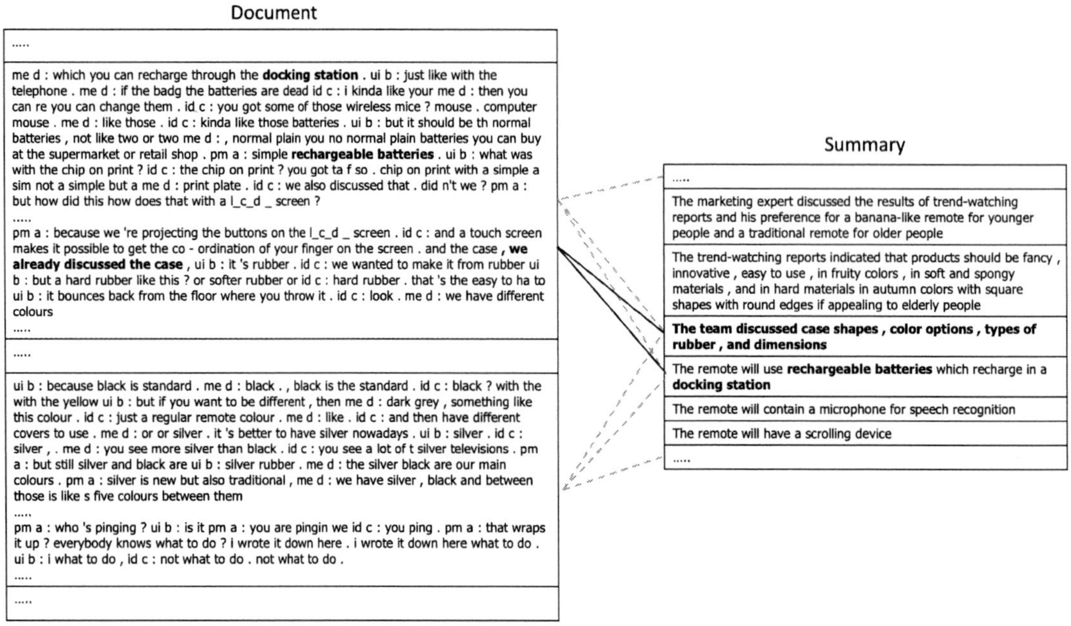

Figure 1: An example from AMI dataset to show an alignment between document segments and target segments. Dotted lines indicate the source-focused aligned pairs, while bold lines represent the target-focused aligned pairs.

method first generates aligned pairs that are relevant to the generation of the final summary. Unlike the previous alignment discussed, the proposed method executes an alignment in a reverse direction. Specifically, the proposed method aligns each target segment with a document segment. By aligning in this reverse direction, we ensure that only relevant document segments are included in the training data for the coarse summarizer. Furthermore, the proposed method incorporates a sub-summary generation contrastive objective (Liu et al., 2021) during training of the coarse summarizer to explicitly model the similarity between the target segment and the document segment. This addition of contrastive objective encourages the coarse summarizer to focus on relevant document segments and target segments and contributes to further improving the summarization quality of the coarse summarizer.

We conduct extensive experiments on six long document summarization datasets to show the superiority of the proposed method. We also compare the proposed method with large large language models-based long document summarization. Experimental results imply that the proposed method contributes to enhancing the efficiency and effectiveness of the multi-stage long document summarization approach compared to the existing method[1].

2 Multi-Stage Long Document Summarization

Let $\mathcal{D} = \{(S_i, T_i)\}_{i=1}^{N}$ be a set of document-target summary pairs, where S_i is the i-th long document and T_i is its corresponding summary. The multi-stage long document summarization approach segments the long document and then summarizes the segmented text in multiple stages because the number of tokens in S_i exceeds the limit of the summarizer. It consists of two stages: C coarse stages and one fine-grained stage. In each coarse stage, an input document is divided into document segments, and then a coarse summarizer generates coarse summaries from the document segments. In the fine-grained stage, a fine-grained summarizer generates the final summary from the last generated coarse summary.

Let K be the number of the maximum input tokens of the summarizer. S_i is divided into multiple segments, each with a length of fewer than K tokens. That is, $S_i = \{s_{i1}, \ldots, s_{in_i}\}$, where n_i is the number of segments of S_i. Similarly, the target summary $T_i = \{t_{i1}, \ldots, t_{im_i}\}$ is also divided into multiple segments, usually split into separate sen-

[1]The proposed method is publicly available at https://github.com/Jinhyeong-Lim/Summ-N-ECS

tences. That is, t_{ij} and m_i are the j-th sentence and the number of sentences in T_i, respectively. To generate training data for the coarse summarizer, Zhang et al. (2022) adopt the ROUGE-based greedy target alignment function, aligning each document segment s_{ij} with a subset of T_i such that the ROUGE-1 score between s_{ij} and the subset is maximized. The training data for the coarse summarizer in the k-th stage is constructed as follows:

$$\mathcal{D}^k_{coarse-s} = \cup_{i=1}^{N} \cup_{j=1}^{n_i} \text{align}_{source}(s_{ij}, T_i).$$

Here, $\text{align}_{source}(\cdot, \cdot)$ is a function to align each document segment with a subset of target segments. Since the alignment is executed for each source segment, all document segments are contained in $\mathcal{D}^k_{coarse-s}$. The k-th coarse summarizer is trained with $\mathcal{D}^k_{coarse-s}$ to minimize the negative log-likelihood (NLL) $\mathcal{L}_{nll}$ between the word distributions predicted by the summarizer and the target segments.

After training the coarse summarizer, a coarse summary is obtained using the trained summarizer from each document segment s_{ij}. All n_i coarse summaries are then concatenated to form a new input for the next stage. The target summary for the next stage is copied from the original target summary. It is worth noting that the number of coarse stages is estimated based on the length of the long document and the characteristics of the summarizer. Further details can be found in Zhang et al. (2022) and Section 4.3.

In the fine-grained stage, the coarse summaries from the C-th coarse stage are concatenated and used as input for the fine-grained stage. Since the number of tokens in the input is shorter than K, a fine-grained summarizer can be modeled similarly to a well-known vanilla abstractive summarizer (Lewis et al., 2020; Zhang et al., 2020). This means that the fine-grained summarizer is trained on the dataset from the last coarse stage and produces the final summary using the last coarse summaries.

3 Improving Multi-Stage Summarization with Enhanced Coarse Summarizer

This paper presents a new approach to multi-stage summarization. The proposed method generates new aligned pairs that include only relevant document segments because the greedy target alignment function (Zhang et al., 2022) generates some pairs that contain irrelevant document segments. In addition, the proposed method incorporates a contrastive learning into the training of the coarse summarizer that a document segment and the corresponding target summary should convey the same meaning, which is not modeled explicitly by the NLL loss (Xu et al., 2022).

3.1 Target-focused Aligned Pairs

To generate aligned pairs that includes the relevant document segments, the proposed method designs a new alignment function. The proposed alignment function focuses on the target segment that each target segment t_{ij} is aligned with a document segment s_{il}, maximizing the ROUGE scores between between t_{ij} and s_{il} (Bold lines in Figure 1. The training data for the coarse summarizer in the k-th stage can be constructed as follows:

$$\mathcal{D}^k_{coarse-t} = \cup_{i=1}^{N} \cup_{j=1}^{m_i} \text{align}_{target}(t_{ij}, S_i), \quad (1)$$

where $\text{align}_{target}(\cdot, \cdot)$ is a function to align each target segment with a document segment. This alignment ensures that irrelevant document segments are not included in the training data.

The training data constructed by the new alignment function, however, has one problem that there is one-to-many mappings in pairs of document segment-target segment, which is also known as multi-modality problem (Gu et al., 2017; Wei et al., 2019). That is, one document segment is mapped to multiple target segments. This can result in the generation of low quality of coarse summaries. To alleviate this problem, the proposed method merges the multi-modal data by concatenating target segments. For example, if the proposed alignment function generates pairs $\{(s_{i1}, t_{i1}), (s_{i1}, t_{i4}), (s_{i1}, t_{i6})\}$, these three pairs are merged into one pair by concatenating three target segments such that $\{(s_{i1}, t_{i1} \oplus t_{i4} \oplus t_{i6})\}$, where $\oplus$ is a string concatenate operator.

3.2 Contrastive Learning with Sub-summary Generation Objective

The summary of a long document comprises multiple sentences, each of which can be seen as a sub-summary. Given that a single long document may encompass multiple subjects, we can consider the coarse summarizer as mapping each subject to its corresponding sub-summary, and these subjects are inherently present within the document's segments. To achieve improved mapping, the proposed method employs contrastive learning with a sub-summary generation objective (Liu et al., 2021).

Table 1: The statistics of data set used in experiments. The document length and summary length are the averaged numbers across the dataset.

Dataset	Size ($|\mathcal{D}|$)	Document length	Summary length	Type	Domain
AMI	137	6007.7	296.6	Dialogue	Meeting
ICSI	59	13317.2	488.5	Dialogue	Meeting
QMSum	1808	9069.8	69.6	Dialogue	Meeting
SummScreen-FD	4348	7605.4	113.7	Dialogue	TV Series
SummScreen-TMS	22503	6420.7	380.6	Dialogue	TV Series
GovReport	19466	9409.4	553.4	Document	Reports

To conduct contrastive learning, the proposed method initially constructs contrastive sub-summary generation pairs, comprising both positive and corresponding negative examples. Positive examples are obtained from data pairs as defined by Equation (1) while their corresponding negative examples are derived by substituting document segments with alternative ones. Here, the method selects the document segment that exhibits the lowest ROUGE score in comparison to the target segment.

Let $\{(s^k_{pos}, t^k), (s^k_{neg}, t^k)\}_{k=1}^{N*m_i}$ be a constructed the contrastive sub-summary generation pairs, where s^k_* and t^k are segments of document and target, respectively. With the contrastive pairs, the proposed method calculates the NLL values as follows:

$$L^{t^k}_{pos} = -\log \Pi_{j=1}^{|t^k|} p(t^k_j \mid t^k_{i:j-1}, s^k_{pos}),$$
$$L^{t^k}_{neg} = -\log \Pi_{j=1}^{|t^k|} p(t^k_j \mid t^k_{i:j-1}, s^k_{neg}),$$

where $L^{t_i}_{pos}$ and $L^{t_i}_{pos}$ are the negative log likelihood values of the positive example and negative example, respectively. t^k_j is the j-th token in t^k. Then, the normalized score is obtained by applying the softmax function to the two NLL values:

$$su(s^k_{pos}), su(s^k_{neg}) = softmax([L^{t^k}_{pos}, L^{t^k}_{neg}]),$$

where $su(s^k_{pos})$ and $su(s^k_{neg})$ represent the normalized scores of the positive example and negative example, respectively, indicating their relative relevance scores.

Then, the sub-summary generation contrastive objective, denoted as $\mathcal{L}_{ctr}$, is defined as follows:

$$\mathcal{L}_{ctr} = \frac{1}{N*m_i} \sum_{k=1}^{N*m_i} \max(0, \delta - (su(s^k_{neg}) - su(s^k_{pos}))),$$

where δ is a margin that the relevance score between a positive document segment and a target segment to be at least larger than the relevance score of the negative example. The δ is set as 1.

The final loss for the coarse summarizer is defined as

$$\mathcal{L}_{coarse} = \lambda * \mathcal{L}_{ctr} + \mathcal{L}_{NLL}, \quad (2)$$

where λ is a hyperparameter to balance the contrastive loss.

4 Experiments

4.1 Experimental Settings

This paper conducts the experiments on six long document summarization datasets: AMI (Carletta et al., 2006), ICSI (Janin et al., 2003), QMSum (Zhong et al., 2021), SummScreen-FD, SummScreen-TMS (Chen et al., 2022), and GovReport (Huang et al., 2021). Table 1 shows data statistics of the datasets. For the query-focused document summarization task using the QMSum dataset, we follow the settings of Zhang et al. (2022) such that the query is concatenated into the beginning of the document at both the training and the inference time.

The proposed method follows the experimental settings of Zhang et al. (2022) except the backbone summarization models. The proposed method adopts the BART-large model, pretrained on the CNN/DM dataset, as the backbone model for the fine-grained summarizer. The backbone model for coarse summarizer in the GovReport dataset is set to BART-large while for other datasets, it is set to DialogLM (Zhong et al., 2022).

All experiments are conducted on one NVIDIA RTX A6000 GPU with a 48 GiB memory. The multi-stage long document summarization with the proposed coarse summarizer is trained for 30 epochs with a batch size of 4. We set the optimizer to AdamW and the learning rate is set to 2e-5 in the coarse stage and 3e-5 in the fine-grained stage. The best checkpoint is chosen by early stopping based

Table 2: Performances of long document summarization on six long document summarization data sets. * denotes the ROUGE-L scores without the sentence split. Best performance is in bold, and second best is underlined.

	AMI			ICSI			QMSum-All		
	R-1	R-2	R-L	R-1	R-2	R-L	R-1	R-2	R-L
HMNET (Zhu et al., 2020)	53.02	18.57	24.85*	46.28	10.60	19.12*	-	-	-
DDAMS (Feng et al., 2021)	53.15	**22.32**	25.67*	40.41	11.02	19.18*	-	-	-
UniLM-CP(Dong et al., 2019)	52.67	19.33	50.55	48.43	12.39	46.24	29.19	6.73	25.52
BART_{Large}-SLED (Ivgi et al., 2023)	-	-	-	-	-	-	34.20	**11.00**	22.00*
DYLE (Mao et al., 2022)	-	-	-	-	-	-	34.42	9.71	30.10
DialogLM (Zhong et al., 2022)	54.49	20.03	50.92	49.56	12.53	47.08	33.69	9.32	30.01
DialogLED (Zhong et al., 2022)	<u>54.80</u>	20.37	<u>52.26</u>	<u>50.11</u>	<u>13.23</u>	<u>47.25</u>	<u>34.50</u>	9.92	<u>30.27</u>
SUMM^N (Zhang et al., 2022)	53.44	20.30	51.39	45.57	11.49	43.32	34.03	9.28	29.48
Proposed model	**54.85**	<u>21.18</u>	**52.28**	**50.27**	**13.38**	**47.30**	**35.31**	<u>10.13</u>	**30.58**

	SummScreen-FD			SummScreen-TMS			GovReport		
	R-1	R-2	R-L	R-1	R-2	R-L	R-1	R-2	R-L
UniLM-CP (Dong et al., 2019)	33.29	6.74	28.21	44.07	9.96	41.73	-	-	-
TopDownFormer (Pang et al., 2023)	**36.84**	**9.19**	31.12	**51.02**	**14.66**	**49.01**	-	-	-
BART_{Large}-SLED (Ivgi et al., 2023)	-	-	-	-	-	-	57.50	26.30	27.40*
PageSum (Liu et al., 2022)	-	-	-	-	-	-	<u>60.04</u>	<u>27.17</u>	<u>57.21</u>
DYLE (Mao et al., 2022)	-	-	-	-	-	-	**61.01**	**28.83**	**57.82**
DialogLM (Zhong et al., 2022)	35.75	8.27	30.76	45.58	10.75	43.31	-	-	-
DialogLED (Zhong et al., 2022)	36.70	8.68	**31.38**	45.22	11.69	42.86	-	-	-
SUMM^N (Zhang et al., 2022)	32.48	5.85	27.55	44.64	11.87	42.53	56.77	23.25	53.90
Proposed model	<u>36.81</u>	<u>9.07</u>	<u>31.21</u>	<u>45.81</u>	<u>11.97</u>	<u>43.35</u>	58.01	25.66	55.30

on the highest average of ROUGE-1/2/L scores on the validation set. The λ in Equation (2) is set to 1.

The proposed method is compared with the previous state-of-the-art methods on the datasets. The performance is measured with ROUGE (Lin, 2004).

4.2 Experimental Results

Table 2 shows the ROUGE scores of the proposed model compared to the baselines. The proposed model outperforms SUMM^N on all datasets, which indicates that the enhanced coarse summarizer in the proposed method improves the multi-stage summarization approach. Furthermore, the proposed model achieves similarly or even better performance compared to other state-of-the-art models. These results demonstrate that utilizing the proposed coarse summarizer in the multi-stage summarization approach is a reasonable solution for long document summarization.

We investigate the effectiveness of target-focused alignment and contrastive learning in the proposed model. Table 3 shows the results of an ablation study. If the coarse summarizer is trained only using $\mathcal{D}^k_{coarse-t}$, the performance is dropped by 1.28 on the AMI dataset and 3.2 on the ICSI dataset compared to the proposed method.

Table 3: Ablation study on test set of AMI and ICSI datasets. Performance is the ROUGE-1 score.

	AMI	ICSI
$\mathcal{D}^k_{coarse-t}$ + contrastive learning	54.85	50.27
$\mathcal{D}^k_{coarse-t}$	53.57	47.07
$\mathcal{D}^k_{coarse-s}$ + contrastive learning	53.79	46.12
$\mathcal{D}^k_{coarse-s}$ (= SUMM^N)	53.44	45.57

However, its performance is better than the one of SUMM^N, which is trained using $\mathcal{D}^k_{coarse-s}$. This implies that the target-focused alignment and the contrastive learning helps improve multi-stage summarization.

4.3 Coarse Summary Analysis

To verify the quality of coarse summaries generated by the proposed method, we compare the coarse summaries at different stages with the target summary. Figure 2 depicts the ROUGE-1 scores of all datasets for each stage. Stage 1 represents the model with only one coarse stage and no fine-grained stage, while Stage i (i > 1) represents i - 1 coarse stages and one fine-grained stage. When comparing the ROUGE-1 scores of the proposed

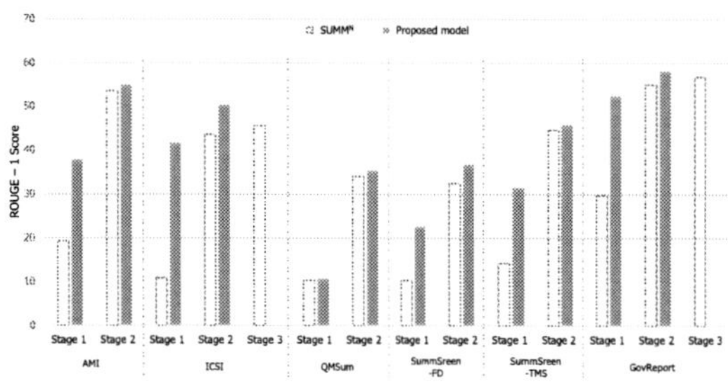

Figure 2: ROUGE-1 scores at different stages.

Table 4: Values for the coarse stage estimation

	ICSI	QMSum	GovReport
d_1	13317.2	9069.8	9409.4
K	1024	1024	1024
c_1 (Ours)	24.9	37.2	38.4
c_1 (SUMM^N)	276.8	68.4	243.2
$\hat{N}$ (Ours)	1 (0.7)	1 (0.7)	1 (0.6)
$\hat{N}$ (SUMM^N)	2 (1.9)	1 (0.9)	2 (1.5)

method with SUMM^N, the proposed method consistently outperforms SUMM^N at all stages. Notably, in the ICSI and GovReport datasets, the proposed method at Stage 2 achieves higher performance compared to SUMM^N at Stage 3. This indicates that our proposed method is more effective than SUMM^N.

We also investigate the effectiveness of the proposed method by estimating the number of coarse stages. In the multi-stage summarization, the fewer the coarse stages performed, the greater the effectiveness of the method. SUMM^N proposes a method to estimate the number of coarse stages. It is based on the length of the long document and the characteristics of the summarizer. The number of coarse stages is computed as follows:

$$\hat{N} = \left\lceil \frac{\log K - \log d_1}{\log c_1 - \log K} \right\rceil,$$

where d_1 and c_1 are the average length of document and coarse segments in coarse stage 1. K represents the maximum input tokens of the backbone model.

Table 4 shows the values used to estimate the coarse stage on three data sets. The estimated number of coarse stages for the proposed model on ICSI and GovReport is smaller than those of SUMM^N. This difference arises because the coarse summarizer in SUMM^N is trained using pairs of a document segment and a set of target segments, whereas the coarse summarizer in the proposed method is trained using pairs of a document segment and a target segment[2]. As a result, the coarse summarizer in the proposed method exhibits a tendency to generate more succinct coarse summaries, which in turn facilitates the generation of superior final summaries.

4.4 Human Evaluation

This paper conducts human evaluation with AMI and ICSI dataset to validate the quality of the generated summaries with respect to fluency and coverage. The experimental settings for the human evaluation follow those of Zhang et al. (2022). Specifically, the quality is assessed through three metrics: Readability, Conciseness, and Coverage. Readability takes into account word and grammatical error rate to assess the fluency of the summary. Conciseness measures how well the summary discards the redundant information, while Coverage gauges how well the summary covers each part of the dialogue.

We compare the results of the proposed method and SUMM^N because both methods are grounded in the multi-stage summarization. For source documents within AMI and ICSI datasets, three human annotators evaluate the quality of the summaries generated by each model. In this process, each annotator reviews the source document, the gold summary, and the generated summary, subsequently rating each summary from 1 to 5 (with higher scores indicating superior quality) across the aforementioned metrics.

Table 5 summarizes the performance of the proposed method and the baseline, SUMM^N. The proposed model outperforms SUMM^N in both the AMI and ICSI datasets. Specifically, the Coverage score of the proposed method is notably higher than that of SUMM^N. It seems that the coarse summarizer in the proposed method effectively generates concise summaries for each document segment, while the fine-grained summarizer captures the essence of each segment more comprehensively. The results of human evaluation experiments demonstrate that the proposed method generates better summaries than SUMM^N.

[2]For the sake of simplicity, there is no one-to-many mappings.

Table 5: Human evaluation scores.

	AMI			ICSI		
	Readability	Conciseness	Coverage	Readability	Conciseness	Coverage
SUMM^N	3.90	3.45	3.48	3.56	3.28	3.33
Proposed model	**4.15**	**3.58**	**3.78**	**3.77**	**3.55**	**4.17**

Table 6: Performances of LLM-based summarization on three long document summarization data sets.

	AMI			ICSI			QMSum-All		
	R-1	R-2	R-L	R-1	R-2	R-L	R-1	R-2	R-L
LongChat-7B-16K (Zero-shot)	26.15	6.77	24.50	18.06	2.07	17.12	23.40	3.86	20.78
Llama 2-13B (Zero-shot)	29.20	6.23	27.77	9.99	0.79	9.46	15.10	1.94	13.40
Llama 2-13B (Few-shot, Source-focused)	28.59	7.09	27.18	23.35	2.62	22.42	21.32	3.16	18.82
Llama 2-13B (Few-shot, Target-focused)	30.49	7.28	29.18	24.66	2.99	23.47	21.48	3.16	19.16
Proposed model	**54.85**	**21.18**	**52.28**	**50.27**	**13.38**	**47.30**	**35.31**	**10.13**	**30.58**

4.5 Comparison with LLM-based Long Document Summarization

Recent studies have shown that while summaries generated by large language models (LLMs) consistently outperform those of fine-tuned summarization methods in short document summarization (Zhang et al., 2023; Pu et al., 2023b), they typically fall short in the context of long document summarization (Yang et al., 2023; Nijkamp et al., 2023; Touvron et al., 2023). For example, ChatGPT achieved a score of 28.34 R-1 on the QMSum dataset (Yang et al., 2023), whose score is below the 35.31 R-1 obtained in our study. According to the study (Nijkamp et al., 2023), the performance of XGen-7B for GovReports was only at 21.28 R-1, which is substantially inferior compared to existing long document summarization methods. The recently introduced Llama 2 (Touvron et al., 2023) also encountered challenges in long document summarization, achieving only a 15.08 R-1 score on the QMSum dataset. Apart from LLMs specifically engineered to handle extended contexts, the majority of LLMs have input context length about 4K (e.g., Llama2-13B). This implies that even when using LLMs, a multi-stage summarization approach remains essential to process long documents.

To probe the efficacy of LLM-based summarization in our experiments, we conducted experiments using the LongChat (Li et al., 2023) and Llama 2 (Touvron et al., 2023) models and evaluated their performance in comparison with the proposed method. We employed two types of LLM-based summarization approaches: zero-shot summarization and few-shot multi-stage summarization. In zero-shot summarization, the model is provided with both a task prompt and the document as input, and then it generates a summary of the given document. In few-shot multi-stage summarization, we replace both the coarse and fine-grained summarizers in the multi-stage summarization with a few-shot LLM summarization model. Here, we also examined two types of few-shot LLMs for the coarse summarizer: a source-focused model, where the few-shot examples are sampled from source-focused pairs, and a target-focused model, where the examples are sampled from target-focused pairs.

Table 6 shows the performance of the LLM-based summarization across three long-document datasets. The efficacy of the summary model using LLMs is inferior to that of existing multi-stage summarization approaches. In other words, LLMs have not yet demonstrated strong performance in long document summarization, indicating an area for future research. Another interesting observation is that when using LLMs for multi-stage summarization, LLMs with few-shot examples from target-focused pairs achieve better performance than those with few-shot examples from source-focused pairs. These results suggest that target-focused pairs play an important role in improving performance in multi-stage summarization.

4.6 Case study

Table 7 shows sample summaries generated by the proposed method and SUMM^N. Both summaries

Table 7: Sample output summary of the proposed method on the AMI dataset.

SUMM^N	The project manager opens the meeting by **recapping the events of the previous meeting**. The marketing expert presents the results of market research , which shows that users want a fancy-looking remote control that is easy to use and has a **fancy look** and feel. **The user interface designer** presents the user interface concept for the remote , which is based on the idea that a **remote** should be simple and user-friendly. The industrial designer presents about the internal components of a remote control. The group discusses using kinetic **energy** to power the device , using a simple battery for the **LCD screen** , and using an advanced chip for the advanced **chip**. The project manager closes the meeting , telling the team members what their tasks will be for the next meeting. $\cdots$ The Marketing Expert will research how to produce a remote that is technologically innovative. The User Interface Designer will look at how to make a remote out of wood or plastic with either a wooden or plastic cover. The Group will not work with teletext. There was a lack of information on the cost of components and materials.
Proposed method	The project manager **recapped the decisions made in the previous meeting**. The marketing expert presented the results of a market study which shows that users of remotes want remotes to have a **fancy look** and feel, are interested in speech recognition, and are willing to pay extra for an **LCD screen**. The interface specialist presents, suggesting that the remote should be user-friendly and attractive, using large buttons, **speech recognition**, and using a little display. The industrial designer presents, presenting the components design. The group discusses the features they would like to include in the remote, including an LCD screen and a kinetic **energy** source. The user interface designer and industrial designer will work together on the look-and-feel design the group will use default materials. The remote will be single curved, single curved or double curved. The case will be made of plastic or rubber. The company will use **wood**. What type of **chip** to use. Whether to have a double curved or single curved case $\cdots$ the device will have a **docking station** for the remote to put the remote in when not in use. what sort of chip the device should have. What kind of display to include. What shape the remote is to be. Whether speech recognition is a good idea or not. Whether the remote has to be a changeable case. **Choosing between an LCD screen or speech recognition.**
Gold	The project manager opened the meeting and **recapped the decisions made in the previous meeting**. The marketing expert discussed his personal preferences for the design of the remote and presented the results of trend-watching reports , which indicated that there is a need for products which are **fancy** , innovative , easy to use , in dark colors , in recognizable shapes , and in a familiar material like wood. The user interface designer discussed the option to include speech recognition and which functions to include on the remote. The industrial designer discussed which options he preferred for the remote in terms of energy sources , casing , case supplements , buttons , and chips. The team then discussed and made decisions regarding energy sources , speech recognition , **LCD screens** , **chips** , case materials and colors , case shape and orientation , and button orientation. $\cdots$ The case covers will be available in wood or plastic. The case will be single curved. Whether to use kinetic energy or a conventional battery with a **docking station** which recharges the remote. Whether to implement an LCD screen on the remote. **Choosing between an LCD screen or speech recognition**. Using wood for the case

capture the content of the source long document and exhibit similarities to the gold summary. However, the summary from the proposed method contains more relevant phrases compared to the one generated by SUMM^N such as "recapped the decision made in the previous meeting" and "choosing between an LCD screen or speech recognition". We posit that the proposed summarizer has the capacity to generate concise coarse summaries, which subsequently facilitate the production of final summaries enriched with key phrases.

5 Conclusion

In this paper, we have demonstrated the effectiveness of enhancing the coarse summarizer in the multi-stage split-then-summarization approach. To enhance the coarser summarizer, the proposed method focuses on constructing target-focused aligned pairs, ensuring that only relevant source segments are included. Then, the proposed method incorporates contrastive learning into the training of the coarse summarizer to reinforce the conveyance of the similar meaning between source and target segments. Experimental results on six long document summarization datasets show that the proposed method helps improve the performance of the multi-stage long document summarization approach.

Acknowledgments

This work was supported in part by the National Research Foundation of Korea (NRF) funded by the Korean Government (MSIT) under Grant 2021R1F1A1048181, in part by the Institute of Information and Communications Technology Planning and Evaluation (IITP) funded by the Korean Government (MSIT) through Artificial Intelligence Innovation Hub under Grant 2021-0-02068.

Limitations

While the multi-stage split-then-summarization approach offers flexibility in processing long documents by adjusting the number of stages, it requires lots GPUs with large memory sizes. In our experiments, we used A6000 GPUs with a 48 GiB memory, and the training process took up to three days per dataset. It is important to note that the proposed model is based on the existing multi-stage long document summarization approach, which means that the memory usage during training is similar to the existing approach, and the footprint remains the same during inference.

Ethics Statement

We have conducted the proposed model training and testing using publicly accessible datasets. To the best of our knowledge, this work does not involve any ethical issues. We believe that this work complies with the ethical code of ACL.

References

Iz Beltagy, Matthew E Peters, and Arman Cohan. 2020. Longformer: The long-document transformer. *arXiv preprint arXiv:2004.05150*.

Jean Carletta, Simone Ashby, Sebastien Bourban, Mike Flynn, Mael Guillemot, Thomas Hain, Jaroslav Kadlec, Vasilis Karaiskos, Wessel Kraaij, Melissa Kronenthal, Guillaume Lathoud, Mike Lincoln, Agnes Lisowska, Iain McCowan, Wilfried Post, Dennis Reidsma, and Pierre Wellner. 2006. The ami meeting corpus: A pre-announcement. In *Machine Learning for Multimodal Interaction*, pages 28–39, Berlin, Heidelberg. Springer Berlin Heidelberg.

Mingda Chen, Zewei Chu, Sam Wiseman, and Kevin Gimpel. 2022. SummScreen: A dataset for abstractive screenplay summarization. In *Proceedings of the 60th Annual Meeting of the Association for Computational Linguistics (Volume 1: Long Papers)*, pages 8602–8615, Dublin, Ireland. Association for Computational Linguistics.

Li Dong, Nan Yang, Wenhui Wang, Furu Wei, Xiaodong Liu, Yu Wang, Jianfeng Gao, Ming Zhou, and Hsiao-Wuen Hon. 2019. *Unified Language Model Pre-Training for Natural Language Understanding and Generation*. Curran Associates Inc., Red Hook, NY, USA.

Xiachong Feng, Xiaocheng Feng, Bing Qin, and Xinwei Geng. 2021. Dialogue discourse-aware graph model and data augmentation for meeting summarization. In *Proceedings of the Thirtieth International Joint Conference on Artificial Intelligence, IJCAI-21*, pages 3808–3814. International Joint Conferences on Artificial Intelligence Organization. Main Track.

Jiatao Gu, James Bradbury, Caiming Xiong, Victor OK Li, and Richard Socher. 2017. Non-autoregressive neural machine translation. *arXiv preprint arXiv:1711.02281*.

Luyang Huang, Shuyang Cao, Nikolaus Parulian, Heng Ji, and Lu Wang. 2021. Efficient attentions for long document summarization. In *Proceedings of the 2021 Conference of the North American Chapter of the Association for Computational Linguistics: Human Language Technologies*, pages 1419–1436, Online. Association for Computational Linguistics.

Maor Ivgi, Uri Shaham, and Jonathan Berant. 2023. Efficient Long-Text Understanding with Short-Text Models. *Transactions of the Association for Computational Linguistics*, 11:284–299.

A. Janin, D. Baron, J. Edwards, D. Ellis, D. Gelbart, N. Morgan, B. Peskin, T. Pfau, E. Shriberg, A. Stolcke, and C. Wooters. 2003. The icsi meeting corpus. In *2003 IEEE International Conference on Acoustics, Speech, and Signal Processing, 2003. Proceedings. (ICASSP '03).*, volume 1, pages I–I.

Mike Lewis, Yinhan Liu, Naman Goyal, Marjan Ghazvininejad, Abdelrahman Mohamed, Omer Levy, Veselin Stoyanov, and Luke Zettlemoyer. 2020. BART: Denoising sequence-to-sequence pre-training for natural language generation, translation, and comprehension. In *Proceedings of the 58th Annual Meeting of the Association for Computational Linguistics*, pages 7871–7880, Online. Association for Computational Linguistics.

Dacheng Li, Rulin Shao, Anze Xie, Ying Sheng, Lianmin Zheng, Joseph E. Gonzalez, Ion Stoica, Xuezhe Ma, and Hao Zhang. 2023. How long can open-source llms truly promise on context length?

Chin-Yew Lin. 2004. ROUGE: A package for automatic evaluation of summaries. In *Text Summarization Branches Out*, pages 74–81, Barcelona, Spain. Association for Computational Linguistics.

Junpeng Liu, Yanyan Zou, Hainan Zhang, Hongshen Chen, Zhuoye Ding, Caixia Yuan, and Xiaojie Wang. 2021. Topic-aware contrastive learning for abstractive dialogue summarization. In *Findings of the Association for Computational Linguistics: EMNLP 2021*, pages 1229–1243, Punta Cana, Dominican Republic. Association for Computational Linguistics.

Yixin Liu, Ansong Ni, Linyong Nan, Budhaditya Deb, Chenguang Zhu, Ahmed Hassan Awadallah, and Dragomir Radev. 2022. Leveraging locality in abstractive text summarization. In *Proceedings of the 2022 Conference on Empirical Methods in Natural Language Processing*, pages 6081–6093, Abu Dhabi, United Arab Emirates. Association for Computational Linguistics.

Ziming Mao, Chen Henry Wu, Ansong Ni, Yusen Zhang, Rui Zhang, Tao Yu, Budhaditya Deb, Chenguang Zhu, Ahmed Awadallah, and Dragomir Radev. 2022.

DYLE: Dynamic latent extraction for abstractive long-input summarization. In *Proceedings of the 60th Annual Meeting of the Association for Computational Linguistics (Volume 1: Long Papers)*, pages 1687–1698, Dublin, Ireland. Association for Computational Linguistics.

Erik Nijkamp, Tian Xie, Hiroaki Hayashi, Bo Pang, Congying Xia, Chen Xing, Jesse Vig, Semih Yavuz, Philippe Laban, Ben Krause, Senthil Purushwalkam, Tong Niu, Wojciech Kryscinski, Lidiya Murakhovs'ka, Prafulla Kumar Choubey, Alex Fabbri, Ye Liu, Rui Meng, Lifu Tu, Meghana Bhat, Chien-Sheng Wu, Silvio Savarese, Yingbo Zhou, Shafiq Rayhan Joty, and Caiming Xiong. 2023. Long sequence modeling with xgen: A 7b llm trained on 8k input sequence length. Salesforce AI Research Blog.

Bo Pang, Erik Nijkamp, Wojciech Kryscinski, Silvio Savarese, Yingbo Zhou, and Caiming Xiong. 2023. Long document summarization with top-down and bottom-up inference. In *Findings of the Association for Computational Linguistics: EACL 2023*, pages 1267–1284, Dubrovnik, Croatia. Association for Computational Linguistics.

Dongqi Pu, Yifan Wang, and Vera Demberg. 2023a. Incorporating distributions of discourse structure for long document abstractive summarization.

Xiao Pu, Mingqi Gao, and Xiaojun Wan. 2023b. Summarization is (almost) dead. *arXiv preprint arXiv:2309.09558*.

Tobias Rohde, Xiaoxia Wu, and Yinhan Liu. 2021. Hierarchical learning for generation with long source sequences. *ArXiv*, abs/2104.07545.

Yi Tay, Dara Bahri, Liu Yang, Donald Metzler, and Da-Cheng Juan. 2020. Sparse Sinkhorn attention. In *Proceedings of the 37th International Conference on Machine Learning*, volume 119 of *Proceedings of Machine Learning Research*, pages 9438–9447. PMLR.

Hugo Touvron, Louis Martin, Kevin Stone, Peter Albert, Amjad Almahairi, Yasmine Babaei, Nikolay Bashlykov, Soumya Batra, Prajjwal Bhargava, Shruti Bhosale, et al. 2023. Llama 2: Open foundation and fine-tuned chat models. *arXiv preprint arXiv:2307.09288*.

Bolin Wei, Shuai Lu, Lili Mou, Hao Zhou, Pascal Poupart, Ge Li, and Zhi Jin. 2019. Why do neural dialog systems generate short and meaningless replies? a comparison between dialog and translation. In *Proceedings of the 2019 IEEE International Conference on Acoustics, Speech and Signal Processing*, pages 7290–7294. IEEE.

Qianqian Xie, Jimin Huang, Tulika Saha, and Sophia Ananiadou. 2022. GRETEL: Graph contrastive topic enhanced language model for long document extractive summarization. In *Proceedings of the 29th International Conference on Computational Linguistics*, pages 6259–6269, Gyeongju, Republic of Korea. International Committee on Computational Linguistics.

Shusheng Xu, Xingxing Zhang, Yi Wu, and Furu Wei. 2022. Sequence level contrastive learning for text summarization. In *Proceedings of the AAAI Conference on Artificial Intelligence*, volume 36, pages 11556–11565.

Xianjun Yang, Yan Li, Xinlu Zhang, Haifeng Chen, and Wei Cheng. 2023. Exploring the limits of chatgpt for query or aspect-based text summarization. *arXiv preprint arXiv:2302.08081*.

Jingqing Zhang, Yao Zhao, Mohammad Saleh, and Peter Liu. 2020. PEGASUS: Pre-training with extracted gap-sentences for abstractive summarization. In *Proceedings of the 37th International Conference on Machine Learning*, volume 119 of *Proceedings of Machine Learning Research*, pages 11328–11339. PMLR.

Tianyi Zhang, Faisal Ladhak, Esin Durmus, Percy Liang, Kathleen McKeown, and Tatsunori B. Hashimoto. 2023. Benchmarking large language models for news summarization. *arXiv preprint arXiv:2301.13848*.

Yusen Zhang, Ansong Ni, Ziming Mao, Chen Henry Wu, Chenguang Zhu, Budhaditya Deb, Ahmed Awadallah, Dragomir Radev, and Rui Zhang. 2022. Summ^n: A multi-stage summarization framework for long input dialogues and documents. In *Proceedings of the 60th Annual Meeting of the Association for Computational Linguistics (Volume 1: Long Papers)*, pages 1592–1604, Dublin, Ireland. Association for Computational Linguistics.

Ming Zhong, Yang Liu, Yichong Xu, Chenguang Zhu, and Michael Zeng. 2022. Dialoglm: Pre-trained model for long dialogue understanding and summarization. *Proceedings of the AAAI Conference on Artificial Intelligence*, 36(10):11765–11773.

Ming Zhong, Da Yin, Tao Yu, Ahmad Zaidi, Mutethia Mutuma, Rahul Jha, Ahmed Hassan Awadallah, Asli Celikyilmaz, Yang Liu, Xipeng Qiu, and Dragomir Radev. 2021. QMSum: A new benchmark for query-based multi-domain meeting summarization. In *Proceedings of the 2021 Conference of the North American Chapter of the Association for Computational Linguistics: Human Language Technologies*, pages 5905–5921, Online. Association for Computational Linguistics.

Chenguang Zhu, Ruochen Xu, Michael Zeng, and Xuedong Huang. 2020. A hierarchical network for abstractive meeting summarization with cross-domain pretraining. In *Findings of the Association for Computational Linguistics: EMNLP 2020*, pages 194–203, Online. Association for Computational Linguistics.

Author Index

Association for Computational Linguistics
209 N. Eighth Street
Stroudsburg, Pennsylvania 18360

ISBN 978-1-7138-8603-7

9 781713 886037

CURRAN ASSOCIATES INC.
proceedings.com